18 95

KARL BARTH
LETTERS
1961-1968

KARL BARTH
LETTERS
1961-1968

Edited by
JÜRGEN FANGMEIER
and
HINRICH STOEVESANDT

Translated and Edited
by
GEOFFREY W. BROMILEY

WILLIAM B. EERDMANS PUBLISHING COMPANY
GRAND RAPIDS, MICHIGAN

Translated from the Swiss edition of Barth's collected works,
Karl Barth: Briefe, 1961-1968, V, Vol. 6, of the *Karl Barth Gesamtausgabe*.
Copyright © 1975 by the Theologischer Verlag Zürich;
second edition © 1978 by the Theologischer Verlag Zürich.

Library of Congress Cataloging in Publication Data
Barth, Karl, 1886-1968.
Letters, 1961-1968.
Translation of Briefe, 1961-1968.
Includes indexes.
1. Barth, Karl, 1886-1968. 2. Theologians—
Switzerland—Correspondence. I. Fangmeier, Jürgen.
II. Stoevesandt, Hinrich. III. Bromiley, Geoffrey William. IV. Title.
BX4827.B3A4 1980   230'.044'0924   [B]   80-29140
ISBN 0-8028-3526-6

230
B284L

208688

CONTENTS

TRANSLATOR'S PREFACE

The present volume is a translation of the letters of Karl Barth written during the final years from his retirement in 1961 to his death in 1968 and collected in the Swiss *Gesamtausgabe* of his works. Details of the editorial procedures will be found in the original prefaces that follow. A few letters, portions of letters, or phrases were composed by Barth himself in English, and these are indicated at the appropriate points.

It should be noted that in the English version several letters (marked by an asterisk in the chronological list in the index, and by brackets in the text) have been rendered either wholly or partially in the form of précis. The reasons for this vary. In some cases the reference is to local or specialized matters which would have little or no interest for the average reader. In others Barth gives much the same news in more than one letter written at the same time, as, for example, in those concerning his health. Others contain more detailed personal greetings which need not be reproduced in full. The policy has been to err if at all in favor of full inclusion, and in all cases the gist has been given so that readers may know whether or not it is worth their while to go to the original for the full version.

Just before the completion of the translation the Swiss editors were able to make available certain important corrections and additions which they were making in the second edition. It has been possible, then, to avoid some errors and fill some gaps in the notes and also to include in the body of the text some additional letters which the second Swiss edition will have in the appendix. In the list of letters and again in the main text a note will be placed beside these letters indicating that in the original they are to be found only in the second edition.

One of the special delights of reading these letters is that while we can still see Barth the theologian, active and alert for all his advancing years and infirmities, we also vividly see Barth the man, stamped with our common humanity, yet no less distinguished by his inimitable individuality. An acquaintance with even a few of these detailed human aspects can give fresh insight and interest to the study of his weighty theological volumes.

Pasadena, Epiphany 1979   Geoffrey W. Bromiley

PREFACE TO THE SECOND EDITION

A new edition of the *Briefe, 1961-1968* is now called for and this gives the editors the opportunity to make some improvements.

First, some errors in the notes have been corrected and some lacunae filled. For the most part this has been made possible by attentive readers and reviewers. Sincere thanks are expressed to them for their valuable help. [These have all been incorporated in this first edition of the English translation. G.W.B.]

Secondly, a number of letters by Barth have been made accessible to the Karl Barth Archive by their recipients since the publication of the first edition in the autumn of 1975. Thanks are expressed to the owners. These new letters have been put in an appendix but numbered in sequence to facilitate their chronological integration. [In the English translation they have been put at the proper points in the text but marked by (second ed.) to show that in the original they will be found only in the Appendix to the second edition. G.W.B.]

The additional letter to Carl Zuckmayer (No. 292a) and the first draft of the first paragraph of No. 302 have also been included. Zuckmayer had asked that these not be published during his lifetime, but after his death in 1977 the full correspondence between Barth and Zuckmayer came out in the volume *Späte Freundschaft* (Theologischer Verlag, Zurich) and they are now given their proper place in the *Gesamtausgabe*.

Schöller and Basel, November 1978   *J.F. and* H.S.

PREFACE TO THE FIRST EDITION

Karl Barth's seventy-fifth birthday on 10 May 1961 marked a decisive break in his life. At the end of the summer term in which it fell he retired. He did so at his own wish. As they had done for his philosopher-colleague Karl Jaspers, the cantonal authorities of Basel-City had allowed him to continue after his seventieth birthday in 1956 and left it to him to decide when to terminate his professorship. In the seven-and-a-half years granted to him after his retirement, in contrast to the preceding four-and-a-half decades of comprehensive activity when he made his chief contribution, Barth appeared only infrequently on the public scene, giving only a few lectures and publishing comparatively little.

Nevertheless, although to those who repeatedly asked for public statements he pointed to his published work, he was not entirely silent in these years. On the one hand he especially valued conversation as a form of expression. He received many individual visitors and also many groups of various kinds from whom he invited questions in advance. In due course transcripts of these discussions will appear in the comprehensive edition of his works. On the other hand he made up for his lack of public appearances by writing letters. Though the number of letters from these final years, even apart from the gaps caused by sickness, is considerably smaller than that from many earlier periods, Barth in old age particularly cultivated the letter and regarded it as the form of writing that was now best suited to him. Thus while he appeared less and less in public, his letter-writing afforded him continued participation in theological and other questions of the time.

It has been resolved, then, to publish important letters from this period as soon as possible after Barth's death in order to meet the request to make the later Barth more accessible. When the decision was made in the summer of 1970 to bring out a comprehensive edition of the works of Barth, Jürgen Fangmeier had almost completed his manuscript of a selection of letters at the request of Barth's heirs. The decision of those responsible for the full edition to integrate the letters into their edition delayed publication for some years. For one thing, the format had to be adjusted to that adopted for the other volumes—a task in which Bernd Jaspert gave valuable help. Furthermore, both the number of letters and also the text of those already included needed to be extended for the sake of completeness. Fangmeier had based his original work on the large but incomplete collection of carbon copies kept by Barth himself, supplemented by only a few others that recipients had made available on request to the heirs or to Fangmeier himself. Hinrich Stoevesandt, an official executor working in the Karl Barth Archive in Basel, was able through his individual efforts relating to this period in Barth's life to increase considerably the number of letters available. He thus came to be associated with Fangmeier in editing the volume.

The present volume offers most of the letters from May 1961 to December 1968. Letters published elsewhere in the *Gesamtausgabe* are omitted. Thus a letter to Bultmann dated December 1963 may be found in the exchange with Bultmann. Those to Thurneysen will come in Volume III of the correspondence with Thurneysen. Some letters will appear in a volume containing Barth's public letters. Finally, a special volume is planned for letters to his two sons overseas, Markus and Christoph, whom Barth kept regularly and explicitly informed about anything important he was doing or experiencing. These letters will serve the same autobiographical function for the final years as those to Thurneysen did for the early years, and thus merit separate publication.

While every effort has been made to achieve completeness, absolute completeness in publishing private letters is not possible—and this is especially true of the later period. First, the ideal—if there is such a thing—is limited by the loss of many letters (how many one cannot say), by the failure to find others, and by the failure of recipients to make others available. Second, even the relative completeness that is technically attainable could theoretically be achieved only if an edition such as this were a matter of purely historical documents, that is, if those concerned—the writer, recipients, and people mentioned in the letters—lived on only in the form of literary reminiscence. But a theoretical ideal of this kind means little in practice. For, finally, Barth naturally wrote many letters that have no abiding significance or have interest only for the recipients. To include these would be superfluous. In cases of doubt we have opted for too much rather than too little. But the principle which led us to leave out some letters has also led us to leave out certain portions of others.

Of these various factors which work against a complete edition, the first and last will always be valid and only the second will eventually cease to obtain. The question whether for this second reason alone we should omit letters from the comprehensive edition of Barth's works, and thus make this extensive and important side of Barth's work available for a long time only in provisional form, was answered in the negative by the many people who served the project as consultants. Work on the material from 1961 to 1968 has vindicated this fundamental decision. Of the great mass of available material, the letters and portions of letters which were thought to be worth publishing in terms of content, but which the recipients would not release for publication, or which the editors judged to be unsuitable because of those directly or indirectly involved, have proved to be a small minority. In the present volume only a few letters of material significance have been totally omitted. And only rarely have we had to use the signs of omission (. . .) which many readers and reviewers found disruptive in the two previous volumes of Barth's correspondence with Thurneysen.

Since achieving the greatest possible completeness necessitates ongoing decisions that the editors of other materials do not have to make, in the course of the work we have often asked ourselves whether we were not going too far in this direction. In cases of doubt we have asked the recipients of letters for their consent to full publication. The generous response usually received has encouraged and strengthened us in our resolve to leave out as little as possible.

Some recipients, in agreeing to publication, have made it a condition that their own names not be mentioned. This has meant eliminating any clues to their identity in the text. In other cases we have not named the recipients when their identity is not essential to understanding and personal matters are touched on. Omitted names of recipients, or of people referred to, are denoted by N.N., and place names which might reveal their identity are denoted by X.

After 1966 Barth dictated most of his typed letters to his assistant Eberhard Busch, who worked for him after his secretary Charlotte von Kirschbaum fell sick. Sometimes he let Busch help in the drafting, and Busch even wrote some at Barth's request and according to his instructions. Two examples containing typical views of Barth have been included in the volume, but in small print and numbered out of the usual sequence. [The English edition has summarized Busch's letters at the points at which they were included in the Swiss edition. They are not in small print.]

Some complete or partial examples of letters written to Barth have been given in the appendix, but these include only letters that are necessary to understand Barth's own letters or that contain replies by authors whose works are discussed by Barth.

As regards the text the rules of the comprehensive edition have been followed. The orthography has been conservatively modernized, although a place is left for some of Barth's peculiarities. The punctuation has also been brought into line. Minor grammatical errors have been corrected, missing words supplied in brackets, and doubtful words marked by (?). Occasionally the text has been smoothed, this being indicated by a footnote. Abbreviations have been written out except where they are common ones or occasionally when they are an intentional stylistic medium.

The editors acknowledge their indebtedness to the sons and daughters of Barth who have given advice on various matters, to the recipients of letters (or their heirs), and the authors of letters in the appendix, who have consented to publication, to Dr. Bernd Jaspert for his cooperation as mentioned, to various people who have helped with the notes, to Reiner Marquard for his work on the indexes of scripture references, names, and works of Barth referred to in the text, to the foundations whose grants have made publication possible, to the National Foundation for Academic Research which supports the Barth Archive and the work of the second editor, and to the Theologischer Verlag, successor to the Evangelischer Verlag which published Barth's work for many years, for the energy and understanding with which it is safeguarding his legacy.

Schöller and Basel, March 1975   JÜRGEN FANGMEIER
                                        AND HINRICH STOEVESANDT

ABBREVIATIONS

C.D.   *Church Dogmatics (Kirchliche Dogmatik)*
CW   *Christliche Welt*
ET   English Translation
EvTh   *Evangelische Theologie*
JK   *Junge Kirche*
LThK   *Lexicon für Theologie und Kirche*
NZZ   *Neue Zürcher Zeitung*
RGG³   *Die Religion in Geschichte und Gegenwart* (3rd ed.)
ThExh   Theologische Existenz heute
ThLZ   *Theologische Literaturzeitung*
ThSt   Theologische Studien
ZThK   *Zeitschrift für Theologie und Kirche*

Letters: 1961-1968

1
Circular Letter to Those Who Congratulated Barth on His Seventy-Fifth Birthday

Basel, May 1961

Dear Friends,

The day when I could look back on a full seventy-five years has come and gone. It has impressed on me afresh what a gift it is to have as many real friends as I have (far away or nearer, all very close in every sense of the term). You have remembered me so richly with letters and telegrams and flowers and other costly presents that our postal authorities almost had to set up a special service to the Bruderholz.[1] It took me some three days to read quietly the written greetings (including sixteen from the place I preach in, where this letter is being duplicated[2]), to take note of this or that book or picture, to play the records for the first time, and to do justice to the fine things which among many others were given for my physical refreshment. Best of all, however, were not the good gifts and words you sent me but what I sensed behind them, what spoke to me through them: your rejoicing with me at something that cannot be taken for granted, namely, that the sun still shines on me; your sharing in my work; your personal affection for me; and in addition your considerable and forgiving patience with my faults and foibles. Many have thanked me for what they suppose they have received from me. Understandably this has moved and comforted me, especially when pastors told me I gave them courage and joy in their preaching. But I can only pass on these thanks to Him to whom alone I myself owe each and every thing. Indeed I am sometimes frightened when I see the amount of free and unmerited grace that has ruled over and in my life, action, and work. It has been almost like something alien, in strange contrast to my own life day by day and year by year in which I have smoked my pipe and have sometimes indulged other appetites, and have rather wheezily thought and written and spoken what seemed to follow next, although always under the impression that I was some distance behind what was really happening. I have always had in

—3—

mind the many who have worked just as hard as I have, or harder, but whose days, unlike mine, have been lived out in obscurity or semi-obscurity. To be "famous" ("the greatest scholar of our time," as I even read as icing on the cake) is all very pleasant. But who will finally be praised? I beg you, then, to continue your kindness to me and to accompany me with your thoughts and encouragements. I also admonish you in all seriousness, don't make a myth out of me, for the angels will certainly not like that and the perspicacious will see through it to my shame. Let each try to do what I have attempted, doing in his own field, better than I have done, a little something that will be to the glory of God and his neighbors. Until the third millennium comes (and beyond) there will be many, many new things in the church and in theology for those of true heart and good will to think and do. For myself, I still have a few things in mind as far as time and strength allow. Starting this autumn, now that forty years have past, I shall no longer be teaching,[3] but if my younger colleagues allow, I shall take part in certain exercises and naturally shall be at my desk, where my much worthier father also lived and worked. C.D. IV, 4 is being prepared but is far from complete. Eschatology? Friends, do not ask or complain or plague me too much about this. Could it not be written by someone else? Haven't many fine symphonies and buildings and theological summas been left unfinished? But I commit these things to God, who knows better than you and I do what is needful for you and possible for me. Our whole office is to praise Him from the depths as best we may. And now I thank you for everything, sincerely sharing your efforts, joys, and sorrows.

With warmest greetings,

Yours,
Karl Barth

[1]The district in Basel where Barth lived at 26 Bruderholzallee.
[2]Basel Prison.
[3]Barth retired at the end of the summer semester of 1961 but taught the winter semester of 1961/62 due to a delay in calling his successor.

* * *

2

To Prof. Kornelis Heiko Miskotte
Voorst, Holland

Basel, 19 May 1961

Dear Heiko,

On 11 May, when, unknown to me, you were in Basel, I read your evaluation of *C.D.* in *ThExh.*[1] The day before yesterday I read your article in *Waagschale*,[2] and today your letter[3] has come. The contents do not wholly surprise me, since on the 14th, although you forbade him to speak about it with me (forbade him!), I had a long conversation with H. Stoevesandt on the matter. What can I say to all this?

Your analytical comparison of the structure of *C.D.* to Moby Dick affected me a lot, for, as one who lives and thinks much less reflectively than you, I found in your presentation much new light on many things I have done in the past and continue to do, as you describe. It pleased me to see myself so perceptively understood in the way that you have and as only a man so insightful as you can. I thank you.

I also thank you for your words about me in the *Waagschale* article. I particularly note your statement that I, or the *C.D.*, am a "phenomenon" for you. And from there it is only a step to your piteous letter evoked by my speech on the tenth.[4] The trouble I gave you is obviously connected with the difficulty caused by my lecture in Hanover[5] and my article in *Theologische Umschau*.[6] From my standpoint these were and are mere statements which are quite clear and have nothing whatever to do with the glory of Moby Dick. I have not heard that anyone else found them troublesome, disturbing, alienating, etc. They are this for you. What really is the problem? I am trying to understand you and have provisionally concluded that I am indeed a "phenomenon" for you, one that you have integrated into yourself, with whose glory you see yourself stand or fall, a veritable image to which for your own sake you must ascribe impregnability. And now you realize to your horror that I let myself—myself or the beloved Moby Dick, whom you see sweeping through the ocean with such consoling power—that I let myself be addressed as one of the good but perishable creatures of God, and that I count on my impregnability only until the coming of the "strong man" who can make all things new and better. You cannot see that indications along these lines—in relation to myself and my work as such, not its basis, object, or content, but my own encircling human efforts—are simply a necessity of life for me, especially in these days when I am so powerfully assaulted by the waves of my reputation, and this is not the first time, but has been so from the very beginning, as you may read in my preface to the sixth edition of *Romans* in 1928.[7] How could I stand before God and man if I did not realize and did not say openly that the "time for everything" of Ecclesiastes[8] applies to the composite of Moby Dick and *C.D.* too? But you think that I am sinning in the matter! Against whom or what? So far as I can see, against you in so far as you have done what you should not have done and made this composite an image. Heiko, do me and above all do yourself a favor. Free yourself from this image with a healthy tug and then rejoice with me that you and I are held up in the hands of God as the very fragile creatures we are in all the finitude of our persons and works.

This, then, is how I see the matter for now. If you object and feel that you have been terribly misunderstood, then I must say to you very seriously: Heiko, why did you go around Basel for two whole days without availing yourself of what may be "the unique opportunity"[9] for a face-to-face discussion, in which, if my version is wrong, you could lead me by the give and take of dialogue to the right one? Heiko, you who are in spirit ten times my superior, what kind of a Narcissus are you that you could throw yourself and your old friend in Basel into such a turmoil of uncontrolled misunderstanding in thought and feeling! It began when you thought I was overtired in that lecture and believed you had heard Lollo v. Kirschbaum[10] speak of I know not what physical infirmities. It is true that I have aged a little, as is natural, but as yet I have strength beyond my deserts.

To sum up, there is nothing about which you and I cannot speak quietly and companionably, and in order that we may do this you must come back to Basel. In this sense cheerfully, sincerely, but not without an admonitory finger,

Yours,

KARL BARTH

[1]K. H. Miskotte, "Über Karl Barths *Kirchliche Dogmatik*. Klein Präludien und Phantasien," *ThExh*, N.F. 89 (1961). Miskotte alludes in this article (10ff.) to the student nickname for *C.D.*, "Moby Dick" (from Melville's novel, 1851).
[2]K. H. Miskotte, "Bij de 75e verjaardag van Karl Barth," *In de Waagschaal* [Amsterdam], 16 (1960/61), 336f.
[3]See Appendix, 1, and also Appendix, 2, for Miskotte's reply.
[4]Speech of thanks on the occasion of Barth's seventy-fifth birthday celebration at the Basel restaurant Bruderholz, 10 May 1961.
[5]K. Barth, *Evangelische Theologie im 19 Jahrhundert*, ThSt, 49 (Zollikon-Zurich, 1957); lecture to the Goethe Society in Hanover, 8 Jan. 1957.

[6]K. Barth, "Möglichkeiten liberaler Theologie heute," *Schweizerische Theologische Umschau*, 30 (1960), 95-101.
[7]K. Barth, *Römerbrief*, 6th ed. (Munich, 1928), p. xxviii. This preface is not found in later impressions. In it Barth answers the charge that he is quietly becoming a man of yesterday by pointing to his awareness from history that successful theologians "ride quickly," like the dead. Nevertheless, he asks that his death not be announced prematurely since he still has time to do better than he has done thus far.
[8]Eccl 3.
[9]Cf. *C.D.* III, 4, §56, 1.
[10]Charlotte von Kirschbaum, Barth's secretary for many years.

*　　　*　　　*

3
To Dr. Geoffrey W. Bromiley
Pasadena, California

Basel, 1 June 1961

Dear Dr. Bromiley,

Please excuse me and please try to understand that I cannot and will not answer the questions these people put.[1]

To do so in the time requested would in any case be impossible for me. The claims of work in my last semester as an academic teacher (preparation of lectures and seminars, doctoral dissertations, etc.) are too great. But even if I had the time and strength I would not enter into a discussion of the questions proposed.

Such a discussion would have to rest on the primary presupposition that those who ask the questions have read, learned, and pondered the many things I have already said and written about these matters. They have obviously not done this, but have ignored the many hundreds of pages in the *C.D.* where they might at least have found out—not necessarily under the headings of history, universalism, etc.—where I really stand and do not stand. From that point they could have gone on to pose further questions. I sincerely respect the seriousness with which a man like Berkouwer studies me and then makes his criticisms.[2] I can then answer him in detail.[3] But I cannot respect the questions of these people from *Christianity Today*, for they do not focus on the reasons for my statements but on certain foolishly drawn deductions from them. Their questions are thus superficial.

The decisive point, however, is this. The second presupposition of a fruitful discussion between them and me would have to be that we are able to talk on a common plane. But these people have already had their so-called orthodoxy for a long time. They are closed to anything else, they will cling to it at all costs, and they can adopt toward me only the role of prosecuting attorneys, trying to establish whether what I represent agrees or disagrees with their orthodoxy, in which I for my part have no interest! None of their questions leaves me with the impression that they want to seek with me the truth that is greater than us all. They take the stance of those who happily possess it already and who hope to enhance their happiness by succeeding in proving to themselves and the world that I do not share this happiness. Indeed they have long since decided and publicly proclaimed that I am a heretic, possibly (van Til) the worst heretic of all time.[4] So be it! But they should not expect me to take the trouble to give them the satisfaction of offering explanations which they will simply use to confirm the judgment they have already passed on me.

Dear Dr. Bromiley, you will no doubt remember what I said in the preface to *C.D.* IV, 2 in the words of an eighteenth-century poem on those who eat up men.[5] The continuation of the poem is as follows: "... for there is no true love where one man eats another." These fundamentalists want to eat me up. They have not yet come to a "better mind and attitude" as I once hoped. I can thus give them neither an angry nor a gentle answer but instead no answer at all.

With friendly greetings,

Yours,

KARL BARTH

P.S. I ask you to convey what I have said in a suitable manner to the people at *Christianity Today*.

---

[1]Professor Geoffrey W. Bromiley of Fuller Theological Seminary, Pasadena, was co-editor and chief translator of the English version of *Church Dogmatics*. At the request of the editor of *Christianity Today*, and as a personal favor to him, Bromiley asked Barth whether he would answer some critical questions put by the American theologians Clark, Klooster, and van Til (see Appendix, 3).

[2]G. C. Berkouwer, *The Triumph of Grace in the Theology of Karl Barth* (Grand Rapids: Eerdmans, 1956).

[3]*C.D.* IV, 2, p. xii; IV, 3, pp. 173-180.

[4]Cf. C. van Til, *The New Modernism* (Philadelphia, 1946), and later, in defense of his view against Berkouwer, *Christianity and Barthianism* (Philadelphia, 1962).

[5]"There are obviously fundamentalists with whom dialogue is possible; only butchers and cannibals are beyond the pale, and even they only provisionally, for there is always hope that they will attain to a better mind and attitude." [Barth's instincts here were not unsound, for it appeared later that the three theologians would have been given the last word in counter-replies to his replies. G.W.B.]

*　　　　*　　　　*

4

To Werner Rüegg
Hombrechtikon, Zurich Canton

Basel, 6 July 1961

Dear Mr. Rüegg,

You are quite right. My answer to that question was not satisfactory in my own view either.[1] This was because I stuck to the strict wording of the question, which was not, as you wrote, whether a Christian can believe in eternal life, but whether, in the light of parapsychology, there is a state beyond which interaction is possible with the dead. In all honesty I could reply to this question only that I had no knowledge of such a state and that the lady who put the question would do better to consider that in both this life and the next it is with God that she has to do.

Naturally there is much more to say about eternal life than that. I cannot be explicit in this letter, but I can at least give you a hint of my thinking on the issue in the light of Revelation and indeed the whole of holy scripture.

Eternal life is not another and second life, beyond the present one. It is this life, but the reverse side which God sees although it is as yet hidden from us—this life in its relation to what He has done for the whole world, and therefore for us too, in Jesus Christ. We thus wait and hope, even in view of our death, for our manifestation with Him, with Jesus Christ who was raised again from the dead, in the glory of not only the judgment but also the grace of God. The new thing will be that the cover of tears, death, suffering, crying, and pain that now lies over our present life will be lifted, that the decree of God fulfilled in Jesus Christ will stand before our eyes, and that it will be the subject not only of our deepest shame but also of our joyful thanks and praise. I like to put it in the fine stanza of Gellert in which he speaks of knowing in the light what is now obscure on earth, of calling wonderful and glorious what took place inscrutably, of seeing with our spirit the context of our destiny with praise and thanksgiving.[2]

This is "what the professor thinks" and this is what he should have said briefly last Sunday to the woman who wanted to know about spirit appearances and to all the other listeners.

With friendly greetings,

Yours,
KARL BARTH

[1]Rüegg wrote a letter to Barth on 4 July 1961 concerning the answer Barth gave to a question on the radio program *What Do You Think, Professor?* Expressing dissatisfaction with Barth's reply, he said that he had expected a decisive reference to the promises, especially of Revelation.

[2]Dann werd ich das im Licht erkennen,
Was ich auf Erden dunkel sah,
Das wunderbar und herrlich nennen,
Was unerforschlich hier geschah.
Dann schaut mein Geist mit Lob und Dank
Die Schickung im Zusammenhang.
(Fourth verse of the hymn "Nach einer Prüfung kurzer Tage")

*　　*　　*

5

To Bishop Albert Bereczky
Budapest

Basel, 18 July 1961

Dear Bishop Bereczky,

The sending of your article on the narrow way[1] not only delighted me as a welcome sign of life from you, but also struck me as the fullest and deepest presentation I have yet seen of your present course and place. And I can assure you that I followed what you said with great inward participation. You especially impressed me by leaving out this time any criticism of the west and simply speaking positively as a Christian about what seemed to be demanded of you step by step. I can now imagine how if I were a Hungarian I might have made choices and decisions which, if not the same as, would be at least very similar to yours. Perhaps as a Hungarian I too would have hesitated to take part in the peace movement which you mention on p. 14[2] because to this day it is not clear to me what the movement means by "peace." But I mention this only in passing.

You may have heard that I have now reached the end of my academic career—seventy-five is a considerable age—and was to have given my last lecture at the end of the summer semester. But things have changed due to political problems ("McCarthy" style) in the election of my successor—I refer to Gollwitzer in Berlin—so that the post will not be filled by winter and I shall be working on a restricted program. Some small commotion has arisen in Switzerland about the matter,[3] but it does not worry me. God will provide in this affair too.[4]

I hope, dear bishop, that you are in good or reasonably good health.

The main thing is the beautiful inner peace which I detected in what you wrote. We all need that.

Thanks for thinking of me. With warmest greetings,

Yours,

KARL BARTH

[1] A. Bereczky, "Unser schmaler Weg," *Communio Viatorum* [Prague], 4 (1961), 5-15.

[2] The reference is not to a specific institution but to a general peace movement which took concrete form in the Prague Christian Peace Conference arranged by J. L. Hromádka.

[3] The press took sides on the issue, with papers like the *National-Zeitung* of Basel for Gollwitzer, and others like the *Neue Zürcher Zeitung* against him.

[4] Gen 22:8.

*   *   *

6
To N.N.
Bonn

Basel, 26 July 1961

Dear N.N.,

Your alarm is unnecessary.[1] You have fallen victim to a rumor. I cannot reconcile what someone told you with what I really said at a session of my society in December 1951 on the ethical problem of war.

We were discussing the distinction and relation between *ethics*, as reflection on what is to be recognized as God's command in a specific time and place, and *ethos*, as the practical decision to be made in a specific time and place by certain people according to their recognition of the command of God.

In reply to a German student I had to maintain that even when, as in modern war, our thinking moves with ninety-nine percent certainty in a particular direction, we cannot and should not set up binding laws.

An American student then chimed in with the question whether the ten principles of the German brotherhoods (*ethos*), which were being much discussed at the time, should be proclaimed to the American government.[2]

My answer was No, unless American Christians were able to say something of the same kind on their own responsibility. The ten principles might give them something to think about (*ethics*), but the decision (*ethos*) must be their own.

This was the point at issue, and it was in relation to it that I gave my opinion as indicated.

With friendly greetings,

Yours,

KARL BARTH

[1]N.N. had heard a rumor that in a seminar for American students Barth had said that America should not unilaterally give up atomic weapons.

[2]For the ten principles, a constituent part of the *Anlage an die Synode der Evangelischen Kirche in Deutschland* of March 1958, see *JK*, 19 (1958), 124f. and *ThExh*, N.F. 70 (1959), 104.

*   *   *

7

To Pastor Emanuel Paskert
Dinslaken

Basel, 26 July 1961

Dear Pastor,

Your letter, friendly remembrances, and account of your obviously vigorous activity have given me much joy, and I thank you for your greetings. I, too, still have lively recollections of the evenings in Bonn.[1] But I have to admit with sorrow that in contrast to you my paltry active participation in music ended long since. In its place I listen with new appreciation to records of Mozart and also Bach and Handel, and I still enjoy music in this passive and undoubtedly limited way. It certainly cannot compare with what you are doing actively according to the program you sent. But my son Christoph, whom you perhaps remember and who is now an Old Testament professor in Jakarta, is still a zealous cellist in that distant equatorial land.

Regarding your mild but definite rebuke regarding H. E. Weber[2] what shall I say? The fact is that in earlier years he made no strong impression on me either positively or negatively. After the war we met on friendly terms in Bonn and I saw that in some important matters he had drawn near to us. A later history of theology will perhaps make clear what happened. What is certain is that I was not led by him to take up again in a different way problems that had been laid aside and even dropped. I had no cause whatever to keep quiet about him, as you put it, for he never spoke to me in any living way. Do not say anything about this to

Mrs. Weber, with whom I have always been on good terms without ever raising the question of her husband's theology.

Friendly greetings to you and yours and best wishes for your work,

Yours,

KARL BARTH

[1]Evenings of chamber music in Barth's house during the Bonn years (1930–1935).
[2]Paskert had expressed displeasure at a campaign of silence in Bonn regarding the former Bonn teacher of New Testament and systematics, Hans Emil Weber (1882–1950), and asked Barth not to have any part in it.

*   *   *

8
To Hans Stern, Editor of konkret
Hamburg

Basel, 27 July 1961

Dear Mr. Stern,

I have received your questions and thank you.[1] I recall that when you first sent them I was so busy that I set them aside. They are so large that each would need a little essay in the form of a manifesto. I cannot, however, produce this kind of thing on request, but only in situations which seem to call directly for a word from me.

Is it really clear to you what a sore point you touch on in Question 4? It is not odd to me that in the face of atomic armaments there should have arisen an isolated and almost sectarian movement in certain circles but that a regular popular movement should not arise, whether in Germany or here in Switzerland, where we set in motion a constitutional initiative against the similar plans of our political and military heads but with great effort could raise only 74,000 signatures in the whole country. What are we to think of this? The movement is certainly not meaningless but highly meaningful. Neither with you nor with us has there been any lack of clear explanation or lively appeal. But in both cases the people have reacted with indifference. Can we be surprised, then, that those who rule us, whether directly or indirectly, are going on with their evil designs as though nothing had happened? I am reminded of what happened in 1933 when it was the people— having eyes but seeing not—that first ignored Hitlerism and then had to put up with it. What they will have to put up with this time if they stupidly accept the atom bomb might well be final. Be that as it may, in your group, too, you will perhaps have to face the unmistakable fact that it is the fate of significant movements to be unsuccessful, that they must be ventured just the same, and that it is only when swimming hopelessly against the stream that one can really live—really live "concretely."

With friendly greetings in this regard,

Yours,
KARL BARTH

¹The publication *konkret* had asked Barth to answer several questions. The fourth concerned a popular movement against atomic armaments in Germany. The movement had not so far been successful and Barth was asked whether it was pointless, as many thought, and if not, why not.

*   *   *

9
To Prof. Ernst Wolf
Göttingen

Basel, 28 July 1961

Dear Ernst,

Lollo,[1] who is my memory and conscience in such matters, has pointed out to me that you celebrate your sixtieth birthday on 2 August.[2] In order that I may not be late in this important matter but do you justice in the calm of festive depth and deep festivity, I am writing you at once.

That you now have sixty years behind you is an important event. And that I have been able to spend half of these years in fellowship with you is for me an occasion of great joy and thanksgiving. You must have seen what specific pleasure it has given me each time you have entered this room. Only rarely and not very clearly, however, have I indicated to you what you mean to me and how much all that you have done for me over this long span has touched me. This time I am going to make it explicit.

When I think of it, you stand before me as the embodiment of what I would terribly like to be but now that my "unique opportunity"[3] has almost passed I certainly never can be: a true scholar, who has not just hit on a few things in and out of season as I have, but has displayed (a) a proper view of creation as a whole; (b) a constantly functioning acquaintance with the literature on every important subject between heaven and earth; and (c) what I find to be an astonishing ability to gather things together in literary form, to develop them, and to expound them succinctly and in the right terms. This is your gift, to which I can only look up, grateful that there is such a thing so close to me.

An observation: Have you really been true to your real bent by becoming, technically at least, a teacher of systematics?[4] I see and understand you as a historian with strong systematic talents and interests, not vice versa (cf. your recent address on Melanchthon, which I found most instructive).[5]

Be that as it may, the chief thing I have never stated properly is my realization of how much you have unselfishly done for me across the years and decades. I am remembering not merely your great and successful efforts to assemble and edit two comprehensive *Festschrifte* for me.[6] The real point is that I could always rely on you to jump in at once for me when necessary or otherwise appropriate. It has depended and still depends on you, not whether my wonderful services for church and theology should rate highly in the upper echelons in Germany but simply whether *any* value should be attached to the murmurings of the old man in Basel, which often seemed to be remote in both time and space. In word and writing you have played your part with a loyalty which puts me to shame. That I realize this is what must be said for once in due order.

When shall we see you again? We so easily lose touch with what is going on in Germany, for example in relation to the brotherhoods,[7] or the Berlin Kirchentag, or Niemöller's activity in East Germany.[8] How much goes on before and behind the wings which cannot be read in any newspaper and which would best be expunged in Christian love. In the Hamburg *Welt* I learned that in Bielefeld, in a kind of museum of the church conflict (should I donate an old pipe?), the original of the Barmen Declaration is on display. Is this really the text that I drew up while the Lutherans slept?[9] And how did it get there?

Meanwhile here in Basel (and in all of Switzerland) we have had our own church conflict about Gollwitzer,[10] in which I have not taken part, but which has revealed the thoughts of many hearts.[11] At the moment those who must decide are on vacation. No appointment to my chair is thus to be expected before the winter. As you may have read, a great occasion was made of my last lecture, with the rector in full regalia, a male chorus, and a broadcast, but in the winter I shall be back on the job with a lecture and seminars. I shall then retire definitely in the new year (naturally by way of Brione).[12] In view of my natural indolence and release from daily pressure the problem of how to continue C.D. still awaits solution. Lollo will undoubtedly have to keep me afloat with drops and showers and encouraging words.

Here, apart from incursions by Americans, Japanese, and others, we had an enjoyable visit from Prof. Steinbauer and his wife.[13] His book—I have received and read the beginning—seems to me to be a good one but could do with shortening.[14] In official Bavaria things are obviously not good in spite or because of Dietzfelbinger.[15] But where in the church are they good?

On 6 August I shall be preaching in the usual place—on the love in which is no fear because it is cast out.[16] I shall be sending on a little work in which I with many others had to answer in telegram style the question, What is the national task of modern Switzerland?[17] I had a friendly telephone call from Heinemann direct from the Bundeshaus in Bonn.[18]

So much for now. We shall be thinking of you on August 2. Lollo will demonstrate this in a separate greeting to you.

My warmest greetings to you and Asta. (Uvo[19] was here recently; how well he has done!)

Yours,

KARL BARTH

[1]Charlotte von Kirschbaum.

[2]In fact, Wolf's sixtieth birthday was on 2 August 1962. In a letter of 31 July 1962, not included in this collection, Barth begins by saying that the past year has simply confirmed what he had said by mistake the year before.

[3]C.D. III, 4, §56, 1.

[4]In 1957 Wolf switched from the chair of church history at Göttingen to that of systematic theology.

[5]E. Wolf, "Philipp Melanchthon. Evangelischer Humanismus," Göttinger Universitätsreden, 30 (1961).

[6]Theologische Aufsätze . . . , ed. A. Lempp and E. Wolf (Munich, 1936) and Antwort . . . , ed. E. Wolf, C. v. Kirschbaum, and R. Frey (Zollikon-Zurich, 1956).

[7]Barth is referring to leadership conflicts at the conference in Frankfurt on 24–25 May 1961.

[8]The 1961 Kirchentag was originally scheduled for Leipzig in East Germany but was moved to Berlin. Niemöller refused to participate and made a lecture tour in East Germany instead.

[9]In preparation for Barmen Barth was on a working committee with Hans Asmussen and Thomas Breit, and while they took a siesta he himself drafted the six theses which were adopted almost unchanged as the Barmen Declaration at the synod on 31 May 1934.

[10]Cf. Letter 5, par. 2 (subsequent references will be to the number of the letter alone).

[11]Cf. Luke 2:35.

[12]The place where Barth regularly took a short vacation after the winter semester, often along with E. Wolf. It is in Ticino Canton.

[13]Karl Steinbauer, Wolfratshausen, Bavaria.

[14]The book, which dealt with Steinbauer's opposition to National Socialism and the Lutheran leaders in Bavaria, was never published.

[15]Hermann Dietzfelbinger, Bishop of the Evangelical Lutheran Church in Bavaria from 1955.

[16]Sermon in Basel prison on 1 John 4:18: "There is no fear in love."

[17]"Welches ist heute unsere grösste nationale Aufgabe?"; answers by ten prominent Swiss citizens in *Zürcher-Woche*, 7 July 1961.

[18]Gustav Heinemann, at that time a delegate in the West German Federal Diet.

[19]Wolf's wife and son.

*   *   *

10
To Marie-Claire Barth
Bogor, Indonesia[1]

Basel, 1 August 1961

Dear Marie-Claire,

Your last letter to Mama, which came this morning, offers me a welcome opportunity to write a few words to you directly.

I can well imagine that parting from the GMPI,[2] which you have served so long and faithfully, has cost you quite a bit, even though you will still play a part in it in a senior capacity. The program of your conference greatly pleased me because it obviously testified to profound and careful preparation. If only all of our conferences in the old church were planned so well and responsibly! Since you must have had a hand in arranging things there, you are really to be congratulated for the work you have now substantially completed. And I may only hope that your growing sons[3] and their father will be the more grateful now that you give yourself chiefly to them.

I was sorry to hear that Daniel took the temporary absence of his mother so badly that his stomach was affected and he even lost weight. Nicolas on the other hand is emotionally and physically stronger. A small exegetical difference of opinion arose here regarding the report given by Christoph. I took it to be quite harmless to hear that Nicolas resembled me, but Lollo thought it meant he showed signs of developing into an unconcerned fellow like his grandfather in Basel. However that may be, Nicolas must have a cup like Daniel's; we will buy it next week. I shall be very glad to see the two and if only they were here would take them out and watch them eat one of the big meringues they make very well around here. You will be able to cope with what follows, won't you?

We are enjoying vacation life along with various little tasks. I shall be preaching in the prison on 5 August.[4] And various guests provide a break. Yesterday we had Paul Tillich, with whom I get on excellently as a man, for all our total theological disagreement. His wife was present too and joined in eagerly and volubly on themes that interested her. She was so much at home with us that she suddenly took off her shoes and stockings and curled up boldly in one of our easy chairs. The things that happen in this vale of tears! A Japanese professor of medicine who also heads a clinic in Tokyo was there too. He knew neither German nor English and since I unfortunately know no Japanese he simply took photographs from all angles and immortalized my lovely voice on tape. The Gollwitzer battle has quieted down for the holidays.[5] There is no foreseeing what will be done after the rest period. Some of the harm has been made good by the fact that fifty-one Zurich pastors have come out for Gollwitzer.[6] The weather vacillates here between hot and cold. Lollo is again wearing the dress with yellow hares you didn't like two years ago—the only thing I have against you!

Enough for now. This was simply meant to be a note of sympathy. Greet Christoph and the youngsters and warmest greetings to yourself,

Yours,

PAPA

P.S. You must not expect anything special in a lecture by me. I am a tired old man whose intellectual forces are rapidly declining.

---

[1]Barth's daughter-in-law, wife of his son Christoph.

[2]Gerakan Mahasiswa Kristen Indonesia (Indonesian Student Christian Movement). Marie-Claire Barth, née Frommel, was student secretary of this organization from 1957 to 1961, before and just after her marriage. She resigned at the 1961 congress, where the theme was "Christ Has Come to Serve."

[3]Daniel (1959) and Nicolas (1960) Barth.

[4]Cf. 9, n. 16.

[5]Cf. 5, par. 2.

[6]"Wir freuen uns aufrichtig ... 51 Zürcher Pfarrer zur umstrittenen Professoren-wahl in Basel," *Tages-Anzeiger für Stadt und Kanton Zürich*, 7 December 1961.

*   *   *

11
To a Theological Student

Basel, 22 August 1961

Dear N.N.,

The photographs you took on 10 May and so kindly sent to me are very good and will always remind me vividly of that morning. I sincerely thank you for them.

When I then at your request recommended you for a Reformed Churches grant I simply assumed that you intended to improve your English in Edinburgh and especially to gain some acquaintance with the Anglo-Saxon theology represented there. If I had suspected you could now ask me, What shall I really do in the land of John Knox? I would certainly not have given my name in support of your application. Is it clear to you that you will bring censure on me—not to speak of others— if you do not do there what you proposed, and do it properly? If you do not do this, but proceed to spin a heap of straw into gold, to use your own expression, then it would be better for you to give up the grant so that it may be passed on to someone more modest.

The same applies to your dissertation plan, regarding which, strictly formally, I would draw your attention to the fact that with us (and other Swiss faculties to the best of my knowledge) you cannot become a doctor without passing the "state examination." So then, even if you think you have the most brilliant academic future, I advise you to face first and to prepare very seriously for the eschaton of the state examination.

This counsel coincides, however, with the only responsible thing I can say to you regarding your plans for theological reformation. I have read your letter twice and have to confess that my head spun worse the second time than the first. Your enterprise, for which you quote Jer. 20:9, has neither head nor tail and where one looks for the middle there is darkness. Before one can say (or meaningfully ask) anything, one must first listen, and before one can write anything, one must first do proper reading. If you cannot or will not learn this, you had better keep your fingers out of not merely academic theology but theology in general. Why should you not be able or willing to learn it? But to do so you must now make this, in the form of practical exercises, your own most urgent task, taking precedence over everything else, and I particularly mean over all high-flying plans for the reformation of dogmatics.

Dear N.N., your present mode of theological, Christian, and human existence worries me as it comes out in your letter—so much so that I can only beg you to take a big sponge, wipe out everything, and begin again at the beginning which, as we know, consists in the fear of the Lord that is the beginning of wisdom.[1]

With warm greetings and good wishes,

Yours,

KARL BARTH

[1]Cf. Prov 1:7; 15:33.

*　　　*　　　*

12
To Dr. Hans-Werner Bartsch
Krümbach über Giessen

Basel, 31 August 1961

[In this letter Barth discussed political matters in Germany relating to the question of nuclear armaments. The complete text and explanatory notes of this and the other summarized letters may be found in *Briefe, 1961-1968*, V, Vol. 6 of the Swiss *Gesamtausgabe.*]

*　　　*　　　*

13
To Mrs. N.N.
Safenwil (Aargau Canton)

Basel, 16 September 1961

Dear Mrs. N.N.,

It was kind of you to send me those lovely flowers. They have been put in various places in our little house and give pleasure to us all. I sincerely thank you.

Please tell your brother that I am with him in his suffering. I can well recall how sad he was when—I think it was in the summer of 1911—he lost his first wife. Yes, you are right; we are all getting older and have not much time left. But all will be well.

What a pity you could not be in Zofingen.[1] I was glad to be in Aargau again. And many amusing things took place; for example, there was a speech by Ernst Widmer,[2] who quietly dug up the fact that they had not been too satisfied with me in Safenwil. And then Elise Diriwächter, as she then was (now Mrs. ? in Dörfli),[3] got up and gave witness on my behalf to all the four hundred people. Markus[4] was also there. He has now been in Chicago for some time. And my sister,[5] whom you remember, came from Bern to be present. Afterwards I went to see the fine new parsonage in Safenwil and was pleased everything is so much more comfortable. But we were usually cheerful and content in the old parsonage, weren't we?

I must be back to work. With warm greetings to you and your husband,

Yours (also a little older),

KARL BARTH

[1]At the Kirchentag there on 10 August 1961 Barth gave an address on "Church and Theology" and met many of his former parishioners from Safenwil.
[2]President of the governing board of the church at Safenwil during Barth's ministry there (1911-1921).
[3]Elise Hilfiker. Dörfli is a part of Safenwil.
[4]Markus Barth, Barth's eldest son, was then a New Testament professor in Chicago. He returned to Basel in 1973.
[5]Gertrud Lindt, née Barth.

*   *   *

14

To Carl Frey
Basel

Basel, 7 October 1961

Dear Mr. Frey,

Unfortunately I cannot comply with the request in your letter of yesterday.[1]

To be sure, I am always thinking of the German problem. The only thing is that I do not wish to express myself in an organ appearing in East Germany.

To be frank, I fear both the way they use for propaganda anything that agrees with their doctrine and also the way they will suppress or disregard any reservations. And is it not true that the peace treaty will come as a fixed thing and the planned world forum will not have the slightest influence on what, when it comes about, will be an event between the Kremlin and the White House?

I thus ask you to excuse me.

With friendly greetings,

Yours,
KARL BARTH

[1]Frey was a Basel journalist who asked Barth to participate in a world forum on the question, Why do you favor a German peace treaty?

*   *   *

15
To Prof. Edgar Bonjour
Basel

Basel, 27 October 1961

Dear Colleague,

You have again given me pleasure by sending me the second volume of your essays.[1] Accept my sincerest thanks for this welcome gift. You know so well what I do not know but what I so greatly want to learn. For this purpose this further volume of your works will serve me well.

The time I usually turn to history is in the night when I should be sleeping but am glad to turn again to the humanities. Would you believe it, the book that occupies me at the moment is an account of the life and works of the Confederate general Thomas Jackson of the American Civil War,[2] and for the sake of accuracy I compare it with other accounts of the same events—no simple maneuver in bed. Another thick tome on Abraham Lincoln[3] was a gift from my son in Chicago and is awaiting me. But I should like to slip in something from Swiss history between them, lest my growing sympathy for the southern "rebels," which has already brought me into disfavor in Switzerland, should gain the upper hand.

Enough! I thank you again and extend my best wishes for your semester's work. With warmest greetings,

Yours,
KARL BARTH

[1]E. Bonjour, *Die Schweiz und Europa. Ausgewählte Reden und Aufsätze*, II (Basel, 1961; Vol. I, 1958).
[2]R. L. Dabney, *Life and Campaigns of Lt. Gen. Thomas J. Jackson (Stonewall Jackson)* (New York, 1866).
[3]C. Sandburg, *Abraham Lincoln. The Prairie Years and the War Years*, one-vol. ed. (New York, 1954).

*   *   *

16
To Prof. Jan Milic Lochman
Prague

Basel, 30 October 1961

Dear Colleague,

Warmest thanks for your friendly and pressing letter of 19 October.[1]

How often and how earnestly I have been invited to Prague and have always had to refuse. Be sure that what is written in Matthew 25:43b carries weight with me. If only I were still as active as some years ago so that I could more easily combine what I have to do here with many important things elsewhere. But the same difficulty constantly arises. You want me in Prague on the twenty-second to the twenty-fifth of January. But dear colleague, I am now engaged in what will certainly be my last semester—one hour of lecturing, two hours of seminars, and four of colloquia. Students from at home and abroad are here, and to the best of my strength I must prepare and hand out the food they need. In addition to that to prepare some special lectures and a sermon for Prague and to fly off there for a week—you will see that others could do this, most others, but I never could, and even less can I do it now with my seventy-five years. The fact that I have undoubtedly written more books than any other living theologian, so that people can read me without seeing me, certainly does not excuse me, or only in part. Somewhere even in my life there could and should be a space for me to come in a flash to Prague, to see again my friends there, and at least in part to satisfy what they expect from me. I would love to do it even now. But things being as they are, it is impossible. My eyes are almost full of tears as I write, but this is the way it is and I can only ask you and Hromádka[2] and Souček[3] and all the good people there to understand so far as they can. Pass on to them my warm greetings, and greetings to you, too,

Yours,
KARL BARTH

[1]An invitation to give lectures and a sermon at a theological conference in Prague, January 1962.
[2]Josef L. Hromádka (1889-1969), professor of systematic theology on the Comenius Faculty at Prague. Cf. Barth's letters to him.
[3]Josef B. Souček (1902-1972), professor of New Testament on the Comenius Faculty.

*　　　*　　　*

17
To Prof. Otto Weber
Göttingen

Basel, 4 December 1961

Dear Friend and Colleague,

I owe you a reply which you are perhaps expecting with some impatience.

Can you believe it? I am not in favor of a German translation of that work *Proclamation de l'Évangile*.[1] It is a translation of the copy of a homiletical colloquium I held in Bonn, I think in the summer of 1933.[2] It would make no sense to translate it back into German. Nor do I want the German original to be published—it must be around somewhere—since it has in it many crudities and blunders which might not make it totally impossible in the French sphere but which should not be allowed on the scene in today's German sphere.[3]

Fellow-humanity will have to wait with some patience for the publication of *C.D.* IV, 4 (not to speak of V).[4] I am now in *mezzo del cammino*,[5] and in what is definitely my last semester I am not teaching ethics but a strange one-hour course, *Introduction to Evangelical Theology*,[6] which gives me as much to do as the four-, three-, and finally two-hour courses gave me when I was working on the *Dogmatics* in my vigorous years. And in April I shall be off to America (provisionally Chicago and Princeton).[7]

As I am writing, someone has left here the record of the last seminar session. It deals with the *Institutes* III, vi, 5,[8] and the final paragraph of the account runs literally as follows:

4. With the above-mentioned exclusion of the division between God and human orders, and the demand for an undivided heart, an ethics in the spirit of R. Niebuhr, and especially one sharing the Lutheran two-kingdoms doctrine, is shown to be inadequate. Yet against expectation, and to the obvious horror of Karl Barth, Otto Weber, Reformed (!) professor of theology at Göttingen, has in his translation given to III, xix, 15 the heading "The Two Kingdoms."[9] This might well be regarded as another confirmation of the thesis that we are influenced by our background. At any rate, pending some deeper insight, the only possible explanation must be provisionally that the German soul is naturally Lutheran.[10]

Tableau!

With sincere greetings and all good wishes,

Yours,

KARL BARTH

[1]K. Barth, *La Proclamation de l'Évangile* (Neuchatel, 1961).
[2]The winter semester of 1932/33 and the summer semester of 1933.
[3]Later the German text, revised by G. Seyfferth, was in fact published with the title *Homiletik. Wesen und Vorbereitung der Predigt* (Zurich, 1966).
[4]A fragment of *C.D.* IV, 4, *The Christian Life. Baptism as the Foundation of the Christian Life*, came out in 1967 (ET 1969). Materials for the rest of the unfinished volume were published as part of the *Gesamtausgabe* in 1975.
[5]Cf. Dante Alighieri, *La Divina Commedia*, I, 1–3.
[6]Pub. Zurich, 1962 (ET 1963).
[7]On the United States tour cf. 23, 30, 34–37, 39–40.
[8]The theme of Barth's seminar in the winter semester of 1961/62 was "The Christian Life in Calvin," the text being the *Institutes* III, vi–x.
[9]J. Calvin, *Unterricht in der christlichen Religion*, II (bk. III) (Neukirchen, 1937; 2nd ed. 1963), p. 412.
[10]On 8 Dec. 1961 Weber replied that it could hardly be contested that in the *Institutes* III, xix, 15 and IV, xx, 1–3 Calvin does in fact present the idea of the two kingdoms, but these are relics of the 1536 edition which are an alien body in the final version.

*　　　　*　　　　*

18
To Pastor H. Poms
Basel

Basel, 7 December 1961

Dear Pastor,

I am sorry you were so thoroughly upset by what I said the previous Monday about Jewish missions.[1]

I wonder, however, if this would have been possible if you had not merely seized on the catchphrase "Better no Jewish missions today," which came, as you recall, at the end of a discussion of other matters. You should have also borne in mind the more explicit and basic presentation which I attempted both of the general relation between Israel and the church in *C.D.* II, 2, §34 (with a minute exegesis of Romans 9–11), and also practically and specifically of Jewish missions in *C.D.* IV, 3, pp. 876ff. Before you correct me on the matter publicly, as the closing part of your letter suggests, it might be well for you to study these passages closely, lest you tilt at windmills. It might be profitable to consult too what Gollwitzer, Kraus, and others said at the Berlin Kirchentag about the whole Jewish question as the most burning issue for Christians today.[2]

If Jewish missions are not actually called Jewish missions (I know of Jews who regard the very term as an insult and I too must reject it as theologically impossible), and if the thing itself is done under another name as exclusively a work of Jews among Jews (i.e., so long as the Gentile church has obviously not taken to heart "The Last of the Righteous" and all it implies),[3] then, dear pastor, agreement between yourself and me will probably be reached quite easily.

My whole concern is (Romans 9:4f.) that Israel as Israel should finally be taken seriously as the starting point of every discussion of what Israel should and should not do.

With friendly greetings,

Yours,
KARL BARTH

[1]On 27 November 1961 Barth was answering questions put by Basel clergy. Poms, a preacher for the Swiss Evangelical Jewish Mission, wrote him on 2 December 1961 asking whether it was for any man to say that the word of the Lord Jesus Christ should be withheld from Israel for a period. Having sung about the rising of the star of Jacob, can we say to Jacob's children that it is for us, not for you, or we will not now tell you anything about it? Must our penitence for the holocaust take the form of silence? Has not this silence become the real sin? In repayment must we sacrifice the small group of Christians engaged in Jewish missions on Christ's commission? Poms said that from conversations with Jewish relatives and friends he knew many Jews who had no greater longing than to hear what they seemed to reject and contest so sharply, the gospel of Jesus Christ.

[2]Cf. the *Dokumente* of the Kirchentag (Stuttgart, 1961), pp. 413-505, and also *Der ungekündigte Bund. Neue Begegnung von Juden und christlicher Gemeinde*, ed. D. Goldschmidt and H.-J. Kraus (Stuttgart and Berlin, 1962).

[3]A. Schwarz-Bart, *Le Dernier des Justes* (Paris, 1959); German *Der Letzte der Gerechten* (Frankfurt/Main, 1960).

*　　　　*　　　　*

19
To a Prisoner in Germany

Basel, 20 December 1961

Dear N.N.,

Your letter of the thirteenth reached me yesterday and moved me greatly. Partly because you refer to my good friend Gertrud Staewen[1] but above all because Christmas is upon us, I hasten to make at least a short reply.

Since you obviously want something from me, you cannot be serious in expecting me to judge you harshly. But can I give you any supporting counsel?

You say you plunge deeply into the Bible in vain. You say you also pray in vain. You are clearly thinking of a "final step" but you shrink back from it. Have I understood you correctly?

First regarding your prayers. How do you know they are in vain? God has His own time and He may well know the right moment to lift the double shadow that now lies over your life. Therefore, do not stop praying.

It could also be that He will answer you in a very different way from what you have in mind in your prayers. Hold unshakably fast to one thing. He loves you even now as the one you now are. . . . And listen closely: it might well be that He will not lift this shadow from you, possibly will never do so your whole life, just because from all eternity He has appointed you to be His friend as He is yours, just because He wants you as the man whose only option it is to love Him in return and give Him alone the glory there in the depths from which He will not raise you.

Get me right: I am not saying that this has to be so, that the shadows cannot disperse. But I see and know that there are shadows in the lives of all of us, not the same as those under which you sigh, but in their way oppressive ones too, which will not disperse, and which perhaps in God's will must not disperse, so that we may be held in the place where, as those who are loved by God, we can only love Him back and praise him.

Thus, even if this is His mind and will for you, in no case must you think of that final step. May your hope not be a tiny flame but a big and strong one, even then, I say, and perhaps precisely *then*; no, not perhaps but certainly, for what God chooses for us children of men is always the best.

Can you follow me? Perhaps you can if you read the Christmas story in Luke's Gospel, not deeply but very simply, with the thought that every word there, and every word in the Twenty-Third Psalm too, is meant for you too, and especially for you.

With friendly greetings and all good wishes,

Yours,

KARL BARTH

[1]Gertrud Staewen, née Ordemann, for many years a social worker in the Tegel prison, Berlin.

*   *   *

20
To Pastor Hans Schädelin
Bern

Basel, 20 December 1961

Dear Pastor,

With much grief I learned yesterday morning of the death of your father.[1] With his fiery, restless, critical, yet as long as I knew him constructive spirit, he was one of the constant forces in my own life. He made an unforgettable impression on me when I visited him for the first time in Rohrbach. And then there were other meetings at which I had reason to be grateful to him for salutary shocks as well as for the encouragement of his participation in my activities. There were also times when I saw him less frequently and even moments of minor confrontation as when he seemed to me to be too "churchly" in terms of the Bern church. I am sorry today not to have tried to see him more in these last years. This was due partly to an undoubted short circuit in detail, by which I put him on much that same line that you and your brother-in-law Stickelberger[2] take on the East-West question. You may be sure, however, that this kind of thing in no way altered the high and friendly regard in which I held him. What his passing will mean for Bern and beyond you are well aware, and much better than I. Seldom are we given the kind of shepherd and leader that he was in the church. What a fifty-year period was that in which in his own unique way he stood in the front line! All I can say to you is that his death has left a truly great gap in my own world. Thinking about him always seemed to me like looking at a mighty fortress. I will never forget how reliably he rushed to my aid in difficult situations—I am thinking of the call to Bern in 1927[3] and the Feldmann crisis ten years ago.[4] Nor can I ever forget the cheerfulness and humor with which he always met me through all the ups and downs.

I ask you to assure your mother of my heartfelt sympathy. With all good wishes for yourself and your work,

Yours,
KARL BARTH

[1]Albert Schädelin (1879-1961), emeritus cathedral pastor and professor of practical theology at Bern.

[2]Rudolf Stickelberger, originally a pastor (1947-1961), later an editor and journalist.

[3]Though championed by Schädelin, this call fell through because of theological and financial problems. Details may be found in the correspondence between Barth and Thurneysen, Vol. II: 1921-1930 (Zurich, 1974), pp. 512ff.

[4]A controversy arising out of Barth's Die Kirche zwischen Ost und West (Zollikon-Zurich, 1949). For details and literature see Briefe, 1961-1968, V, Vol. 6 of Gesamtausgabe, letter 20, n. 4.

*   *   *

21

To Prof. Karl Gerhard Steck

Basel, 24 December 1961

Dear Friend,

After reading your "hand-out"[1] on the controversy with [the Romans][2] I had a desire to address you as *Vir doctissime*, as we do here at doctoral graduations. I found it to be a materially excellent as well as practical paper. Send it also to Hans Küng, who is continually sawing away at the same trunk from the other side (Gartenstrasse 103, Tübingen). Yesterday I was in Geneva, not among the ecumenists, but to meet Christoph and his wife, who with their two sons (who speak and understand only Indonesian) have come to spend eight months in Europe. Thanks for your letter and its news. I am now doing what is definitely my last semester and in April I am going with L.[ollo] to America for a while: lectures in Chicago and Princeton and visits to some battlefields of the Civil War of a hundred years ago.[3] I shall be coming back with the impetus of the rebel yell (do you know what that is?) into the theological doings and affairs over here. With greetings (also from L.) to you and yours and the necessary good wishes,

Yours,
KARL BARTH

[1]K. G. Steck, "Die römisch-katholische Kirche und die Ökumene," *Botschaft und Dienst*, 4 (1961).
[2]Partly illegible.
[3]Cf. 23, n. 1.

*   *   *

22
To Dr. Martin Niemöller
Wiesbaden

Basel, 7 January 1962

Dear Martin,

You are celebrating your seventieth birthday[1] and will receive many tokens of grateful sharing in your life. So far I have not received the announced book of pictures illustrating it (what a good idea!).[2] But you can be sure that you are before me in a very living way and that with many, many others I rejoice that you were and are still there in our tangled age, in that distinctive way that has been given you. That you are like a *rocher de bronze* would not be quite the right simile; rather, you are like a magnetic needle which is always moving but always points unerringly upwards and forwards. I hope you outlive me so that I may always say how good it is that along with the many vacillating figures there is also a Martin Niemöller.

The past year has brought you unusual things: the sudden and painful loss of your good life's partner,[3] with whom we had become accustomed to see you since 1945; and then (how vigorous you are!) your participation in the New Delhi Conference and your giddy ascent there into the supreme council of the ecumenical movement.[4] And now I suppose—it is said of you that God alone knows where you are at any given moment—that you are in your Hessian diocese[5] doing everything that can be done to support, to set in motion, and to pacify. May you enjoy success in all things, to God's glory and the healing of our confused heads and troubled hearts, both there and elsewhere, not least in the east zone which God loves[6] and to which you have special access.

And now you are seventy and have reached the first of the limits set in Ps 90[7] while I am already on the way to the second. Do we want to do a little more, Martin? And will there be granted us a little span to do it? Perhaps we have done what we were to do by way of participation in the history of the church and the world and life in general. But ordering this is not in our hands. And so long as we are not told from above to stop, neither you nor I would wish to discontinue our course, even though it is with softly slowed down engines rather than full steam ahead. You will note the little admonition (I am not the only one to whisper it to you) not to overdo things, so that, as Thurneysen[8] puts it so well, you may be kept for the church a little longer, as we usually say with some caution in relation to veterans and jubilees.

Enough, for you will have enough to read in these days and weeks. You know it will always be a joy to me to see you here and think of you elsewhere. In April and May I am planning to go to America for the first time, with a limited program but with anticipation and real curiosity, and I will certainly come upon your tracks there.

With warmest greetings,

Yours,

KARL BARTH

[1] 14 January 1962.

[2] *Der Mann in der Brandung. Ein Bildbuch um Martin Niemöller. Mit einem Geleitwort von Albert Schweitzer*, ed. H. Mochalski (Frankfurt/Main, 1962).

[3] Mrs. Else Niemöller, née Bremer, had a fatal accident 7 August 1961.

[4] The Third World Council of Churches at New Delhi, 19 November–5 December 1961. Niemöller was here elected one of the presidents of the World Council.

[5] The Evangelical Church in Hesse and Nassau.

[6] East Germany. The phrase, which Barth liked to use, was coined in the fifties by a theologian resident there.

[7] Ps 90:10.

[8] Eduard Thurneysen (1888-1974), one of Barth's closest friends, was at this time emeritus cathedral pastor and professor of practical theology at Basel.

*   *   *

23

To Prof. John E. Smith, Yale University
New Haven, Connecticut

Basel, 7 January 1962

Dear Colleague,

You have not yet received a reply to your kind letter of 20 December. Let me first thank you sincerely for the gracious invitation you extended to me on such generous terms. In other circumstances it would be a great pleasure for me to give the two lectures you ask for at Yale and to take the opportunity to stay for a time at the college.

But you will have already learned from Prof. Formann and Mr. Holden, whom I have written in the meantime, that to my regret it is not possible for me to visit Yale.

My plan for the U.S.A. visit had to be from the very first a greatly limited one.[1] I shall spend a week in Chicago, where my son works,[2] and a week in Princeton, where there is a jubilee celebration. Then I shall visit as a tourist a few places that are historically important to me, returning to Europe in the middle of May. I beg you to understand that if I were to come to Yale too it would be hard for me to turn down invitations I also have to other places. But to undertake a big tour with many visits would be beyond the powers of my no longer youthful age (seventy-six).

I am sure you will not take this as any disparagement of your invitation and offer. It is not a question of my sincere *velle* [will] but my limited *posse* [ability].

With warm greetings and best wishes for your work in the New Year,

Yours,

KARL BARTH

---

[1]On his United States tour Barth, accompanied by Markus and Christoph and Charlotte von Kirschbaum, visited Chicago for small group discussions (7-12 April), Dubuque for discussions in the seminary (13-14 April), Chicago for lectures one through five from his *Evangelical Theology* (15-28 April), Princeton on the occasion of the 150th anniversary for the same lectures as in Chicago (28 April-5 May), Gettysburg and Washington for political discussions (5-8 May), Richmond and Civil War battlegrounds (8-14 May), San Francisco for the same lectures as in Chicago and Princeton at San Anselmo Seminary (14-16 May), and New York for discussions with prison officials, civil rights leaders, and professors at Union Seminary (23-26 May). He flew back to Switzerland on 26 May 1962.
[2]Markus Barth.

*   *   *

24
To N.N.

Basel, 13 January 1962

Dear N.N.,

Your letter to Lollo on 23 Dec., and the sending of Lord Dowding's book, were obviously meant for me too and so I will tell you briefly what I think of the book. Your good mother wrote to tell us that I would shake my head when I read your letter. One might say that I did so, especially at *God's Magic!*[1] But shaking the head is not strong enough. To be sincere, I have to say that I read it with horror.

I will not enter into the question of the presupposed possibility and reality of survival after death, of communication with the dead, or the help we can give them and they can give us, because I have to declare myself totally incompetent in such matters. I have never had, and presumably never will have, encounters with Egyptians who died 3000 years ago or with pilots who crashed during the war, and Lord D. himself, although he has astonishing things to tell us in this regard (pp. 21-31; 49-58), puts little weight on this side of the matter but rather lays all the emphasis on what we are supposed to get out of such encounters. "By their fruits you shall know them"[2] (p. 10).

I might also put to you the following question: Dear N.N., how do you distinguish between the five talks of the Egyptian in 1945, which are reproduced in the book, and the best of liberal preaching which you may hear in any canton as well as Basel, and which Lord D., if he had been to church more diligently, could have heard from many people in the Church of England without having to summon up voices from the beyond? Could what was said really make an impression on you? And could you expect it to make an impression on me? This is precisely the kind of religious talk that for good reasons I have left aside for the last forty or fifty years. [. . .] And are we now to listen to such talk again just because it comes from the beyond?

A few examples:

I read on p. 18 that prayer is only another word for thought.

On pp. 19 and 48: the redemption of man must take place through man.

On p. 33: we have to realize and accept the immanence of God in ourselves and all our fellow creatures.

On p. 33: men, not God, made the earth.

On pp. 46, 48, and 58: we must distinguish between a Christ spirit and Jesus, who is simply its completest form.

On p. 49: each of us is a part of God and so each is also a part of other men.

On p. 58: religion is action in accordance with enlightened self-interest.

Do I have to say to you that this is poor stuff, that these are not even new but old and indeed the very oldest heresies? If nothing better or more clever is to be had from the beyond, then I want no communication from there, nor should you, dear N.N., whom thus far I have always thought of as someone receptive to good theology.

You see I am simply shocked, and deeply shocked, to find you taking the way of spiritualism after your express declaration: Nothing more than Jesus Christ. The matter is all the worse because with you it is obviously bound up with astrology too. [. . .] If only I could still call you back.

With warm greetings,

Yours,
KARL BARTH

[1]Lord Dowding, *God's Magic* (London, 1962).
[2]Matt 7:16, 20.

*　　　　　*　　　　　*

25
To the Institute of the Sacred Heart of Mary
Hannut, Belgium

Basel, 12 February 1962

Dear Teachers and Students,
Most Venerable Sisters,

You have had the great and ingenious goodness to send me an address which you have all signed and in which you have expressed, in words that sincerely touch me, your Christian sympathy with the theological work whose design has formed and characterized my life to this day.

It surprises me and yet also fills me with joy to learn from your message that news of my doings has reached you too.

You are right to tell me that much of the route to the unity of the church is laid when we come together again in *love*. Being the friend of many Roman Catholic theologians, I add that I am happy to affirm that in *truth* as well we have come closer on both sides than could ever have been imagined fifty years ago. One thing is certain: the more both your theology and ours concentrate on the person and work of Jesus Christ, true God and true man, our sovereign Lord and only Savior, the more we shall find ourselves already united in spite of some important differences. Do you not also think the day will one day come when we shall no longer speak of Roman Catholic and Protestant Christians but simply of Evangelical Christians forming one body and one people? *Veni Creator Spiritus.*

With this prayer and hope I salute you, all of you, teachers and taught. My desire is that the common work of your Institute may be done to God's glory and the benefit of humanity.

KARL BARTH

*   *   *

26
To Pastor Dorothee Hoch
Riehen near Basel

Basel, 3 March 1962

Dear Miss Hoch,

Thanks for your proposal for a baptismal service.[1] I like it very much. Only the baptismal instruction on the first page causes me some disquiet. Would it not be better to leave out the allusion to infant baptism, since it is mythology to think any witness is imparted to babies?

Some material for further reflection on this part of the text:

The Lord Jesus Christ had Himself baptized in the Jordan to confirm His complete fellowship with us sinners and His complete readiness to live and die for us in the service of God.

Hence His command to His disciples: Go into all the world. . . .

Our baptism is the sign that we have heard His Word, that we rejoice that we may belong to the covenant set up in Him between God and man, that we are thankful to Him and ready to follow Him in love, that we pray God He will make us truly free to do this.

With friendly greetings and all good wishes,

Yours,
KARL BARTH

[1]Stimulated by Barth's doctrine of baptism, the recipient had drawn up a liturgy for baptisms at the Basel Hospital for Women, and asked Barth to evaluate it.

*　　　*　　　*

27
To Mrs. Gertrud Staewen
Berlin[1]

Basel, 15 March 1962

Dear Gertrud,

I am thinking of you, too. Do not let yourself be overcome by the demons you have fought so stoutly all your life. And remember that I am retired like you and have only a little left to say. The time must come when we—our generation—will have had our time and opportunity and made it more or less fruitful. "The Lord alone is King . . .":[2] Have we not always stood for this both to those who are free and to those who are in prison?[3] Thus! [. . .]

Early today I recommended to an older (or no longer young) lady with pains in her legs that she should follow my countermeasure of raising the feet. But raising the head and heart is more important.

Your old friend greets you,

KARL

P.S. On a letter that came today I was addressed as the late Professor of Systematic Theology!

[1]Appended to a letter by Charlotte von Kirschbaum, 15 March 1962.
[2]From the last verse of Paul Gerhardt's "Du, meine Seele, singe . . ."
[3]Alluding to G. Staewen's prison work.

*　　　*　　　*

28
To Prof. W. H. Schultze
Braunschweig

Basel, Bruderholzallee 26, 26 March 1962

Dear Colleague,

Sincere thanks for what you told me about your great-grandfather Wegscheider,[1] which I did indeed find most interesting. What I wrote about him rested solely on reading his Latin dogmatics.[2] I willingly acknowledge that figures of his apparent onesidedness could have had dimensions one needs to know to do justice to them. I will now be even more restrained when talking of him than I thought I was then (over thirty years ago), in spite of the term "philistine."[3]

With friendly greetings,

Yours,

KARL BARTH

[1]Julius August Ludwig Wegscheider (1771-1849), professor of theology and philosophy at Halle, a leading proponent of theological rationalism.
[2]K. Barth, *Protestant Theology in the Nineteenth Century* (1932/33 lectures; Zollikon/Zurich, 1947), pp. 475-481.
[3]Barth, *Protestant Theology*, p. 481.

*   *   *

29
To Church Councillor Wolf-Dieter Zimmermann
Berlin

Basel, 28 March 1962

Dear Councillor,

I must reply to two letters you sent me.

1. On 12 March you asked about my reaction to the article "A Conversation with Karl Barth" which appeared in the *Evg. Pfarrerblatt*.[1] It would take us too far afield to go into details. I can only say that it corresponds to neither the spirit nor the wording of what the author heard me say. His account of what I thought I heard the author himself say in that conversation is also totally inexplicable to me. I must reject any co-responsibility for the publication.

2. On 26 March you asked concerning the contents of the recording.[2] We are dealing here with what is a matter of principle for me. Only in the context of its delivery is a sermon, strictly, what it is meant to be. If its context in the narrower sense is bypassed to give it a wider audience through print or radio or on a record, then for decades—so far as printing is concerned—I have thought I should insist that it appear only with the preceding and following prayers (both composed *ad hoc*), because for me this threefold middle portion of an evangelical service constitutes an inseparable whole. Even better, when it is possible on the radio or

on a record, we should have the whole service, including the introduction, congregational singing, and the benediction. Thus the sermon (which is not a lecture) should be kept in its full setting even for those who are absent, or, as on a record, kept in its context for the listeners when it is played again. I do not see this as a questionable procedure but a good one. And I have been assured by many who play the records of that sermon how pleasing it is to them—even if only in imagining the real action—to range themselves with the prisoners, to pray with them, and, at least in one instance, to join in their singing. And when the record was played to the prisoners themselves, they looked as if they would stand up again for the prayers. What more do you want? It is another question, of course, whether this can be done with the more complex and fixed Lutheran liturgy. At any rate my own view is that if we are to have recordings at all, then we should record sermons with as much as possible of their natural setting.

With friendly greetings,

Yours,

KARL BARTH

[1]J. Berger, "Gespräch mit Karl Barth," *Evangel. Pfarrerblatt* (publ. by the Alliance of Evangelical Pastors in East Germany, 1962), Part I, pp. 67-69; Part II, pp. 83-85.

[2]Cf. 9, n. 16. Zimmermann asked Barth why, contrary to the previous practice of West German radio, he also wanted on the record the liturgical parts of the worship service.

*   *   *

30
To Prof. Charles C. West
Princeton, New Jersey

Basel, 1 April 1962

Dear Dr. West,

Your letter and the need to answer it are much on my mind.[1] I was never very good at accepting special tasks. And my last semester with all its usual and unusual concerns has gone by without my getting round to the essay assigned to me for the V. 't H. *Festschrift*. Furthermore, having had no hand in preparing for New Delhi[2] as I did for Amsterdam and Evanston, I seem almost to have slept through it, so that I am now too little in the picture to speak with any competence. Since I have now become a marginal figure in ecumenical circles—and

theology in general is more tolerated than really listened to in them—
is it really necessary that you should have a contribution from me to
the *Festschrift?* In my view people like Niemöller or Hromádka or Ernst
Wolf, who are close to things, have much more important things to say
than I do. I am very grateful for your observations on what might be
expected of me in America, but my aims, so far as I have any, are more
modest than you assume and do not in any event include political
prophecy. Unavoidably my view will emerge that American policy toward Russia ought to have been different even from 1918 on. More
important to me, however, is in the first instance simply to listen and
observe. It is enough that I shall be presenting a little theology not of
the general American pattern. As you may have heard, the American
past (1861-65!) also interests me. Perhaps the experience my American
friends and foes will have with me will be that of putting a little child
in their midst.[3] For my part I have already had a good and encouraging
experience with the Paris correspondent of *Time* magazine, who has visited me here more than once and interviewed me in their usual style.[4]
I hope I shall meet more clever people of this kind.

   With friendly greetings for now and hoping to see you soon,

Yours,

KARL BARTH

[1]West had asked Barth to participate in a *Festschrift* for W. A. Visser 't Hooft, then
General Secretary of the World Council of Churches.
[2]Cf. 22, n. 4.
[3]Mark 9:36.
[4]"Witness to an Ancient Truth," *Time*, 20 April 1962, pp. 59-65.

*   *   *

31
To Prof. D. F. Fleming
Nashville, Tennessee

Basel, 2 April 1962

Dear Colleague,

   Forgive me for taking so long to reply to the double dispatch of your
work on the Cold War[1] after sending such friendly personal greetings
on 16 Dec.

   In fact I have been waiting a long time for such an independent and competent survey of the relation between America and Russia and between the West and the East in general. I am one of the few here who in relation to western policy has been able to follow only with profound concern the development that has taken place since the second world war. Your work is important to me because it shows plainly that what has happened since 1945 has its roots in much earlier mistakes. How glad I would be if it could be put on the desks of the editors of all the papers that shape public opinion in my country in what is to me a fatal way. Perhaps you do not know that I am "only" a theologian and not an expert in history or politics. Thus I do not think I have the competence to express publicly any judgment on such an important work as yours. I must be content simply to refer to it from time to time. But I have given the second copy to my very reliable colleague the historian Edgar Bonjour, who will certainly make significant use of it.

Now that I have become professor emeritus, at the end of this week I am starting for the first time on a little lecture tour in the U.S.A. and am eagerly awaiting what I shall hear there in person about the matters that are of common concern to us.

For the time being I thank you heartily for the confidence you have shown in me by sending me your book. With high regard for your courage and achievement,

Yours,
KARL BARTH

[1]D. F. Fleming, *The Cold War and Its Origins, 1917-1960*, 2 vols. (London, 1961).

*   *   *

32
To Bishop Albrecht Hege
Heilbronn

Basel, 3 April 1962

Dear Bishop,

Please excuse me for keeping you waiting so long for a reply to your letter of 19 February. In these months I have been claimed by the winding up of my academic work and all that it has entailed. I also wanted to give your request serious consideration.[1]

All things considered, I would rather not accede to it. The date is a bad one for me, but that is a secondary reason that could perhaps be dealt with. The decisive point is that if I were to speak at your conference I would be in what is for me an ambiguous situation. In my view, what you have in mind when speaking of "the process of dissolution in evangelical theology" (Bultmann, etc.)[2] has been too closely associated with the disturbing political, ecclesiastical, and ecclesiastico-political reaction in West Germany since the war for me to speak about the one and say nothing about the other. Once in Württemberg I was put in what seems to me to have been a similar ambiguous situation,[3] and I do not want to go through it a second time. To be specific, where people are against Niemöller I will not be against Bultmann, for while I am that with all my heart, I am also for Niemöller with all my heart.

So please take it in good part if I would rather not accept your invitation.

With kind regards,

Yours,

KARL BARTH

[1]The invitation was to give a lecture on the reason for the present process of dissolution in evangelical theology.

[2]On the controversy with Bultmann cf. esp. Barth's *Rudolf Bultmann. Ein Versuch, ihn zu verstehen*, ThSt, 34 (Zollikon-Zurich, 1952) and the *Barth/Bultmann Briefwechsel 1922-1966*, ed. B. Jaspert (Zurich, 1971).

[3]Barth probably has in mind the event at the Paul Gerhardt-Gemeinde in Stuttgart (14 March 1954) when he answered questions put to him.

*   *   *

33
To Pastor Friedrich Middendorff
Schüttorf

Basel, 5 April 1962

Dear Pastor,

Since I am leaving for a short stay in America the day after tomorrow, I do not want to leave your letter and enclosures (of 4 March) unanswered.

I agree wholeheartedly with all that you tried to write upon the consciences of the pastors of your church and earlier the synod.[1] You are fortunately not the only one to think and speak in this way today. But we cannot hide the fact that in this whole complex of questions (and not this alone) we are now up against a wall that is worse than the Berlin wall, that we and what we stand for, in Switzerland as well as Germany, are reaching and convincing only a very small minority of people in either church or world. How is it? I cannot assume an almost general hardening, but I do ask, without for the moment seeing my way clearly, what it is that we have not done too well. We have lived through the two wars, outlived Hitler, taken part in the church conflict, and introduced a better theology than that which preceded ours. But we must now attempt to call a true "Halt" and "Proceed" to a general reaction (I am including the Bultmannian movement in theology too). The whole situation calls for a new song to be sung to the Lord.[2] Can we sing it? Or do we need other people coming from a point that is still concealed from us? Or must all of us—old as well as young, wise as well as foolish—pass under a great judgment that will teach mores to those who come after us? These are things one can reflect on and I do it very often . . . , then finding it best to read a Psalm or a hymn by Paul Gerhardt (e.g., "Du bist ein Mensch, das weisst du wohl . . ." ["You are a man, you know that well . . ."]) and to sigh or hope accordingly. That this puts us to shame a little in comparison with Niemöller, who still rushes like an arrow from a bow to this target and that, is clear to me. Yet perhaps there have to be a few people who openly admit that they have lost the breath for further expectorations and adjurations, so that they seek with the greater longing the breath from above, which alone can do things, and will finally and assuredly do so.

In any case let us not be upset to be in that minority or even to be alone.

Greetings and all good wishes,

Yours,

KARL BARTH

---

[1]Middendorff had sent out a circular letter criticizing the neutralism of pastors in the face of mass means of destruction and anti-communism. In a letter to Barth he had bemoaned a general reactionary movement and an inclination to conformism in the Evangelical Church.
[2]Ps 98:1.

*　　　　*　　　　*

34

[Letters 34-39 contain English phrases by Barth, indicated by asterisks]
To Max Zellweger
Basel[1]

Chicago, 18 April 1962

Dear Max,

Your letter of the fifteenth, hopefully labeled "1," has reached me and overwhelmed me by the kind precision with which you are acting for me there and keeping me abreast of things. Many, many thanks for the trouble you are taking for me. I am glad that everything is in good hands there; Markus is taking care of us here with similar *allround efficiency.*

Time magazine with my picture, the open tomb (or even at a pinch, Lollo thinks, the entry to a wine cellar!), the article and all its more or less suitable information, and even the picture at a *night club* here, which I hope will not cause too great offense in Basel,[2] will soon be available and for sale there too. Vanity of vanities.[3] What people have spent on the scraps of information of which it is composed would form a good bundle in "bread for brothers" or in the form of a contribution to the Basel City Mission. The telephone has been ringing continuously here; Markus, however, knows how to keep people *at bay.* As yet I have not appeared in public, although things will really break loose the week after Easter. Lollo watches like a lynx that I am not overtaxed, or do not overtax myself.

Yet an awful lot has already happened in these first one and one-half weeks. We have probably made more personal contacts than you made during your own notable American trip.[4] Apart from the unavoidable *interviews* (the real press conference comes only on Good Friday, which is not observed in any way here), I have spent an evening with Markus' students, another with seven interested Jews, another with Roman Catholic theologians, and yet another with a group of prominent business men, who were all very open and also explained to me the *steel crisis* into which we have come at just the right moment. Could I perhaps get a post on the board of a company here?[5] That would be "the hammer." And with whom did we have breakfast the day before yesterday—with whom? With Billy Graham, who again was very pleasant personally, though I told him *openly speaking* that I did not like his performance in the football stadium in St. Jakob.[6] We were then photographed together and the news-hungry press will not delay in publicizing this picture too.

Last Friday we were in Dubuque staying in an expensive motel (*Holyday Inn*), and I had a whole evening of discussion with the seminary faculty, who were a little hesitant at first, but who gradually laughed and were tardily merry, as Rilke put it.[7] The following morning we went to a fine vista-point overlooking the Mississippi. Back in Chicago I was able to satisfy my curiosity about the Civil War (1861–5) in a bookstore specializing in the subject and also in a historical museum. I also saw inside a captured German U-boat, saw half the world from the Prudential Building, and then spent the evening in an existentialist theater and the night club to which the picture in *Time* bears witness. What the picture does not show is that I had a discussion with the performers on the relation betweeen judgment and grace. The man on the far right is a Buddhist (note Christoph too in the background). In the meantime I have taken part in a lecture and two seminars conducted by Markus. And yesterday Christoph for his part gave a very learned and impressive lecture to two hundred students at McCormick Seminary. My impression is that the two boys do this much better than I myself do, so that the *great old man* can quietly and without loss slip into retirement, especially because here that old man can perform only with intelligible but very rough English.

Max, all in all I really like America. The people I have met so far are all so free and open and lively that I can overlook or make allowance for the obvious trash. (Television, which we watched one evening, was a real abomination!) [. . .] Even to see the flowing traffic on the broad streets is quite a pleasure, but you learned to know and enjoy this enough for yourself. So far I have not been smitten by homesickness for Switzerland. [. . .]

Yesterday a black professor asked me: *Which is your impression of that strange place, called the United States?* I gave a very restrained answer both to him and to others who put the same question—yes, the blacks too.

[Family greetings]

Good Friday has not yet come. On that day Markus is to give a sermon in the university chapel at the odd hour of twelve noon to one. He is at work on it now.

With thanks,

Yours most truly,

PAPA

[1]Barth's son-in-law.

[2]The portrait on the title page of *Time* has in the background an empty tomb with the stone rolled away, and on the ground a crown of thorns, with the caption: "The goal of human life is not death, but resurrection." Among the illustrations is a picture of Barth in a restaurant with the caption: "Barth with secretary and Second City actors in Chicago. A Calvinist—but not a gloomy one."

[3]Eccl 1:1.

[4]The Zellwegers had visited the U.S.A. in the fall of 1961.

[5]Barth had sometimes asked his son-in-law in jest whether he could not find him a post on an industrial board of directors.

[6]Barth had met Billy Graham in the summer of 1960 shortly before Graham preached in the football stadium at Basel.

[7]R. M. Rilke, *Die frühen Gedichte* (Leipzig, 1898), p. 6.

*   *   *

35
To Max Zellweger
Basel

Wranglers Roost, near Phoenix, Arizona, 19 May 1962

Dear Max,

Unlike you I have not been very faithful in writing. But I just couldn't do it. Every day the last six weeks has been literally filled up from morning to night, and so I have left the European correspondence almost completely to Lollo and Christoph. I wish I could show you what I now see before me. Yesterday we came here in five hours by car from the Grand Canyon. We are a little off the *high road* at a ranch that takes visitors. This afternoon we shall return by jet from Phoenix to Chicago. After a few days of rest and review we shall go to New York for some last visits and sightseeing. What I see before me here is a charming court surrounded by low buildings, in which are growing palms and those crazy cactuses we know from your pictures. Above is a cloudless sky. Markus and Christoph have gone for a morning ride, while we older illustrious persons are simply here admiring things and waiting for what happens next.

Max, America, which we have sampled a little in the midwest, east, and west, is a fantastic affair, a world in which much is astonishingly alike and much astonishingly unlike. When people ask for impressions of America one's mouth simply closes; there is no knowing where to begin, since generalizations are certainly wide of the mark. I shall be in the same difficulty in Basel. But gradually all kinds of details will emerge until only a few remain; yes, this is what America was and what it will be for me in this life. I have, however, been asked everywhere to return and if possible stay a year and teach on the most fabulous terms. I would indeed prefer Princeton or Richmond or San Francisco, from which we have just come, to the University of Basel. I was not only charmingly received everywhere but also intelligently questioned (in three big press conferences with the whole apparatus of photos, films, and television), and heard and applauded by thousands (!!); what appeared in the papers was in part good and in part tolerable. In Virginia I saw everything or almost everything I wanted to see relating to the Civil War. I even shot a one-hundred-year-old musket and hit the target; this special interest of mine aroused some gratitude. We were also with the Swiss ambassador in Washington[1] [. . .] but not in Philadelphia so we could not visit R. Serkin.[2] But I cannot tell everything.

At seven on Sunday morning, if all goes well, we shall land at Kloten, where we set off, on Swiss Air; what an unearthly hour for you. If you want to meet us as you saw us off, nine (or later) will do, since customs and passport, plus a good cup of coffee in Swiss style, will take some time there. You can reach and inform us from the twenty-third to the twenty-sixth at Union Theological Seminary, Broadway at 120th St., NY 27 (NY). But if this task curtails even to the smallest degree your Sunday morning peace or keeps you from an important service, do not perform it. We can reach our destination with the good old SBB.[3]

Markus and Christoph have now come back from their ride and are sporting in a *swimming pool* under the open sky; they and Lollo greet you.

Yours most sincerely,
PAPA

P.S. Christoph says I am the most capable of pleasure in the whole family—I hope not the one who seeks it most. I certainly cannot deny that the life, the land, and the people have given me uncommon joy in these weeks.

---

[1]August Lindt.
[2]The pianist Rudolf Serkin, who when in Basel taught Barth's daughter Franziska, Max Zellweger's wife.
[3]Swiss Railways.

*   *   *

36
To Pastor Martin Schwarz
Basel[1]

In flight with TWA from Richmond to Chicago, 19 May 1962

Dear Chief,[2]

In New York I am to visit a third prison. All in all Spitalstrasse 41[3] is better than what I have seen here so far. But this is only one part of my experiences. At the moment I am flying at 12,000 m above the earth. The prisoners in San Francisco (mostly blacks) to whom I spoke, send greetings to ours. They sang well and lustily for me.

All good wishes, *so long,*

Yours,
KARL

[1]Barth's contribution to a joint letter from C. v. Kirschbaum, Karl Barth, and Christoph Barth.
[2]Schwarz was chaplain at Basel prison and set up Barth's sermons there.
[3]Basel prison.

*   *   *

37
To an Assistant at Radio Basel

Chicago, 22 May 1962

Dear Dr. Meyer,

Sincere thanks for your friendly letter. I hope to reach Kloten on 27 May and to go from there to Basel.

But think about it: I cannot go on the air there with my American experiences. For one thing, I know just enough about the land to know how much more one has to know to speak of it meaningfully and responsibly. For another, I would rather be quiet for a while in Switzerland after the experiences of the early part of the year.[1] Third, I have been surrounded for seven weeks here by such a cloud of *publicity* that I would like to return to a corresponding anonymity at home.

I ask you to take this in good part. With friendly greetings,

Yours,
KARL BARTH

*   *   *

38
To Pastor Ulrich Hedinger
Fällanden (Zurich Canton)

Basel, 6 June 1962

Dear Pastor,

Your book on the concept of freedom in *C.D.*[1] was the first thing I read after returning from the U.S.A., and I do not want to delay telling you what pleasure it gave me to get to know your enlightened and enlightening work. I do not praise merely the care with which you studied my Moby Dick. I am not glad merely that you saw it from this standpoint and were able to approve on the whole its movements in the ocean. I also realize—all the relevant passages are marked with a little arrow—what questions and more or less explicit criticisms you have expressed in detail. There can be no thought now of a total retraction, but if possible I shall have to consider such worthwhile objections as yours when I possibly continue the work.

I. A. Dorner, to whom I owed much in the matter of God's immutability,[2] deserved mention in your presentation, and even more so W. A. Mozart, for whom I wrote a commemorative essay under the title of "Mozart's Freedom,"[3] and who throughout the years and decades has contributed something very important toward relaxing me.

However that may be, thanks that you took so much trouble—and with so much success—in this inquiry. Someone some day will have to go into the literature about me, which has long since become too involved for me. And I can definitely predict that he will give a place of special honor to your book. [. . .]

I hope to see you again some time. With friendly greetings,

Yours,

KARL BARTH

[1]U. Hedinger, *Der Freiheitsbegriff in der* K.D. *Karl Barths* (Zurich, 1962).

[2]*C.D.* II, 1, pp. 490-522. On p. 493 Barth observes that he owes much to the inspiration of Dorner (1809-1884) in this section.

[3]K. Barth, "Mozarts Freiheit. Ansprache bei der Gedenkfeier im Musiksaal in Basel am 29. Januar 1956," in *Wolfgang Amadeus Mozart, 1756/1956* (Zollikon, 1956), pp. 33-50.

*   *   *

39
To Pastor Emeritus Ernst Hubacher
Bern

Basel, 6 June 1962

Dear Friend,

How glad I would be to cooperate with you.[1] But the time is not opportune. I have already resolved firmly not to publish my American impressions in articles, lectures, etc. (except in Basel prison),[2] partly because I want to be quiet again here after the enormous publicity surrounding me there, but also because I now know just enough about America to see that I would need to know a good deal more to speak responsibly about it. I do not like the thought, then, of putting things on a candlestick again as the project in *L. und Gl.* would do. If this must be done, follow *The Christian Century* of 16 May and *Christianity Today* of 25 May, who described things fairly objectively and in their ways sympathetically.[3] But even in these articles there are far too many of the inflated words about me that they love over there but that Swiss readers would not find edifying. Would it not be enough to tell your readers that I flew and travelled about the country for seven weeks, saw the Grand Canyon, the Atlantic, and the Pacific, heard a good deal and said a good deal, and finally on the *St. James River* in a ruined Civil War fort shot a one-hundred-year-old musket and to the honor of the Swiss army even hit the target—an event which with some good will might even be regarded as symbolic of my other activities and successes? But is this really necessary? I unfortunately do not have, or do not yet have, photos of the kind you want, although over there I was snapped unceasingly with and without flash bulbs and in all kinds of situations. Vanity of vanities! And only now comes the worst thing of all: the essay by Milton Mayer[4] has sunk without a trace in the flood of paper which has washed around me with special force these last months, so that you must meet that ever restless contemporary with something other than this copy. I ask you to excuse me! in both respects!
 With sincere greetings,

Yours,
KARL BARTH

---

[1]Hubacher had asked Barth to put at his disposal materials for an account of the American trip in the journal *Leben und Glauben*.

²On 14 June 1962 Barth spoke about his American trip to the inmates of Basel prison.
³Cf. *The Christian Century*, 79 (1962), 615ff. and 685ff.; *Christianity Today*, 6 (1962), 847-851.
⁴Lent by Hubacher to Barth. Hubacher had asked for it back because he wanted to use the article in dialogue with a third party.

*   *   *

40
[written in English]
To Dr. James I. McCord
President, Princeton Theological Seminary
Princeton, N.J.

Basel, 11 June 1962

Dear President McCord,

You have not heard a word of me since our memorable last meeting on the battlefield of Gettysburg. So many things have happened in between. But believe me, I have not forgotten—we have not forgotten—Princeton Theological Seminary: the agreeable week we have spent in that wonderful landscape in spring's full glory; the kindness and generosity with which you have received, housed and nourished, and entertained us all, the whole group of travellers; the clever and efficient organisation of the work, which to do I had the privilege and the pleasure in such a famous place. Thank you for all, what you, your wife, your colleagues, and the very devoted young men in your guesthouse have been and done for us. Our memory of Princeton is singular.

Do you understand that I wonder sometimes whether my activities in those seven weeks in the U.S.A. have achieved something more serious than the—so to say—sensational personal impact I seem to have made (if *Christian Century*, *Christianity Today*,[1] etc. are right) on certain people; or whether what I have tried to say over there has been wiped out by other equally headline worthy encounters and events—whether the usual talk on "religion" is going on and on after as before? But maybe it is too soon to ask such questions?

The book you presented me at Gettysburg (Stewart, *Pickett's Charge*)[2] is excellent, the most accurate and livid account I have ever read of that decisive afternoon in July 1863.[3] Did you know that what may be called the failure in general Lee's command and conduct on that day was (highly probably) due to the fact that he was badly suffering (very untimely!) from intestinal troubles? Again, *hominum confusione, Dei providentia!*

May I ask you to say my—our!—greetings to *all* those who made our days in Princeton so enjoyable: including the faithful angel-guardians who watched on my door, while the "murderer" was supposed to lurch about[4]—including also the boys who made me an honorary member of their baseball team; and especially to Mr. Andrews who brought us from Princeton to Gettysburg and Washington. You allow me certainly to write this letter also as a kind of "Encyclica" to all those good people at your place.

With my best wishes for the success of your important work, in respect and friendship,

Yours,

KARL BARTH

P.S. I hope that the parcel containing some valuable remnants of our existence in Princeton—among them more books dealing with the Civil War and the Baseball tricot!—is safely on its way to Europe. One never knows whether the intercontinental mail functions as it should do!

[1] Cf. 39, n. 3.

[2] G. R. Stewart, *Pickett's Charge. A Microhistory of the Final Attack at Gettysburg, July 3, 1863* (Boston, 1959).

[3] The battle at Gettysburg on 7 July 1863 marked the turning point in the American Civil War. The Union forces drove the army of the Confederates under General Robert E. Lee into retreat.

[4] At a reception in New York on 1 April 1962 an uninvited intruder had to be forcibly ejected. He left with the threat "I'll get him in Princeton" and on his chair was found a piece of metal pipe. Barth was thus put under guard for about 12 hours. It later turned out that the supposed assailant merely wanted to draw Barth's attention to his musical talents and that the metal pipe was part of a camera tripod.

*   *   *

41
To Prof. Dietrich Ritschl
Reigoldswil (Baselland)

Basel, 11 July 1962

Dear Colleague,

I read in a train your work on the black issue[1] which you so kindly sent me and I am pleased both by the line you took and developed and also by the care and caution with which you worked. Shouldn't it be published in English, since in the main—if not exclusively—is it not to Americans that you wanted to offer some insights?

Perhaps we shall see one another some time; I shall probably be here with no major breaks until the middle of August.

With thanks and friendly greetings,

Yours,
KARL BARTH

[1]D. Ritschl, *Nur Menschen. Zur Negerfrage in den amerikanischen Sudstaaten* (Berlin, 1962).

*　　　*　　　*

42
To Prof. Hans Rheinfelder
Munich

Basel, 14 July 1962

Dear Colleague,

Please forgive me for being so long in answering your kind letter of 16 June.[1]

How I should like to give the glad Yes! you want, but for various reasons I cannot do so. The most important one is that while I am naturally pleased to be called an expert by you, and to know that you liked my Rousseau essay,[2] I have to admit to you that since that excursion more than thirty years ago I have never studied Rousseau closely. Thus I not only do not know the books that have been written about him since, but the life and work of the man himself have so far faded from view that it would be audacious of me to venture out as I should have to do if I accepted your most flattering commission. You must excuse me for having devoted my time and energy in the past decades almost exclusively to my main task as a dogmatician, though not without asking at times whether I would not in a second life dedicate myself fully to history, for which I have such an uncanny liking. Goethe, who would have been the climax of the "Background," was missed out only because the semester in which I gave the series (the disastrous year 1933) came to an end first.[3] From that period I also have all Voltaire's writings (seventy-one volumes). A pity—or perhaps not—that by human judgment I cannot make a further incursion into this field of yours. I write this merely that you may believe that I do not lack the desire to accept your commission, but only the required impudence.

In thanking you for the confidence you placed in me, I beg you to take my refusal in good part.

With high regard and friendly greetings,

KARL BARTH

[1]An invitation to give an address in Munich on the occasion of Rousseau's 250th birthday.
[2]In Barth's *Protestant Theology in the Nineteenth Century*, §5.
[3]The *Protestant Theology* was made up of Barth's lectures in Bonn in the winter semester of 1932/33 and the summer semester of 1933.

*   *   *

43
To Dr. Robert Leuenberger
Safien-Thalkirch (Grisons Canton)

Basel, 15 July 1962

Dear Dr.,

Thanks for your letter of the eighth and for sending your essay,[1] which I knew already from that issue of *Reformatio*.

I can join Mr. Vogelsanger[2] in praising the cleverness of your article. It is indeed a little too clever to please me. But why should we quarrel? We were and are radically apart in our view of the two matters you discussed. That Swiss participation in general atomic armament might be crazy and offensive, and that the way my succession was handled here in Basel was just an example of the darkest of Swiss mediocrity, obviously affects you in neither head, heart, nor nervous system. And so you were and are in a position soberly to counterbalance yes and no, pro and contra, issuing compliments and censures both right and left, inviting all good citizens and Christians to see their faults, to be kind to one another, and to keep on talking as if nothing had happened. In neither matter can I look down from such a high mountain or observation tower. In the German church conflict first Bodelschwingh[3] and then Marahrens[4] and his crowd spoke from such places and dabbled in ecclesiastical politics. But what is that to you? We are now in 1962 in

Switzerland—"All quiet on the Potomac" as they said for a time in America one hundred years ago—and we have time and peace and obligation and opportunity simply to be clever and to talk cleverly. You can be so clever that you never even dreamed, for example, of asking whether it is fitting, as one who is obviously not involved, to quote against others what I, as one who was involved, said in 1935 against myself and my friends.[5] Now it may well be indeed, and again as one concerned I will not exempt myself, that by God's will things in the Swiss church and Swiss theology are to go downstream in this new direction.

I will thus content myself with a note to set the historical record straight.

1. Having served twenty-five years on the Basel faculty, I can only state that never in that period have I thought there was a homogeneous school ("the pure doctrine of a strict theology of revelation") under my direction.[6] Each of my colleagues in theology could affirm, and would have to do so, that in this whole period we lived and taught together (in only too untroubled fashion) and that I was simply one professor among others, more often in a minority than a majority as I recall. That Cullmann and I opposed the Bultmann school on very different presuppositions is a simple fact. Neither with him nor any other faculty member did I enter into resultant alliances or decisions (such as now take place in the reverse way in Zurich). The presence of Baumgartner was enough to assure some open opposition to me.[7] And on at least two important occasions I even differed from my friend Thurneysen. I took no part in the negotiations for my successor, was not consulted by anyone as to my views or wishes, but know that what the faculty was after in this matter was not the continuation of a Basel school along my own theological line, but—and this is something very different—that my replacement be a man of corresponding weight. Gollwitzer (the first suggestion) would have been such a one, or Ernst Wolf, or Kreck, or according to the opinon of the faculty Max Geiger, who was named with Gollwitzer and Kreck in its second proposal.

2. It is not true, then, that the faculty made Gollwitzer the first and sole nominee. It put forward three names. Gollwitzer was made the sole nominee by the expert commission and the curators (with Zschokke's cooperation![8]). Then on the council the ophthalmologist Rintelen intervened, instructed by his friend Stickelberger of the *Weltwoche*, until finally the sole nominee was no nominee.

In this light there is no point to the much too pious as well as much too clever conclusion to your article.

Dear Dr., I have the highest regard for the dedication and skill which you have brought to your work in Basel.[9] But I have no sympathy for your activity as a mediator in the organ of the Evangelical Church Union, which has become in practice an organ for the Swiss John Birch Society. Do not be cross with me if I tell you this openly,

With friendly greetings all the same, and all good wishes for your well-deserved vacation,

Yours,

KARL BARTH

[1]R. Leuenberger, "Pro et contra. Bemerkungen zu einer politischen Kontroverse in der Kirche," Reformatio, 11 (1962), 276-296.

[2][P.] V[ogelsanger], "Nachwort," Reformatio, 11 (1962), 306.

[3]Friedrich von Bodelschwingh (1877-1946) was chosen in 1933 for the newly instituted position of Reichsbischof but had to yield to Ludwig Müller, whom Hitler wanted.

[4]August Marahrens (1875-1950), bishop of Hanover (1925-1947), was chairman of the Provisional Directorate of the German Evangelical Church, whose establishment on 22 Nov. 1934 led to the protest and withdrawal of Barth, Hermann Albert Hesse, Karl Immer, and Martin Niemöller.

[5]Leuenberger, 296.

[6]Leuenberger, 292.

[7]Walter Baumgartner (1887-1970), Old Testament professor at Basel, was a friend of Bultmann.

[8]Dr. Peter Zschokke was minister of education in Basel (city) Canton.

[9]Leuenberger was head of the Kirchlich-Theologische Schule in Basel, which he had recently helped to found.

*　　　*　　　*

44
To N.N.

Basel, 16 July 1962

Dear N.N.,

"Who (or what) is God for you?" I call this a good short question. But I can give only a short and, I hope, good answer.

First note two things:

In no case is God a "what" that one may peep at close up or at a distance and value or disparage as one pleases. God is a "Who."

And He is not who He is "for me" or "for you" (according to our ideas of Him) but in His own reality and truth, above both you and me, for all men, for the whole world. And hence also for you and for me!

Who is God? I have no original answer to give you to this question, but can affirm Him only as He has shown and expressed Himself before us, apart from us, and therefore for us.

Thus He is our, your and my, Creator and Lord, who judges and has mercy on us, our Father and Redeemer. It is thus that He revealed and reveals Himself in the history of Israel and in Jesus Christ, to which witness is given in scripture. Think carefully about each of these words, yet not according to your own opinion, but as you try to read the Bible and pray a little. Each of these words is a pointer to God Himself.

In conclusion, another little lesson. I am glad you have put so much confidence in a stranger like me. But we must not "worship" any man—except in the person of Him in whom God Himself became a man.

With friendly greetings and all good wishes,

Yours,
KARL BARTH

P.S. I have written rather a lot of books, thick and thin, in which you can find further explanations of what I have only indicated here.

*   *   *

45
To Prof. Kornelis Heiko Miskotte
Voorst (The Netherlands)

Basel, 16 July 1962

Dear Heiko,

Through our common friend Hinrich[1] in Bremen I hear that you have had many physical troubles and have had to entrust yourself to the skill and knives of doctors. May I express my sympathies and also the hope that what surgeons can do, and also the loyal work of nurses, have interested and edified you as they did me when I was in a similar circumstance in 1944.[2] And may I express finally my sincere wishes for your swift and full recovery. On the general and special fragility of human life you will have had your own thoughts at this time, far more profound ones than I could set before you, and so I will spare you anything more along these lines. It will be good to hear that you have come back to the land of the living well and cheerful.

In the meantime I have experienced and done all kinds of things about which there is much to tell. My departure from my Basel chair in the spring became a kind of dishonorable discharge, as came out plainly in the unwillingness to supply a successor in whom I could in any way take pleasure. But only yesterday a wise old friend advised me not to upset myself but simply to—wonder. A good formula, is it not? Everything has indeed been wonderfully strange. In contrast my American journey (with L. v. Kirschbaum, my Indonesian son, and the other who now lives there) can simply be called wonderful: magnificent vistas of land and sea, moving encounters with all kinds of people, the full satisfaction of my curiosity about the sites of the Civil War, lively discussions with theologians as well as secular people of every type, astonishing attendance at my lectures. That after seven weeks I should come back exhausted to this little house was natural and yet also a sign that something had happened. Now I must get back to Moby Dick, but you know from your own experience how hard it is as an emeritus not to enjoy day by day all kinds of central and peripheral reading and to leave God's works to Himself or to others who think they know everything far better. I now have about ten honorary doctoral hoods[3] (all to be put in the wardrobe in heaven!), thirteen grandchildren, and for fourteen days even a great-grandchild.[4] Surely you are now well again and happy about me.[5] If after your convalescence you can expressly tell me the latter I should be very pleased.

With warm greetings,

Yours,
KARL BARTH

[1]Hinrich Stoevesandt, who translated several of Miskotte's works.
[2]Hernia operation.
[3]See K. Kupisch, *Karl Barth in Selbstzeugnissen und Bilddokumenten* (Reinbeck bei Hamburg, 1971), pp. 143-145.
[4]Olivier Schopfer, b. 8 July 1962, son of Pierre Schopfer and Ursula, née Zellweger.
[5]See 2 and Appendix, 1.

*   *   *

46
To Prof. Erich Fascher
Berlin

Basel, 16 July 1962

[In this letter Barth told Fascher he had seen two of Fascher's students (Gottfried de Haas and Traugott Vogel), thanked the Berlin faculty through him for sending as a gift the book *Ikonen* by K. Onasch (Berlin, 1961), and said he would be offering some private colloquia which the two students might attend.]

*　　　　　*　　　,　　　*

47
To Councillor Prof. Albert Krebs
Wiesbaden

Basel, 16 July 1962

Dear Councillor,

It is high time that I should finally answer your friendly letter of 13 April.[1]

In penal matters I had the chance while in America to make at least some investigation of the situation there (in Chicago, San Francisco, and New York). Most impressive to me was Rikers Island (north of Manhattan), where Mrs. Kross is commissioner in charge and is doing some notable reforming work. I would very much recommend that you get in touch with this woman who knows her goal so well and is so energetic. She has a German secretary with whose mediation you might perhaps contribute to her paper.

Regarding your flattering desire for an article from me on the problem of official oaths, I unfortunately do not feel in any position to comply. To say something worth while I should have to study the materials afresh and I cannot do this in the foreseeable future.

Please excuse me, with fond memories of Fulda,[2] and warmest greetings,

Yours,
KARL BARTH

---

[1] A request to contribute an article on official oaths to the *Zeitschrift für Strafvollzug*.

[2]Site of the Evangelical Conference on Prisoners' Aid (10 May 1959) at which Barth answered questions; cf. U. Kleinert, ed. *Strafvollzug. Analysen und Alternativen* (Munich/Mainz, 1972), pp. 46-52.

*   *   *

48
To Pastor Helmut Goes
Stuttgart-Uhlbach

Basel, 17 July 1962

[Barth first thanked Goes for some sermons, which he called good proclamation ("... if only this term were not ridden to death by our friend Hermann Diem!")[1] both for their content and careful preparation. He continued ...]

As regards further attention to "the lady in the crinoline," *C.D.*, we must wait and see. You will not believe how content I am just to be able to read so much so peacefully in my allotted retirement, spiritual and secular things in motley sequence—often overcome by big yawns when I listen to the endless prattle of the existentialists—and then to write a little letter or two as I am doing now. But I realize—and Lollo is always whispering something of the same to me—that this cannot last. I am now back to the original situation in which I finally did two commentaries on Romans with no students.[2] For the moment, since our Indonesians are still here,[3] and are out and about, I still have an excuse not to take the matter too seriously.

[Barth then mentioned that some photos had come showing him at various points at Gettysburg. One photo was of a monument to Luther in the Lutheran seminary where Lee had his headquarters.] Luther is sitting with an open Bible, but is looking past it, and I am standing with crossed arms reflectively before or under him. "I know not what it meaneth."[4]

Hoping to hear from you, and if possible to see you, with warm greetings,

Yours,

KARL BARTH

[1]Cf. esp. H. Diem, *Theologie als kirchliche Wissenschaft* (Munich, 1955), II, 4.
[2]K. Barth, *Der Römerbrief* (Bern, 1919); *Der Römerbrief* (Munich, 1922). In distinction from these volumes Barth first delivered the text of *C.D.* in the form of lectures, so that his professional work advanced the literary production. When the lectures ended

with the summer semester of 1961 work on the *C.D.* ceased, apart from IV, 4 (*Fragment*), which came out in 1967 (ET 1969).
[3]Christoph and his family.
[4]The first line of Heine's "Lorelei" ("Ich weiss nicht, was soll es bedeuten . . .").

*   *   *

49
To Prof. Helmut Gollwitzer
Berlin

Basel, 31 July 1962

Dear Helmut,

A letter to you is long overdue. Your letter to Lollo reminded me that it must now be written.

We both learned with concern that your other eye might be a bad one too and need medical attention. We hope that you get good news in Bonn and that for the moment your acute anxiety may be relieved. In your eye-troubles I cannot help but think that you see ten times more with your threatened eyes than hundreds and thousands do with unthreatened ones. God will provide.

Neither you nor I—as those most concerned in the events at Basel—can ever forget the year 1962. But you may be able to perhaps somewhat more easily than I. I understand and grant that there will be rejoicing in Berlin at the outcome of the affair, because you will stay more directly in touch with German questions than if you had to worry about the problems and petty irritations here and accept the much reduced thrust and attendance and response you would certainly encounter. For me, however (remarkably the shock only began to hit me properly after our return from America), the affair is "a document of the shame of our age."[1] As the conclusion of my twenty-five years in Basel it is a dishonorable discharge, and above all it is a painful disappointment, for I would have been genuinely glad to have you so close, to see my teaching chair (I taught standing the whole twenty-five years) occupied by you, and to have the chance to keep participating in a little academic work (in the form of common colloquia and the advancement of my remaining seven doctoral candidates) in cheerful activity on the margin of your own teaching. But all this has fallen through. I was already diligently reading the theological-political essays and addresses you so kindly dedicated to me[2]—am I mistaken in thinking that the quiet but notably emphatic tone in which you express yourself in the large preface is connected with your impressions of our Swiss humanity?—and I can only say what fools they are in Basel and all Switzerland to have let slip the irretrievable opportunity to bring such a mind and head and heart among them, and to have done so with such shameful prejudice. The only light in the darkness is that the faculty put you first to the very end, though they should have done so more firmly in the second round. [. . .] Concerning the ultimately decisive power of the press and the political parties, one can only say: "The work of moths and destruction." Basel University has been greatly spoiled for me. I will still offer a few private colloquia in the neighboring restaurant but there will be a monotonous blank on the lecture list.

With many others, especially Lollo, you will naturally tell me I should give myself the more energetically to work on *C.D.* Yes indeed, if only I had not been gripped by a lassitude bordering on acedia in relation to the whole theological scene. In the face of the thrust of our theological existentialists I increasingly feel only more disgust and abhorrence. [. . .] But that is what is demanded today. Does it make much sense to write a thirteenth and fourteenth volume if I could not stop this deluge with my previous twelve volumes? Are not other and new voices such as your own (I am pleased by your ontology and theology[3]) needed to check it? Meanwhile I [. . .] sit at a little table in the corner laughing in an artful but friendly fashion, knowing the facts, getting a respectful hearing—but in the end not listened to.[4] And this very day I have been looking into the works of our friends Kreck and O. Weber,[5] who bravely manage to say some good things for all the ifs and buts, but they too—I can only hide my face—seem as if they had learned nothing, absolutely nothing, of what can be fruitfully said and argued theologically. This comes not out of all the familiar dialogues old and new, even granting an implicit or explicit regard to what this or that person had to say and still has to say, but comes only out of the matter itself and with our faces set toward Jerusalem.[6] If, however, Kreck and Weber, both good people, have not at least methodologically taken over even this from me, what is the good of my butting in again? Shouldn't we suppose that I have had my day and, as Miskotte has been suggesting, that I am now invited, "in an oriental rest that defies all activists," to look on a little and see how others plan to use the time still given to them? Especially since I have in fact been a *great-*grandfather for a few weeks now!

Lollo cannot stand this kind of thinking. She will be angry when she reads this, call me ungrateful, and try to stop me from sending the letter if possible. But this is the way it is and I had to tell someone this. I am reading among other things the London sermons of Zinzendorf (in a 1756 edition, the year of Mozart's birth)[7] and I take great delight in the onesidedness and bold originality of these works, each of which is far superior to the irksome stuff turned out by the Ebelings, Fuchses, etc. My reading and authority in matters concerning the American Civil War has also increased to such a point that I was asked in all seriousness to write an article on its theological relevance. I shall not do this. But there are in fact interesting parallels between the North and South of those days and the West and East of today. Similarly, after the victory of the North, the Switzerland of that time went with the weather-vane as modern Switzerland has done since the overthrow of Hitler in 1945. And to link the times I myself fired a shot from an old muzzle-loader at Fort Harrison on the James River and triumphantly shattered a green bottle.

Do you know what I fear will happen if I get back to work on *C.D.*? That now that I am outdated I will go back to the provocative style of the second *Romans*,[8] in which case all the fine books written about me would have to be rewritten or be given a greatly incongruous concluding chapter. But enough. Who knows what might yet be set in motion? I liked the pictures of Brione,[9] although Lollo has not given me any of them. Come back again in person, you and your wife Brigitte, and meanwhile affectionate greetings,

Yours,
KARL BARTH

[1]A slightly inaccurate quotation from the first line of Schiller's *Rousseau*, which reads "monument," not "document."

[2]H. Gollwitzer, *Forderungen der Freiheit. Aufsätze und Reden zur politischen Ethik* (Munich, 1962).

[3]Cf. H. Gollwitzer, *Die Existenz Gottes im Bekenntnis des Glaubens* (Munich, 1963; ET 1965).

[4]Barth is alluding to "Das Verhör," in *Sonntagsblatt f.d. Ev.-Luth. Kirche in Bayern*, 29 July 1962.

[5]W. Kreck, *Die Zukunft des Gekommenen. Grundprobleme der Eschatologie* (Munich, 1961); O. Weber, *Grundlagen der Dogmatik*, Vol. II (Neukirchen, 1962).

[6]An allusion to G. Tersteegen's hymn, "Kommt, Kinder, lasst uns gehen" (1738). Cf. Luke 9:51.

[7]N. L. Graf von Zinzendorf, *Einiger seit 1751 von dem Ordinario Fratrum zu London gehaltenen Predigten* ... (London and Barby, 1756); cf. *Hauptschriften*, ed. E. Beyreuther and G. Meyer (Hildesheim, 1963), V.

[8]Cf. 48, n. 2.

[9]Taken on vacation together in March 1962.

*   *   *

50
To Prof. Walter Kreck
Bonn

Basel, 31 July 1962

Dear Colleague,

Now retired, I have finally found time to look more closely at your eschatology[1] than when I sent a not very satisfactory postcard acknowledging its receipt.

I can no longer say that I do not see what you are getting at. It is due to the style of the work that it first seems ambivalent to the reader. But if he reads on, following the many curves in your path, then he can no longer be in the dark concerning your purpose, at least regarding the main question of the relation between the history, the present, and the future of Jesus Christ. I would have to be totally deceived if in answering this basic question, or shall we say more cautiously this formally basic question, you and I were not looking in the same direction.

I do not feel quite so sure, of course, about your answer to what I might call the materially basic question of eschatology, the question of what is properly to be understood by the coming of the Lord which is still ahead, and which in spite of every "already" is still "not yet." In very many places, all of which I have underlined, you say that this coming will be the—shall we say, radical, universal, and definitive— manifestation of the Christ event which has until now been self- attested in its history and its present only in its concealment. But some- where an eschatology has to say something precise about this "coming." That claim *would be* something precise. Do you want to say this, in- terpreting carefully in view of the fullness of the biblical language, yet without addition or subtraction? If so, then materially, for all our con- ceivable differences, I could follow you very well. But I am not so sure as I should like to be whether you really want to be tied down to saying this, in light of your text with its constant "buts" and "on the other hands."

But this leads me to my real objection to your book. It concerns the style of the work. By your express declaration you wanted to do a bit of dogmatics. Have you really done this? You say very impressively on p. 9 that it is not a matter of what is said by Luke or Paul (!), Luther or Calvin, Bultmann or Barth, but of "the truth." If only you had carried out this program. If only you had told us directly, without elucidative excursuses in exegesis, dogmatic history, and theological history, what you hold to be "the truth" in this matter. Instead, from p. 14 to the end we find you in the kind of debate with Luke and Paul, and also with Luther and Calvin . . ., all of which ought to be behind one in dogmatics, mentioned perhaps implicitly or even at times explicitly, but not given the status of the main theme as it is in your book. What you offer us are very interesting and above all very learned meditations on dogmatics, on the dogmatics which should have begun just where you break off; it is no accident that your first chapter (on the main types of eschatology) made the strongest impression on me. I read your text with a real hunger for theses, but in the main I found only wrestlings with all kinds of partly true or partly false hypotheses, antitheses, or even syntheses, and to that extent I remained hungry.

Perhaps when I make this objection you will find some consolation if I tell you that I have exactly the same objection to make against the dogmatics of O. Weber.[2] Do you not see that the matter—upon which there can be no serious differences between you and me—would sound very different in both your presentations if, looking directly at Jerusalem,[3] you had worked methodologically with a very different freedom—identical with a very different dogmatic strictness—and thus been able to confront our comfortless existentialists in a very different way?

Do I need to ask your pardon for speaking so openly? I take it rather that you will like this better than if—as I do with a good conscience—I were to write merely that you have composed what is in its way a very fine and in every respect an instructive book.

With all good wishes and greetings,

Yours,
KARL BARTH

P.S. The strife here about my successor, in which you were involved a little, was a scandal that stank to high heaven. I wanted to spare you by not speaking any more about it in this letter.

[1]See 49, n. 5.
[2]See 49, n. 5.
[3]See 49, n. 6.

*   *   *

51
To Werner Finck
Munich

Basel, 31 July 1962

[Barth had been asked by Finck, whom he saw acting (in a cellar in Munich) in 1932, "the year before the flood," to take part in a televised show called "Cheerful Hopelessness" or the like. In this letter Barth asked to be excused, having no desire to be televised in Germany and feeling no need to prove his sense of humor. He suggested that if a theologian was wanted Diem would do a better job.]

*   *   *

52
To Prof. Leo Schrade

Basel, 4 August 1962

[In this letter Barth thanked Schrade for sending an article on Haydn, noting he had found new insights in it, but was not convinced that Mozart had not preceded Haydn in the movement from baroque to classical music. Thus far what had been impressive to him in Haydn had been even more impressive in Mozart, but he was ready to learn from someone who knew the field so much better. See L. Schrade, "Joseph Haydn als Schöpfer der Klassischen Musik," *Universitas*, 17 (1962), 767-778, and for the full text of the letter *Gesamtausgabe, Briefe*, V, p. 89.]

*   *   *

53
To Theological Student Clemens Besmer
Bern

Near Eggiwil, 17 August 1962

Dear Mr. Besmer,

I was sincerely pleased to have your letter of the fourteenth. The question why my voice does not seem to get through although my books and writings are in so many hands and are also being read concerns me too. But when I see how nebulous are the theories that are preferred by so many people today, I am not too worried that the sun which I think I have seen can be obscured very long. I am also thankful that here and there are people like you—perhaps not all that few—who have the mind and heart not to be led astray even now but with uplifted head to go ahead on the only possible way.

The *Evangelical Theology*[1] will soon be out now.

With sincere thanks and friendly greetings,

Yours,
KARL BARTH

[1]See 17, n. 6.

*　　　*　　　*

54
To Prof. Günther Dehn
Bonn

Walchensee, 13 September 1962

Dear Friend,

At this peaceful spot, as a guest (with Lollo) of Ernst Wolf, I have read first the book of Gottfried Mehnert which you quote,[1] and then your own recollections that you so kindly sent me[2]—all at one sitting (only with difficulty has Lollo got me moving on little walks). Mehnert (who annoyed me only a little) I do not know, but I know you and so I want to write you at once to thank you and to say that I have read it all with great sympathy.

Three things in your book impressed me either afresh or as a new experience: 1. the amazing course of that part of world and church history in which it has been your lot to be present and to play a part—and which has been my lot, too, in my own place and office; 2. the structure of your Christian life, a life shaped both by the peace and disturbance of this time of ours, marked by all its secular and religious ungodliness, yet a life not abandoned but gloriously and wonderfully ruled over by God; and 3. you yourself, Günther Dehn, according to the spirit and the flesh in all your unrepeatable uniqueness. You are wrong to think (p. 222) that you could give me nothing. Throughout the decades you have been to me a comforting and admonishing example, both in the impregnability and overwhelming strength of your material and personal loyalty and in the distinctive combination of deep seriousness and the lightest cheerfulness. How could I refrain from saying this expressly for your eightieth birthday? It must be at least hinted at again here since your life and the sober humility of your picture of yourself have again sincerely and profoundly influenced me.

The number of faces[3] (including some known to me closely, others more distantly, and others not at all) that you present in these recollections either to the left or right of your path is astonishing. So, too, is the sympathy and restraint with which you speak of all the moving events and people. That one becomes wise and mild in old age and in looking back, but that the fire still glimmering beneath the ashes has not simply been put out, is my experience too. With the accompanying advantages and disadvantages, pencil strokes replace those of charcoal, pastels replace oils, the ocarina the trumpet. But everything is recognizable as it was, as it is, and as it will be eternally in the light (and before the face) of God, according to my understanding of eschatology.

Biedermann did not belong to Bern but to Zurich![4] Bousset was not a Swiss theologian as the index says but seems to have been a German Huguenot. God, according to 1 Cor 5:19,[5] reconciled the world to Himself, not Himself to the world. [. . .]

On the other hand it seems quite right that it should be brought to light in what a primitive state you first found me (was it 1906 or 1907?) in Bern.[6] I vaguely remember that I was strictly reprimanded by my father after that evening. I appeared in a similar light to others, too. That is the way it was.

Who in the world is Ursula Cardinal (!) von Widdern?![7] Lollo and I came up with the idea she might have been the prodigy you often extolled after the second world war (now greatly matured).

Lollo is just going to begin your book. Who knows, she might write you too. At the moment she is reading one of the works of the very fascinating Simone de Beauvoir, the friend of Sartre. She sends greetings with me. Shall we be able to see and speak with you personally again? I have just been in America and am now resting.

Most sincerely,

Yours,

KARL BARTH

[1]G. Mehnert, *Evangelische Kirche und Politik 1917-1919* . . . (Düsseldorf, 1959).

[2]G. Dehn, *Die alte Zeit: die vorigen Jahre. Lebenserinnerungen* (Munich, 1962).
[3]Cf. Goethe's *Faust*, I, v. 520.
[4]Alois Emanuel Biedermann (1819-1885), incorrectly called a Bern dogmatician by Dehn.
[5] 2 Cor 5:19; the German text incorrectly has 1 Cor 5:19.
[6]On p. 143 Dehn tells of a visit to Barth's parents in Bern. Karl Barth, who was then a theological student, would not be drawn into a discussion of ecclesiastical and theological matters but was interested only in his student union.
[7]Dehn mentions her in the preface (p. 6) as an assistant in proof correction.

* * *

55
To Prof. Martin Fischer
Berlin

Basel, 26 October 1962

Dear Colleague,

Disorganized in my dealings with humanity and the Christian world by foolishly breaking my arm,[1] I have not yet answered your kind letter of 5 Sept. Look, I cannot do what you want.[2] Meditations are a literary genre I have never tried and it is surely too late now to learn the special skill required. Since I myself find it hard to meditate on sermons I give, I do not see how I can help others in this regard. Hence "I pray you, have me excused."[3]

I can understand there has been some relaxation in Berlin now that Cuba with its bases seems to have become for a while the focus of objective and subjective world tension.[4] But the pause will be short enough.

With kind regards and best wishes and greetings,

Yours,
KARL BARTH

[1]On 16 Sept. 1962, while staying with E. Wolf in Walchensee, Upper Bavaria, Barth fell and broke his right arm. He spent some time in a hospital in Bad Tölz, returned to Walchensee on 11 Oct. and Basel on 21 Oct.
[2]Fischer had asked Barth to contribute to a book of sermon meditations.
[3]Luke 14:18f.
[4]The Cuban missile crisis at the end of October.

* * *

56
To Bishop Hermann Dietzfelbinger
Munich

Basel, 27 October 1962

[In this letter Barth thanked the bishop for his sympathy, referred with gratitude and respect to the work of the doctors and nurses in the hospital at Bad Tölz, said he had been visited by a Franciscan and by two Lutherans, with whom he joined in worship, and told how, heavily bandaged, he had taken part in a little theological conference, so that his relationships in Upper Bavaria had been warm and happy.]

*　　　*　　　*

57
To Prof. Paul Althaus
Erlangen

Basel, 28 October 1962

Dear Colleague,

It is high time to thank you for the friendly card you sent me at Bad Tölz. In spite of the adverse occasion, I was glad to get to know the land and people there. I remember with great gratitude the hospital and its staff. I also made good contacts with the Catholic and Lutheran churches. I have now been back home eight days, a bit damaged but recovering. The frailty of human life has been concretely made clear to me these last weeks; high time at our age, is it not? [There follow references to *Evangelical Theology*, the Basel succession, and the American tour.] I am now trying to adjust to retirement and make myself relatively useful by means of a few colloquia. I certainly cannot write novels (like the astonishing E. Hirsch).[1] But Mozart is still ringing out; I now have almost all the available Mozart records. So I do not need a "primal revelation"[2] and am all the more sure of the order "Gospel-Law."[3] This will become clear to you, too, in heaven. Thanks again for your sympathy and be assured of my best wishes.

Yours,
KARL BARTH

[1]Emanuel Hirsch (1888-1972) had been a colleague of Barth at Göttingen (1921-25). He retired in 1945, became blind soon after, but published many novels and stories as well as theological works.
[2]A central concept in Althaus's theology.
[3]The usual Lutheran sequence espoused by Althaus was "Law-Gospel." Cf. K. Barth, "Evangelium und Gesetz," ThExh, 32 (Munich, 1935); ThExh, N.F. 50 (1956).

*   *   *

58
To Franz Sanders
Bremen

Basel, 29 October 1962

Dear Mr. Sanders,

Thanks for your letter of the twenty-third. I have neither time nor strength for a full answer. In the Evangelical Church there are many kinds of professors, and some odd ones, and thus we find an E. Stauffer, too.[1] You do not need to worry about him, for I do not think he has much influence. In any case the truth is strong and vital enough to assert itself again and again over against all professors. My position regarding East and West is not as simple as W. Simpfendörfer presents it and as it obviously appears to you, too.[2] Even in dreams I have never spoken of the dark West and bright East but said rather that it would be better for the bright West to repent instead of constantly bemoaning the dark East. Perhaps you can find a copy of my work of a year or so ago, *Brief an einen Pfarrer in der DDR*,[3] and try to understand directly what and how I think. Do you know my medical friend Prof. Karl Stoevesandt, Kohlhökerstr. 56 in Bremen? Perhaps a talk with him might be helpful.

Are you by any chance a relative or descendant of the famous Sanders of the awakening?[4]

With friendly greetings,

Yours,

KARL BARTH

[1]In his letter Sanders had told Barth he had been unsettled by E. Stauffer's book *Jesus, Paulus und wir* . . . (Hamburg, 1961).
[2]Sanders had also asked about Barth's position in relation to East Germany, referring to W. Simpfendörfer, "Dunkler Westen—Heller Osten," *Evangelischer Digest*, 4, no. 9 (Sept. 1962), pp. 16-24.

[3]K. Barth, *Brief an einen Pfarrer in der Deutschen Demokratischen Republik* (Zollikon, 1958).
[4]Barth had in mind the preacher Immanuel Friedrich *Sander* (1797-1859).

* * *

59
To Dr. Eberhard Jüngel
Berlin

Basel, 3 November 1962

Dear Dr. Jüngel,

I have just reread with close attention your essay on analogy,[1] and must not delay letting you know how pleased I am with this fine work. You undoubtedly express better than I could have done myself what I have thought and think on the subject. The discussion has now passed a turning point and it certainly cannot go back again. My local analogy specialist, Grover Foley, who has already won merit in dialogue with H. U. v. Balthasar,[2] has, of course, some reservations about your essay, but so far he has not expanded on them to me. I myself find you obscure in relation to E. Fuchs,[3] whom I have not yet been given the grace to understand. Do you know J. F. Konrad's *Abbild und Ziel der Schöpfung?*[4] I like it and will learn from its Old Testament monitions. But so far his basic objection (and agreement, too)—to the extent that he deals with Fuchs—has not revealed itself to me. I would like to know what my friend H. Vogel says about the conclusion to your article[5] and whether he will still develop a doctrine of paradox. Be that as it may, thanks for your great—and undoubtedly successful—efforts in this matter.

Furthermore, I have not thanked you for your great New Testament work.[6] This should be done, although I have not yet taken it in hand as is due.

With all good wishes for your future work and friendly greetings,

Yours,

KARL BARTH

[1]E. Jüngel, "Die Möglichkeit theologischer Anthropologie auf dem Grunde der Analogie," *EvTh*, 22 (1962), 535-557.
[2]Cf. G. Foley, "The Catholic Critics of Karl Barth—in Outline and Analysis," *Scottish Journal of Theology*, 14 (1951), 136-155.
[3]Jüngel, esp. 552. Like H. Vogel, Fuchs had been one of Jüngel's theological teachers.

⁴J. F. Konrad, *Abbild und Ziel der Schöpfung. Untersuchungen zur Exegesis von Genesis 1 und 2 in Barths* K.D. *III, 1* (Tübingen, 1962).

⁵Jüngel, 556f., sketches as a possible reply to his and Barth's doctrine of analogy that of H. Vogel, which would replace analogy by paradox.

⁶E. Jüngel, *Paulus und Jesus. Eine Untersuchung zur Präzisierung der Frage nach dem Ursprung der Christologie* (Tübingen, 1962).

*   *   *

60
To a Former Student in America

Basel, 7 November 1962

Dear N.N.,

Your request for a confidential recommendation puts me in some difficulty.

The time of your study here is well in the past, so that a friendly recollection of the good impression I then had of you would hardly have the concreteness necessary for this purpose. Since then you have followed a course as scholar and teacher on which I could not accompany you in detail. I must admit that after your last visit here with your wife I was not very sure where to place you in terms of your present theological development and orientation.

Above all I do not see how I could speak positively about the plan you sketch in your letter for work on Heidegger, Tillich, and Bultmann. According to your description this plan seems very problematic to me. That there are parallels and connections between these three contemporaries does not make them a triumvirate, nor especially does the fact that they once taught together in Marburg (only briefly as I recall).[1] I find a sure relation (which changed a good deal with time) only between (the younger) Heidegger and Bultmann. Relating Tillich (being) and Bultmann (time) to Heidegger (being and time)[2] seems to me to be a construction that none of the three would accept, and for which I could not assume co-responsibility regarding either you, the two foundations, or a wider public by recommending your plan. You will certainly find among modern theologians and philosophers in Europe and America some authorities who take a different view from mine and who will thus be able to lend you impressive support in approaching the two foundations. Unfortunately I myself am not in a position to render you this service.

I ask you not to be cross with me for this—*ultra posse nemo obligatur*. With friendly greetings to yourself and your wife,

Yours,

KARL BARTH

[1]Rudolf Bultmann, 1921-1951 (New Testament); Martin Heidegger, 1923-1928 (philosophy); Paul Tillich, 1924-1925 (systematic theology and philosophy of religion). [2]*Sein und Zeit* (Halle, 1927) (ET 1962).

*   *   *

61

To Prof. Ernst Wolf
Göttingen

Basel, 8 November 1962

Dear Ernst,

Many thanks for your letter of the fifth. Your news of the many things you have already done depresses me, for the only relatively useful thing I have done was to conduct yesterday the first session of my English colloquium. It included fifty to sixty participants, among them an eight-year-old child brought along by his mother, who could not get a baby-sitter. Next time one or another infant will surely appear seeking information on the basic concepts of ethics and so forth. Also depressing is the fact that I am now totally delivered up to the views and hands of various women, older and younger, regarding exercises I must do for my arm. Thus I can only decline with sorrow in the matter of the Easter march.[1] Since we do not have this undoubtedly promising form of expression in Switzerland,[2] I do not belong among its sponsors. It also seems a bit odd to me to have sponsors for Easter marches who let others battle with wind, weather, distance, and police, while they are content to march along in spirit.[3]

The "Reise-Colleg" of that old Göttingen student[4] is most informative; I read a few pages at a time and get more and more into the picture. This evening will be my first "society," for which some fifty are enrolled (including a group of Ebeling's students from Zurich). Tomorrow evening will be the first gathering of a little circle in which my remaining doctoral students will discuss their respective projects. From Rome I hear via Cullmann that they are discussing the liturgical schema[5] and even the *sub utraque*. Lollo, with me, greets you both. We think often about Walchensee. Max Geiger[6] has just come back tired but happy from fourteen days of military service in the mountains in which he not only threw hand-grenades but instructed and delighted his comrades with accounts from the Book of Job. Lollo has told me plainly (apropos Job) that of all the men she has met I am the most unwilling to suffer. So the image of my character vacillates in history.[7] But who and what does not vacillate today?—among other things the dogmatics of Trillhaas,[8] which he has just sent me and to which I have replied with a somewhat sweet-and-sour card. That it is better than his ethics[9] might be somewhat dubious praise. If I were Luther I would add something about the likely imminence of the last day. So I will leave it there.

With most sincere and grateful greetings to you and Asta,

Yours,
KARL B.

[1]Wolf had been asked to remind Barth that he had been invited to sponsor the Easter march against atomic weapons.
[2]The first Easter march in Switzerland took place in 1963 and took place every year up to 1967.
[3]An allusion to the Nazi Horst-Wessel song.
[4]*Vorlesungen über Land- und Seereisen, gehalten vom Herrn Professor Schlözer*, according to the notes of the student E. F. Haupt (winter semester 1795/6), ed. W. Ebel (Göttingen, 1962).
[5]Barth's Basel colleague Oscar Cullmann was an evangelical observer at Vatican Council II in Rome. For the resultant *Constitutio de Sacra Liturgia* see *LThK*, 2nd ed., Suppl. Vol. I (1966), pp. 14-109.
[6]Max Geiger, professor of church history at Basel, had accompanied Barth home from Walchensee on 21 Oct. 1962 after Barth's accident there (see 55).
[7]Barth is quoting from Schiller's *Wallenstein*, Prologue, vv. 102f.
[8]W. Trillhaas, *Dogmatik* (Berlin, 1962).
[9]*Ethik* (Berlin, 1959).

*　　　*　　　*

62
To Prof. Oscar Cullmann
Rome

Basel, 25 November 1962

Dear Friend,

Many thanks for your card from Monte Pincio (an unforgettable association for me).[1] You can imagine that it is with the closest attention and even with "burning concern"[2] that I receive from the holy city the news filtering through from the fringe of the mystery council,[3] and I anxiously await your direct reports. Your activity among the "other" council fathers (as we read in the paper yesterday) must be considerable. What has been decided about St. Joseph greatly pleased me.[4] Is not the relationship between J. and Jesus Christ ("foster-father") a much more exact model for the church than Mary's relationship is? (cf. Pius IX, *Quemadmodum Deus*, 8 Dec. 1870).[5] A Jesuit, Fr. L. Filas,[6] whom I met in Chicago, gave me instant approval in this. Some mariological ideas would then, of course, require careful modification. Will there be any headway on the second schema before 8 Dec.?[7] Here the *Dies academicus* has taken its usual course, but without me. My private colloquia at the Bruderholz come round with almost uncanny frequency.[8] I do not know what is going on at the Petersplatz and Rheinsprung.[9] At noon today I am seeing the four Czechs.[10] Has the *Spiegel* affair[11] been "mirrored" in Rome too?

With sincere greetings,

Yours,

KARL BARTH

[1]Here in 1934 Barth wrote part of his *Nein! Antwort an Emil Brunner*, ThExh [Munich], 14 (1934).

[2]Allusion to the encyclical with this title (Pius XI, 4 March 1937).

[3]Vatican II (11 Oct. 1962–8 Dec. 1965).

[4]St. Joseph was put in the canon of the mass by the decree *De S. Ioseph nomine Canoni Missae inserendo* of the Roman Congregation of Rites, 13 Nov. 1962.

[5]By the decree *Quemadmodum Deus Iosephum* Pius IX had declared Joseph to be a patron of the church. For Barth's view see his "Über die Annäherung der Kirchen. Ein Gespräch zwischen Karl Barth und T. de Quénétain," *JK*, 24 (1963), 304-309.

[6]Francis L. Filas, professor in the department of theology, Loyola University of Chicago, author of many books about St. Joseph. Cf. his *Joseph: The Man Closest to Jesus: The Complete Life, Theology and Devotional History of St. Joseph* (Boston, 1962), p. 462: "In a conversation in Chicago with the author of the present book (April 27, 1962), Dr. Karl Barth used substantially these words, 'If I were a Catholic theologian, I would lift Joseph up. He took care of the Child; he takes care of the Church.'"

[7]*On the Sources of Revelation.* Debate on this had begun on 14 Nov.

[8]The reference is to the "society," the English and French colloquia, and the doctoral seminar, which took place either at Barth's home or in a restaurant close by.

[9]The university buildings.

[10]The Czech theologians Professors J. B. Soucek and J. H. Lochman and Pastor J. Cihak, accompanied by the Swiss theologian Hans Ruh.

[11]Several reporters and the editor of *Der Spiegel* ("The Mirror") were arrested on suspicion of treason after publishing a critical account of maneuvers; cf. *Der Spiegel*, 16 (1962), no. 41.

*   *   *

63
To Miss Annie Hirzel
Locarno

Basel, 28 November 1962

[In this letter Barth told Miss Hirzel he had sent her some illustrated magazines, brought her up to date with his recent activities, and sent her a check for her seventy-fifth birthday to help her hold her head above water in the rising tide of inflation. He went on to quote from Gerhardt's hymn "Die güldne Sonne" (1666): "After the roaring of the sea and whistling of the wind there shines the welcome face of the sun." He then added: "I have noted you do not like being addressed out of the hymnbook. So translate the lines into your own speech."]

*　　　　　*　　　　　*

64
To Mrs. Helene Bürri-Fahrni
Hunibach near Thun

Basel, 30 November 1962

[Having received some photographs and a cake from Mrs. Bürri-Fahrni, the pastor's wife, Barth noted that the picture of Niesen above Lake Thun was much more refreshing than a studio portrait of himself, and that the cake was more genuine, because closer to God's creation, than the theological literature composed on his desk. He was, however, sending a copy of the portrait after his *Einführung*, as a token of gratitude and a pledge that one day he would come in person "if God wills and we live" (James 4:15).]

*　　　　　*　　　　　*

65
To Superintendent Udo Smidt
Detmold

Basel, 11 December 1962

Dear Superintendent,

I have just received the copy you kindly sent of the imposing jubilee edition of the Heidelberg Catechism.[1] Apart from its external magnificence (is the weapon on the front that of the princes of the Palatinate?), it has been very well and serviceably done. May it be read and valued as well! By the way, what has become of the translation of the HC into modern German,[2] on which I was once asked to give an opinion but which I do not remember seeing in print? It would be much more desirable than the other things that come out of Germany. But there reign Bultmannians of all colors and the indestructible Adenauer in politics. We hope things will not end up in another mess. For the moment we will focus on Christmas—and the more so the darker the scene becomes.

With sincere thanks and greetings,

Yours,
KARL BARTH

[1]*Der Heidelberger Katechismus. Jubiläumsausgabe 1563/1963* (Essen, 1963).
[2]A modern edition had come out the previous year: *Der Heidelberger Katechismus. Für den Jugendunterricht in evangelischen Gemeinden vereinfachte Ausgabe* (Neukirchen, 1961).

*   *   *

65a
To Dr. Arnold Buchholz
Cologne

Basel, 12 December 1962

Dear Dr. Buchholz,

I would like to be of service to you.[1] But unfortunately I am not one of the ten who knew the man. It could be I saw him once on the streets of Zurich. But who could know at that time . . . ? To my regret, then, I can return only a negative report.

Respectfully yours,
KARL BARTH

[1]Buchholz was planning to collect some personal reminscences of W. I. Lenin. He had been told Barth was one of approximately ten persons who knew Lenin and had asked for his cooperation in a letter dated 10 Dec. 1962. Barth's reply has been included here because the rumor has been revived that Barth knew Lenin personally. [The late inclusion of the letter in the Swiss edition accounts for its non-sequential numbering.]

*   *   *

66

To Dr. Johann-Friedrich Konrad
Bonn

Basel, 17 December 1962

Dear Dr. Konrad,

Someone has whispered to me today that you were waiting in some suspense for my reaction to your book *Abbild und Ziel der Schöpfung* that you sent me.[1] Insofar as I can say something about it, I will do so gladly.

The first thing undoubtedly is to express my serious recognition of the industry and perspicacity with which you have studied me, your unmistakable and sincere desire to do justice to my efforts, and finally your bold attempt to go on from *CD*, which the younger generation is not only allowed but commanded to do.

But I falter[2] here already—if I am to say something to the point.

It is clear to me behind veils of tears that in your investigation you bury in a kind of mass grave almost all my fine expositions of Genesis 1 and 2. To make up my mind with what right you do this I should have to resume studies which I pursued in the final stages of the second world war; it is doubtful whether I would be able to do this. However, the shots with which you have flattened those expositions do not come primarily from your knowledge of the Old Testament but from your knowledge of systematic theology. And unfortunately I have to say to you that in this respect my eyes are holden: I do not see what you are getting at when you say I should everywhere have kept the covenant and reconciliation apart, nor do I understand the christological presuppositions which are obviously normative for you. In particular, the concept of a sacred history of language, which controls your presentation, imparts no clear picture of me. For this reason I can also make nothing of the schema of purpose and goal[3] to which you wish to convert me, and neither can I do anything with it so far as concerns your supposed elucidation of the concept of analogy. I have passed on your book to my young students with the request that they help me, but I received no enlightenment from them. Since I want to like your work and praise it, this is too bad, but so it is. Is it connected with the fact that in what you say I seem to hear again the voice of the theology of E. Fuchs, with which, in view of its kaleidoscopic and glossolalistic character, I have so far been able to achieve only a rather obscure and troubled acquaintance?[4]

If advances beyond *C.D.* are to be in this direction, I can contemplate future developments only with astonishment, as the famous hen did the duckling she hatched. But perhaps I am mistaken in locating you at this point. If I had known what was coming when I saw Professor Kreck[5] this autumn, he might have told me something which would explain matters.

I really wanted to send a letter, too, to your father,[6] who sent such kind greetings through you. Perhaps I may return his greetings through you with my thanks for his extolling of my sermons in *ThLZ*, though I must deeply deplore the way he handled those of Fritz Dürst just after.[7] Tell him this man is the preacher I like best and listen to regularly in these parts.

But enough! Do not be cross if my thanks for your work sound hollow. Perhaps you will succeed in some future work in being more enlightening to me than you are in this one, no doubt through my own fault.

With all good wishes for Christmas and friendly greetings,

Yours,
KARL BARTH

[1]See 59, n. 4.
[2]J. W. Goethe, *Faust*, I, v. 1225.
[3]Barth really meant Abbild (not Absicht) und Ziel, the title of the work.
[4]Barth was now hard at work on Fuchs, and one of Barth's students, J. Fangmeier, was doing a study which was later published as *Ernst Fuchs. Versuch einer Orientierung*, ThSt, 80 (Zurich, 1964).
[5]Konrad's mentor. Barth had met him in Josefstal on 2 Oct. 1962.
[6]Joachim Konrad, professor of practical theology at Bern.
[7]J. Konrad, "Neuere Predigtliteratur," *ThLZ*, 87 (1962), 801-812. The survey covered Barth's *Den Gefangenen Befreiung* (803f.) and F. Dürst's *Aus seiner Fülle. Predigten* (Zurich, 1960; 804).

*   *   *

67
To Prof. Fritz Buri
Basel

Basel, 18 December 1962

Dear Colleague,

Christmas must not get any closer before I thank you for the weighty gift you made me by sending the second volume of your *Dogmatics*.[1]

As is proper in Advent, let me begin with the positive things I can say about it.

I sincerely admire your achievement in writing these five hundred pages in addition to your work as head pastor.[2] So far as I know, none of your predecessors or other Basel clergy has ever been capable of this.

I also admire sincerely your heroism in as it were placing yourself between all stools: you annoy former liberal friends by the garb of orthodoxy with which you clothe yourself; you annoy positive theologians by that garb's undeniable transparency; and finally you do not try in any way to keep in with me, whom in your friendly accompanying letter you describe as either openly or secretly your chief debating partner. Thus I see you as one of the old Swiss knights of Urs Graf[3] striding defiantly through the land or as one of your beloved stone figures in the minister staring fixedly ahead. I always have some liking for such an attitude.

But you will not be surprised if I go on to say for the sake of your own person and destiny as well as the content that I am sorry—again sincerely—not to see so much work and character put in the service of a better cause.

Concerning the content first, it is understandable that from the very first step, and then as I read on and on, I cannot follow you. You love the word "incredible." Your christology, wrapped like a bit of chocolate in the silver paper of your anthropology, is quite "incredible" to me— painful though it is to have to say so. In your Jesus Christ, who first and last seems to be only the most important cipher of a "Christian faith," I unfortunately cannot recognize the one I know by this name,[4] for all the beauty with which you have decked him. I see two consequences of the vacuum I think I see here at the heart of your theology. First, your christology is for you neither a permission nor a constraint to cross the limit of your traditionally very individualistic anthropology in the direction of the fellow-man or neighbor. One notes with sorrow that you have no longer kept up with "religious socialism," as Lüdemann has not kept up with it.[5] Thus the house of Christian faith whose self-understanding you seek to define is, if you will pardon me, much too musty a place. Again, your christology obviously does not suggest that your dogmatics ought to offer a simple but clear and rather cheerful[6] confession of the Christian faith. Rather, it seems as if the most pressing concern of faith's self-understanding lies in the morose, scholastic controversies which dominate your five hundred pages from beginning to end. Where are we given occasion to strike up a Gloria or at least utter a beatitude? But how can there be an occasion for this if the Savior (yes, dear colleague, the Savior)—in Basel one says "the Lord Jesus"—is all in all only a cipher of our own little Christian faith?

Now for the personal side. Allow me to tell you openly that you deeply grieve me. This is what I usually say when complaints about you reach me. I am no psychologist. But I cannot see you as the great tree you so easily seem to be. I note that in the faculty and the community you often appear to be painfully isolated. For that reason I gladly take up your suggestion that we should meet again personally. Don't be afraid I might slip it over on you again that a professional conversion is what you really need. But tell me and explain to me this and that, and I will listen, muttering but open and sympathetic. How about an evening in the week after Christmas or New Year? Your wife, with whom I always get along well but whom I have not seen for some time, could perhaps come too, but no one else. Will you come to me, or shall I take a mini-taxi, now my favorite mode of transportation, and come to Augustinergasse?[7]

Be that as it may—I am ready for all good things, though I do not include approval of your dogmatics.

With friendly greetings, also to your wife, and best wishes for the festal season,

Yours,
KARL BARTH

[1]F. Buri, Der Mensch und die Gnade, Vol. II of Dogmatik als Selbstverständnis des christlichen Glaubens (Tübingen, 1962; Vol. I, Vernunft und Offenbarung, 1956).

[2]Buri was head pastor (formerly antistes) at Basel Minster and also Professor of systematic theology.

[3]Swiss goldsmith, painter, draftsman, and illustrator (c. 1485-1527/8).

[4]In the MS Barth corrected "think I know" to "know."

[5]Hermann Lüdemann (1842-1933), professor of systematic theology in Bern, proponent of theological liberalism. L. had come to know Swiss religious socialism but found no place for it in his theology.

[6]In the MS Barth corrected "fröhlichen" to "vergnügten."

[7]Buri lived at Augustinergasse 11.

*   *   *

68

To Prof. Joseph L. Hromádka
Prague

Basel, 18 December 1962

Dear Joseph,

When the three men who came to us from Prague like the three wise men from the east were on the point of returning to you, having left outstanding impressions everywhere, I wanted to give them a letter to you as our friends Schwarz and Ruh had done.[1] It now follows as my postscript to what they will have let you know.

The three will have told you that on Sunday afternoon, in a small circle here in Basel, we spent a profitable time on Joseph theology, in this case the interpretation of the political theology or theological politics of Joseph Hromádka. Shortly afterward I saw your essay "The Crisis is Past?" in your church newsletter of November 1962.[2] You will already have had two letters from Basel on it. All things considered, it seems important to me, too, to say something to you about it. It is one of the many fine things about you that one can speak openly to you without having to fear losing your desire for new and better fellowship; such can be the only terms on which to disagree.

Dear Joseph, I am referring to the quality in you which has disturbed me in your public statements for years. In this latest essay it struck me almost like a blow: in its negative mode, there is the lack of any higher place above the clouds of ideologies, interests, and forces which confront and conflict with one another in the cold war; and in its positive mode, there is the arbitrariness with which you not only champion one of the fronts personally but also expect the church and the world to do the same. Evangelically, what I regard as right and even commanded in the modern situation is precisely what our friend Lochman has set forth in exemplary fashion (far better than I could) in his essay "Balance of European Humanism" in *Junge Kirche*.[3] That is that our attitude should be one in which, with our Word and for the sake of God, we can be in helpful solidarity with man as such, and therefore with those of the left and the right, those who suffer and those who strive, the righteous and the unrighteous, Christians and atheists, the followers of humanisms A, B, C, and D. What I see you doing when your theology—as it should— becomes political is something different: you pressure us and other contemporaries with the demand that we should discover the newly developing world of freedom and peace represented in the figures of

Nikita, Mao, and even Fidel, and see in the figure of John [Kennedy] an incarnation of the old social and political order that has been outdated since 1917 and is now crumbling away. My hair stands on end at this black and white depiction and the demand that we should adopt it.

I will not quarrel about the concrete political tasks that you set (implicitly and explicitly) in your essay, although I have various reservations and amendments in relation to each of them. This would lead to a political discussion that cannot be our purpose. It is rather a question of the method and style of your presentation, in view of which I cannot suppress my old suspicion, familiar enough to you, that your attitudes and corresponding Christian admonitions are determined entirely by a point of view which is materially identical with that of the one Leviathan that is striving for power today, except that, and this is very important, for you this point of view is undergirded by a reference to Jesus Christ and holy scripture, though I cannot see it. Dear Joseph, do you not realize that Emil Brunner, Reinhold Niebuhr, and other western fathers defend their western outlook with the same method and in the same style, and being able to do this they thus bring on the scene their crusade against communism, so that you and they are waging the cold war in just the same way? From the outset I could see in the well-known bird of Picasso only an anti-American hawk and not a dove that can bring comfort to all people[4]; hence I could never take seriously or support the so-called World Peace Movement (about which we have heard remarkably little recently). You should have seen to it that the Prague Peace Conference, which was really inspired and led by you, stood under a distinctly different sign from that hawk.

Martin Schwarz and Hans Ruh have told you, or hinted to you, how difficult you make it for us, your western friends, when you take the line you do in this last essay and give it such clear and disturbing emphasis. I cannot think that this is just a tactical move. It really has a supremely strategic character. The benighted people in the newspapers and *Weltwoche* and *Reformatio* etc. will again cry *Quod erat demonstrandum* when this essay falls into their hands—may all the good angels prevent it. We will certainly not give up on you. But so long as such announcements come from you, how can we make it clear to them and to others in the Christian and secular world on this side of the iron curtain that the issue for us (and basically for you, too, is it not?) is neither an anti-communist nor a communist peace but the peace of God which is above all understanding[5]—and therefore righteousness (in the biblical sense of the word) both against all and on behalf of all?

Dear Joseph, how I would rejoice to hear (as the finest Christmas present) that you have achieved a breakthrough—a true and powerful breakthrough in this direction.

With all good wishes for the festal period, now as before and in all circumstances,

Faithfully yours,
KARL BARTH[6]

[1]See 62, n. 10.
[2]J. L. Hromádka, "Die Krise ist vorbei?" *Die protestantische Kirchen in der Tschechoslowakei*, 9 (1962), no. 9, pp. 61ff. (on the Cuban missile crisis).
[3]J. M. Lochman, "Bilanz des europäischen Humanismus," *JK*, 23 (1962), 651-660.
[4]From 1948 on Pablo Picasso often painted doves (symbolizing peace) for posters at communist peace congresses.
[5]Phil 4:7.
[6]For Hromádka's reply, see Appendix, 4.

*　　　*　　　*

69
To Prof. Hans Küng
Tübingen

Basel, 19 December 1962

Dear Colleague,

I suspect that the episcopal staff, whose bearer is hidden among the haloes of the other participants in this blessed council in miniature,[1] belongs to you, that you then are the coming man so finely depicted. Provisionally, then, I hopefully congratulate you on your naming as *peritus*.[2] Do you know I am one of the few Protestants who is not annoyed but pleased that Joseph has been put in the canon of the mass?[3] His function as foster-father of Christ makes him a much more appropriate patron of the church than the *theotokos*, who is usually mentioned in this connection. It would be good if on your Christmas journey to Switzerland, you could look in on me and whisper to me some council secrets. You can imagine I have followed the proceedings thus far with "burning concern"[4] but not without some confidence.

With warm greetings and all good wishes,

Yours,
KARL BARTH

[1]Barth was writing on a card which depicted Lucas Moser's *The Saints Crossing the Sea* (1491) on the Magdalene altar of the church of Tiefenbronn near Pforzheim.
[2]A theological expert at Vatican II, appointed by John XXIII.
[3]See 62, nn. 4-6.
[4]See 62, n. 2.

*   *   *

70
To Prof. Ernst Wolf
Göttingen

Early January 1963

Dear Ernst,

As a first greeting in the New Year I am sending you two documents from my immediate and more distant past. That of 1933 Lollo claims as her possession and would like to see again some day.[1] More freely, however, I send you that of 1962, because "this man" is so plainly recognized in it "as a Protestant" and yet so finely shown to be "filled with paradisal peace."[2]

The first waves of direct news from the council will have reached you, too. What are we to make of the fact that John XXIII has struck a medal with the inscription *Ubi Spiritus Dei, ibi libertas*[3] (in the nineteenth century the favorite text of our theological Liberals!)? Has the millennium already drawn near?

With sincerest greetings from Lollo and me to Asta [. . .][4] and yourself,

Yours,
KARL B.

[1]Barth sent one of the accompanying letters (1 July 1933) with *Theologische Existenz heute* (Munich, 1933) to the Prussian Minister of Science, Art, and Culture, Dr. Rust, to Chancellor Adolf Hitler, and to Dr. Krummacher. Wolf copied the letters before returning them and published them in *EvTh*, 23 (1963), 389-391.
[2]Barth is referring to the way a Roman Catholic describes him in a letter responding to an article of his on "Gottes Geburt" in *Wir Brückenbauer*, 21 (1962), no. 51.
[3]2 Cor 3:17.
[4]Not fully decipherable.

*   *   *

71

To Pastor A. Brune
Frondenberg (Ruhr)

Basel, 9 January 1963

Dear Pastor,

When I try to elucidate the relation between A and E by referring to that between M and B,[1]

1. by M and B I naturally do not mean the men thus named, so that the man M (as A) is put above the man B, but I have in mind their music in its characteristic substance and form;

2. nor do I mean that M = A and B = E, but I am simply comparing the relation of A to E with that of M to B.

A comparison (which is not an equation) is possible when there is at least some (more or less clear) similarity between the things compared.

A similarity between the relations of A and E and M and B seems to me to exist to the extent that on both sides we have the contrast between a being engaged in liberated self-giving to another and a being engaged in striving to grasp another while still seeking liberation.

(In the sentence that you found confusing I was only doing methodologically what I find constantly done in the synoptic parables [which are not equations].)

With friendly greetings,

Yours,

KARL BARTH

---

[1]Brune had asked Barth to explain the statement in his *Evangelical Theology* that Agape stands in relation to Eros as Mozart does to Beethoven.

*   *   *

72

To Prof. Ernst Wolf
Göttingen

Basel, 13 January 1963[1]

Dear Ernst,

Thanks for your letter. We were sorry to hear Asta is not well again. Give her our remembrances and greetings. We have heard about the

Frankfurter Tagung[2] from von Oppen and Schellong[3] who visited us here. But we are not clear as to events there or the underlying motives and emotions. K's doctorate has been decided and will be made public at the end of the term.[4] I shall be very pleased to contribute a sermon to his *Festschrift*. Those of 23 Dec. and 31 Dec.[5] will reach you, and in the foreseeable future I shall be preaching there again. You can select what you think is suitable.[6] You may also disclose the documents of 1933[7] to astonished posterity. A possible title might be: "My friend, learn to understand this aright: this is the way to deal with witches."[8] The paradisal peace with which I am filled[9] has just been disturbed a little (a) by one of the colds I usually suffer from at this time of the year, and (b) by reactions in the broader family circle. The English translation of *Evangelical Theology* has finally come out (along with the French and Japanese).[10] Meanwhile I remain in a mostly receptive frame of mind. I have read a work by Heinz Zahrnt on the historical Jesus[11] which you obviously value, though the author is unknown to me, but having considered it I find it rather slim. My son Christoph would quote: "This is what so greatly provokes us Catholics." He himself is provoked at the moment by the difficulties in getting a certain car from Australia to Java. So everywhere there is obviously not a little to sigh about. Give Asta our greetings and best wishes. Greet your fine Uvo and friendly greetings from Lollo and me to yourself (always . . .[12] remembering ? Upper Bavaria),[13]

Yours,

KARL BARTH

[1]Date on postmark.

[2]Conference of the Church Brotherhoods (5-6 January 1963) on the oath and emergency legislation.

[3]Otto Albrecht von Oppen, pastor in Datteln, and Dieter Schellong, pastor in Gütersloh.

[4]Professor Karl Kupisch, Berlin, was being given an honorary doctorate at Basel.

[5]Sermons on Luke 1:53 and 2 Cor 12:9, publ. in *Rufe mich an . . .* (Zurich, 1965), pp. 68ff.; 78ff.

[6]In fact not a sermon but an essay by Barth ("Überlegungen zum Zweiten Vatikanischen Konzil") formed his contribution to the *Festschrift* when it finally came out under the title *Zwischenstation* (Munich, 1963).

[7]Cf. 70, n. 1.

[8]Goethe's *Faust*, I, v. 2516f.

[9]Cf. 70, n. 2.

[10]K. Barth, *Evangelical Theology: An Introduction*, tr. G. Foley (London, 1963; also New York, 1963); French trans. by F. Ryser (Geneva, 1962); Japanese trans. by T. Kato (Shinkyo Shuppansha, 1963).

[11]H. Zahrnt, *Es begann mit Jesus von Nazareth: Die Frage nach dem historischen Jesus* (Stuttgart/Berlin, 1960).

¹²Indecipherable.
¹³Reference to the vacation in Wolf's house; cf. 55f.

*   *   *

73
[written in English]
To Leonard V. Fulton
El Cerrito, California[1]

Basel, 14 January 1963

Dear Mr. Fulton,

Martin Luther had once been asked what to do suppose we had reason to believe that the Last Day might be very near? Luther's answer: I would go, plant a small young apple tree, and then wait and see. Well, here is your little Timothy! Tell him (more by your example than by words) what is the matter with faith, hope, and love! Teach him how to become a peace-maker in his next surroundings, a pleasant individual before God and before his neighbors! Let him grow up as a man who has nothing to fear. That will be your contribution to international peace. By doing so (and by praying that it may be done in the right way!) you will make a better use of the time (still left to you and us all) than by speculating about what may happen. Do you see my point?

My greetings to you and to young Timothy!!

KARL BARTH

[1]Fulton had asked Barth (and other prominent people) for advice on how, at the right time, to give his then two-year-old son an answer to the question: "How can I and other men of my standing work concretely for international peace?" and had added, "For the Timothies everywhere, I ask this."

*   *   *

74
To Prof. Hiderobu Kuwada
Tokyo

Basel, 22 January 1963

Dear Colleague,

Sincere thanks for your serious and interesting letter. I remember your visit to us clearly and gladly and am pleased to have contact and discussion with you again in this way.

If I correctly understand your letter about conditions of peace I can only express my happy agreement with the substance of what you say.

You state that for peace on earth it is not enough that we protest against war and preparation for it, nor even against nuclear war, nor against every form of nationalism, imperialism, and capitalism, as is done by friends of peace in Japan and their left-wing supporters, and as is done in laudable fashion in so many peace movements in all countries. You would understand and accept that the task in the work for peace you are given as a Christian and a theologian is a different one and a special one. You refer to the inner realities which underlie war and all preparation for war, mentioning specifically the envy, hatred, and pugnacity that controls men. You connect these fatal inner realities with the Christian concept of original sin. You say that even a world that does not wage war could not be a good and truly peaceful world without liberation from these evil inner realities. You wait for true peace as a gift of God consisting of a reconciled relation between man and man as well as between God and man, so that no place is left for the inner realities that lead to war.

I not only have no objections to this; I accept it with full conviction. But allow me to state the same thing in accordance with the measure of my own theological thinking and in my own words.

I would begin by recalling that in holy scripture, which is normative for me, the word peace is identical with the much broader concept of salvation. This is why you and I cannot agree that there is no more to a fruitful peace movement than battling against war and a military ordering of the relations between peoples. The salvation that includes peace within it is what at the end of your letter you call God's great reconciliation: the reconciliation of the world with God which includes the reconciliation of men with one another. And I would stress the fact that this is the reconciliation which God has already accomplished in the history of Jesus Christ, in His life and passion, and already manifested in His resurrection from the dead. It is the reconciliation which does not first have to be made by us but which has been established by God, and whose light does not first have to be kindled by us but already shines as God's light. In Jesus Christ God and man and man and man are already at peace, not as enemies, but as true comrades and companions. In Him salvation is already present and at work. In Him this gift of God has already been given—it simply waits to be received by us.

What the world lacks is the knowledge and awareness of our human responsibility for that peace which is not just a beautiful idea but the reality that God has set up and revealed within world history. The pity is that the nations live with eyes and ears closed to it. But so long as they do not see and hear God's gift, they cannot and will not take it, and so long as they do not take it, war and many other evils will come. Why do they miss it? Why do they not see and hear it, why does our world continually show itself to be a world of war? I seek the blame for the disasters that constantly threaten the world afresh less in the corruptions that have become man's second nature than in the laxity of the Christian churches throughout the world in fulfilling their special task of proclaiming to men the objective reality of salvation, and therefore of peace too, by word and also by example, and doing so with the clarity and definiteness, the joy and consistency, that are commensurate with this great matter.

What should be done? We can and should continually insist that peace is better than war. We can and should continually refer today to the dreadful experience of Hiroshima. We can and should continually admonish ourselves and others that we must love and not hate one another and therefore not kill one another. All this is fine and good. But it seems obvious to me that in the last resort none of it brings any help. What the world needs is the revolutionary knowledge that by the love with which God has loved it, it is freed from the unhappy necessity of seeking its salvation in any national, political, economic, or moral principles, ideas, and systems (whether western or eastern), and therefore of seeking it in the unavoidable cold or hot wars. The world is liberated for a life of man with God as his Father and his fellowman as his brother. It is thus liberated for a life which makes war in any form superfluous, abolishing and excluding it. The world must recognize that by the love of God in Jesus Christ it is already a liberated world. But how can it see itself as this liberated world, and conduct itself as such, if Jesus Christ is not proclaimed to it as its Lord and Savior in a completely different way from heretofore?

Conditions of peace? In this matter there is only one condition whose fulfilment would truly guarantee peace on earth. Christians are usually quick enough to say that the nations must be converted to faith in Jesus Christ. This is true. But something else must precede it. The nations—and this applies to Christians and Christian churches themselves—must be *called* to Jesus Christ in such a way that their eyes and ears are opened, that they cannot withstand and evade knowing the reality of salvation and therefore of peace, that the irrefutable truth of the covenant between God and man and man and man will be written on their hearts and consciences as the law of their conduct. What must be done is this: Christians and the Christian churches must call the nations in this way to faith in Jesus Christ. But how can they call to this faith so long as they are not certain of it themselves in a new way, much more definitely, soberly, and courageously? What needs to take place today in the interests of peace is in the first instance an awakening, an inner renewing, a spiritual reformation, and to that extent a conversion of Christians and the Christian churches themselves—a conversion to the truth of their own message. Among other things a good deal of better theology is needed. Thus, dear colleague, we come to face the contribution that you and I must make to peace among the nations. You had this in view when you wrote about the special way you were trying to work for peace in Japan. If I have properly understood you, I might now add: Let us be our own personal peace movement both there and here, in our prayers and in our studies in the service of the completed work and spoken word of God, whose power and light are the only hope of peace, but a victorious hope.

I believe that in all this I have not said anything different from what was on your mind when you wrote your letter. I greet you, then, in the fellowship of genuine brotherliness,

Yours,
KARL BARTH

*   *   *

75
To Prof. Karl Linke
Friedberg

Basel, 26 January 1963

Dear Colleague,

Thanks for your kind letter.[1] But I cannot co-operate, being of the opinion that the heroes of the present situation should decide this chariot-race among themselves (at the risk of men and horses falling)— but having no hope that a true "Lazarus, come forth"[2] will result. I thus beg you to excuse me.

Yours,
KARL BARTH

¹ On behalf of the paper *Stimme der Gemeinde* Linde had asked Barth, along with Braun, Ebeling, Käsemann, Kreck, Mezger, and Pannenberg, for an exposition of the raising of Lazarus in John 11:1-45 in order to acquaint readers with the present theological situation.
² John 11:43.

*　　　　*　　　　*

76
To Prof. Carl Iversen
Copenhagen

Basel, 20 February 1963

[In this letter Barth thanked Prof. Iversen and the University of Copenhagen for awarding him the Sonning Prize (for European Culture) for 1963 and promised to be there to receive it on 19 April.]

*　　　　*　　　　*

77
To Pastor Friedrich Elsässer
Biberach

Basel, 25 February 1963

Dear Pastor,

I have received and read your memorandum on the Council. I, too, am neither an optimist nor a pessimist in this matter. But I await developments more quietly than you. By counterreformation I understand a Catholicism oriented and shaped in opposition to the Reformation (Trent). They have long since finished with this in my view. Let us see to it that we do not set up a Protestantism that is itself oriented and shaped in opposition to Rome, and so forth. Since your memorandum smacks a little of this, I am not totally satisfied with it, though many things in it [. . .] have my full approval. Be careful that you do not leave with the people you are addressing the impression of being a Don Quixote tilting at windmills.

All good wishes for your work and friendly greetings,

Yours,
KARL BARTH

*　　　　*　　　　*

78
To Dr. Richard Lienhard
Zurich

Basel, 4 March 1963

[In this letter Barth refused an invitation to write about the nuclear initiative of the Swiss Social Democratic Party for a referendum on atomic armaments for Switzerland, his main problem being that he would have to criticize the party, or its leaders, for rejecting a first initiative, and had yet to be convinced of its present seriousness.]

*   *   *

79
To Dr. Martin Meyer
Lenzburg (Aargau Canton)

Basel, 5 March 1963

[In this letter Barth declined an invitation to give an address in Lenzburg on the mission of Switzerland, pleading that he felt no constraint to do this and that the time had come for the younger generation to be called on in matters of this kind.]

*   *   *

80
To Dr. B. A. Willems, O.P.
Nijmegen (Netherlands)

Basel, 6 March 1963

Dear Dr. Willems,

Sincere thanks for kindly sending me a copy of your little book about me.[1] I have affectionate recollections of you at the time you studied here and my impression of your presentation agrees with these. I do not read Dutch fluently enough to have read all the ninety pages thoroughly. But I have taken some random samples and noted everywhere how sure is your grasp of essentials and how lovingly you speak of me. Your presentation is another fine example of the new atmosphere between confessions about which we hear so much through the first session of Vatican II. I think you are right—Hans Küng is also of this opinion—that the most serious difference is to be found in the field of ecclesiology, and the next in the right understanding of the Chalcedonian mean between Alexandria and Antioch. What will you say when I tell you I am one of the few Protestants who was not annoyed by the insertion of St. Joseph into the canon of the mass? I find this biblical figure, movingly obedient and ministering, much more suited to be the protector (and exemplar!) of the church than Mary, with whose function that of the church is not to be compared.[2] I cannot assume John XXIII had this in mind with his move toward a Joseph theology. But is it not permissible and perhaps even obligatory to think further in this direction and then perhaps to reach further clarifications in ecclesiology as well?

Another word about your work: I did not like your picture on the back at all. As for mine on the front: well, my hair has since become a good deal more grey or white and there are now other visible signs of my seventy-seven years. At the last there remains only *sperare in Dominum*.

With sincere greetings and all good wishes for your work,

Yours,
KARL BARTH

[1]B. A. Willems, O. P., *Karl Barth. Een inleiding in zijn denken* (Tielt/Den Haag, 1963; German trans. Zurich, 1964).
[2]Cf. 62, 69.

*　　　*　　　*

81
To Prof. Josef L. Hromádka
Prague

Basel, 6 March 1963

[In this letter Barth explained why he had not been able to come to Prague as had been hoped. The suggested program had been over-expanded, Barth did not like to speak extemporaneously, he had no prepared lectures like those he had used on the American tour, and in his view it was best for him to focus on his work with students and his preaching in Basel prison, letting the younger generation take over wider responsibilities.]

* * *

82
To Franz Heiniger
Zurich

Basel, 8 March 1963

[Invited by Heiniger to be a patron of the Swiss Youth March against atomic armament, Barth declined on the grounds that he had refused to sponsor a similar German march and that marching young people do not need the "patronizing" of older nonmarchers.]

* * *

83
To Pastor Walter Feurich
Dresden

Basel, 16 March 1963

[Barth had heard that Feurich had not been too well and was in a difficult situation, being attacked on both sides. He extended sympathies, told him why he himself had not been able to go to Prague, and promised to give any help possible.]

* * *

84
To Pastor Artur Mettler
Neuhausen (Schaffhausen Canton)

Basel, 17 March 1963

[In response to a letter in which Mettler had told him that reading the *Evangelical Theology* had recalled the old days, Barth asked Mettler to fill him in on his recent doings and explain why he had dropped out of sight. "You do not in any way owe me an *apologia pro vita tua*. You should simply be aware that I should like to hear about you if you for your part are inclined to tell me."]

* * *

85
To Dr. Herman Bizer
Rosenfeld (Württemburg)

Brione (Tessino Canton), 29 March 1963

Dear Dr. Bizer,

I do not usually judge either men or teachings hastily. But I do in fact object to the Roman *and* and the Evangelical (or not really Evangelical!) "faith *and* baptism."[1] I regard baptism, in brief, as an act, a confession, a prayer of faith, or of the obedience of faith—not as a "means" of grace and salvation, not as a "sacrament." Your brother[2] will hardly be satisfied with me on this point.

With friendly greetings,

Yours,

KARL BARTH

[1]Bizer had written a letter on 27 March 1963 saying how pleased he was to read that Barth had condemned the Catholic *and*, and asking if he also condemned the Evangelical *and* in "faith *and* baptism."
[2]Ernst Bizer (1904-1975), professor of church history at Bonn, Herman Bizer's *cousin*.

* * *

86
To Prof. Umberto Campagnolo
General Secretary of the European Society of Culture
Venice

Brione (Tessino Canton), 3 April 1963

Dear Mr. Campagnolo,

Let me begin by saying how much I admire both the indefatigable zeal shown in your efforts regarding the problem of culture and the intensity of your attempts to bring together such different and opposing minds to consider this problem. St. Mark's Square, Venice, will perhaps be celebrated one day as the Vatican dedicated to the cult of this deity. I have to like and admire you.

Forgive me for not replying earlier to your request of 5 February.[1] Since our last meeting[2] I have become a fairly old man (seventy-seven years!) living in retreat, although this is broken again and again by too many visits, consultations, and correspondence of all kinds, so that I have to choose carefully between what I can do and what I can't.

Now, participating in your symposium on "Culture and Religion" is one of the things which does not escape my interest but is beyond my powers, given the limits of time and leisure now at my disposal. I have so often discussed these things that any who might be interested in knowing my views can easily find them in the context of my published works. I should not like to repeat myself yet again. Would the success of this exercise in "understanding" ["comprendre"] not be better served if you were to turn to representatives of the younger generation? The day of their responsibility has come, while grandpas like myself will have the benefit of listening and learning to what extent and in what way their seed will prove to be useful or not.

This, dear Mr. Campagnolo, is the sum of my reflections on your request and the reason why I beg to be excused.

Kind regards to yourself and Mrs. Campagnolo—we have affectionate remembrances of you both—and best wishes for your fine work.

Yours,

KARL BARTH

[1]Campagnolo had asked Barth to contribute to a symposium on "Culture and Religion" in his paper *Comprendre*.

[2]Barth had taken part in a conference of the society in Venice in 1956 (29 March– 1 April).

*   *   *

87
To Mrs. Gertrud Staewen
Berlin

Basel, 27 April 1963

Dear Gertrud,

Yes, don't be despondent! Good news! God is not dead. He does not have to retire in the autumn (like Konrad Adenauer). He does not intend to do so in two years (like Nikita Khrushchev). If we still live, we are upheld well.

Next week there is to be a Berlin-Basel week here during which the Berliners will entertain us with theater, music, and even sermons, Kupisch[1] will give a lecture, your Willy Brandt will give us the creeps with horror stories about the wall, and (as a climax) the Berlin zoo will help ours to new glory with the gift of some wild animals. All that is really lacking is for you to bring greetings and sympathy to our Basel convicts from their Berlin counterparts.

Tell me, good Gertrud, do you have financial worries as well? If so, that God's kingdom may not be in word only but also in power,[2] I can and will very gladly help you out.

As concerns Christoph,[3] first *he* and then *we* must have expressed ourselves badly. The decisive point for me is that (on records or not) I can say something only when I have, not just something, but something *definite* to say, and when I *have to* say it, and so unfortunately I am no good at rhetorical flights in the void. Tell him this is the way I am made, and as a gifted psychologist he will understand.

With all good wishes,

> Yours,
> KARL (now prematurely
> described in the paper
> here as the eighty-year-
> old scholar).

[In a postscript Barth asked Mrs. Staewen to think sometimes of incidents from their youth. For details see *Gesamtausgabe, Briefe*, V, p. 141.]

---

[1]K. Kupisch, *Kirche und soziale Frage im 19. Jahrhundert*, ThSt, 73 (Zurich, 1963).
[2]Cf. 1 Cor 4:20.
[3]Dr. Christoph Staewen, son of the recipient, was planning a series of records with the title "Voices of our Time." He wanted Barth to contribute but Barth persisted in his refusal.

*   *   *

88
To Prof. Carl Iversen
Copenhagen

Basel, 30 April 1963

[On 19 April 1963 Barth had gone with his son-in-law Max Zellweger to receive the Sonning Prize in Copenhagen. He wrote this letter to say that the prize money had reached his bank, and that he planned to give half of it away to relief organizations. He thanked Prof. Iversen and his colleagues for the award, for his generous reception, and for the kind words spoken in his honor. He passed on to Mrs. Iversen the name of a novel he had told her about, *A Shade of Difference*, by Allen Drury, and concluded with renewed thanks and greetings.]

*   *   *

89
To Prof. Niels Hansen Søe
Gentofte (Denmark)

208688

Basel, 30 April 1963

[In the first three paragraphs Barth expressed his thanks to Søe for his words at the Sonning award and for an evening of discussion at Søe's home, sending greetings and good wishes to his wife. He then continued:]

I have asked myself how it is that my attitude to the question of infant baptism—which is really only a peripheral problem for me—constantly gives rise in Denmark to the special interest which you showed in it that evening. It can hardly have anything to do with Kierkegaard. Is it the influence of Grundtvig,[1] which I do not properly estimate among you? However that may be, I look back on that evening with pleasure, and do not doubt that in the next life, if not in this, we shall reach agreement on that disputed point.

With all good wishes then—until we meet again,

Yours,
KARL BARTH

[1]Nikolai Frederik Severin Grundtvig (1783-1872), Danish pastor, poet, historian, and educator.

*   *   *

90

Basel, 27 May 1963

Dear Mr. Miller,

Thank you for your long letter;[1] I appreciate your deep interest in a question which has always been important for me. As far as I can see, I think I am in agreement with all that you say on the necessity of not giving up your belonging to the Jewish community. That Israel remains the root into which the Christians are grafted (Romans 11) has always [been] a central theme for me, and I wonder that you should hold such convictions so strongly in a seminary whose teachers have long been at odds with me precisely on this point. I wish you all perseverance in your plans and a wholesome influence on the all too self-sufficient "Christianity" of your country,

Yours truly,
KARL BARTH

[1]Miller, a theological student of Jewish origin at Union Theological Seminary, had asked Barth how a Jewish Christian could best make his confession of Jesus Christ in the Jewish community.

*   *   *

91

Basel, 22 June 1963

Dear Colleague,

Thank you for your kindness in sending me the triptychon by you and the two other Kurts.[1] What you say fills me with a certain distress. You hint several times that my whole theological work suffers from a fatal weakness in this matter. I have always believed that the problem of art or the arts must be dealt with in connection with the eschatological apocalypse. I attempted to outline something along these lines in the earliest version of my ethics.[2] In the meantime all kinds of attacks have made me aware that most unfortunately I have no feeling at all for modern art (in all three of its branches!) as you describe it in your book. I have not passed a negative judgment on it and do not recall having ever said a bad word about modern art. It is just a sad fact that I have no understanding, no eyes, no ears for it. It must be very painful for you three, who so kindly take issue with me, to hear this. But this is the way it is, and it is for me a serious reason not to write *CD* V, in which I should have to speak about the matter. At this point I do not want to make do with my small understanding of the classics in the three areas. There are other reasons, but this one, too. Perhaps I am too deeply embedded in the nineteenth century. But I see from your book that not a few among your heroes are my contemporaries. Perhaps in heaven what is now hidden from me will be disclosed, but it is a pity it doesn't happen now. In short, I remain *anapologētos* in this field and am only glad I have a philosopher brother[3] who is more at home in it and can thus be more helpful to you.

Please do not see this as an indication of any lack of respect for your endeavors. I admire the seriousness with which all of you tackle the problem: the only thing is that where it counts I cannot go along with you nor enter into discussion with you.

An incidental question: how is it that none of you have taken into account the theological aesthetics of H. U. von Balthasar, the first two volumes of which are already available?[4] This does not mean that I myself felt wholly satisfied with it!

With all good wishes for your further work (which you will from time to time make available to your fellow-workers) and friendly greetings—also to your wife,

Yours,

KARL BARTH

---

[1] K. Marti, K. Lüthi, and K. von Fischer, *Moderne Literatur, Malerei und Musik. Drei Entwürfe zu einer Begegnung zwischen Glaube und Kunst* (Zurich/Stuttgart, 1963).
[2] Ethics Lectures 2 (Winter Semester 1928/9 and 1930/31). Part 1 (Summer Semester 1928 and 1930) has been published in the *Gesamtausgabe* as *Ethik 1, 1928*, ed. D. Braun (Zurich, 1973) and Part 2 as *Ethik II* (Zurich, 1978). Cf. K. Barth, "Die Kirche und die Kultur" (1926), in *Die Theologie und die Kirche* (Munich, 1928, pp. 364-381; ET 1962).
[3] Heinrich Barth (1890-1965), professor of philosophy at Basel.
[4] H. U. von Balthasar, *Herrlichkeit. Eine theologische Aesthetik*, Vol. I (1961); Vol. II (1965); Vol. III (1965-1969).

*　　　*　　　*

92

To Prof. Ronald Gregor Smith
Glasgow

Basel, 28 June 1963

Dear Colleague,

Sincere thanks for what you wrote me eight days ago.

First and supremely for your very fine study of Hamann and Kierkegaard.[1] I admire the depth with which you have penetrated into the thinking of both, and to the extent that I know their thinking I can only agree with your findings. If you have written more like it—I vaguely remember a theological work which began with a dialogue with a blackbird[2]—I too would award you an honorary doctorate. Congratulations on this honor which you have received in what was once for me beloved and almost holy Marburg.

But I am already at the point where my thanks and the affection with which I think of you from Bonn days must be combined with a heavy question-mark. You too—*et tu, Brute!*—are one of the many who think the future well-being of theology is to be sought in some kind of link between me and the Bultmann school. For me this is a "salvation history" which is highly problematic and needs the sharpest demythologizing. Either, dear Mr. Smith, the wedding sermon I once preached for you in that rose-colored church on the Rhine[3] (I no longer remember the content) must have been a very poor exposition of John 11:25—or you yourself must have understood it very poorly. Can you not see that a choice has to be made today between (1) an . . .[4] unimproved anthropological ontology, and a consequent return to the darkest nineteenth century (*Honest to God*—O abyss of banality!); and (2) a seriously improved ordering of the relation between the object and subject of theology, followed by the advance (beyond fundamentalism and liberalism!) to a spiritually (*pneumatikos*) enlightened and enlightening evangelical-ecumenical proclamation. No, apparently they cannot see this any more in Glasgow than in the totally reactionary West German Republic. How then can I repress a profound sigh? But from the very fact of this letter you will see that I do not on this account cease "to speak to you."[5]

I shall have to think about your question whether I would write a foreword to Balthasar.[6] In contrast to most of the books written about me his book is really significant. But "a good introduction"?[7] I think and I have to say that it misses by a hair's breadth what I had and have in mind. Do you know the second edition with its important new preface?[8] Is Collins a Roman Catholic house?

Gloege's[9] report that I am about to write on Goethe is a freely invented legend. Nowadays I too have daily dealings with a blackbird which wakens me up each morning from the roof of our neighbor's house.

My warmest greetings to your wife Käthe and greetings and all good wishes to yourself,

Yours,
KARL BARTH

[1]R. G. Smith, "Hamann und Kierkegaard" (lecture at Marburg on 12 June 1963 on the occasion of his receiving a doctorate), published in *Zeit und Geschichte. Dankesgabe an R. Bultmann zum 80. Geburtstag* (Tübingen, 1964), pp. 671-683.
[2]*Still Point* (London, 1943).
[3]The wedding of R. G. Smith and Käthe Wittlake in Oberkassel on 13 June 1947.
[4]"Auf Grund einer" stricken from MS.
[5]Smith had feared this might happen because of his Marburg doctorate.
[6]Smith had arranged with Collins for an English translation of Balthasar's book *Karl Barth* and had asked Barth to write a foreword.
[7]In his letter of 20 June 1963 Smith had asked for "a brief foreword to this book, presumably telling people that you still think this is a good introduction to your thought."
[8]Second ed. (Cologne, 1962), pp. i-x.
[9]Gerhard Gloege, then professor of systematic theology at Bonn.

*   *   *

93
To Prof. Joseph L. Hromádka
Prague

Basel, 10 July 1963

Dear Joseph,

It is high time we continued our correspondence, and first a reply to your letter of 13 May.[1] Last Sunday we celebrated Eduard Thurneysen's seventy-fifth birthday here,[2] and on this occasion Georges Casalis[3] and Matthias Thurneysen[4] talked to me very firmly about you. So I can be silent no longer.

Remarkably, it is just twenty-five years since I wrote my first and famous Hromádka letter.[5] The second of 18 December 1962[6] apparently troubled and saddened you and others more than I had expected. As I have only now come to see, it was ill-fated.

One reason is that, in a way that is unclear to me, it has achieved wide publicity, especially in West Germany. Can you tell me more exactly who claims to have read it there? For my part I can simply assure you that I showed it to only two people, Martin Schwarz and Hans Ruh, both known and well-disposed to you, both beyond suspicion. And I now hear that those around you in Prague have given definite assurances that nothing came from there. Is our correspondence censored and made available to third persons, such as our common well-wishers in West Germany? However that may be, this time (as distinct from the autumn of 1938) I had meant to write you a purely private letter, not intending in the least to pass on my difference with you to those it does not concern but to whom it might give pleasure. There could be no question of wanting any breach of solidarity with you in relation to some third parties.

Another fatal factor was that my letter coincided with my turning down the visit to Prague.[7] It had nothing to do with this nor vice versa. I see now—and am sorry this could happen—that in Prague it might have appeared, and in part had to appear, as if my criticism of you were related to my declining. Look, none of you really knows how tired I am at this stage of life. Composing books, lectures, sermons, etc. has always been for me a very laborious task, eating up days and weeks, and undertaken only with very real anxiety—how often I have envied others who could dash them off, and even dictate them into a machine. And when an avalanche comes such as that which threatened in Prague and then in East and West Berlin, I am gripped by a kind of panic in which the only thing I can do is run off. I also consider that for over forty years I have said and written what I have to say and write on all the important themes. Younger people may now take up the larger tasks; what remains for me is to answer various questions in smaller circles, to read doctoral dissertations, to conduct doctoral examinations, to preach to the convicts, to write this and that smaller essay, etc. My personal situation produced the refusal which it now seems has caused such concern in Prague and especially to you.

One reason certainly did not lead me to it, namely that of strengthening, as you write, the circles in your church which are critical of you and which, as you later say, cannot handle the present situation and do not even have the resolution to wrestle boldly on the spot with your problems. Do you really think it would have pleased me to be welcomed by such reactionaries at your expense?

Dear Joseph, how are we going to avoid continually speaking past one another? My point in relation to you has nothing whatever to do with anti-communism, anti-sovietism, etc. Is that not made clear by the fact that here in the West and especially in Switzerland I have for

eighteen years been continually suspected of the opposite? I have therefore been attacked and calumniated, directly and explicitly so by Niebuhr[8] and Brunner,[9] not to mention countless lesser minds of various
calibres. No, I have never confessed myself to be a procommunist, or
acted as such, for reasons we might best discuss over a cup of coffee or
a glass of wine, but which are not important to us now. I have, however,
always spoken out loudly and consistently as an opponent of western
and especially Swiss anti-communism: against the cold war,[10] atomic
armament,[11] ten years ago against the remilitarizing of West Germany,[12]
in 1945 in favor of limited cooperation with certain communists in
connection with Free Germany[13] (though my experiences in this field
were not good ones)—all with the result that I have been treated here
almost like a bête rouge,[14] and finally with the result that my academic
work ended with the rejection of the candidacy of Gollwitzer, which
was unpopular for the same reason.[15] And now you come and certify
that the actuality and urgency of what I wrote you bears the impress of
my western homeland, that I live in irrational fear of your Eastern European world, etc. How have I managed to give you this impression
which is so out of keeping with the whole of my present life—even
though I may sometimes have admitted to you that in spite of all that
displeases me here I would rather not live there?!

As concerns my past and present relation to you, the point is simply
this: After my experiences in Switzerland with the religious socialism
of Kutter and Ragaz, and after going to Germany in 1921 and what I
went through there in 1933f., I have an extreme allergic reaction not
only to all identifications but also to all the drawing of parallels and
analogies between theological and socio-political thought in which the
superiority of the *analogans* (the gospel) to the *analogatum* (the political
insights and opinion of the theologian concerned) is not clearly, soberly,
and irreversibly maintained and does not remain visible. Where the
relative importance of the two is reversible, there I speak—as I did not
do in my last letter—of a philosophy of history which does harm to
theology and Christian proclamation. Recently Lochman has said very
plainly about you that you are certainly not a historical philosopher in
the cloak of a theologian but a genuine theologian in the occasional
cloak of a historical philosopher.[16] This is what I think, and by it I mean
that you assume the cloak of a man who can treat the two sides of that
analogy as though they were reversible, and whose theological music
sometimes has for that reason an impure (or, shall we say, a less pure)
sound. "Sometimes"—yes, only sometimes, on the not infrequent oc-

casions when you undertake to require not only of your Czech friends but of all of us *urbi et orbi* that we should master the historical situation theologically in the light and by the hand of your political analyses, taking it seriously exactly as you see it for the sake of the way of Jesus Christ. Now whether their interpretations are good or not (and I do not regard them as good), I have to concede that fellow-christians like Niebuhr and Brunner think and desire the same thing in their own ways. My point in relation to them—and to you too—is that I wonder if anyone (in western or eastern fashion) really interprets the historical situation in such a way that *in* that same situation (in its actual form and not as it is in their analyses) there can be spoken and heard the Christian *witness* to the kingdom which, deriving from neither the western nor the eastern world, seeks to be spoken and heard in both. This is what I once battled against in Germany; this is what I battle against on both the right and the left today—or, better, *for* that which Pope John XXIII now represents better than I on both the right and the left. There—I think I was speaking about this transcendent place in my last letter—I should like to see you, too. To my grief I do not see you there, because I always find you (now again in your memorandum on the German question)[17] occupied with onesided analyses which others can counter in the same vein and with the same validity. If the Peace Conference, instead of engaging in such analyses both on the right and on the left, would only get to the real point on both sides along the lines of Casalis' essay,[18] which greatly pleases me! Is this really the voice of a western man picking holes in an eastern man? Or is it really the objection made against you on all sides, as you claim in your letter to me? Is it really impossible for you, from all you have known of me, to understand me more substantially and less trivially in this matter?

I shall show this letter only to Martin Schwarz, who as the chief authority on the Peace Conference ought to know about it. Hans Ruh, having passed his examinations *summa cum laude*, has disappeared in the direction of England. You need not hurry to answer this letter. But knowing my suspicions of the police[19] you might be so kind as to let me know on a card that you have received it and when and in what circumstances.

So for now with warm greetings and with the same sentiments as ever,

Yours,
KARL BARTH

[1]See Appendix, 4.

[2]An early celebration on 7 July (the birthday was the tenth).

[3]Thurneysen's son-in-law, professor of practical theology on the Free Faculty of Protestant Theology in Paris and at the time vice-president of the Prague Peace Conference.

[4]Thurneysen's son, pastor in Zurich-Schwamendingen.

[5]"Brief an Prof. Hromádka in Prag" (19 Sept. 1938) in *Eine Schweizer Stimme* (Zollikon-Zurich, 1945), pp. 58f.

[6]See 68.

[7]Cf. 81.

[8]R. Niebuhr, "Why is Barth Silent on Hungary?" *The Christian Century*, 74 (1957), 108-110.

[9]E.g. E. Brunner, "Wie soll man das verstehen? Offener Brief an Karl Barth," *Kirchenblatt f. d. ref. Schweiz*, 104 (1948), 180-184.

[10]E.g. K. Barth, *Die Kirche zwischen Ost und West* (Zollikon-Zurich, 1949).

[11]E.g. K. Barth, "Es geht ums Leben," *SOS. Zeitung f. weltweite Verständigung*, 7 (May 1957), 2.

[12]E.g. K. Barth, "Fürchtet euch nicht" (letter to W.-D. Zimmermann on 17 Oct. 1950); also "Gedenken—heute!" *EvTh*, 14 (1954), 533-543.

[13]E.g. K. Barth, "Wie können die Deutschen gesund werden?", *Eine Schweizer Stimme*, pp. 371ff. In a letter appended to this writing Barth told a German who emigrated to Switzerland to join the Movement (in Exile) for a Free Germany: "Don't be afraid if you meet a few communists there. You will also have to live with communists in the Germany of the future. Do so quite freely now."

[14]Cf. 20, n. 4.

[15]Cf. 5, n. 3; 37, n. 1; 43; 49.

[16]J. M. Lochman, "Die Bedeutung geschichtlicher Ereignisse für ethische Entscheidungen," *ThSt*, 72 (Zurich, 1963), p. 15, n. 3.

[17]J. L. Hromádka, "Memorandum on the German Question," *Christian Peace Conference*, 4 (May 1963), 83ff.

[18]G. Casalis, "Reconciliation through Christ as Basis for Living with Others," *Communio Viatorum*, 6 (1963), 103-116.

[19]Cf. complete text of 105, *Gesamtausgabe*, V, 6.

*   *   *

94
To H. Israelsen
Copenhagen

Basel, 12 July 1963[1]

Dear Mr. Israelsen,

If you knew how many letters I receive daily as an old man, and how hard it is even to read, let alone answer them all, you would understand why you have not heard from me before in regard to your interesting letter of May.

Your presentation of the relation between God's omnipotent grace and free human will and especially human sin did indeed interest me—

and first because it is not often a man in your calling[2] has the time, ability, and desire to wrestle with such serious problems as you do in the manuscript you sent.

I am pleased to be able to assure you that in my view you are on the right track in your discussion both as a whole and as regards the main point. Perhaps you should be a little more on guard against the inclination to treat the relation like an equation which with some good will and understanding can be solved. Grace should not be regarded as a kind of institution, nor sin as a necessity, nor freedom as a possibility man always has. But you do not really mean that. And I agree with you that in these great mysteries it is not a matter of contradictions but of the great harmony of the will and works of God. Do not stop testing and correcting your insights by holy scripture. Then, being sound in what really counts, you can and should live and represent a comforted life.

With friendly greetings and all good wishes,

Yours,
KARL BARTH

[1]Two dates, 30 June and 12 July, are mixed together, but the latter seems to be the right one.
[2]A railway official.

*   *   *

95
To N.N.

Basel, 12 July 1963

[In this letter to a lady who had written describing her difficulties in Germany after 1945, Barth admitted that his generation had done a poor job and that with the demand for atomic armament things were not much better in Switzerland. Since she lived near Basel he invited her to come and see him personally.]

*   *   *

96

To Superintendent Dr. Walter Herrenbrück
Leer (East Friesland)

Basel, 13 July 1963

[Barth first apologized for his tardy reply to a letter of 12 February, especially now that he did not have the excuse of *C.D.*, the lady in the crinoline. He continued:]

You asked me—I learned to my surprise you are in the eventide of your executive work[1]—for advice on what the churches should do about the work of the Bultmannians (I call them the company of Korah[2]) which spreads like a stain on blotting-paper.

Well, like you I deplore the fact as such. We have in it a pompous return of the nineteenth century, which young people today do not know in its original form, and in relation to which the *C.D.*, like other books, must wait its time (has the new edition of the first edition of the Romans reached East Friesland yet?[3]). I also take this fact as a sign that "we"—our generation and yours—did not do our job so well that God did not see fit to bring against us on every hand what he is now giving us to understand through the lips of *nebalim*.[4] I also ask whether in the circles of church government a little searching of conscience might not be in order as we look back on what was perhaps too easy a triumph of grace.[5]

Presupposing all this, we can and should quietly affirm the unmistakable poverty, thinness, and even futility of this whole undertaking which claims so much and at first seems to be so successful. I ask you: Compare Bultmann with Schleiermacher, Ebeling with Wilhelm Herrmann, and Herbert Braun with D. F. Strauss! And now the rosy-cheeked Bishop of Woolwich with his *Honest to God*! If the minds of men are not hopelessly devastated by the strontium dispersed in the atmosphere, it will surely become evident to some and even many, and perhaps fairly soon, that the emperor is naked, to quote Andersen's child. A second rule for church leaders is that they should realize this first and should not let themselves be bullied by the youngsters who are to be examined by them and are under their care, nor set up solemn discussions of Robinson—O those endless discussions!—such as that which Lilje recently introduced.

A third thing: Do not do anything that might smack even a little of suppression or persecution. Everywhere the Bultmannians long for this, like Ignatius of Antioch[6] thirsting for martyrdom at the hands of irritated pietists and fundamentalists and upper and lower church courts. Confessing and other congregations should be instructed in this regard that the Bultmannians be left thirsty so far as this drink is concerned. Let them stew with themselves and others as long as they like in the juice of their hermeneutics, their talk about talk (the speech event),[7] their demythologizings, etc., and hold out before them the table which is prepared for us according to Ps 23:5. As I have learned these past years from my experiences with Ebeling-saturated students from Zurich who come each Thursday to my colloquium in Basel, after the *ars amandi* that now inspires them they will acquire a longing for a proper love story with some sap to it. The job of wise church leadership is to entangle them in such a story—Barmen I and Heidelberg Cat. 1[8] not just declaimed but practiced.

This then is what I would whisper in your ear in answer to your question from Seir (Isa 21:11). [Barth now asked what might happen as a result of Herrenbrück's retirement to a parish in Hanover. He expressed a desire to hear from him, but did not want questions about *C.D.*] I have an allergic reaction to these, irritably referring to the thousands and thousands of pages with which I have already pleased and provoked mankind.

With warm greetings,

Yours,

KARL BARTH

[1]After twelve years as superintendent, Herrenbrück took a pastorate in Hanover, 1 November 1963.

[2]Cf. Numbers 16.

[3]K. Barth, *Der Römerbrief* (unaltered reprinting of the first edition of 1919; Zurich, 1963).

[4]I.e., fools.

[5]An allusion to the title of G. C. Berkouwer's study of Barth's theology.

[6]Ignatius (c. 110) looked forward eagerly to his martyrdom in Rome.

[7]A central concept in the theology of Ebeling and Fuchs.

[8]Barmen Declaration (1934), Thesis I; Heidelberg Catechism (1563), Question I.

*   *   *

97

To Prof. Herbert Kubly
Zurich

Basel, 16 July 1963

Dear Colleague,

I have read your new novel,[1] and as I must admit to my shame have found out from reading it, and from personal details taken from it, who it was I was talking to when you visited me some weeks ago.

Why, in the questions you put and in which I later recognized the author of this book, why did you not make it plainer who you were in what you had to say? I can only hope that, measured against the problems that concerned you, I did not seem too gauche to you.

Your book is most stimulating, even to the limit of the tolerable. Did that horrible scene toward the end of the story have to be described so explicitly? But you know better than I do the relations and people to whom you wanted to hold up the mirror and you judged that only in this extreme form could you bring out the supratemporal element you aimed to express. I could certainly accompany your "Christian" with great sympathy. And I was interested in particular by the—yes, the "Christian" thread which runs through the book. Something there, so far as I could understand it, touched a sympathetic chord. But you will not take it amiss if I suggest that your theology needs some improvement. You have become too much an American in taking the common view that like all religion (I hate the word) the Bible and the Christian tradition is a kind of Bern dish—I take it you know what that is—from which all can serve themselves as they think good or as they desire. All too easily this leads to fatal levelings and exaggerations. But this criticism does not alter the fact that on the whole I was moved by your novel and wish it good sucess.

With friendly greetings (and hoping that in your book on Switzerland[2] I will not fare too badly under your sharp pen),

Yours,

KARL BARTH

P.S. I should have told you that I am one of the few on this side of the Atlantic who has a special interest in the Civil War. I regard Bruce Catton as one of the best writers on this subject.[3]

---

[1]H. Kubly, *The Whistling Zone* (New York, 1963).

[2]H. Kubly, *Switzerland* (New York, 1964).
[3]Barth had several works by Catton; for a list see *Gesamtausgabe, Briefe*, V, p. 162.

*   *   *

98
To Mrs. N.N.
Basel

Basel, 17 July 1963

[A letter of condolence to Mrs. N.N. on the loss of her husband Fritz, with whom Barth had served in the army, who had always been a good and cheerful comrade, and whom, Barth assured her, she had brought back into a living relation to the Christian faith.]

*   *   *

'

98a
To Prof. Ronald Gregor Smith
Glasgow[1]

Basel, 17 July 1963

Dear Dr. Smith,

My difference from Balthasar has nothing whatever to do with the ecumenical question. It is simply that, like many Protestants, he is interested in certain philosophical structures of my theology instead of in the theology itself. But I do not want to criticize him publicly for this and therefore I would rather not write the foreword. English readers can see it themselves—or not see it!

I was glad to hear there is the possibility of seeing you and your wife here in August. Let us know in good time so that we may avoid conflicts. Perhaps you will see the blackbird on my neighbor's roof, with which, as with all God's creatures that refrain from regarding the self-understanding of their faith as the theme of theology, I have a warm relationship. Until then, sincere greetings and good wishes to you and your wife Käthe,

Yours,
KARL BARTH

[1][The Swiss editors added this letter during the printing of their first edition; this accounts for the nonsequential numbering, which the English edition follows for the sake of reference.]

*　　　*　　　*

99
To the Reverend Marion W. Conditt
Temple, Texas

Basel, 12 August 1963

[Conditt had asked Barth to write a foreword to his book *More Accept-able than Sacrifice. Ethics and Election as Obedience to God's Will in the Theology of John Calvin* (Basel, 1973). In his reply Barth expressed pleasure that Conditt was now in the preaching ministry and congrat-ulated him on the birth of a daughter, Carla, a sister for his son Calvin. He declined, however, to write the foreword, partly because he did not recall the work well enough, but primarily because he thought younger scholars should now stand on their own feet and perhaps not be stamped so expressly and visibly as Barthians. He closed by saying that in ex-amining an American doctoral candidate on 2 July he had asked him what took place in America on 1-3 July 1863, but sadly neither he nor his waiting wife and mother-in-law knew—the answer being the battle of Gettysburg!]

*　　　*　　　*

100
To Prof. Franco Bolgiani
Turin

Basel, 12 August 1963

[Bolgiani, professor of church history on the Faculty of Letters and Philosophy at the University of Turin, had asked Barth for an evaluation of the theological significance of E. Peterson (1890-1960), formerly of Göttingen and Bonn and a convert to Roman Catholicism. Barth an-swered that he had known Peterson personally only in Göttingen (1921-24), where he had found him an eccentric, isolated, but distin-guished figure. Theologically he had been impressed most by his theo-

—113—

ries about angels, although he had found them debatable; cf. *C.D.* III, 3, §51.]

*   *   *

101
To Prof. Martin Werner
Bern

Basel, 15 August 1963

Dear Colleague,

I have just seen your review of my *Evangelical Theology* in the *Theol. Umschau.*[1] I did not expect you to join the ranks of those who have lauded it to the skies. But I also did not expect that you would leave me with not a dry stitch, and destroy me so totally. I would rather have supposed that despite your understandable rejection of all my work I should have experienced at your hands at least a minimum of "reverence for life."[2] I am almost alarmed by the fury with which you have obviously accompanied my path all the past decades. Do you not find it a little sad that it seems destined that we two rather elderly people should have to look forward to parting from one another in this way?

Be that as it may, with friendly greetings,

Yours,
KARL BARTH

[1] M. Werner, "Karl Barths *Einführung in die evangelische Theologie*," *Schweizerische Theologische Umschau*, 33 (1963), 84-87.
[2] Werner's theological work is built on this central concept of Albert Schweitzer.

*   *   *

102
To a Young Relative

Basel, 16 August 1963

[N.N. had written Barth asking for financial help and direction as to serving God. In this letter Barth sent the former but said that he could not help her with the latter until she learned the meaning of service in general. She had done dilettante college work and had been moving restlessly from place to place so that he would not be surprised if the next letter were to come from some spot on the shores of the Caspian Sea. He advised her to take any job that would mean discipline and obligation so that through learning what service is she might learn what it means to serve God.]

*　　　*　　　*

103
To Marie-Claire Barth
Bogor, Indonesia

Basel, 17 August 1963

Dear Marie-Claire,

If I understand things properly you are at the moment a grass-widow. It can be no substitute for you to get a letter from your aged father-in-law, but since I unexpectedly received one from you (7 August) I want to say how much it pleased me to be addressed by you in such a full and friendly way—the prophetess Huldah[1] in Bogor stands so clearly before me (much more so than the biblical one, about whom even our learned Christoph has no solid information). It is most edifying for me to see how you two and the young folk around you are so vigorous and active. When one cannot say that of oneself, one realizes for the first time how good it is to be at work. Not only are you a church adviser, an important office in which I wish you much joy and success, but you are also writing a commentary on Second Isaiah, in which you will immediately come upon Jerusalem, which is to climb a high mountain as a preacher.[2] What a pity it is to be in Indonesian, which will be unintelligible to me (until eventually in heaven I will understand this language, too). And then from early to late you are the faithful guardian and teacher of Daniel, Colas, and Kätherli, whose pictures moved me greatly. If only I could see them again and have a comfortable familiarity with them! From Christoph's article in *Evg. Theol.*[3] I have noted with respect how well he has been able to keep abreast academically in those distant parts. If only we knew what would happen when you fold your tents there and return to no less dark Europe. I still recall the strong vote of your father[4] that his daughter was not destined to end her days in a manse. But what position and work will open up appropriate to your own and Christoph's worth and ability?[5] In the generation following that of Daniel and his brother and sister little Olivier Schopfer is now attracting attention (he is at the moment in Basel). What kind of days will they see—all these young people who are now marching on the scene. But we are not to worry about tomorrow[6] and so we may leave all these questions open and refer the decisions to a higher court.

Am I mistaken, dear Marie-Claire, if I get the impression that your letter drifts toward the point at which you begin to speak about Teilh. d. Ch.?[7] I can see that this man and his work have become important to you, not least in relation to your father. He seems to commend himself to others, too (Georges Casalis, for example), as a possible (!) point of contact with modern man.[8] It is remarkable how the trend in this direction constantly appears in otherwise enlightened Christian circles. That I should always scent new mischief there, and therefore have such an allergic reaction and not join in (in this case either), may well be my special task in this century. It may well be related to this that it makes me sad to see people far and near running after new approaches in this direction.

As concerns T. de C. I let myself be oriented first by the book *Le milieu divin*.[9] Now it seems at first quite harmless when you write that what you find so exciting in him is not the theological material but the anthropological and palaeontological. Why should we not learn from a man who knows so much about these things? But then (even according to your own presentation) he moves on at once from his scientific observations to the unfolding of visions of a cosmos that is rising up from darkness to light; to the concept of a gigantic development in whose context Christ too plays an important role at certain places—but in such a way that he too must accept being evaluated and understood in terms of the context. This is precisely what Gnosis in every age has done with Christianity—always with the intention of bringing in what is distant from it and finally elucidating it. Anthroposophy is doing the same today, and so is the Bultmann school with its existential theology (which has strangely reached its climax with the *Honest to God* of the rosy-cheeked Bishop Robinson of Woolwich and the hundreds of thousands who swallow it). This is also the aim of so-called spiritualism, whose task it is to prepare us for increasing light after death by means of increasingly intensive purifications, our body being scornfully left behind here below. Always new and giant snakes by which the poor gospel of the Old and New Testaments must let itself be gulped down—and always with lofty eulogies on the way this will help to spread it among the children of the world. Believe me, dear and good Marie-

Claire, the *Milieu divin* of your T. de C. is a giant gnostic snake of this kind—a giant snake compared with which the brave rationalism and moralism of Brunner's eristics is a harmless blind-worm. If I said No! then as loudly as I could,[10] do I not really have to do so now?

Do you know what pleased me best in this part of your letter? The almost incidental information, quite new to me, that your father is reading the gospels every day. Why not leave him quietly in that school when you will probably annoy him again with T. de C. and at worst might even lead him into error? I don't know whether I can really warn and restrain you. But one thing you must promise me, that you will later tell Daniel and Colas and Kätherli that grandpa remained adamant on this point even to his old age. Perhaps then, impressed by the latest boa constrictor appearing around 2000, they will quietly laugh at me, as even today aunt N.N. in her love and concern can only "pardon" me—but perhaps not.

Meanwhile with warm father-in-law greetings,

Yours,

PAPA

[1]This was Barth's name for his daughter-in-law after he heard her speak in public in 1962 (cf. 2 Kings 22:14).
[2]Isa 40:9.
[3]C. Barth, "Grundprobleme einer Theologie des AT," *EvTh*, 23 (1963), 342-372.
[4]Professor Edouard Frommel of Geneva.
[5]Christoph Barth became Old Testament professor at Mainz in 1967.
[6]Cf. Matt 6:34.
[7]Pierre Teilhard de Chardin.
[8]The point at issue in the Barth-Brunner debate of 1934.
[9]P. Teilhard de Chardin, *Le milieu divin* (1926); *Oeuvres*, Vol. IV (Paris, 1957).
[10]K. Barth, *Nein! Antwort an Emil Brunner*, ThExh, 14 (Munich, 1934; ET *Natural Theology*, 1946).

*   *   *

104

To a Roman Catholic Instructor in Religion in the Rhineland[1]

Basel, 18 August 1963

Dear Mr. N.N.,

My position on the question of conversion is fundamentally this: Even if there is cause for great dissatisfaction with one's church, one should stay in it in the hope that new movements will come and resolve to do one's best in relation to these. Only in this way could I myself have been and continue to be a member of the Evangelical Reformed Church. I do not regard the situation in Roman Catholicism today as hopeless in spite of the three last dogmas[2] (and many earlier ones). In John XXIII the papacy found a surprisingly new face. Nor is it impossible that in the continuation of the Council (or apart from it) important internal changes will come which might be promising for the Roman Catholic Christian.

All the same I can understand it if someone cannot go on in practice but has to explode, i.e., convert, in his concrete relation to those three dogmas (and other things that go too far). In such cases one must do it in God's name. One cannot and should not live against conscience. You will realize, of course, that in Old Catholicism as in any other communion you will come across many things you don't like but have to make allowances for. But if the *Munificentissimus Deus*[3] has become the climax of the intolerable for you, then out you must go whatever the cost.

Perhaps I might put to you the following test: You mention the probability that if you raise the questions that properly trouble you, you may be set aside, i.e., relieved of your duties as a religious instructor. My advice is: Let this happen. In your teaching and elsewhere say what you have to say in the acknowledgment and confession of your Christian faith. Who knows whether the worst will really happen to you today. But if it should, then the time has come, not to submit *laudabiliter*, but to quit.

With friendly greetings and all good wishes,

Yours,
KARL BARTH

[1]Published (in German) under the title "Brief aan een roomskatholieke Religionslehrer" in *Kerk en Theologie*, 18 (1967), 266f.

[2]The dogmas of the immaculate conception (1854), papal infallibility (1870), and the assumption of Mary (1950).

[3]The Bull of Pius XII on 1 Nov. 1950 which officially proclaimed the dogma of Mary's assumption.

*   *   *

105
To Prof. Georges Casalis
Antony / Seine

Basel, 18 August 1963

Dear Georges,

Sincere thanks for your letter of the twelfth from Cameroon. Unfortunately the only address you gave was the place-name Yaoundé, and since I have recently had many laboriously written letters come back to me marked addressee unknown, I am sending this to Paris where as so often you have left your wife Dorothee sadly alone. She will perhaps be glad to read the letter and send it on to where she knows you are.

I was delighted to hear that the old theologian pleased that Dominican. Naturally we cannot know whether the October talk will do as well.[1] Let us wait and see. So you are now in Cameroon, fraternizing with black archbishops, and introducing folk there into some of the mysteries of *C.D.*[2] Georges, I am struck with amazement at the breadth of your radius of activity, with which I can compare only that of your father-in-law, who even from Kapf went restlessly to and fro preaching and burying and marrying.[3]

The expansion of my illuminating treatment of religions which you have undertaken in discussion with the people of Cameroon does not please me too much. Where do you find in the Bible the slightest trace of a theory according to which the fact of religions is a sign to faith that man is made for fellowship with God? This is the first step on the way that leads back to our old plight and you should not help our black brethren on to this path.

Protestantism! I have had to write a letter to a Roman Catholic teacher in the Rhineland who is thinking of conversion and I have advised him against it unless he is silenced and thus forced out in practice. Hans Küng, who was here with me for some enjoyable hours, displayed a dampened but still evident optimism regarding the continuation of the Council, so that if one is on that side it might be worth while hanging on in spite of everything.

Georges, I am a little disturbed that you seem to set such high store by Teil. de Ch. I had to write a letter about him yesterday to my fine daughter-in-law in Indonesia, née Frommel, who seems to be even more captivated by that man and his work than you, and who hopes that by way of his scientific observations, philosophical constructions, and religious visions, she will be able to reach the heart of her father, who has a total aversion to the church, theology, missions, etc. Always apologetics at the root of Gnosis! For having read the book *Le milieu divin* (and having no desire to read further), it seems unmistakable to me that in T. de C. we have a classic case of Gnosis, in the context of which the gospel cannot possibly thrive. The reality that is supposedly manifest there, and that we are supposed to believe, is the deity of evolution—naturally decked out with the name of Jesus Christ, as always happened and still happens in Gnostic systems.

Lollo and I had a similar but even sadder experience recently in X, where we found Aunt N.N., not at all low, but very uplifted: uplifted in contemplation of a spiritual process in which she sees dear Uncle N.N. and other dead people freed from all corporeality and moving higher into the light from darkness. As she shares that experience she can look back only with sympathy on me and my feeble theological efforts, as a student who has been advanced to a higher class looks back on one who has been left behind. She also showed me that to be able to speak about these glories I should have to read not only the one book I got to know with horror[4] but 20 (twenty) others.

[In the rest of the letter Barth filled Casalis in on his problems with Hromádka; cf. 68 and 93. Having suffered so much for not being anticommunist, he wondered whether Hromádka had ever done or suffered anything in opposition to antiwesternism. Since he was too tired to be rushing off to Prague, he thought perhaps the younger generation would now have to achieve a proper understanding. He closed with a reference to A. Malet's book on Bultmann, *Mythos et Logos. La pensée de Rudolf Bultmann* (Geneva, 1962), but had no time left to comment on it.]

[1]The reference is to Casalis's television interviews with Barth on 12 May, 22 Oct., and 7 Nov. 1963. In his letter of 2 Aug. Casalis told Barth of an approving letter received from the Dominican J. P. Liégé relating to the first interview, which was later published as K. Barth, "La théologie, le monde et la vie," *Réforme*, no. 1002 (30 May 1964), p. 11; German *JK*, 25 (1964), 700-702.

[2]In a course for African pastors in Yaoundé on African religions and the Christian answer, Casalis held a seminar on *C.D.* I, 2, §17.

[3]Eduard Thurneysen, who used to take his vacations at Kapf im Emmental, Bern Canton.

[4]Cf. 24.

*   *   *

106
To Pastor Hannelotte Reiffen
Grossneuendorf (Oderbruch, East Germany)

Basel, 19 August 1963

Dear Mrs. Reiffen,

Let me begin by saying how pleased I was to get your letter of the seventh because it shows me how conscientiously you are following your difficult calling. [. . . Barth expanded on this a little.] But you do not want to hear such general praise from me but professional advice in a very difficult situation—advice which it is even more difficult to . give.

As you depict it you have not been baptizing infants any more for quite a time. You have come to an understanding with the church council that it is fundamentally (theologically) impossible. Two couples have thus postponed baptizing their children. But a third couple insists on it. You could decline because they are not church people, but you are uneasy about this because for you rejection of infant baptism as such stands in the background, and your church council will not support you in it. Have I read the situation aright?

If so, my view is that having gone so far you cannot draw back; when you have put your hand so energetically to the plow you must not look back,[1] and particularly not in relation to your conscience and the congregation. In a more extensive exposition of that synodical resolution[2] you must declare that for *you* adult baptism is the *only* legitimate possibility alongside which *you* can see no other, so that no infants can or should be baptized by *you* in Grossneuendorf. This position will be understood even if not accepted by everybody, whereas any other could only cause confusion on every hand. I could not speak so definitely in every case. In yours the issue seems to be clear. Perhaps East Germany, in which so much responsibility now rests on the congregations and their pastors, is destined to be the place of progress in this matter too, this being impossible in West Germany where in their sheer security the churches are under the threat of spiritual indolence. A decision like yours will directly or indirectly have relevance there too, so that I think it appropriate in the general interest to encourage you to go further along the lines of your resolve thus far. Let me hear from you again.

Commending you to God and with warm greetings,

Yours,

KARL BARTH

[1]Cf. Luke 9:62.

[2]The belief that in 1960 or 1961 the Synod of Berlin and Brandenburg had passed a resolution permitting adult baptism was apparently erroneous, according to a letter of Mrs. Reiffen to the editors.

*　　　　　*　　　　　*

107
To Pastor Johannes Hamel
Naumburg

Basel, 19 August 1963

Dear Pastor Hamel,

Thanks for your letter about the ten articles.[1] It is true I have been asked (by the Brandenburg Reformed) to write a theological evaluation of this document, and for some weeks I have been wondering what to think and say.[2] For a good while I knew nothing about its origin and even less about its implications in church politics and I intended to speak about its theological content as it were in a vacuum. In your letter, however, I have heard various people warning me how easily I could put my foot in it in this matter.

It was clear to me from the outset that this is a two-front war and that the ten articles are a substantially good development in this situation. What I miss in them is a thoroughgoing christological and then eschatological centering and a certain tautness of thought and expression. It also seems questionable to me that the document is being passed off as not just one but *the* direction for the church today, being thus invested with an authoritative character [. . .] which in its day was never claimed for Barmen. A comparison with Barmen is demanded, as emphasized resoundingly in *Christian Century.*[3]

Reading Kloppenburg's essay with its hypocritical title[4] has suggested to me that I should muffle though not suppress my critical considerations. For in truth I have no mind to bring water to the mills of the assimilators, migrants as you so instructively describe them, so that when I begin to write on this delicate matter I will as much as possible avoid anything that might be used in this way. It is my view, too, supported by the impression gained in my difficult correspondence with the otherwise so estimable Hromádka, [. . .] that in the East, in spite of the abomination of Dibelianism, greater danger threatens from this side. The offense offered to the shades of Bonhoeffer (in propagation of Bultmannianism) surpasses all limits.

Rest assured: I am in a position to follow what you say and hint at, and will do all I can, if not to ward off further disaster, at least not to promote it. I would be grateful to you if you could give me at least an outline of where those who have commissioned me (the Brandenburg Reformed) are to be sought in this whole matter.

With warm greetings,

Faithfully yours,
KARL BARTH

[1]*Ten Articles on the Freedom and Service of the Church*, adopted at a conference of church leaders in East Germany in 1963, text in *JK*, 24 (1963), 329-334.
[2]K. Barth, "Theologisches Gutachten zu den Zehn Artikeln über Freiheit und Dienst der Kirche," *EvTh*, 23 (1963), 505-510.
[3]Germanicus (pseudonym), "East Germany," *The Christian Century*, 80 (1963), 989.
[4]H. Kloppenburg, "Kein befreiender Glaube," *Kirche und Mann*, 16, No. 8 (August 1963).

*   *   *

108
[written in English]
To Adelaide B. McKelway
Hanover, New Hampshire

Basel, 21 August 1963

Dear Mrs. McKelway,

We were glad to have your letter with all its good tidings concerning your new settlement and with the nice pictures taken here and at the station the moment we said farewell. I like it to hear, that Paul Tillich is satisfied about the manner your husband has treated him.[1] This is exactly what I wished: that that necessary attack on Tillich's abominable theology should be made in the indirect way of an absolutely fair representation of its trend and particularities. The satisfaction of Tillich is so to say the test for the fact, that your husband has in so far succeeded. Tell him my congratulations: I hope that the book will be well received among the theologically interested people in the States. Your announcement concerning the expected baby is indeed very exciting. May it become a brave boy or a beautiful girl and may it see peaceful days before and after the time-mark of the year 2000. Play and sing him Mozart so soon as possible and if it is a boy, your husband should teach him even so soon how to smoke a real pipe.

Grover Foley, the hero of so many meetings in the Bruderholz-restaurant, has been examined and has left Basel also. He has a kind of professorship in Austin, Texas. So one after the other of our American friends are going. We miss you—nobody cares now to take us to the church of Pfr. Dürst—but not only for that reason! Well, I am busy with two new books of Bruce Catton on the Civil War, and my son Markus (now in Pittsburgh) has sent me these days an exciting novel *Seven Days in May*[2] dealing with the Pentagon in Washington. So America is always present here.

My best wishes and greetings are going to you, dear Mrs. Adelaide and of course to Mr. "Sandy"!

Faithfully yours,
KARL BARTH

[1]A. J. McKelway, *The Systematic Theology of Paul Tillich. A Review and Analysis* (Richmond, Virginia, 1964).
[2]Fletcher Knebel, *Seven Days in May* (New York, 1962).

*   *   *

109
To Pastor Dieter Schellong
Gütersloh[1]

Basel, 11 September 1963

Dear Pastor,

Confound it, what an overheated atmosphere you live in in Germany—one man's hand against another's.[2] How then can there be rational, let alone spiritually sound common thought and speech? The point is I have been asked by the moderator of the Brandenburg Reformed to write a theological evaluation of the ten articles. Naturally I already knew them and various noises from the tumult they caused had reached me. But I did not have to worry about that. And so I set to work without regard for the confounded politics or church politics and to the best of my knowledge and conscience tried to answer the question clearly put to me concerning the theological content of the articles. I have now done this and described *sine ira et studio*, with favor to none and hostility to none, what I regard as good and as less good in the document. And since I thought the matter might be of general interest, and to prevent anyone in East or West quoting whatever might suit his purpose, I have sent it to Ernst Wolf to be published in his autumn number.[3] There the matter must rest. I have not written for or against the different groups nor tried to mediate between them but have simply spoken a calm word on the matter. Whether successfully or not is another question, but I could not in any circumstances refrain from doing it, even at the risk of being misunderstood and misused by one side or the other or both, in view of the fury of their mutual opposition. Tell this to those in whose name and on whose commission you have written me.

[Barth closed the letter with personal matters.]

With warm greetings to you and yours,

Yours,
KARL BARTH

[1]Schellong had asked Barth, if he was publishing anything on the *Ten Articles*, not to oppose the countertheses, "Theologische Sätze . . . ," *Kirche in der Zeit*, 19 (1964), 181ff.
[2]Cf. Zech 14:13.
[3]*Evangelische Theologie*; cf. 107, n. 2.

*   *   *

110
To Dr. Albert von Erlach
Hertenstein (Lucerne Canton)

Basel, 11 September 1963

[In this letter Barth referred to the services held in connection with the air crash on 4 Sept. 1963,[1] and alluded to Luther's "In the midst of life. . . ."[2] He expressed sympathy with von Erlach at his wife's troubles,[3] and hoped for a meeting, perhaps in Lucerne. Barth also said he had just consulted a heart specialist, was too tired to go on with *C.D.*, thought "most people have not yet read, or read only in part, the twelve fat volumes already issued," and was pleased he could still smoke his pipe.]

[1]The crash claimed eighty lives.
[2]Based on the medieval antiphon: "In the midst of life we are in death."
[3]Emilie von Erlach (née Qeerleder), d. 4 January 1964.

*   *   *

111
To Prof. Jean-Jacques von Allmen
Neuchatel

Basel, 16 September 1963

[Barth had been asked by von Allmen to make available a portrait and a recorded conversation with Hans Küng for the Swiss Exposition at Lausanne in 1964. Barth replied in this letter with an emphatic refusal: "No, I cannot and will not collaborate," arguing that this had been his policy from Safenwil days, and that while a portrait might have been permissible in 1939, when he had figured among "distinguished Swiss abroad"(!), he could not play an active part in increasing the divine displeasure at self-conscious Swissness. He wondered what Küng's reply would be; as it turned out, he declined also.]

*   *   *

112
To Prof. Jean Roche
Paris

Basel, 18 September 1963

[Roche had written to Barth to tell him the University of Paris had decided to confer on him an honorary doctorate of letters and humane sciences. In his reply Barth thanked him for the honor, said that God willing he would come to Paris with his son-in-law Max Zellweger for the ceremony on 7 November, gave travel details, promised to wear his professorial robe, and hoped he would not have to make a speech.]

*   *   *

113
To Prof. Hans Küng
Tübingen

Basel, 19 September 1963

Dear Colleague,

Having sat for an hour at my empty desk reflecting on your phone call, I will answer you with no delay.

The possibility of the invitation[1] not only interests me greatly but also pleases and honors me—not least because it seems that in Bea's secretariat[2] the fear of me as a wild man seems to have been overcome. Express my sincere thanks to those who have commissioned you and let them not doubt that if things were different I would come to Rome with no less alacrity [*alacritas*] than suavity [*suavitas*].

But unfortunately it cannot be done. To be able to participate worthily among the observers or in wider circles I would need much more than ten days' time[3] to enter even to some degree into the whole affair. And then I look at my calendar for the end of September, October, and December and find that I am more than tied up with engagements—including two important ones in Paris[4]—from which I cannot now withdraw. This brisk gadding about, which you as an active young man can do, is no longer for me. And finally I wonder whether, even if things were different, my health would stand up to the rigors of St. Peter's and its environs. Please convey this in suitable terms to those who have commissioned you and please have me excused.

I shall always be pleased to hear from you and even more to see you—though better not as a pair of ecumenical exhibits.[5]

With warm greetings,

Yours,
KARL BARTH

[1]Küng had been asked by the Roman authorities to phone Barth asking whether he would come to the second session of Vatican II as an observer.
[2]Secretariat for Christian Unity under the leadership of Cardinal A. Bea.
[3]The second session of Vatican II was from 29 Sept. to 4 Dec. 1963.
[4]Cf. 112 and 120.
[5]Cf. 111.

*　　　　*　　　　*

114
To Andre Sandoz
La Chaux-de-Fonds

Basel, 19 September 1963

Dear Sir,

The exclusion of women from parochial and synodical councils is undoubtedly an arbitrary convention—an anomaly which in our church, as in others, deserves only to be abolished.

I enclose a clipping which might interest you.[1] On 6-7 July Zurich decided in favor of women voting in the church.

With regards and good wishes for your work,

Yours,
KARL BARTH

[1]From *Wir Brückenbauer*, 6 July 1963; a special page, "Die Frau in der Kirche," including Barth's "Warum sollte es im Kanton Zürich anders sein?"

*   *   *

114a
[second edition]
To Prof. Heinrich Vogel
Berlin

Basel, 8 October 1963

Dear Friend,

Your Nicaenum[1] has arrived and I make haste to thank you for this further fruit of your intellect. You will not take it amiss that I began reading at the end, i.e., with pp. 196-215.[2] These sections are in many respects most worthy of "praise."[3] And the consensus between you and me is so broad and deep that in fact I am *not* clear where I am really supposed to seek[4] the disagreement mentioned on pp. 211ff.[5] But why the "only"[6] at the bottom of p. 211 ("not only of the revelation")?[7] Is *everything* already *accomplished* in the death of Jesus Christ while less than *everything* has yet been objectively *revealed* in his resurrection; is it as yet only concealed from our eyes? "It is a matter of the reality of the newly made creature in a new being and nature not yet proper to us"? "In a new light that does not yet enlighten us," I could understand. But as your sentence runs I cannot understand it. Fortunately on p. 212 you again speak of "knowledge that understands," of a new eye and hearing, of "direct knowledge." Is it not in this light that we are to understand what is meant by the new corporeality? We must have another discussion of all this some day, either on your next visit to Switzerland[8] or with a new eye and hearing—in some very different place. With sincere greetings, also to your wife, and with thanks again for your gift,

Yours,
KARL BARTH

P.S. During these days I have had a fruitful time with another significant contemporary, namely, Heiko Miskotte.

¹H. Vogel, *Das nicaenische Glaubensbekenntnis. Eine Doxologie* (Berlin/Stuttgart, 1963).

²Vogel deals here with eschatology on the basis of the Nicene "And I look for the resurrection of the dead and the life of the world to come. Amen." For many years eschatology had been the theme of a friendly debate between Vogel and Barth. Cf. H. Vogel, *Freundschaft mit Karl Barth. Ein Porträt in Anekdoten* (Zurich, 1973), pp. 57-62.

³The German word is "Rühmung" which, with its suggestion of glory, is a central term in Vogel's theological aesthetics: *Der Christ und das Schöne* (Berlin, 1955); also *Die Rühmung. Psalmen und Kirchenlieder* (Berlin, 1948).

⁴In the original Barth made the slip of putting "ist" (to be sought) for "habe."

⁵"In the future world of God it is not only a matter of the revelation of our past being in time, the being that has been given and reconciled by God, as Karl Barth stated in his anthropology. It is a matter of the reality of the newly made creature in a new being and nature not yet proper to us . . . ," p. 212n.

⁶Cf. n. 5.

⁷Cf. John 19:30.

⁸The two were on vacation together from 3 October to 7 October 1963 in Gyrenbad by Turbenthal (Zurich Canton).

*   *   *

115
To Dr. Walther Morgenthaler
Muri near Bern

Basel, 15 October 1963

[Morgenthaler, a psychotherapist and old friend of Barth's, had sent the latter copies of his book *Der Mensch Karl Marx* (Bern, 1962). Having thanked him for these, Barth expressed the view that it was rather too acute a study. He asked whether one could correctly depict a past figure for whom one has no liking at all. Instead of offering a list of vices, should one not try to read partly through the eyes of Jenny von Westphalen, Marx's wife? And also take the age and circumstances into account? And study the work of Marx in its own right and not in abstract psychological or psychoanalytical fashion? According to Morgenthaler's method we would all be sorry creatures. Barth referred in closing to having sent a copy of his little work on Mozart (1956) and wondered if Morgenthaler might be interested in the *Protestant Theology in the Nineteenth Century*. Regarding the Mozart, he said that his medical colleague Albert Schüpbach had asked him why he bothered with theology when he could write fine pieces like this (Schüpbach, however, died in 1955!).]

*   *   *

116
To a Young Acquaintance

Basel, 16 October 1963

[The writer had told Barth briefly of her criminal record, new friend, and emigration to Canada. In reply Barth found it hard to give advice for lack of details, and asked if she was still in the Evangelical Fellowship and what her relation to it was now. He wondered if young people were really better helped in such small groups than in the more tepid atmosphere of the organized churches. He had sensed things were not going too well when the writer was in Basel and assured her of his continuing interest and concern.]

* * *

117
To Ruth Barth
Bryn Mawr, Pennsylvania

Basel, 16 October 1963

[Having tendered thanks for a recent letter, Barth here expressed surprise at the freedom of student choice in American colleges. He wondered if the recipient ought not to look at other possibilities before aiming to be a "fiction-writer," mentioning his own reading of the black writer James Baldwin. He asked for more information concerning her Christian pilgrimage as a test case of someone not baptized in infancy. In answer to a question he said he did not regard her as an optimist, nor was he himself, but was often depressed.]

* * *

118
To Miss Annie Hirzel
Locarno

Basel, 18 October 1963

[Barth first referred to his coming trip to Paris and then to Bièvres where he would have discussions with fifty French pastors. He then offered felicitations on the recipient's seventy-sixth birthday and enclosed a check in addition to a parcel already mailed. He advised Miss Hirzel not to waste her slender resources on the sentimental upkeep of family gravestones, which are simply a witness to corruptibility. Regarding his own health, Barth noted he had as yet no traces of serious illness, acknowledging, however, "we must all go as we came. But then we shall truly be in the best hands."]

*　　　　*　　　　*

119
To Pastor Hans Riniker
Lenzburg (Aargau Canton)

Basel, 25 October 1963

Dear Pastor,

I should have thanked you long ago for the fine article on the era of Barth,[1] which according to one well-known church historian is now finally over. And I am reading today your careful discussions of Buri's *Dogmatics* and Gollwitzer's book.[2] All this has greatly pleased me. Do we know one another personally—pardon my forgetfulness. Were you perhaps a student here? Undoubtedly it is for me a salutary experience to see that good theology is still being done in Lenzburg (in 1912 or 1913 I gave a lecture there to Aargau pastors on the personality of God);[3] indeed, this is better theology than we were capable of in those distant days. The difference between Schleiermacher (he too aimed to think historically!) and Bultmann is not one I would draw as sharply as you do. The decisive thing in both is anthropocentricity or the lack of what might be called a real distinction between God and man. Go on courageously and prudently (how you are to be envied being only thirty-three). Things are already going well.

With friendly greetings,

Yours,

KARL BARTH

[1]Perhaps H. Riniker's " 'Der Stellvertreter,' " in *Kirchenblatt f. d. ref. Schweiz*, 119 (1963), 294-298, though this refers only incidentally to Barth on 296. Was Barth confusing Riniker with G. Blocher, "Karl Barth—ein Zeitgenosse," ibid., 258-266?

[2]H. Riniker, "Die Existenz Gottes. Zu zwei theologischen Neuerscheinungen" (F. Buri's *Dogmatik*, II [Bern, 1962] and H. Gollwitzer's *Die Existenz Gottes im Be-*

kenntnis des Glaubens [Munich, 1963]), *Kirchenblatt f. d. ref. Schweiz*, 119 (1963), 322-326.

[3]K. Barth, "Der Glaube an den persönlichen Gott" (lecture to the Aargau Union of Pastors in Lenzburg, 19 May 1913), *ZThK*, 24 (1914), 21-32; 65-95.

*   *   *

120
To Prof. Georges Casalis
Antony/Seine

Basel, 28 October 1963

Dear Georges,

It is wrong that I should have left you for almost eight days without a word of thanks and happy remembrance. The four days in Paris[1] were a time of unusual refreshment for me. And it is of you especially that we think. How many hours and how much effort we cost you in addition to your many other burdens! How well you took us about in your unassuming but speedy little car! Above all, how fine it was to talk to you, and to find such understanding in big and little things alike, from the first steps to the pool of Bethesda[2] to the last glass of wine! We did not delay passing on enthusiastic news of you to the Birsigstrasse.[3]

In these circumstances it is hard to say whether my second Paris trip to the great Mandarins of the Sorbonne[4] has any chance of being anywhere near so successful. But my son-in-law is already looking forward to it "anonymously," as he likes to say, a fine dress-coat is already waiting to be put on, and this will probably be the last time I shall have to take part in a show of this kind.

Now a practical question in relation to the future. There was talk of another television appearance.[5] On which of the three days (6-8)? We shall be there by 1 P.M. on the sixth, and then the whole afternoon will be free. We leave at 5 P.M. on the eighth, and shall be free before that. So it seems best to me not to put the appearance on the seventh, when some pressure might arise between the morning ceremony and the evening banquet, but to arrange it sometime on the sixth or eighth. You will know how to fix it with your unique wisdom and resolution. But I wanted to express to you my own concern.

In the meantime I have read attentively your work on the church.[6] How can I not agree with you when I gave the concept of the church the same orientation in *C.D.* IV? But mark you, I am not wholly satisfied with this presentation, for this almost necessary orientation seems to leave us with the total kenosis of the church in favor of its head Jesus Christ and therefore of the world, which is good. Yet in the New Testament the church, so far as I can see, has *in* this kenosis (and therefore *in* this, its origin and goal) its own teleology, misery, and glory. In the high flights of your presentation this seems to be shortchanged in spite of the fine things you say in this dimension toward the end. You must perhaps take care that you do not slip into an ecclesiological Ebionitism which could all too easily change into an ecclesiological Docetism. Perhaps in the three days ahead—or even in the television discussion—we could talk about this a little.

Greet my fine honorary daughter-in-law,[7] your likable children, and the little American lady, to whom Lollo and I did not say an express goodbye; Lollo adds her warm greetings.

Until later,

Yours,
UNCLE KARL

[1]Barth was in Paris 19-22 Oct. with Charlotte von Kirschbaum, spent two days of discussion with French pastors in Bièvres, and was interviewed on French television on 20 Oct. with G. Casalis, whose guest he was.
[2]Cf. John 5:2ff. Barth is referring to his morning bath.
[3]The Thurneysens lived on this street in Basel.
[4]6-8 Nov. 1963; see 112.
[5]Cf. 105, n. 1.
[6]G. Casalis, "L'Eglise 'réduite à sa plus simple expression'" (1963), in *Vers une église pour les autres* . . . (*Studies in Evangelism by the World Council of Churches*, collected by G. Casalis, W. H. Hollenweger, and P. Keller; Geneva, 1966), pp. 73-75.
[7]Dorothee Casalis, née Thurneysen.

*　　　*　　　*

121
To Präses Kurt Scharf
Berlin

Basel, 28 October 1963

Dear Präses,

Have I or have I not answered your letter of 8 October, or have I just dreamed I did so? I am disturbed to find no corresponding mark on it and seriously fear I have not done so. The firm of G and C[1] wrote me afresh on 16 Oct., all signed, sealed, and blustering. I have no intention of playing their game but have put their demand where it belongs, in the wastepaperbasket. I am surprised at your patience in having anything to do with these excited shouters and think you should quietly make an end where I have not even begun.

Have you studied my little theological evaluation of the ten articles?[2] Obviously only the second or third part of what I say will be read or noted or quoted there (in both West and East). And I shall be praised (or blamed) by the one lot for extolling the articles and praised (or blamed) by the other lot for so sharply criticizing them. I am unable to find my way in this hectic and extremely unfair discussion and for the future will regard silence as my better part.

Warm greetings to you, dear Präses, and all good wishes for your work,

Yours,
KARL BARTH

[1]Two North Germans who had attacked Scharf for a lecture he gave at Kiel and who were trying to drag Barth into the debate.
[2]Cf. 107, n. 2.

*　　　*　　　*

122
To Mrs. Charlotte Gelzer
Basel

Basel, 30 October 1963

[A letter of condolence to Mrs. Gelzer on the death of her husband. Barth had known Heinrich Gelzer when in Safenwil, and though the two differed he had always respected him as a representative of the Pietist tradition to which some of Barth's ancestors had belonged and to which he himself expressed indebtedness. He assured the widow of his friendship and was confident she would meet the new situation "in the strength of all that had most deeply united" her to her husband.]

*　　　*　　　*

123
To Prof. Oscar Cullmann
Rome

Basel, 30 October 1963

Dear Friend,

Thanks for your instructive letter of the twelfth.[1] And in the meantime we have been able to read and see you in a very delightful way in the *Nat.Zeit.*[2] I believe all Basel was instructed, encouraged, and honored by this contribution. It struck me at once that your epitaph should read: O. C., confidant of three popes. *Perge modo.* When I read the opening address of Paul VI,[2a] I wondered in my pride if this man had perhaps read the *C.D.* It served to bring about my deserved and salutary humbling that it was in part from the springs of *Christ and Time*[3] that the healing visible in him had come. Certainly astonishing things are now taking place behind the wings in the Roman church. What goes on at the council will undoubtedly have repercussions, too, on those more hidden processes, and it is undoubtedly worth while following the work of the council attentively from a distance, or, as is your lot, from close by. I said to Balthasar[4] some years ago that I could have no objection in principle to a statue of Mary if instead of on the altar it were put on a level with the congregation and had its face turned toward the altar. According to your latest report on the integration of mariology into ecclesiology, a development of this kind seems to be under way.[5] A pity that the majority voting for this was not larger.[6] One of the best bits of news for me was that the fathers (and observers?) in St. Peter's were not allowed to smoke cigars and cigarettes—though sin does not commence with the cigarette, as I recently told a Salvation Army officer from Nimes who was visiting me—but they were allowed to smoke pipes. Here is an example for you: If you were a good pipe-smoker, your time-line would not extend in such an unauthorized way to infinity.[7] Am I mistaken in getting the impression that since your last letter, in spite of the difficulties for our Catholic friends that you rightly stress, you now view the council more hopefully? Any word from you will be interesting. But you have more important things to do there than write letters.

What is there to report here? The waves of the Hochhuth and Bovet scandals have now settled a little.[8] The Swiss people have demonstrated their famous common sense in the elections by returning the parties in much the same strength to Bern. By a small margin (he lacked only one hundred votes) my successor H. Ott just missed being elected. From the nineteenth to the twenty-second I was with 120 pastors in Bièvres and from 6-8 Nov. I shall be back in Paris with my son-in-law Max Zellweger to receive the Doctor of Letters.[9] Things are buzzing around me as in a hive. I had thought retirement would be more restful.

Again enough for now. I almost asked you to give my greetings to the pope. But don't delay to pass them on to our lively Hans Küng.

All the best to you. Don't overdo things so that you may be kept for the church.

Warm greetings,

Yours,

KARL BARTH

[1] Cullmann was in Rome as an observer at Vatican II.

[2] An interview with Cullmann in *National-Zeitung* [Basel], 27 Oct. 1963, p. 3.

[2a] [Numbering of Swiss edition] Paul's speech at the opening of the second session of Vatican II, 29 Sept. 1963.

[3] O. Cullmann, *Christus und die Zeit* (Zollikon-Zurich, 1946; ET *Christ and Time*, 1964).

[4] Hans Urs von Balthasar.

[5] Cf. the *Dogmatic Constitution on the Church* published a year later, chap. VII.

[6] The votes for putting the schema on Mary in that on the Church were 1114, the votes against 1074, and 5 votes did not count.

[7] A reference to Cullmann's interpretation of the NT view of time. He had corrected it in the 3rd edition (1962); cf. the Preface.

[8] A reference to Hochhuth's play *The Deputy* and to the attack of Moral Rearmament on Theodor Bovet, head of the Christian Marriage and Family Institute in Basel.

[9] Cf. 112 and 120.

* * *

124
To Hans Otto Rosenlecher
Dortmund

Basel, 30 October 1963

[The recipient was thinking of a denominational change, but in his reply Barth advised against it unless he could not continue where he was, since he would find much to disillusion him in the new body and in Barth's view "it is best for each of us to be faithful to the Lord in the church in which he first opened our eyes to him."]

* * *

125
To a Convict in Germany

Basel, 31 October 1963

[Barth apologized for not writing earlier, mentioned that Gertrud Staewen was not well and could not do her usual visiting, and expressed pleasure that the recipient was reading his books and attempting practical and not just theoretical hearing. He mentioned his preaching in Basel prison, his next visit to be on Christmas Eve at five o'clock (on John 16:33), when he would be on the air in Germany as well as Switzerland. He closed by wishing his reader peaceful days and nights and the reality of the coming and presence of the true Son of God and Man in the approaching Advent season.]

*   *   *

126
To Thomas Wipf
Zurich

Basel, 31 October 1963

Dear Mr. Wipf,

Your letter of 11 Oct.[1] has gone unanswered far too long.

The present situation (the council and the inner movements behind it) is a warning that we must state the differences carefully. Are there really irreconcilable antitheses? Or are there differences only in emphasis?

Evangelical: Unconditional precedence of God's free grace over against the "good" being and action of men (even Christians).
Roman Catholic: Tendency to reverse this relation.

Ev.: The Bible has strictly the first word over against church tradition.
R.C.: Tendency to understand the Bible in the light of tradition instead of the opposite.

Ev.: The church is God's people within which are certain ministering functions ("offices").
R.C.: Inclination to regard these as a priestly hierarchy around which the people (the "laity") must gather.

Ev.: The church's unity rests on God's living Word (in Jesus Christ through the Holy Spirit), and only incidentally on legal ordinances.

R.C.: Inclination to understand spiritual order in terms of a legal order.

Ev.: Central significance of proclaiming (preaching) the biblical gospel.
R.C.: Prevailing concentration on administering the so-called "sacraments."

Ev.: Respect and gratitude for the existence of good examples of the Christian life.
R.C.: Veneration and invocation of the "saints."

Ev.: Centrality of Jesus Christ as true Son of God and Man.
R.C.: Apparent sharing of this centrality by Mary as the human mother of God.

Here are seven points where you may safely proceed so long as you are careful. Care is required for two reasons:

1. because many things are fluid in modern Roman Catholicism and may lead to agreements and then to modifications of the total picture;

2. because we Evangelicals for our part are not on top of our own cause and must look out lest the first might become last and the last first.

With friendly greetings and all good wishes for your project on 22 Nov.,

Yours,
KARL BARTH

---

¹Wipf had asked Barth for help in making a report on the main differences between the Roman Catholic and Protestant confessions.

*   *   *

127
[written in English]
To James E. Andrews
Princeton, New Jersey

Basel, 1 November 1963

Dear Mr. Andrews,

Thank you for your kind letter from 13 Sept. Gettysburg is always present to my mind. And so is the generous help you gave me on that remarkable day in May 1962 unforgotten.[1] Since then I have read a good deal more about what happened there in 1863. Do you know the big and very carefully written *Centennial History of the Civil War* by Bruce Catton?[2] I studied the two first volumes. The third, in which he will deal with Gettysburg, is not yet in print. June last summer I was haunted by the idea: I should write in a Swiss paper something about the tragedy of 1-3 July one hundred years before. I did not do so, because I felt myself troubled by the coincidence of the events in Alabama, etc.[3] That very moment I found myself not able to praise the bravery of the Confederates of 1863. So the article has remained unwritten!

Concerning our Swiss battlefields: They are far less cultivated than those I have seen in America: No guides, no panoramas, no cannons, no regimental monuments, no unearthed bullets. . . . A stone with a simple inscription, sometimes an enclosed pyramid of skulls (!), sometimes a rom. cath. chapel; after the battle of Sempach (1386) they have built one specially for the memory of the killed *enemies*! That's all. But if you come over I shall try to show you some of the places, maybe also Kappel, with the spot where Zwingli died.

No objections to be made concerning the tapes of my American lectures.[4] I hope that also Mr. Cohen[5] will agree to your proposal.

Will you give my greetings, please, to President McCord. He told me about a review of my book on Anselm by the novelist John Updike.[6] I am wondering, what he may have said and I would appreciate it very much to have a copy of his article.

With all my best wishes for your work,

Truthfully yours,
KARL BARTH

---

[1]Andrews took Barth to see the battlefield on 5 May 1962; cf. 40.
[2]Cf. 97, n. 3.
[3]Racial disturbances.
[4]Andrews had asked permission to play tapes of the Princeton lectures; cf. 23, n. 1.
[5]Of Holt, Rinehart and Winston, the American publishers of *Evangelical Theology*.
[6]J. Updike, "Faith in Search of Understanding," *The New Yorker*, 12 Oct. 1963, pp. 203-210; reprinted in *Assorted Prose* (Fawcett Crest Book; Greenwich, Conn., 1966), pp. 212-219 (on Barth's *Fides quaerens intellectum* (Munich, 1931; 2nd ed. Zollikon, 1958; ET London, 1960).

*   *   *

128
To Pastor Hans Heinrich Brunner
Zurich

Basel, 11 November 1963

Dear Pastor Brunner,

I am a little disturbed by what your father has written about me in the new edition of *Wahrheit als Begegnung*,[1] pp. 45f.: every statement a wild distortion, and that after I had thought he and I could end our days in a kind of truce.[2] Could this not be discontinued or prevented? Certainly I will not react to it publicly. But as I did not want to address him personally, which might have excited him unnecessarily, I thought I should at least tell you that I take no pleasure in this rekindling of ancient anger.

With friendly greetings,

Yours,

KARL BARTH

[1] E. Brunner, *Wahrheit als Begegnung* (Zurich, 1938; second enlarged ed., 1963).
[2] A personal reconciliation had taken place between Barth and Brunner in Nov. 1960. On earlier controversies cf. 62, n. 1 and 93, n. 9.

*   *   *

129
To Pastor Hans Heinrich Brunner
Zurich

Basel, 21 November 1963

Dear Pastor,

Thanks for the really good letter you sent in reply to my inquiry.

I learned from another source how much trouble you have taken in the matter. So my inquiry neither could nor should imply any criticism of you.

My complaint was not so much at the tone of the statements in *W.a.B.*[1] as the caricaturing of myself and more generally the fact that your father cannot stop provoking me.

But you are right: This is part of the burden of his age and in this regard I cannot accuse him.

My own age ("an alert and active life")[2] you should not depict in such glorious terms. In possible contrast to your father's it is characterized by the fact that in the main I can now take part in the theological vanity fair[3] only as a spectator. This is not an ideal position.

Thanks for the copy of *Kirchenbote* you sent.[4] I like what you say there.

A question in conclusion. Some weeks ago—before seeing *W.a.B.*— I asked Erwin Sutz,[5] who has been rushing to and fro all his life as pontifex between your father [and me], whether your father would be pleased if on some occasion—still to be found—I visited him personally. With his usual zeal Sutz thought he would. But I would like to hear from you whether this would be your opinion, too. In any case I shall not react publicly to *W.a.B.* and would certainly not do so at a personal meeting. I wonder, though, whether your father might be more provoked than pleased by such a meeting. There is no hurry. But I would be grateful for any hint you might give me in this regard. Again I do not want to omit anything that might give such a meeting between us a happier note.

With friendly greetings and—as you think it appropriate—with kind regards to your mother,

Yours,
KARL BARTH

P.S. The Basel *Kirchenbote* has trapped me neatly with the thoughtless article "Karl Barth says Yes."[6] But I have reacted to it only with a phone call to the person responsible.

---

[1]Cf. 128, n. 1.
[2]A quotation from H. H. Brunner's letter to Barth, 18 Nov. 1963.
[3]The German editors see a reference to Thackeray's *Vanity Fair*, but perhaps Barth was really thinking of Bunyan's *Pilgrim's Progress*.
[4]*Kirchenbote f. d. Kanton Zürich*, 29, No. 11 (1963), pp. 6f.
[5]Zurich pastor, a student of both Barth and Brunner.
[6]*Kirchenbote. Für d. Glieder d. evang.-ref. Kirche Basel-Stadt*, 29, No. 11 (1963). The reference is to Barth's positive attitude to the ten articles (cf. 107, n. 2). The "Yes" recalls Barth's *Nein! Antwort an Emil Brunner* (Munich, 1934).

*　　　*　　　*

130
To Prof. Paul Tillich
Zurich

Basel, 22 November 1963

Dear Paul Tillich,

You must be surprised, and I must apologize, that I have not previously answered your letter of 25 October.[1] Now you say you will be visiting me on December 1. You will be very welcome at the hour suggested.

Where shall we begin when we sit down together again? With the infirmities of age which obviously afflict us both? Or with the Ground of Being[2] which unconditionally affects us both? Or with your difficulty—I mean my own difficulty in reading your books? Or with the battle of Gettysburg and Lincoln's address there, which I find so moving? Or with the terrible book by the Bishop of Woolwich?[3] Or with the comical Hermeneutical Institute which Zurich has built around Mr. Ebeling and which now has the honor of housing you? Or with the question whether you will soon catch up with me in having a great-grandson?[4] Be all that as it may, I am pleased that on 1 December I shall walk with you from heaven through earth to hell "in considered haste," as Father Goethe foresaw.[5]

With friendly greetings,

Yours,

KARL BARTH

[1]Tillich was a guest lecturer in Zurich and had suggested a meeting with Barth.
[2]The central concept in Tillich's theology.
[3]J. A. T. Robinson, *Honest to God* (London, 1963).
[4]Cf. 45, n. 4.
[5]J. W. Goethe, *Faust*, "Prelude" (v. 241f.).

*　　　　　*　　　　　*

131
To Pastor Karl Handrich
Lachen-Speyerdorf (Palatinate)

Basel, 22 November 1963

[Handrich had asked Barth for help with a eucharistic confession (see Appendix, 5 and 6) and in this hasty letter Barth sent him a corrected version to serve as the basis of the final text (see Appendix, 7). Barth's version runs as follows:

"As we now take and enjoy bread and wine together in accordance with his direction, we find comfort and joy in the presence of his body broken for us and his blood shed for us, and therefore in the promise of our life in his coming kingdom.

We confess in doing this our thanksgiving for the reconciliation of the world with God that has taken place in him.

We also confess herewith that we are bound together as brothers and sisters who must love and assist one another as such.

And we affirm herewith our hope in his final manifestation in which he will come and make all things new."]

*   *   *

132
To Mrs. N.N.
Denmark

Basel, 28 November 1963

[In this letter Barth first thanked Mrs. N.N. for sending copies of the Danish translation of his book on Mozart. He noted that they too were under the shadow of Kennedy's assassination on the twenty-second. In reply to concern about theological controversies he pointed out that they were no better or worse, and no more superfluous, than controversies in other areas of life. Regarding the source of the funds for the Sonning Prize, which N.N. said was very questionable, Barth answered that a reporter had told him this, but he was not worried, since he was putting the money to good use in charities and paying off the mortgage on his house. In any case there is no completely untainted money anywhere. He closed the letter with personal matters and Advent and Christmas greetings.]

*   *   *

133
To Paul Tillich
Zurich

Basel, 3 December 1963

Dear Paul Tillich,

Since I was unable to hear you the day before yesterday either at mid-day or in the evening[1] (though I did not lack for detailed reports of what you said), I am now sending on yet another greeting to Zurich. It is for me a very special phenomenon that we understand one another so well and cordially at the human level, but materially—and don't try to offer me a synthesis; in so doing you would only strengthen me in my opinion!—we can only contradict and oppose one another from the very foundation up.

May I submit to you here what I told the students from undeveloped nations who met here in Basel in April?[2] In contrast to the other speakers (especially our constitutional lawyer) I kept strictly to the assigned quarter of an hour. Thus this is really a short address which as such has some chance of being read by you. I received the greatest applause among the students of any of the prominent speakers.[3] According to you this cannot possibly happen. Nevertheless!

For the continuation and conclusion of your work at Mr. Ebeling's wonderful Institute,[4] and especially for Christmas (*hic Verbum caro factum est*),[5] my good wishes, indeed the very best.

With warm greetings,

Yours,

KARL BARTH

[1]Tillich gave two lectures in Basel on 2 Dec. [not 1 Dec. as Barth's dating would indicate]. He visited Barth the previous evening.

[2]K. Barth, "Das Christentum und die Religion" (lecture on 27 April 1963 at a reception for three hundred foreign students, largely from Asia, Africa, and South America), *Acta Tropica*, 20 (1963), 26-262; *Kirchenblatt f. d. ref. Schweiz*, 119 (1963), 181-183; *JK*, 24 (1963), 436-438.

[3]The constitutional lawyer Max Imboden and the biologist Adolf Portmann also spoke at the reception.

[4]Cf. 130.

[5]The inscription at the grotto of the annunciation in Nazareth. Tillich had seen it on a recent trip to Israel and told Barth he did not like its too concrete allusion to John 1:14.

*   *   *

134
To Prof. Grover Foley.
Austin, Texas

9 December 1963

[Barth apologized for not writing before, expressed pleasure and surprise at Foley's car, assistant, and secretary (more than he himself had ever had), and warned against an over-strict regimen, which had "often led to schism and heresy." Barth referred to the good theology of Deschner, but also the existence of the company of Korah in the persons of Paul van Buren and S. Ogden—all in the remarkable state of Texas. After a short mention of the shattering effect of Kennedy's death and the problem of theodicy it raised, he then went on to speak of a recent article by Foley on Bishop Robinson:]

I notice in *Christian Century* the waves you have stirred up with your article on the fatal Woolwich.[1] It certainly does not seem to have made you many friends there (I told you so!). I have since asked myself whether I should not have warned you more definitely not to inaugurate your public activity in America in this way. You have dared (and this amused me so much I have nothing to say against it)—you have dared to handle in the best tradition of Basel Shrove-Tuesday a matter which seems to be a terribly serious "question" to innumerable foolish contemporaries, including, for example, Bultmann and the director of C. Kaiser,[2] to whom I wrote a letter of protest. Right you are! But surely America is not, or not yet, accustomed to humor of this sort! And this your first act as a doctor newly back from Basel! Oh, Dr. Foley, instead of presenting the soft reply of a positive counterthesis to Woolwich in a modest and non-polemical way, have you not done exactly what the mob likes to expect from a Barthian so that it may regard itself as excused and justified if it skulks in the undergrowth? But I ought to have given you this advice before you left Basel. Do not take what I say as censure but only as a sigh: If only we had first discussed the wisdom of what you attempted.

Have you followed the proceedings at Vatican II? The pope's summons to christological concentration was remarkable.[3] We heard nothing like it at either Amsterdam, Evanston, or New Delhi. For the rest, the difficulties of root and branch reformation have just begun to appear and to exert an influence, so much so that Hans Küng has confessed to serious disillusionment. One cannot but be concerned as to how it will go. But at least there is still hope. [. . .]

In *ZThK* 3 Bultmann has written a fairly weak article[4] in which it looks as though he had been aiming all along at the point where Woolwich, Braun, etc. are now operating.

[Barth closed the letter with news of his colloquia—how he had to cut short a brash student from Zurich who referred to "good old Paul"—and Christmas greetings from himself and his wife and Charlotte von Kirschbaum.]

[1]G. Foley, "Religionless Religion," *The Christian Century*, 80 (1963), 1096-1099; cf. the expanded version in *EvTh*, 24 (1964), 178-195.
[2]Kaiser published the German trans. *Gott ist anders* (1963).
[3]Cf. 123, n. 2a.
[4]R. Bultmann, "Der Gottesgedanke und der moderne Mensch," *ZThK*, 60 (1963), 335-348; also in *Glaube und Verstehen*, IV (Tübingen, 1965), pp. 113-127.

*   *   *

135
To Prof. Hermann Diem
Tübingen

Basel, 2 January 1964

[Barth congratulated Diem on his election as Rector Magnificus for the year 1964/65 and imagined him presiding at solemn academic banquets with his wife, a former student of Barth's at Göttingen, sitting beside him as Annelise Magnifica decked out in her new finery. Contemplating this new "stage on life's way" for Diem, he said he had put the newspaper clipping and picture in one of Diem's books on Kierkegaard.]

*   *   *

136
To General Secretary Gerald Götting
Berlin

Basel, 3 January 1964

[Barth thanked Götting, General Secretary of the Christian Democratic Union of East Germany, for his Christmas greetings and the gift of a book on church architecture—a welcome token of fellowship beyond frontiers, walls, and curtains. He expressed hope for truer understanding than had seemed possible a year before and, while not an optimist, could not but feel things might work out better between Moscow and Washington in 1964, and people might all learn not so much to fight for peace as simply to live for it.]

*   *   *

136a
To Prof. Heinrich Vogel
Berlin

Basel, 11 January 1964

Dear Heinrich,

Were your ears burning last Friday evening (the ninth)? At that time a young scholar in my most intimate circle was reviewing your eschatology.[1] There was rejoicing that in your later utterances (Nicaenum) you have evidently softened your harsh earlier statements.[2] It was again found to be an open question whether and how far the continuity of the will and work of God the Creator (John 1, Col 1, Heb 1) is threatened by your absolutizing of the majesty of death,[3] as also the *tetelestai* of John 19:30. And your Christology (the impeccability, impassibility, and immortality of the human nature of Christ)[4] gave rise to a suspicion of Docetism or Monophysitism. Think about this. Unfortunately I did not hear personally from my student Hans Ruh, who is still in his way an excellent fellow, how you tangled with him in Budapest.[5] What I hear about the whole Prague affair is only partly enlightening, as is the matter of the sermon preached in Budapest by George Casalis, whom I value highly but who has some fads which so far, fortunately, are only slight.[6] The fact that the Chr. Kaiserverlag, against the advice of Ernst Wolf, and solely for the thirty pieces of silver to be expected from a best-seller, has published the miserable work of Bishop Robinson[7] is a scandal that stinks to high heaven. And have you read Bultmann's latest article in *ZThK*?[8] Alas, Heinrich, 1964 will still produce many things which will demand of us (beyond all our detailed differences) both constancy and resistance.

With sincere greetings,

KARL BARTH

[1]All the participants read the eschatological section of Vogel's *Das nicaenische Glaubensbekenntnis* (cf. 114a, nn. 1 and 2) and Dr. Eberhard Busch, who has supplied this information, gave the report.

²In his review Busch emphasized that in his work (p. 204) Vogel stresses the personal identity of the old and the new man in the resurrection, this being a shift away from his strong earlier emphasis on discontinuity (cf. H. Vogel, *Gott in Christo* ... (Berlin, 1951, p. 1032).

³Cf. Vogel, *Gott in Christo* ..., pp. 508ff., 1020ff. In the first passage Vogel criticizes the distinction made by Barth between the death that God willed with creation as man's natural end and death as penalty and judgment (cf. *C.D.*, III, 2, pp. 625ff.).

⁴Cf. H. Vogel, *Christologie*, I (Munich, 1949), pp. 272-310; *Gott in Christo* ..., pp. 655-659, 665-667.

⁵Barth's doctoral student Hans Ruh was then a theological consultant at the Gossner-Mission in East Berlin. The dispute with Vogel, which came to a head at a meeting of the committee preparing for the Second International Peace Conference at Budapest (2-5 January 1964), had to do with organizational matters in Ruh's work in Berlin.

⁶Casalis preached on 5 January 1964 in connection with the meeting referred to in n. 5. His sermon was on Isa 60:1-9 and he delivered it in the Reformed Church, Calvin Square, Budapest. An extract was published in *Christliche Friedens konferenz*, ed. International Secretariat of the Christian Peace Conference, No. 9 (March 1964), p. 211. How Barth already had information about it by 11 January 1964 is not known.

⁷Cf. 96.

⁸Cf. 134, n. 4.

*   *   *

137
To Pastor Emeritus Eduard Burri
Hünibach near Thun

Basel, 21 January 1964

Dear Pastor,

Regarding the reader's letter to *Die Tat*,¹ I have in a sense found it normal that with the many signs of fellowship that have given me pleasure in my retirement I should be continually reminded of the zone of anger which still surrounds me. That someone should see me as a cabaret artist is a new experience for me. But there may be something in it! Do not delay sending me *Leben und Glauben* when your defense comes out in it.² With warm greetings to you both, also from L.v.K.,

Yours,
KARL BARTH

¹The Zurich paper *Die Tat* had published a letter from a reader who did not like Barth's Christmas sermon on the radio ("Aber seid getrost! Predigt über Johannes 16:33," in *Berner Predigten*, 10, No. 1 (1964); rpt. in K. Barth, *Rufe mich an! Neue Predigten aus der Strafanstalt Basel* [Zurich, 1965], pp. 107-119). The writer had described him as a cabaret performer masquerading as a parson, had wondered what the convicts must have thought of this kind of sermon, and had found it so poor that he could not listen to anything else on the radio the whole Christmas season.

[2]The above letter was printed again in *Leben und Glauben. Evang. Wochenblatt* [Laupen], 8 Feb. 1964, p. 3, along with a reply from E. Burri-Fahrni, which had first been sent to *Die Tat* but had been rejected by them.

*   *   *

138
To Dr. Carl Gunther Schweitzer
Bonn

Basel, 27 January 1964

[Schweitzer had written Barth a letter criticizing his depiction of Hegel in the *Protestant Theology*. Barth apologized for not replying on the ground that so much was written about him and to him that he could not answer everything. He continued:]

Hegel has not claimed much of my time since I wrote about him in 1932.[1] I read somewhere that like a blind hen I found the right corn in him and this amused me. But if I now have to read that I didn't understand him, I must try to put up with this too. I still have to get down to a serious reading of Seeberger's book.[2] My philosopher brother Heinrich, who goes for Schelling, has set it aside with marked indifference. That Hegel could still have a future, as I predicted in that early work, I still regard as probable, although in the meantime the flood of existentialism has risen higher and higher. Where I stand will be well known to you: I believe more than ever that as a theologian one should know philosophy but should not in any sense become or be a philosopher.

With all good wishes and greetings,

Yours,
KARL BARTH

[1]The text of the book reproduces the lectures of 1932/33.
[2]W. Seeberger, *Hegel oder die Entwicklung des Geistes zur Freiheit* (Stuttgart, 1961). Schweitzer had referred Barth to this book, which he thought to be "irrefutable."

*   *   *

139
To Pastor Arnold Bittlinger
Klingenmünster (Palatinate)

Basel, 4 February 1964

[Bittlinger had invited Barth to give a lecture on Thesis 3 of the Barmen Declaration at an Evangelical Week devoted to the theme of "The Barmen Declaration after Thirty Years." In declining Barth gave three reasons: his dislike for this kind of lecture; his inability to get about; his belief that the Barmen Declaration should be put into practice and not brought out like an old flag every five years or so, waved a little before not very interested young people, and then carefully preserved in a chest again. If Barmen were a living thing again, the younger generation could very well speak about it. Incidentally Barth also refused to write an article for this anniversary, and his refusal was published as an open letter: "Statt eines Gedenkartikels," in *Die Kirche. Evang. Wochenzeitung* [Berlin], 31 May 1964, p. 1 (cf. the *Gesamtausgabe, Offene Briefe*).]

*　　　　*　　　　*

140
To Pastor Karl Handrich
Lachen-Speyerdorf (Palatinate)

Basel, 4 February 1964

[Barth thanked Handrich for some materials on the Third Reich, asked after his health, and resisted his attempt to persuade Barth to join in the Barmen anniversary on the same grounds as in the previous letter, especially the third: "What can all the solemn talk about Barmen mean when the most alert of young theologians today amuse themselves by gorging on the quails handed to them by Bultmann, Ebeling, Fuchs, Braun and more recently this awful *Honest to God* man from England?" Barth enclosed a photograph of great-grandfather walking with great-grandson and sent his greetings and best wishes to Handrich and his wife.]

*　　　　*　　　　*

141
To Pastor Emeritus Adolf Maurer
Brütisellen near Zurich

Basel, 5 February 1964

Dear Pastor,

You do not weary me, as you suspect, tireless and prudent editor of the *Zwingli Calendar*, but I, to whom you turn with such hope and confidence, should long since have wearied you by being so frequently unable to meet your requests.

If only something important or interesting that I might write and send you for the required purpose would strike me. But look, much though I have written in my life, nothing ever came easily or quickly from my pen or typewriter. And a special difficulty is that I can never really write at request but only when something in myself constrains me to do so. Let us wait and see whether there will be such an impulse before the end of April. If so, I will not fail to let you know.[1]

With friendly greetings and all good wishes,

Yours,
KARL BARTH

[1]Barth did not in fact write anything for the 1965 *Calendar* as requested.

*   *   *

142
To Mrs. Elaine Shaffer Kurtz
Gstaad

Basel, 5 February 1964

[Barth thanked the recipient for sending word that her husband had been impressed by his Christmas sermon and sent her a copy. He also acknowledged the gift of a record of Mozart's Concerto in C, K 299, for flute and harp, and the promise of tickets for two concerts in Basel, though he doubted whether he would be fit to go, and noted that the works would be from the Romantic period, he himself being, musically, an eighteenth-century man who found Beethoven extremely tedious, and those after him even more so.]

*   *   *

143
To Sister Lina Siegrist
Riehen near Basel

Basel, 5 February 1964

[Barth thanked the recipient for her letter and a picture of Safenwil church, where he had confirmed her about fifty years before, this reminding him of the three hundred or so he had confirmed there and of all his students in the years after 1921. He expressed regrets they had met so seldom in Basel but pointed to the earlier pressure of work and now in his retirement his restricted mobility.]

*   *   *

144
To Prof. Oscar Cullmann
New York

Basel, 14 February 1964

Dear Friend,

I was greatly pleased by your greeting from Union Theological Seminary. I myself would not like to have to live in that pseudo-Gothic structure which stands in such a paradoxical relation to the theology pursued in it. But the ways of humanity are always strange.

Regarding the council, I was discreetly asked to come last autumn via Hans Küng.[1] But I do not see how I can usefully join the corps of observers in the third round, quite apart from the fact that in health I hardly feel up to flitting to Rome and back. So I thank you for your suggestion but would rather follow the proceedings from a distance through the wealth of sources made available by the press, as I have already done with great interest so far.

What do you think of the Canadian radio inviting me to give a six-minute oracle this Easter along with Montini, Ramsey, and Hromádka?[2] We only need Athenagoras.[3]

I am wholly at one with you in a basic aversion to the Bultmannitis that is spreading everywhere in both the old world and the new. Certain signs suggest to me that in the foreseeable future the deluge might perhaps recede. But however that may be, in your place I would not engage so much or so forcefully in written and verbal polemics with this movement. [. . .] I have often found that the best way of fighting theological opponents—apart from a few brief flashes of lightning—is to let them be ("Thou preparest a table before me in the presence of mine enemies," Ps 23:5), and to go on quietly with one's own little piece—*à prendre ou à laisser*—since one only gives them an undesired boost among readers and hearers by continually mounting explicit attacks.[4] Don't be cross at me for trying to speak to you along these lines.

May things go well with you in America. Markus will be here for a few weeks in April.

With warm greetings,

Yours,

KARL BARTH

[1] Cf. 113.
[2] Pope Paul VI, the Archbishop of Canterbury, and Professor Hromádka of Prague.
[3] Patriarch Athenagoras of Constantinople.
[4] Cullmann's reply has been lost, but he informed the editors that he had told Barth he could not develop his own position except in antithesis to the existential exposition of Bultmann. Barth's reply to the reply has also been lost, but he apparently expressed some agreement on this point.

*   *   *

145
To Prof. Fritz Lieb
Degersheim (St. Gall Canton)

Basel, 20 February 1964

[Barth sent best wishes to Lieb on his illness and hoped he would adjust to retirement as Barth himself was having to, unable to continue the *C.D.* as many people were pressing him to do. He recalled that forty years before Lieb had regarded his doings as trivial and suggested that everything now was trivial, the problems of Assyriology, geology, and theology, the doings of Macarios in Cyprus, and the unending flow of books, compared with Lieb's recovery, which a pipe might help if it were allowed!]

*   *   *

146
To Prof. Hermann Diem
Tübingen

Brione, Hotel della Valle
9 March 1964

Dear Hermann,

A certain Mr. Bammate of UNESCO has urgently pressed me to take part in a symposium on the relevance of Kierkegaard, to be held in Paris on 23 April. G. Marcel, J. P. Sartre, Jaspers, and other lions will be taking part in the festival. I have definitively refused, but not without suggesting that you are the man for the job. I don't know whether he will follow my pressing advice but he has at any rate taken note of it and may write you in a day or so. Since a representative of Evangelical Protestant churchmanship and theology is wanted at the forum, you will not be able to treat the matter lightly.

Thanks for your last piece on Kierkegaard.[1] With warm greetings from this familiar place to yourself and Annelise,

Yours,
KARL BARTH

[1]H. Diem, "Kierkegaard und die Nachwelt," *Neue Sammlung*, 4 (1964), 38-50.

*   *   *

147
To Prof. K. H. Miskotte
Voorst (The Netherlands)

Basel, 2 April 1964

Dear Friend Heiko,

I was so pleased to get your card with its good news about Glasgow.[1] I, too, was given a D.D. there, in the summer of 1930. The existentialists are now in control there (in contrast to Edinburgh). But (apart from their theological error) they are not bad people and all honor to them that they want to honor you. On Easter Day I preached here (in the prison). I hope the result[2] will not be as bad in your eyes as it sometimes seemed earlier. Markus has come for a month. Christoph is having trouble in Jakarta with the foolishly conservative Bible Society over his new translation into Indonesian.[3] There are always troubles. But Heiko M. (unlike the gods) will not keep silence.[4] We always remember Gyrenbad with pleasure.[5] Your wife has my full sympathy and admiration. It must certainly be no easy thing, but always interesting, to be your wife.

With warmest greetings to her and you,

Yours,

KARL BARTH

[1]The University of Glasgow was awarding Miskotte an honorary D.D.

[2]K. Barth, "Als sie den Herrn sahen," *Basler Predigten*, 27, No. 12 (April 1964), printed in *Rufe mich an* (Zurich, 1965), pp. 120-130 (preached on 29 March 1964, Barth's last sermon).

[3]Christoph Barth was working on an Indonesian translation of the OT.

[4]Allusion to Miskotte's book *Wenn die Götter schweigen. Vom Sinn des AT* (Munich, 1963; Dutch 1956).

[5]Barth and Miskotte had spent their holidays together here in October 1963; it is in Zurich Canton.

*   *   *

148

To Prof. Walther Eichrodt
Münschenstein near Basel

Basel, 4 April 1964

Dear Friend,

I was very pleased to have your note of 27 March, for, frankly, I was not a little surprised by the news that you could read my last book[1] with so much agreement. Strange, is it not, that we can live close by so long without noting how close we are. I am really grateful you can think of me in this way.

I hope you and yours have had a good Easter. On the festal day I tried as usual to preach to the spirits in prison.[2] How good that the important work of your son-in-law has now come out,[3] along with the dissertation of a remarkable Bavarian student, who let himself be carried away into a theological interpretation of Mozart.[4] I am curious to see whether such remarkable works will emerge from the school of my successor.

My regards to your wife, with whom I recently had a good quarter of an hour here, and warm greetings to yourself, with best wishes for your work,

Yours,

KARL BARTH

¹The reference is to *Evangelical Theology*.
²Cf. 1 Peter 3:19; cf. 147, n. 2.
³D. Braun, *Erwägungen zu Ort, Bedeutung und Funktion der Lehre von der Königsherrschaft Christi in Thomas Hobbes' Leviathan* (Zurich, 1963), Vol. I of *Der Sterbliche Gott, oder Leviathan gegen Behemoth*.
⁴K. Hammer, *W. A. Mozart—eine theologische Deutung. Ein Beitrag zur theologischen Anthropologie* (Zurich, 1964).

*   *   *

149
To Prof. Friedrich Wilhelm Kantzenbach
Neuendettelsau

Basel, 4 April 1964

Dear Colleague,

I was pleased to have your letter of 20 March and I have glanced through or read the collection *Zeugnis und Zeichen* you so kindly sent me.¹ The fact that you were a student and are now a disciple of my unforgotten friend Georg Merz² binds you to me from the very first, but especially what you tell me about your development and position in the present theological situation, which has again become so cloudy (*Honest to God!*). If only it were not so difficult to reverse the dominant trend without having to make common cause with some finally very distasteful fundamentalists and having to conduct water to their mill. Your generation will have a big and by no means easy job in this regard.

Yours,

KARL BARTH

¹F. W. Kantzenbach (ed.), *Zeugnis und Zeichen. Reden—Briefe—Dokumente* (Munich, 1964). This included three pieces by Barth: "Der Christ in der Gesellschaft" (1919 lecture), pp. 149-160; "(Ein) Wort an die Deutschen" (1945 lecture), pp. 221-234; "Kirche Jesu Christi" (1948), pp. 234-244.

[2]For Barth's friendship with G. Merz (1892-1959), ed. of *Zwischen den Zeiten* (1923-1933), see the Barth/Thurneysen letters, I and II (Zurich, 1973/4).

*　　　*　　　*

150
To Pastor G. de Ru
Rotterdam

Basel, 4 April 1964

Dear Pastor,

I have received your friendly letter of 21 March and also your book on infant baptism[1] and thank you for both and especially for the good will shown in your letter. Materially, I have to say that I sincerely deplore the fact that obviously the many things (exegetical, dogmatic, historical, and practical) that I and others have brought against infant baptism have finally made no impression on you, so that your discussion amounts only to a confirmation of the *status quo*. How the church will have to be shaken up before it sees, both apart from all else and in connection with all else, that it is highly questionable to try to build itself up with an ocean of baptismal water. But how can I help respecting as such your conviction that this is right?

With greetings and best wishes for your work,

Yours,
KARL BARTH

[1]G. de Ru, *De kinderdoop en het NT* (Wageningen, 1964).

*　　　*　　　*

151
To Pastor Robert Meister
Bümplitz (Bern Canton)

Basel, 4 April 1964

[Meister had written to Barth deploring the way people used his theology for their own ends and urging him to go on with *C.D.* as Farel had pressed Calvin to stay in Geneva. Barth replied that he was cheered by those who, like Meister, were making good and honest use of his work, but he was now seventy-eight, not thirty as Calvin had been when Farel challenged him, and production came less easily at this advanced age. Nevertheless he might do an installment of IV, 4 (C.D. IV, 4: *Fragment*, 1967).]

*   *   *

152
To Pastor T. C. Frederikse
Wassenaar (The Netherlands)

Basel, 12 April 1964

[Frederikse had written thanking Barth for his work and in reply Barth expressed his own thanks, first to the Giver of all good gifts who had permitted him to do it, and then to those who had proved receptive to it. With regard to modern theological trends, he expressed his confidence that they would pass (*nubicula est, transibit*),[1] though "that is in other hands."]

---

[1]This saying of Athanasius on his fourth banishment in 362 should run: *nubicula est et cito pertransibit*.

*   *   *

153
To Pastor Martin Storch
Hanover

Basel, 26 April 1964

[Barth first expressed great appreciation for Storch's book, *Exegesen und Meditationen zu Karl Barths Kirchlicher Dogmatik* (Munich, 1964), which he had finished reading the previous evening. He then continued as follows:]

There are a terrible number of books about me on both sides of the ocean, but not many to which I attach too much importance, either by virtue of their evaluation (favorable or unfavorable) or their description and characterization of my work, or for which I foresee any lengthy future. Your own book is important because it so quietly and clearly shows me in dialogue with my age and therefore, in connection with my own course, offers implicitly what is almost a history of German Evangelical theology in the middle of the century. The general situation will be greatly illuminated if many (including, may one hope, some of the great ones) read the book with the same diligence and orderliness with which you have written it. And if the mist rises, and the time becomes ripe for the younger generation to look back to today, your book will certainly be a pointer for all who have eyes to see.

The house of C. Kaiser has gained real merit by publishing it and thereby lessened a little, though not fully expiated, the crime it perpetrated in producing the outrageous work of the figurine Woolwich. I did not know you had been working on the book for six years and so I am the more surprised at the result. And what a large coal of fire the Lutheran Church of Hanover has placed on my head by helping in the production of the work, as I read in the preface.

Like many others you call on me to continue *C.D.* For various reasons I cannot promise this. But I might manage a fragment—the fairly complete section on baptism.

[Barth closed the letter by referring to the Sonning Prize and the way he had spent the award.]

*　　　*　　　*

154
To Pastor Werner Tanner
Kronbühl (St. Gall Canton)

Basel, 28 April 1964

[Barth agreed with Tanner in deploring the poor theology in a recent lecture by Martin Niemöller ("Die gegenwärtige Theologie und der Religionsunterricht" [1 Nov. 1962], *Stimme der Gemeinde*, 15 [1963], 649ff.). But one had to remember that in the decisive years when Niemöller should have been studying theology he had been sinking allied ships. The synodical sermon by Prof. M. Mezger ("Wo geschieht Gott?" [11 Nov. 1963], *Stimme der Gemeinde* 16 [1964], 133-138) was equally bad. Barth had protested to the paper and intended to tackle Mezger if he could find him: "One never knows whether he is in Wiesbaden, Australia, or Canada."]

*　　　*　　　*

155
To Pastor Werner Bauer
Musberg near Stuttgart

Basel, 29 April 1964

[Barth expressed agreement with Bauer's view that war memorials in churches are a form of paganism. He advised Bauer, however, to omit the statement "our wars were sin" in a declaration he had written, since the word "our" might open the door to stupid objections.]

*   *   *

156
[written in English]
To President James A. Jones
Union Theological Seminary
Richmond, Virginia

Basel, 7 May 1964

Dear President Jones,

Not—as you have put it most kindly in your letter from 30 April—some weeks, but some months ago you wrote me at the request of your faculty and trustees to invite me to become [for] 1964/65 the first "distinguished professor" of Richmond's Union Theological Seminary. Excuse my long, all too long, silence! I had indeed to consider carefully the possibility of the enterprise involved in the acceptance of your invitation. Your proposal was so honorable and its terms so remarkably generous. My sincere thanks go to you and to those in whose name you have written. My memories of the days I spent [in] 1962 in your Seminary and especially in your home with you and Mrs. Jones, and also of your visit in my modest house, are perfectly agreeable. Richmond is a lovely and for me (I have continued to read Civil War literature) in a particular way interesting, yea, exciting place. And how should I not be eager to learn more and more specifically about the situation, the minds, the moral and political tendencies, sorrows, and hopes of the Christianity, the churches, the younger and elder theologians in Virginia? I should very, very like the idea to come, to open my eyes and my ears anew and to do some useful work with you, your colleagues, your students, and the ministers of your country.

Alas, it can not be done. There are difficulties (part of them even difficult to explain) which are—taken all together—not to be overcome: the rather unsatisfying physical conditions of an elderly gentleman; a considerable amount of literary work, which cannot be done but on my own desk in my own study; my regular meetings with a large number of German-, English-, and French-speaking students, whose continuity should not be broken so long as I have the stamina to do the job; troubles in the European theological world asking more or less for my presence on the spot; also some slight complications of a more personal character. Do not make out of these allusions a tragic picture, especially not when you have to tell the fact to your faculty and to your trustees: the fact that—I am really sorry about [it]—taken all together I find myself not able to do what you are asking for and so to accept your glorious and inviting offer.

Thank you also for your kind birthday greetings! I shall never forget the tenth May 1962: the day beginning with the song of your students and my lecture, while in the afternoon I found myself at the feet of the monument of Stonewall at Manassas-Bull Run—him sitting on a horse much too beautiful compared with the efficient but very poor mare on which the "historical" Stonewall Jackson was riding. Well, well, it is to be feared, that also the shot I fired so successfully on the border of the James River has been the last one of my performances of that kind. I shall certainly always remember the moment during the dinner you gave us in your home, when Mrs. Jones stood up waving an ancient Virginia-Dollarbill crying aloud: "The South will rise again!" And I remain proud of that other paper on which I find myself recognized as a lawful citizen of the late C.S.A. But will the South (and the North) "rise again," before an honest, clear and lasting solution has been found out of the race problem? Found out, acknowledged and practised! As far as I can see: then and only then it will be allowed to think and to say that, for example, the 15,000 who charged with Picket the third July 1863, the poor Union prisoners in Andersonville, that further Abraham Lincoln and—John Kennedy have not suffered and died in vain. Human history takes a terribly long breath to achieve but one of those seemingly simple and necessary steps. God knows better what is *really* happening. But there may be moments and opportunities also for human knowledge and action, which should not be missed. Excuse me: but the developments on the American scene are so important for us all!

How are you? Is everybody well: Mrs. Jones, your son and his wife, your daughter and her husband in New York and the little one who sat on my knees in 1962?

Again—I regret that I am such an unuseful fellow for you. Accept my excuses and my most cordial greetings to you, to Mrs. Jones, to the members of your faculty. I am so glad to hear that you are satisfied with the activities of Rissi![1] May we see you in Europe when you realise your plan to make a trip to East Asia?

> Truly yours,
> KARL BARTH

[1]Matthias Rissi, previously a pastor and NT tutor in Basel, had taught at Union, Richmond, since 1963.

*   *   *

157
Circular Letter to Those Who Sent Congratulations to Barth on His Seventy-Eighth Birthday

Basel, May 1964

To all who sent me letters, cards, telegrams, flowers, food, drink, tobacco, and every kind of spiritual refreshment for 10 May

Dear, affectionate, loyal Friends,

The day when I became seventy-eight has now gone. But the mailman, whom I always put to a good deal of trouble at this time of the year, is still bringing me stragglers of the great host that first reached me by May first. I am especially touched and ashamed in the face of all these tokens of sympathetic remembrance because I am no greater performer in honoring the birthdays of others nor do I do as well as I should like even in my general correspondence (often even in pressing matters). Please do not be cross if I reply to the individual greetings of 10 May with a countergreeting that goes out to many others, too.

I did indeed take sincere pleasure in each of the things that were written or sent to me. I realize that only a few can share in so large and sincere a response to their life and work. And having been for so long regarded as hardly respectable or acceptable, I am the first to be amazed at this and to be sincerely grateful for it. What I want to say to you all is especially that this year, too, 10 May brought me so much of the joy and comfort and encouragement which one needs increasingly in old age and which one may less and less expect and anticipate as something deserved, but must accept only as a gift. You have given me this gift again, and I thank you for it. That among the many things that came was a bundle of moving letters from the prison inmates written in response to my sermons there was a particularly cherished gift, as others among you will certainly understand.

I liked it that not a few of those who congratulated me took the occasion to tell me a little about their own situations and activities. All of you have had to carry greater or lesser burdens. But there have never been wanting greater or lesser lights, and especially the great enlightenment that is given us all. I sympathize with all that has been said or hinted at respecting your burdens and only wish it were humanly possible to give specific encouragement and advice where it is necessary. You all realize that I know I am in the same boat with you. In this boat we all have to keep strong and row as hard as we can, though fortunately we do not have to steer.

I have especially received from you so many good wishes for my own future. These were and are most appropriate now that I am ineluctably approaching the upper limit of the span of human life laid down in scripture.[1] Obviously I pictured aging as easier when I was not yet so far advanced in it, and thought the so-called retirement in which I now find myself would be a good deal more pleasant. But I will not expand on that here. I have no reason to raise complaints but every reason to be thankful. The spring sun still shines on me as on so many others, just and unjust.[2] I am rather frail but not ill. I am still loyally provided and cared for. I still take pleasure in the well-being and good upbringing of my bigger and smaller grandchildren and not least of my happy great-grandson. I still listen to Mozart. I still find pleasure in smoking my pipe. I am hardly a producer any more, but I am still a keen consumer of spiritual goods of every quality. I still have the freedom to be greatly incensed or amused as I listen to the "speech-event" on the theological market, which I follow attentively (and whose loudest participants I usually describe as the company of Korah[3] or the united figurines of all lands). The traditional free discussions in German, English, and French still follow their varied course in the Bruderholz restaurant or in the house here, with lively participation. As it appears from many of your letters, my books are still read with industry and profit. I still have many (sometimes too many) visits—even from whole groups of pastors and students from abroad who roll up in cars with important questions. In spite of some signs of the beginning of the

KARL BARTH

break-up of this earthly tent, I am not yet done for.[4] Not yet! On 10 May you strengthened my joy, so that I am content, not in myself, but in all these tokens of the goodness of God.[5] Herewith I commend all of you also to him.

With warm greetings,

Yours,

KARL BARTH

[1]Cf. Ps 90:10.
[2]Cf. Matt 5:45.
[3]Cf. Num 16.
[4]Cf 2 Cor 5:1; Lam 3:22.
[5]Cf. P. Gerhardt's hymn: "Fröhlich soll mein Herze springen," v.10: "Nun kann ich mich durch dich wohl zufriedengeben."

*   *   *

158
To Pastor Daniel Pache
Lausanne

Basel, 22 May 1964

Dear Pastor,

I have not disavowed in principle the contents of the text of *C.D.* quoted in the pamphlet *La guerre et la paix*[1] and also in your publication *L'objection de la conscience.*[2] The only thing I regret is that I did not take into serious consideration the possibility of atomic armament and atomic war, which by its very nature calls into question even what I had called an adequate reason to make war legitimate—including the military defense of Switzerland. Defense of our Confederation by atomic weapons would imply an inner contradiction. In the face of this eventuality conscientious objection needs serious discussion.

With all good wishes,

KARL BARTH

[1]K. Barth, *La guerre et la paix* (Geneva, 1951), from *C.D.* III, 4, pp. 450-470, trans. J. de Senarclens.
[2]*L'objection de la conscience* (Lausanne, 1964). This pamphlet, published by the

Social Commission of the Free Evangelical Church of the Vaud and Jura Cantons, included passages from *C.D.* III, 4, pp. 462 and 466ff.

*   *   *

159
To Prof. Josef L. Hromádka
Prague

Basel, 6 June 1964

Dear Brother and Friend,

You are on the point of celebrating your seventy-fifth birthday. I should like to be among the host of those surrounding you on that day to give personal witness to their respect and gratitude and love for you. But I am three years older than you and much less mobile when it comes to long journeys. So the only option is to give these lines to our good friend Martin Schwarz.

I must tell you, however, that I am thinking of you and sincerely taking part in everything that will affect you on this day as you look back and look ahead. Your way of life has been marked both by the originality, bravery, and joy with which you have chosen to follow it and by the versatility and constancy which you have been enabled to display in all its stages, in spite of a good deal of serious and less serious pressure. The limitation of time and restriction of possibilities given to us men will apply increasingly to you as to me. But according to what we have come to learn about you, you will not do badly in the service yet required of you, but will always remain the pioneer you have been and still are in your own church and the churches of the world, hoping in the Lord and therefore continually mounting up with wings like the eagle.[1] Thus we who are now among the old can acknowledge (as the title of Bonhoeffer's well-known book shows[2]) that the resistance which is commanded of us and which we have to render, not in surrender but in confirmation of that hope, can also one day take the form of submission. To the best of your knowledge and conscience you were obedient to the one who called you, and you will continue to be so whether in resistance or submission. The best, however, is that he who called you is himself faithful beyond all that we can think or conceive.[3]

Bound up with you in this promise, and with warmest greetings,

Yours,
KARL BARTH

[1]Cf. Isa 40:31.
[2]D. Bonhoeffer, *Widerstand und Ergebung* (Munich, 1951; ET *Letters and Papers from Prison*, 3rd ed. 1973).
[3]Cf. 1 Thess 5:24.

*   *   *

160
To Renate Barth
Granitola, Sicily

Basel, 8 June 1964

[In this reply to a letter from his daughter-in-law, wife of Hans Jakob Barth, Barth commented on her description of Granitola and the journey through Italy, gave news of family affairs in Basel, and referred to the controversy about the procurement of Mirage jets for the Swiss army.]

*   *   *

161
To Dean Heinrich Lang
Schwäbisch Gmünd

Basel, 21 June 1964

Dear Dean,

Sincere thanks for your lines of 16 June and your letter to the young theologian.[1] One would like to know how your son, having hoped to give you a fit by sending Robinson's book, reacted to it.[2] I like your presentation because of its simplicity, gentleness, and definiteness. You are right to see in the whole matter a counterrevolution. As I see it, not just in Robinson but already in Bultmann and his disciples it resembles a car whose tires have punctured, so that there is no air left and it has to run on the rims. Many people find this a wonderful way to travel. But I do not think it will have any great future.

With friendly greetings and all good wishes,

Yours,
KARL BARTH

[1]H. Lang, "Brief an einen jungen Theologen," *Evangelium und Kirche. Rundbrief*

d.Evangl. Bekenntnisgemeinschaft in Württemberg, No. 1 (1964), pp. 7ff. The young theologian was the author's son, who had sent his father a copy of *Honest to God*.

²Cf. B. Lang, "Robinson aus der Sicht eines jungen Theologen," *Evangelium und Kirche*, No. 2 (1964), pp. 28ff.

*   *   *

162
To Pastor Werner Tanner
Kronbühl (St. Gall Canton)

Basel, 21 June 1964

[Barth thanked Tanner for a reception held by a group of St. Gall pastors in honor of himself and E. Thurneysen on 17 June 1964. He called on the younger generation to press ahead but found comfort in the fact that the most important statements his generation had made both abroad and at home had not been issued in vain.]

*   *   *

162a
To Prof. Georges Casalis
Antony/Seine

Basel, 26 June 1964

Dear Georges,

I have just read No. 3 of your *Semeur*.[1] I have received the irresistible impression that these students are people who neither can nor will study. Work bores them (p. 65).[2] Instead they walk about (p. 63),[3] living the kind of life described on pp. 56f.[4] This does not prevent them from acting like gravediggers, not only for the whole Sorbonne (pp. 47f.)[5] but also for such venerable old men as J. P. Sartre (pp. 97f.)[6] and also—poor theology to find itself proclaimed "dead" with Barth—myself.[7] And to call all this "the search for a new ethics!"[8] And to publish it all under the auspices of the Fédé[9] of which, if I am not mistaken, you are the president.

What does all this mean? I implore you, Georges, to try to make these poor sheep understand—by your teaching and example—what it is to study, not in order to pass examinations, but because of the necessity and beauty of serious and regular intellectual work the savor of

KARL BARTH

which seems to be strange to the authors of this journal. In this sign—
under the standard of this arrogant bohemianism—you will not con-
quer,[10] whether against Gaullism or against (or for!) Communism.

With sincere greeting to you, to dear Dorothee, and to your very
congenial family,

Yours,
O[NKEL] KARL

[1]*Le Semeur* was the journal of the French Federations of Christian Student Unions
(called Fédé for short). The title of No. 3, 1964, was "Students."
[2]D. Joubert, "La vie quotidienne, source de la théologie . . . ," pp. 58-69: "The student keeps his distance from all that. Work is boring. . . ."
[3]Section 2 of the previous article (p. 63) has at its head as a motto a short dialogue
by Michèle Bernstein which closes as follows: " 'No,' said Giles, 'I walk about. For the
most part, I walk about.' "
[4]A. Frugier, "La journée d'un étudiant à Bordeaux," pp. 56f. This article describes
the daily life of a student, which consists for the most part of visiting cafes, restaurants,
and cinemas and playing cards and table tennis.
[5]T. Willm, "La Sorbonne assassinée," pp. 47-55.
[6]A. Frugier, "A moi SARTRE! Deux mots," pp. 87f. The author makes fun of an
interview of J. P. Sartre with *Le Monde.*
[7]The article by D. Joubert mentioned in n. 2 begins with the sentence: "With Barth,
theology is dead." It includes an observation that begins as follows: "If we intend to
become the gravediggers of Barthianism, it is because we are its grateful heirs."
[8]On the inside of the back cover the issue carries the caption: "*Le Semeur.* Cahier
de recherche pour une nouvelle éthique."
[9]Cf. n. 1.
[10]Allusion to Constantine's vision of the cross just before the battle of the Milvian
Bridge in 312: *In hoc signo vinces.*

*   *   *

163
To Prof. Hans Küng
Tübingen

Basel, 11 July 1964

Dear Colleague,

Do you know Michael Serafian's book *The Pilgrim* (New York,
1964),[1] in which the line chosen and followed by Paul VI in Council
affairs is subjected to an (apparently) uncannily exact analysis and criticism? According to this view the idea of John XXIII has been smoothly
repudiated and rejected by his successor, and with it the whole project
of Cardinal Bea. But you know your way about in this labyrinth better
than I do, and so I hope to see you again one day (at Sempachersee?).[2]

Have you also read *The Shoes of the Fisherman* (London, 1963) by Morris West? At least for entertainment, another exciting book (the possibility of a decidedly eastward oriented papacy) in the form of a novel. Thanks for your article on Swiss Catholicism.[3] Great that in spite of your deanship, the Council, etc., you were able to write it, so that our discussions in the car were not finally for nothing. Whenever I pass the caves on the north side of the Bruderholz I never fail now to think of their former inhabitants.[4]

In health, I am sometimes on the rims after having done pretty well most of my life. I find a good deal of pleasure in the presence of my son Markus from Pittsburgh.

Greet Miss Zurmühle.[5] I shall never forget 17 April.

With all good wishes,

Yours,
KARL BARTH

[1]Michael Serafian was a pseudonym for the former secretary of Cardinal Bea.
[2]In Küng's home city of Sursee (Lucerne Canton), where Küng usually stayed between semesters.
[3]H. Küng, "Die katholische Schweiz," *Civitas. Monatsschrift des Schweizerischen Studentenvereins,* 22 (1966/67), 579-588.
[4]On 17 April 1964 Barth had visited Küng in Sursee. In conversation on their return together he had encouraged Küng to write the article. Jokingly, they had called some of the caves the dwellings of the original—Catholic—inhabitants of Basel.
[5]Odette Zurmühle, Küng's secretary from 1960 to 1967.

*   *   *

164
To Pastor Paul Deitenbeck
Lüdenscheid

Basel, 13 August 1964

[Asked by Deitenbeck to respond to the theological situation of the day, Barth replied that he saw no reason to treat it too seriously, since the "garden figurines" so far had only repeated the eighteenth and nineteenth centuries, and he had made his position clear enough on these and did not need to state it again in relation to the rather naive Bishop Robinson. A true believing community "should not be too quickly flabbergasted by a handful of pompous professors and a few hundred excited students and candidates who for a short while (as in every century) think they must raise their cock-a-doodle-do and who must not be given the satisfaction of being made martyrs. The Bible, not to speak of God, has already withstood other attacks and will withstand this one too." In conclusion Barth quoted Zwingli's slogan: "Not to fear is our armor" (*Der Hirt* [1524], in *Werke*, ed. M. Schuler and J. Schulthess, I [Zurich, 1828], p. 651; *CR*, XC, p. 39).]

*   *   *

165
To Dr. Friedrich Schmid
Blaubeuren

Basel, 14 August 1964

Dear Dr. Schmid,

I have read your book[1] to the end and must not delay thanking you for it (also for the dedication) and saying how pleased I was with it. You have worked the theme out very well and clearly and have thus made an important contribution to our scattered modern "dialogue" which so needs to be put together. If only the great teachers (e.g., the one in Zurich,[2] not to speak of your countryman who threshes empty straw in Mainz[3]) and also many of the excited students, candidates, and vicars would have the grace to read and ponder your book seriously! But in order for that to happen, the level of work, which in my view has sunk considerably in favor of endless prattle—would have to rise seriously. So you too must be patient.

In your Part II it struck me for the first time that I might have done better thirty years ago to direct my frontal attack against Gogarten instead of the much weaker Brunner, whom you surprisingly (but rightly) disregarded. [. . .]

I realize that you had to accept material limits. But I wonder whether it is not a pity that from Vol. IV you did not at least include IV, 3, because there I intentionally tried to take up again the theme of I—but now, as it were, directly from the center. But you have expounded everything very clearly.

What are your next literary plans?

[Barth closed the letter with a remark on his health, and family news and greetings.]

[1]F. Schmid, *Verkündigung und Dogmatik in der Theologie Karl Barths. Hermeneutik und Ontologie in einer Theologie des Wortes Gottes* (Munich, 1964).
[2]Gerhard Ebeling.
[3]Manfred Mezger.

*   *   *

166
To Pastor Emeritus Dr. Otto Lauterburg
Wohnheim Grünau, Wabern (Bern Canton)

Basel, 19 August 1964

[Replying to a letter from this old friend, Barth recalled their school days seventy years before in Bern, a visit Lauterburg paid him in Safenwil, and Lauterburg's commitment to the work in Saanen (Bern Canton), which he had pursued for forty-one years. Though they had moved off in different directions, Barth assured him of sincere and sympathetic respect for his achievements. He noted in conclusion that after decades of almost unbroken health he had not been at all well this summer.]

*   *   *

167
To Dr. Robert Leuenberger
Basel

Basel, Bethesda Hospital, 30 August 1964

Dear Dr. Leuenberger,

You were very kind to send me your *Reformatio* article on Robinson's book.[1] I thank you, having read it attentively twice.

Criticism?[2] What kind of criticism? I do not like your presentation as a *whole*.

Naturally from p. 466 on you say many true and important things. Twice I even came upon the word *alternative* and on p. 475 I even read the statement that in this matter there can be no compromise. But what is a compromise if not the unresolved juxtaposing of the truth and untruth in the bishop's book with which you leave those who read the book and the article? And how are we to understand the alternative you present to the book (not simply as the finding of relatively unimportant theological blunders [p. 461] but as a real alternative) if you concede that there is in Robinson something evangelical and even a powerful modern statement of Christian truths (p. 460).

For me Robinson's book is a painful proof that the theology of the eighteenth and nineteenth centuries is still, "with all its crimes broad blown, as flush as May,"[3] "as though nothing had happened."[4] The whole upshot of the work of Bultmann and Tillich is simply to set this light on a candlestick again. In this connection your essay shows how the old familiar mediating theology can also celebrate its happy revival. In a paper bearing the proud name *Reformatio* and published by the Evangelical Church Union!

[Barth closed by saying he was well looked after but "not even at the pool of Bethesda can I call good (or half-good) what I regard as bad."]

With friendly greetings (also to your wife),

Yours,
KARL BARTH

[1]R. Leuenberger, "Ehrlich vor Gott! Bemerkungen zu dem Buch von John A. T. Robinson: *Gott ist anders* (*Honest to God*)," *Reformatio*, 13 (1964), 456-477.
[2]Leuenberger had asked Barth for criticism.
[3]*Hamlet*, III, 3 (Barth alludes to the German translation of A. W. von Schlegel).
[4]Cf. *Theologische Existenz heute* (Munich, 1933), p. 3.

*   *   *

168
To Pastor Richard Karwehl
Osnabrück

Basel, Bethesda Hospital, 1 September 1964

[Barth reported on his health problems, mentioned the good treatment he was receiving at Bethesda Hospital, and the grace and peace he was experiencing. He also referred to the fine books about him written by M. Storch and F. Schmid, expressed hope that the trees of the garden figurines would not reach to heaven, mentioned a remarkable book on Hitler by H. B. Gisevius, and closed with a reference to the visit by Markus Barth and his family.]

*   *   *

169
To Prof. Emil Brunner
Zurich

Basel, Bethesda Hospital, 26 October 1964

Dear Friend,

My sincere thanks for your letter of sympathy. Since early in the year I have not been well and at the end of August I had to come here, to the bank of the pool of Bethesda, and finally have surgery. Thanks to God and my able and determined urologist I have come through as de Gaulle did and before him Hindenburg and Clemenceau. Now some complicated after-treatment is necessary, which I have borne and bear thus far with a cheerful spirit.

As regards the sick theology of our day, I believe that even on the human level I see signs of the deluge receding.

When I am on my feet again, I will watch out for the first opportunity to visit you, as I have planned to do long since.

I greet you with all good wishes for a maximum of physical and psychical and spiritual resistance and cheerfulness,

Yours,
KARL BARTH

P.S. I have never in my life been seriously ill before and in these months have had much to learn in every respect.

*　　　　*　　　　*

170
To Dr. Otto Lauterburg
Wohnheim Grünau, Wabern

Basel, Bethesda Hospital, 29 October 1964

[Barth thanked the recipient for his concern, told him how well he was being treated, and hoped his wife was making progress. He said he had not attended the Expo, which was hardly necessary since he was on display, and wondered what the angels thought of it.]

*　　　　*　　　　*

171

To Pastor Richard Karwehl
Osnabrück

Basel, 8 November 1964

[Barth first reported on the complications after his prostate operation and commented on his excellent treatment, which showed that there was much to be said for the Evangelical background of the institution. He then went on to speak of some of the books he had read:]

Miskotte, *Der Weg des Gebets*[1]; J. Moltmann, *Theologie der Hoffnung,*[2] both a stimulating and an irritating book, because the young author makes an energetic attempt to deal with the eschatological aspect of the gospel better than the old man of Basel did in Romans and *C.D.* I read him with great openness but hesitate to follow him because this new systematizing—though there is much to be said for it—is almost too good to be true. But the book is worth reading. So is that by F. Schmid on ontology and hermeneutics in *C.D.*[3] (all published by C. Kaiser in penitent recognition of their fall in issuing *Honest to God*). In the evening, along with a little wine, I read the ponderous tome by Fieldmarshall von Manstein, *Verlorene Siege.*[4] . . .

[Barth hoped to begin his classes again in 1965 and resume work on *C.D.* IV, 4 (Fragment), which his doctors encouraged him to do. One American, interested in the functions of his lower organs, observed, "The Lord will preserve you to do more work." In closing he noted that he had begun studying theology sixty years ago that fall.]

[1] K. H. Miskotte, *Der Weg des Gebets* (Munich, 1964).
[2] J. Moltmann, *Theologie der Hoffnung* (Munich, 1964); ET *Theology of Hope*, 1967).
[3] Cf. 165, n. 1.
[4] E. von Manstein, *Verlorene Siege* (Bonn, 1955).

*　　　　*　　　　*

172

To Prof. Jürgen Moltmann
Bonn

Basel, Bethesda Hospital, 17 November 1964

Dear Colleague,

It was most kind of you to have a copy of your *Theologie der Hoffnung* sent to me. During my stay in the hospital, which is to end the day after tomorrow, I had the leisure to read it all at once and assimilate the basic contents. It is time for me to express my thanks not only for the attention shown to me but also for the instruction and stimulation I received from reading your work. May I say a couple of words about the impression it made on me? I have been looking for decades—I was looking even in the twenties—for the child of peace and promise, namely, the man of the next generation who would not just accept or reject what I intended and did in theology but who would go beyond it positively in an independent conception, improving it at every point in a renewed form. I took up and studied your book with this expectation, and at the beginning of my reading I seriously asked myself whether Jürgen Moltmann, who, as far as I recalled, was as yet unknown to me personally, might not be the man. I have in fact been impressed not only by your varied scholarship but also by the spiritual force and systematic power that characterize your book. This attempt, as I foresaw, had to be ventured one day, and the critical insights you have brought on both the right and left hand must and will carry the discussion further. It is to be hoped that note will be taken of you in all circles. I am glad to see how you deal with some earlier efforts to portray me and to note what you say about the present state of knowledge concerning me.

But, dear Dr. Moltmann, I do not find in your *Theology of Hope* what is really needed today to refine *C.D.* and my own theological thrust. I will not hold it against you, as Gollwitzer does,[1] that your book gives us no concrete guidance on ethics in this sphere, determined and bordered by the eschaton. Nor does it seem any more important to me that one looks in vain for a concrete eschatology, i.e., for an elucidation of such concepts as coming again, resurrection of the dead, eternal life, etc. You obviously did not intend to write an eschatology, but only the prolegomena to one and to the corresponding ethics. My own concern relates to the unilateral way in which you subsume all theology in eschatology, going beyond Blumhardt, Overbeck, and Schweitzer in this regard. To put it pointedly, does your theology of hope really differ at all from the baptized *principle* of hope of Mr. Bloch?[2] What disturbs me is that for you theology becomes so much a matter of principle (an eschatological principle). You know that I too was once on the edge of moving in this direction, but I refrained from doing so and have thus come under the fire of your criticism in my later development. Would it not be wise to accept the doctrine of the immanent trinity of God? You may thereby achieve the freedom of three-dimensional thinking in which the eschata have and retain their whole weight while the same (and not just a provisional) honor can still be shown to the kingdoms of nature and grace. Have my concepts of the threefold time (*C.D.* III, 2, §47.1) and threefold parousia of Jesus Christ (*C.D.* IV, 3, §69.4) made so little impact on you that you do not even give them critical consideration? But salvation does not come from *C.D.* (I started out here when reading your book) but from knowledge of the "eternally rich God"[3] with whom I thought I should deal (problematically enough). If you will pardon me, your God seems to me to be rather a pauper. Very definitely, then, I cannot see in you that child of peace and promise. But why should you not become that child? Why should you not outgrow the inspired onesidedness of this first attempt in later works? You have the stuff (and I congratulate you on this) from which may come a great dogmatician who can give further help to the church and the world.

Tell your wife I read her essay on Fontane with great interest.[4] In spite of my well-known suspicions of the North German plain I am a great admirer of this noble Prussian and constantly turn to his novels afresh.

With friendly greetings, renewed thanks, and all good wishes for your—future,

Yours,
KARL BARTH[5]

[1]On the cover of the first edition.
[2]E. Bloch, *Das Prinzip Hoffnung*, 3 vols. (Frankfurt/Main, 1954-1959).
[3]Cf. the second verse of M. Rinckart's (1586-1649) "Now Thank We All Our God" (in English: "this bounteous God").
[4]E. Moltmann-Wendel, "Hoffnung—jenseits von Glaube und Skepsis. Theodor Fontane und die bürgerliche Welt," *ThExh*, N.F. 112 (1964).
[5]For Moltmann's reply (4 April 1965) see Appendix, 8.

*　　　*　　　*

173
To Corps Commandant Dr. Alfred Ernst
Muri near Bern[1]

Basel, Bethesda Hospital, 18 November 1964

[Barth assured Ernst of his prayers in the matter of his recent appointment to command the 2nd army corps and accepted it as God's will that he had not become chief-of-staff as Barth and many others had hoped. He told Ernst that he saw Switzerland's role, from its beginning until the present, as that of "one great compromise," so that it was no wonder a middle line should have been taken on the present matter. Yet, Barth believed, "this eternally mediocre Switzerland will be loved as such and in a pinch defended." He would not destroy Ernst's recent letter on the matter, as Ernst asked, but would see that it was not published. He closed his letter with an account of his illness and recovery, and in a postscript mentioned that he had read *Verlorene Siege* by von Manstein, "who was obviously a good soldier but a child in politics."]

[A response to Ernst's letter of 11 November 1964; see Appendix, 9.]

*   *   *

174
To Prof. Wolfhart Pannenberg
Mainz

Basel, 7 December 1964

Dear Colleague,

What must you have thought of me on your visit to us with your wife a while ago when I advised you with well-meant zeal and exaggeration not to publish anything for ten years until you had become clear as to what you wanted and had in mind? Your great work on christology, which you have so kindly sent me,[1] must have been already finished then, and perhaps already in print. I have studied it in one sitting and see plainly now that you know very well where you want to go. Only too well, I must add, for the material decision which I regarded in our earlier meeting as merely experimental and provisional has been acted upon in this book with such breadth and clarity that it is hard to see how you could reverse it without a 180-degree conversion. And now that you have so definitely made the decision, we are theologically—and you yourself will not disagree—very different if not separated people.

I have every reason to respect and admire most sincerely a good deal in your achievement: Your astonishing breadth of reading in the exegetical, historical, and philosophical fields; the constancy with which you are able to stick to your course through all the thickets; the critical acumen that never fails in detail, and with which you are able to establish and safeguard yourself on both the right hand and the left. Your book is a venture of unusual significance.

And mark you, Dr. Pannenberg, I have read it—as some weeks ago I read the *Theology of Hope* of Jürgen Moltmann[2]—with the sincere curiosity whether I might be dealing at last with the child of peace and promise whose work would represent a genuine superior alternative to what I myself have attempted and undertaken in theology the last forty-five years. For a long time I have been waiting for this better option and I only hope I will be alert and humble enough to understand and recognize it as such should it come my way. But in your project, too, I am not yet able to see it, believing rather that for all the originality with which you have ventured and executed it we have a serious regression to a mode of thinking which I cannot regard as appropriate to the matter and am thus unable to adopt.

My first reaction on reading your book was one of horror when on the very first page I found you rejecting M. Kähler in a way which led me to suspect that, like others, you—and you with particular resolution and with an orientation toward a Jesus who may be found historically—intended to pursue a path from below to above. Obviously your intention did not offer you occasion to reflect that our common friend H. Vogel stopped at his admittedly very substantial analysis of the below, and never gave us the second part of his christology[3] which was to deal with the above reached from the below. I wrestle in vain with the question by what right you manage to rest the doctrine of the revelation of God enacted in Jesus, indeed the very existence and life of God and Jesus' identity with him, on the basis of the figure of your historical Jesus and his message and commitment to God, confirmed by his resurrection from the dead—all of which is much weaker in substance than Vogel's historical Jesus. As Biedermann already saw and said,[4] we know that the resurrection may be reduced historically to objective visions of the disciples and the brute fact of the empty tomb.[5] Is not this to build a house on the sand—the shifting sand of historical probabilities moving one way yesterday and another today? And if you think you are not dealing here with sand but with solid rock, does this not consist finally and properly of Jewish apocalyptic, in whose context you think we can explain both the pre-Easter Jesus and the risen Lord? Is it in the light of this that you explain the recognition and acknowledgment of a general ordination of man to a being that transcends his life and death? In its positive content is your christology—after the practice of so many modern fathers—anything other than the outstanding example and symbol of a presupposed general anthropology, cosmology, and ontology? I have looked in vain in your exposition for new shores, for something better than this return to the old shores. I concede to you with praise the formal point that on your proposed way you have followed a consistent course from below to above, or from the general to the particular— beginning with the shadowy figure of your historical man Jesus (beyond the only historically sure fact of the New Testament text) you could not come to any other result. Over against this I believe that for all its difficulties the christology of the early church is much more promising. I expect your position and my own will be improved on when we have a more energetic and careful treading of the path from above to below, from the particular to the general. In the meantime, if you will pardon the harsh expression, I can only regard your own path as reactionary.

I cannot think you expected any other attitude from me. It alters in no way my thanks for your stimulating and instructive work—nor the fact that so far as time and strength permit I shall follow your future career with close interest.

My regards to your wife and friendly greetings to yourself,

Yours,

KARL BARTH[6]

[1] W. Pannenberg, *Grundzüge der Christologie* (Gütersloh, 1964;ET 1968).
[2] See 171 and 172.
[3] H. Vogel, *Christologie*, I (Munich, 1949).
[4] A. E. Biedermann, *Christliche Dogmatik* (Zurich, 1869), pp. 520-527, esp. 525f. (2nd enlarged ed., Berlin, 1885, pp. 417-425).
[5] The two preceding sentences are one grammatically incomplete sentence in the MS.
[6] For Pannenberg's reply on 9 May 1965 see Appendix, 10.

*   *   *

175
To Prof. Emil Brunner
Zurich

Basel, 29 January 1965

Dear Friend,

We are in a small way companions in suffering, as I had a stroke on 13 Dec., and as a result was being treated in Bethesda Hospital until this morning. I could speak again after a few hours, my first intelligible word being Zacharias.[1] I can read and do so with pleasure. But I can write only with difficulty, as you may see from these lines.

Many thanks for sending me your piece on G. Keller.[2] I admire the fact that you could still do this. I lost all sympathy with the man some forty years ago and have never read him since. The direct result of reading your work was that I had the epigrams, the Zurich short stories, the legends, and the two volumes of Leute von Seldwyla brought to me in the hospital and read them off as though they were all completely new to me. I found good entertainment in them. But alas the author did not endear himself to me any more this second time. And—forgive me—in relation to these works, your own thesis did not enlighten me, at least. I could agree on "bourgeois desire and virtue," though even this did not always add up—but eros and conscience seem to me to be too heavy cargo for this boat. Note that I am not making any polemical observations regarding p. 33.[3] So mild have I become in my old age!

Just one question: Do you really regard the work by Fritz Buri[4] (he does not use a double "r") a good one (p. 30)? I myself once found in it an unbelievable blunder: the pastors in Verlorenes Lachen were described as Swiss Ritschlians, though apart from all else the story was written in the 1850's when Ritschl still thought and worked along Tübingen lines. Even with the best will in the world one could not have been a Ritschlian then, not before 1886 or the beginning of the '90's, in the great period when we were born or getting our first breeches. A book which contains nonsense like this cannot be a good one, and in this case there are other reasons too.

Be that as it may, thanks again, very best wishes, and sincere greetings,

Yours,
KARL BARTH

[1]Cf. Luke 1:5ff.
[2]E. Brunner, "Eros und Gewissen bei Gottfried Keller," 128. Neujahrsblatt zum Besten des Waisenhauses Zürich für 1965 (Zurich, 1965).
[3]Brunner alluded here to the significance of conscience for Keller from the standpoint of natural theology.
[4]F. Buri, Gottfried Kellers Glaube. Ein Bekenntnis zu seinem Protestantismus (Bern, 1944).

*　　　*　　　*

176
To Pastor Emeritus Otto Lauterburg
Wohnheim Grünau, Wabern

Basel, 31 January 1965

[Barth described his stay in the hospital, his conversations with his Roman Catholic doctor on Vatican II and Mozart, and his reading, including Keller. Lauterburg's pacifism had posed for Barth the serious question whether he should have resisted military service in 1940 when Hitler was at the gates. He believed that war would have been justified then as a last resort but regarded conscientious objection as a real possibility and even a necessity in case Switzerland were involved in nuclear war, though no sane person could think of this. Therefore alternative forms of service would be right, though consistent antimilitarists would have to resist these too.]

*   *   *

177
To Pastor Emeritus Oscar Moppert
Basel

Basel, 7 February 1965

[Moppert had asked Barth to explain why H. J. Iwand, a theologian he respected, had not mentioned the Jewish persecution in his letters to R. Hermann from 1933 to 1945. In a firm reply Barth said there was no sense in trying to trace protests against this and that in private letters, since in Germany as in Switzerland information about the persecution was limited. He noted that the Swiss had nothing to be proud of in their own conduct at the time; the Basel Student Union had produced an anti-semitic piece in the years before the war, and it was thus most unsuitable to throw doubts from Basel on what Iwand did and suffered and spoke and did not speak during that whole period. Barth also took the occasion to criticize Moppert sharply for the way he dealt with J. Fangmeier's book *Erziehung in Zeugenschaft* (Zurich, 1964) in *Basler Nachrichten*, 15 January 1965, p. 9.]

*   *   *

178
To Michael Rücker (Theological Student)
Urdorf (Zurich Canton)

Basel, 7 February 1965

Dear Mr. Rücker,

Thanks for your good wishes of 25 January. I reply to your questions:[1] 1. I have not answered E. Brunner's criticism because it should be clear to any attentive reader of his books and mine that in him and me two basically different concepts of "reality," and especially of "real man," are operative.

2. In E.B. "real" man is man as sinner; in me he is man who in spite of his sin is accepted and affirmed by God in grace in J.C.

3. Affirming man in J.C., God affirms man's original created being (oriented to his being in J.C.).

4. To this degree God's self-revelation in J.C. is the revelation of "real man," from whom we must not abstract away theologically (as E.B. does).

With friendly greetings,

Yours,
KARL BARTH

[1]Rücker had asked Barth about his response to Brunner's criticism of his anthropology in *C.D.* III, 2. Cf. E. Brunner, "Der neue Barth. Bemerkungen zu Karl Barths Lehre vom Menschen," *ZThK*, 48 (1951), 89-100.

*   *   *

179
To Corps Commandant Dr. Alfred Ernst
Muri

Basel, 16 February 1965

[Barth brought Ernst up to date on his health, mentioned his new status with the sisters when they heard that Paul VI had sent greetings and his assurance of prayer, looked forward to a visit from Ernst on 27 February, and noted how little he enjoyed reading the newspaper with both its foreign and also its Swiss news.]

*   *   *

180
To Prof. Martin Fischer
Berlin

Basel, 17 February 1965

Dear Colleague,

I cannot yet engage in larger writing projects. But your letter of 5 February must not go unanswered any longer.

I have entered into your discussion of infant baptism[1] with attention and respect. But at the decisive point I simply cannot understand what you are advocating. What is a committal of children to God through the work of the community, its baptizing with water? I can see such a committal only in the work of God himself, of his Word and Spirit, to which the community and the baptized have to respond: as in their proclamation in general, as with their whole faith and hope and love, so also with their baptism, so also with their celebration of the Lord's Supper. Is it not wholly grace that the community may have the freedom and power for this obedience? And how do you arrive at the idea of an operation of baptism which can just as well imply the condemnation as the salvation of the baptized? Such a theologoumenon may perhaps be derived from Luther—but from the New Testament, too? It surprises me that the debate between Gollwitzer and Harder, Koch, etc.,[2] which you must surely know, has not made more impression on you. But I will keep your discussion in view. May I thus briefly send you warm greetings and best wishes for your work,

Yours truly,
KARL BARTH

[1] With his letter Fischer had sent a two-page MS "Von der Freiheit zur Kindertaufe," later published in "Thesen über Kinder- und Mündigentaufe," Part II, *Pastoraltheologie,* 57 (1968), 372f.

[2] The theses of G. Koch and G. Harder, and the countertheses of H. Gollwitzer, drawn up for a regional synod in West Berlin in 1964, were published as Part I of the documents cited in n. 1, 357-371.

*   *   *

181
To Christine Barth[1]
Zollikofen, near Bern

Basel, 18 February 1965

Dear Christine,

You have had to wait a terribly long time for an answer to your letter of 13 Dec.—not because of indifference, for I am sincerely interested in your welfare, and that of your mother and sisters, and am always pleased to have good news from Zollikofen.

Has no one explained to you in your seminar that one can as little compare the biblical creation story and a scientific theory like that of evolution as one can compare, shall we say, an organ and a vacuum-cleaner—that there can be as little question of harmony between them as of contradiction?

The creation story is a witness to the beginning or becoming of all reality distinct from God in the light of God's later acts and words relating to his people Israel—naturally in the form of a saga or poem. The theory of evolution is an attempt to explain the same reality in its inner nexus—naturally in the form of a scientific hypothesis.

The creation story deals only with the becoming of all things, and therefore with the revelation of God, which is inaccessible to science as such. The theory of evolution deals with what has become, as it appears to human observation and research and as it invites human interpretation. Thus one's attitude to the creation story and the theory of evolution can take the form of an either/or only if one shuts oneself off completely either from faith in God's revelation or from the mind (or opportunity) for scientific understanding.

So tell the teacher concerned that she should distinguish what is to be distinguished and not shut herself off completely from either side.

My answer comes so late because on the very day you wrote, 13 Dec., I had a stroke and had to spend several weeks in the hospital.

With sincere greetings which you may also pass on to your mother and sisters,

Yours,
UNCLE KARL

[1]Barth's grandniece.

*   *   *

181a
[second edition]
To Prof. Ernst Staehelin
Basel

Basel, 23 February 1965

Dear Ernst,

Congratulations on the completion of your great work.[1] Sincere thanks for the copy you sent me, in which I read with interest things old and new, known and unknown. I paid special attention to your sketch at the end.[2] In your place I would have felt, of course, some need for a fuller explanation and linking of the terms and concepts used. But I am not in your place and each may and must follow his own path and have his own style of thought and speech.

What further mischief might be brewing in the next faculty meeting in relation to the field of "Systematic Theology"?[3] I am glad that I now have no more than an indirect part in what happens in this part of "fallen creation."[4]

My physical condition is improving remarkably. My only problem is that I am not yet fully presentable or capable of action. But I have been doing well for some time, and so I can and should just be thankful.

With friendly greetings,

Yours,
KARL BARTH

[1]Staehelin had sent Barth the seventh and last volume of his collection, *Die Verkündigung des Reiches Gottes in der Kirche Jesu Christi. Zeugnisse aus allen Jahrhunderten und allen Konfessionen* (Basel, 1965; previous vols. from 1951). This last volume deals with the period from the middle of the nineteenth to the middle of the twentieth century.

[2]Chapter 69, "Sixty-five Theses on the Kingdom of God as the Editor's own Witness," pp. 597-613.

[3]The question was answered by an invitation to the meeting of the faculty on 24 February 1965 when Item 5 on the Agenda was "Second professor for systematic theology." In fact there was nothing to give Barth occasion for alarm, as the minutes show.

[4]In Staehelin's work "Fallen Creation" is the heading of theses 10-21, p. 600.

*   *   *

182
To Prof. Helmut Gollwitzer
Berlin

Basel, 12 March 1965

[Barth first brought Gollwitzer up to date on his illnesses, mentioned his inability to deal with the mass of correspondence, and thanked God for his many years of health and vigor. He continued:]

No, I have never yet heard the voice which whispered to Thomas: "You have written about me well." I continually have to ask myself why I did not state and express everything in such a way as to make impossible in advance the dreadful scenes you had to live through in Mainz. I read the volumes *Post Bultmann locutum*[1] and I had the impression of hearing a voice from Auerbach's cellar or even lower regions, particularly in relation to Braun (and his colleague Mezger is almost worse). You might well have confronted him more head-on. But your charisma is different. And perhaps, indeed, the way out of the impasse is not that of a Quos ego, which I am waiting for and which, having said what I had to say how I had to say it, I myself can no longer advance, like that of Neptune in Idomeneo. For the rest I have the impression even without it that the limits of Bultmannian concern (O these concerns!) and confusion are gradually becoming visible and that some of our much discussed younger scholars are kind enough even to read *C.D.* and not just to talk about it without having read it. You, too, don't expect much of Pannenberg (whose christology I read thoroughly in Bethesda) unless he has the grace to undergo a radical conversion? I think that even the ravens I see on the top of a high tree from my seat here, though they do not do "biblical work," but whose wisdom I see in other things,[2] do not regard this work on christology as a good book.

I read with pleasure your clever survey of the baptismal question. Steady dripping will one day wear away this stone. Why is Martin Fischer, who is so excellent in other things, as G. Merz used to say, and whose work I took to heart, so obstinate in this matter? What was the dear Lord thinking about when in his inscrutable wisdom he also created Lutheranism, which is again and again a snare to the Germans?

[Barth now gave some family news, mentioned a discussion of Moltmann's *Theology of Hope*, and said he had received proofs of Jüngel's book[3] which criticized Gollwitzer in terms of *C.D.* He also reported that his former writing desk was now an object of devotion in the library

of Pittsburgh Theological Seminary, having been replaced by one worthy
of a bank-director.]

[1]*Post Bultmann locutum. Eine Diskussion zwischen Prof. D. H. Gollwitzer, Berlin,
und Prof. D. H. Braun, Mainz, am 13. Februar 1964 in der Johannes-Gutenberg-Univ.
zu Mainz am Rhein*, 2 vols. (Hamburg-Bergstedt, 1965).
[2]Original text unclear.
[3]E. Jüngel, *Gottes Sein ist im Werden. Verantwortliche Rede vom Sein Gottes bei
Karl Barth. Eine Paraphrase* (Tübingen, 1965).

*   *   *

183
To Prof. Wilhelm Loew
Mainz

Basel, 3 March 1965

[Barth gave an account here of his physical ailments, expressed sympathy with Loew in his troubles, spoke of his great-grandson, commented on the irrationality of German politics, and told Loew he was
now reading Goethe again, especially in comparison with Mozart. Contemplating death, Barth spoke of moving very near and "looking at the
point where one can count only on hope, in which, of course, one may
still be cheerful." He also told Loew that Mainz now reminded him of
Braun and Mezger. "Shall we live to see the end of the blossoming of
the company of Korah to which they belong? It seems the apocalyptic
vision of Father W. Herrmann, in which positive and liberal theology
share a common grave,[1] must be fulfilled again. At the moment we are
dealing with a remarkable restoration of the situation around 1910.
Only a new Martin Rade[2] is missing from the picture."]

[1]W. Herrmann, "Christliche-protestantische Dogmatik," *Die Kultur der Gegenwart. Ihre Entwicklung und ihre Ziele* (ed. P. Hinneberg), Vol. I, Sec. IV, 2 (Berlin/Leipzig,
1906), pp. 583-630.
[2]M. Rade (1857-1940), an uncle of Loew's wife, had taught both Barth and Loew at
Marburg.

*   *   *

184
To Prof. Ernst Wolf
Göttingen

Basel, 23 March 1965

Dear Ernst,

I am not yet completely well but remarkably better and so you will be very welcome here. If Monday 5 April is convenient, you can be helpful to us in a little gathering (three to five P.M.) of older and younger scholars in which we shall be dealing with chapter five of Moltmann's *Theology of Hope*. So far I have found the book an interesting but unripe fruit, though much better than Pannenberg's *Christology*. At the moment I am at work on the second volume of Käsemann.[1] He seems to be on the right lines. If only he would explain somewhere to what class of beasts or plants the mythological figure of the historian belongs.

With warm greetings also from Lollo and to Asta,

Yours,
KARL BARTH

[In a postscript Barth asked Wolf if he knew Hans Kressel's biography of Simon Schöfel,[2] a priceless specimen of Lutheranism.]

[1]E. Käsemann, *Exegetische Versuche und Besinnungen*, II (Göttingen, 1964).
[2]H. Kressel, *Simon Schöfel* . . . (Schweinfurt, 1964).

*   *   *

185
To General Secretary Gerald Götting
Berlin

Basel, 23 March 1965

[Barth apologized for not replying earlier to Götting's letter of 14 Dec. 1964, and thanked him for sending a calendar of icons. He commented on the foolish foreign policy of Bonn but recommended *Blätter für deutsche und internationale Politik* (Pahl-Rugenstein Verlag, Cologne, from 1956 on) as a ground of hope.]

*   *   *

186
To Mrs. Ludmilla Gowalezyk
Augsburg[1]

Basel, 7 April 1965

Dear Mrs. Gowalezyk,

That seventy-nine years ago I was baptized as an infant—like the vast majority of all Christians from the third or fourth century on—is one of the many disorders from which the church suffers. I have opposed this disorder. But I have never maintained that baptism administered in this disorder is not valid baptism. What was said to me back then, unfortunately without my being asked or able to reply, *was* said, and therefore I do not see why I should replace that baptism by another and second one. I regarded and still regard it as more correct and important to take my one baptism very seriously. Part of this requires calling on the church to remedy the disorder in the future.

With friendly greetings,

Yours,
KARL BARTH

[1]As a member of a community teaching believer's baptism the recipient had expressed to Barth her pleasure at his repudiation of infant baptism and asked him why he did not have the courage to be baptized afresh.

*   *   *

187
To Prof. Ernst Sommerlath
Markkleeberg/Leipzig

Basel, 8 April 1965

[As editor of *ThLZ* Sommerlath had asked Barth for a piece, for example, one on Mozart and Goethe, and also for a review of Hammer's book *Eine religiöse Deutung Mozarts*. Barth declined on grounds of health and referred to a good review of Hammer in *NZZ* on 14 March.]

*   *   *

188
To Prof. Hans Küng
Tübingen

Basel, 22 April 1965

Dear Dr. Küng,

Perhaps you will be interested in the enclosed survey of the Council, not least in view of the statement by the Westphalian peasant.[1]

I have read with even more pleasure your meditation on freedom.[2] A sufficiently enlightened Evangelical Christian could have written all of it—or almost all. But who concretely are the superiors and who the subordinates? Precisely at this important point your text seems to go astray on p. 38. Even with the best will in the world I could not understand what you say there.

We remember your visit with pleasure. Come again.

With warm greetings,

Yours,
KARL BARTH

P.S. Greet Miss Odette Zurmühle, too, and tell her how much we like her.

[1]Though Küng could not recall what paper the extract was from, he remembered the peasant saying, "Let those in the Council at Rome decide what they will, I remain a Catholic."

[2]H. Küng, *Kirche in Freiheit* (*Theologische Meditationen*, 6; Einsiedeln, 1964).

*   *   *

189
To Prof. Alfred de Quervain
Zollikofen near Bern

Basel, 28 April 1965

[Barth told Quervain of his medical problems but expressed thanks for the skill of his doctors and the friendly and patient care of the deaconesses and other sisters at Bethesda hospital. He still had no desire to write and could do little but keep up with what was going on in the theological world.]

*   *   *

190
To Sister Louise Gallmann
Riehen

Basel, 1 May 1965

Dear Sister Louise,

Your charming bouquet of flowers has reached me safely and I thank you sincerely for them. That you could not come personally is a source of grief, but you see, my state of health is not of the best and visits have to be limited to the most essential.

I read with great pleasure what you told me about the answers of your children under instruction.

And now you, too, have begun reading Teilhard de Chardin. You have a remarkable liking, and also the gifts, for such excursions in foreign lands.

So far as I know not much has remained of the so-called scattered sayings of Jesus. I agree that it is puzzling that in the Gospels there is hardly a passage where one can think of him as having laughed. There must be a reason for this but off-hand I could not name it.

With friendly greetings and all good wishes,

Yours,
KARL BARTH

*   *   *

191
To Prof. Ernst Wolf
Göttingen

Basel, 6 May 1965

Dear Ernst,

In the newspaper yesterday (5 May) I read the report of an academic festival in the German capital in which I am to be honored by Bonn University, but since I cannot take part due to the state of my health you are to give a lecture about me at this event early in June. To me the news in every detail is "fabulously *new*," as Albert Lempp used to say.[1] Can you tell me briefly what is going on and what is to go on?[2] Television here already seems to know of the arrival of an "important personality" on 10 May and is holding itself ready to capture the scene.

With warm greetings (also to Asta),

Yours,
KARL BARTH

[1]Albert Lempp (1884-1943), proprietor of the C. Kaiser Verlag, Munich.
[2] On 16 July 1965 the Theology Faculty of Bonn University celebrated the thirtieth anniversary of the dismissal of Barth from his Bonn professorship by the National Socialist state. Wolf gave a lecture (unpublished) on "Karl Barth's Entlassung. Die Tragödie einer Fakultät."

*   *   *

192
To Prof. Eberhard Jüngel
Berlin

Basel, 3 November 1965

Dear Dr. Jüngel,

I was pleased by the message of sympathy sent by you and your seminar and noted with interest your attempt to think out the sacrament and sacraments.[1] Everything seems to be in good order if I read and understand it aright. I could wish, of course, that the word sacrament could be commemorated in Evangelical theology for some decades only for irenical and polemical purposes but not used any more constitutively. A languages hostel might well be the right place for such a purification. Have you by chance heard anything about Bultmann's present life and work? Since Paul Tillich's death[2] he and I are the last and rather decayed pillars of an older generation. What is Ernst Fuchs doing? I have had only vague accounts of his further wanderings.[3] As for me, I was provisionally released five days ago from the hospital,[4] where I had some wonderful experiences (for a full four months)[5] as an object of modern medical science. I am now trying to resume contact with the rest of the world, both Christian and secular. With sincere greetings and thanks (also to the promising young people who signed the manifesto with you),

Yours,
KARL BARTH

[1]E. Jüngel, "Das Sakrament—was ist das?," *EvTh*, 26 (1966), 320-336. Jüngel had sent Barth the theses, 334-336.
[2]Paul Tillich died on 22 Oct. 1965.

[3]On 11 Dec. 1965 a discussion took place in Barth's home between himself and Fuchs, J. Fangmeier and H. Ott also taking part.
[4]Bürgerspital, Basel.
[5]19 June to 29 Oct. 1965.

*　　　*　　　*

193
To Pastor Richard Karwehl
Osnabrück

Basel, 5 November 1965

Dear Unforgotten and Unforgettable Friend,

[Barth reported to Karwehl on his illness, his need of a catheter, and his inability to do certain things. However, he gave thanks for his recovery, said he could do all the more important things, and told of his reading theology, singing hymns, smoking his pipe, and reading not only the Bible but also—Goethe.]

*　　　*　　　*

194
To Prof. Niels Hansen Søe
Copenhagen

Basel, 6 November 1965

Dear Colleague,

I understand you will celebrate your seventieth birthday on 29 Nov. Being now not far from the other limit set in the Psalm, I must not fail to salute you on that day and express my sincere good wishes for the years still granted to you.

Concerning baptism and some other articles of faith, we have not been and are not of the same opinion. But we are one in trusting the promise which is given us in the articles. And you should know that I have always respected and valued your work from afar.

Excuse me if I must be content with these few lines. I have a four month stay in the hospital behind me in which I had to practice Christian ethics[1] as best I could.

In sincere fellowship,

Yours,
KARL BARTH

[1]An allusion to Søe's chief work: *Christliche Ethik. Ein Lehrbuch* (Munich, 1949; 2nd ed., 1957); Danish original, *Kristelig Etik*, 1942.

*　　　　*　　　　*

195
To Pastor Günter Schwenzel and Mrs. Lieselotte Schwenzel
Darmstadt

Basel, 8 November 1965

[Barth told the Schwenzels about his illness but was thankful to God and men that he was still alive and could read, talk, smoke, sing psalms and chorales, listen to Mozart, and rejoice in his fourteen grandchildren. He had had a long and refreshing phone conversation with Gollwitzer, who was at the time in St. Blasien in the Black Forest, and heard a broadcast from an unfamiliar place in Zurich Canton which was not a flop but a sign that the good Lord is not dead as theological fools say.]

*　　　　*　　　　*

196
To Prof. Ernst Wolf
Göttingen

Basel, 15 November 1965

[Barth thanked Wolf for a card from the Walchensee, for a letter, and for a copy of his speech on 16 July (cf. 191, n. 2), which he had shown to Christoph and Marie-Claire Barth. Barth had three observations on the address (with its publication in view):]

1. The sub-title "tragedy" seems to me to be too weighty for the depicted proceedings. Would not "tragi-comedy" or the like be enough?

2. I have never forgotten for a moment that I am Swiss. I was a true dual citizen, and with the cunning all of us then exercised, and had to exercise in every matter, I could play on this or that of my two nationalities as the *kairos* required.

3. You write that during the Third Reich you never gave the required Hitler salute. But I have a pretty little photo (the setting seems to be the room on the Franziskanerstrasse in Bonn) which shows you bashfully but unmistakably making the salute.[1] Perhaps other copies of this photo have survived the storms of the period. Be careful, then, that no one trips you up with it.

[Barth went on to speak of his reading Goethe and a big volume on the American Civil War. He also noted what he called "the foolish book of the son Haering (Tübingen) on his father [T. Haering, 1848-1928] with his many sorties against me." He expressed pleasure at a recent declaration of the German Evangelical Church on relations with the East and then went on to give a detailed account of his medical problems. He mentioned the fate of his old desk,[2] and closed by mentioning the inscription (*Hic verbum caro factum est*) which Tillich had found in Nazareth and did not like. Tillich, he said, "will now know better, and one day we [. . .] shall know even better."]

[1]In his reply on 22 Nov. 1965 Wolf explained that when the photo was taken he had given an address on the question of academic salutation and as a result had never exchanged the salutation with his classes either in Bonn or Halle.

[2]Barth's desk has stood in the foyer of the library of the Pittsburgh Theological Seminary since 1964. Barth himself wrote the inscription; see Appendix, 11.

*　　　*　　　*

197
To Prof. Oscar Cullmann
Rome

Basel, 25 November 1965

Dear Friend,

Sincerest thanks for your letter of the twenty-first. What you think of the Council (forward, backward, etc., and then a few centimeters or millimeters again in the right direction) corresponds exactly to my impression from a distance. I follow all that goes on very intently. Gerhard Sauter, whom I have known very well so far, has just sent me his book on the future.[1] I have not yet looked into it. Yesterday, I received Hermann Kutter's book on his father,[2] brought by the author. Since my discharge from the hospital I have had some good days, God be praised. But I shall no longer be able to teach or write anything of significance. Yet on 12 Dec., in the watchful presence of my (Roman Catholic) physician, I hope to preach again to the spirits in prison.[3]

With all good greetings and wishes,

Yours,
KARL BARTH

[1]G. Sauter, *Zukunft und Verheissung. Das Problem der Zukunft in der gegenwär-tigen theologischen und philosophischen Diskussion* (Zurich, 1965).
[2]H. Kutter, Jr., *Das Lebenswerk Hermann Kutters* (Zurich, 1965).
[3]The engagement finally had to be cancelled.

*　　　*　　　*

198
To Prof. Katsumi Takizawa
Fukuoka (Japan), at Göttingen

Basel, 12 January 1966

[Barth thanked the recipient for a gift of flowers and an accompanying letter, describing him as a loyal student and friend. He explained that he was now looking into the family tree with a view to an autobiography, but did not expect this to be translated into English or Japanese. He had decided to do no more work on *C.D.*]

*　　　*　　　*

199
To Pastor Martin Gabriel
Halberstadt

Basel, 14 January 1966

Dear Pastor,

Not until yesterday did I come upon the friendly letter you sent my wife on 26 November 1965. Sincere thanks for your sympathetic re-membrances. Those were indeed testing times that I had to go through (three times to the hospital and two operations), and perhaps they still lie ahead. But I have always said and still say to myself continually that the good Lord and the angels probably wanted and continue to want to see whether I am able in a small way to live out some of the fine things I have written about these past fifty years. For the moment at least, I can still sit at my desk, read, do a few minor things, and enjoy the much love shown me by near and distant friends.

I did not know the little work by Claudius that you sent. It is very good and I will put it in my own exposition of the Lord's Prayer which came out in 1965.[1]

If I am not mistaken Halberstadt was the place where I gave my lecture on Wilhelm Herrmann to the Friends of the Christian World in 1925.[2] An inspired man of that persuasion opened the service before the address with the words from Goethe about the sun singing its song in ancient style. . . .[3] Those were the days!

Greet Schröter,[4] Langhoff,[5] and others in East Germany who would like to be greeted by me. Sincere greetings to yourself,

Yours,
KARL BARTH

[1] Matthias Claudius, *Über das Gebet, an meinem Freund Andres*; K. Barth, *Das Vaterunser nach den Katechismen der Reformation* (Zurich, 1965); trans. from the French, *La prière* . . . (Neuchatel/Paris, 1949).
[2] K. Barth, "Die dogmatische Prinzipienlehre bei Wilhelm Herrmann" (lecture at Hanover on 13 May and Halberstadt 17 May 1925), in *Die Theologie und die Kirche*, II (Munich, 1928), pp. 280-284. Cf. K. Barth/E. Thurneysen, *Briefwechsel*, Vol. II, *1921-1930* (Zurich, 1974), pp. 330f.
[3] Goethe, *Faust*, Prolog im Himmel (v. 243f.: "Die Sonne tönt nach alter Weise in [Barth adds "der"] Brudersphären Wettgesang."
[4] Dr. Fritz Schröter (1904-1973), from 1955 to 1971 Senior of the Reformed Churches in the Evangelical Church of the Province of Saxony.
[5] Pastor Heinz Langhoff, from 1957 to 1972 Moderator of the Reformed Churches in the Evangelical Church of Berlin-Brandenburg.

*   *   *

200

To Corps Commandant Dr. Alfred Ernst
Muri

Basel, 15 January 1966

[Barth referred to his reading of Alice Meyer's *Anpassung oder Widerstand* (Frauenfeld, 1965) on Swiss policy toward Hitler in 1940: "a good book by a woman who still cannot do what any fool of a man can do and often does not do, i.e., vote." He learned from it the role of a certain Captain Ernst in advocating resistance and of the importance of his own lesser role at the time. He reported to Ernst the illness of Charlotte von Kirschbaum; he could do only minimal work now that he had to be his own secretary. In a long postscript he told the story of his being awarded "The King's Medal for Service in the Cause of Freedom" in 1952. As a state employee he was not allowed to receive the award, but the British consul told him that "when the king has conferred a medal on someone it is conferred, and it will thus remain in Basel" (cf. the illustration in

C.D. IV, 1, p. 312). After his retirement he went to the consulate, the medal was bestowed, and he wore it proudly when receiving the Sonning Prize in Copenhagen and the honorary doctorate in Paris, though not when he was operated on in Bethesda Hospital!]

*   *   *

201
To Corps Commandant Dr. Alfred Ernst
Muri[1]

Basel, 22 January 1966

[Barth had learned that Ernst had had to cancel a lecture through sickness and sent good wishes for his recovery. He recalled the animosity he had aroused in some circles by his censored lecture "Im Namen Gottes, des Allmächtigen!" (*Eine Schweizer Stimme, 1938-1945;* Zollikon-Zurich, 1945) on the occasion of the 650th anniversary of the Swiss Confederacy. In reply to Ernst's remark that in assessing the situation in 1940 one must seek the truth somewhere in the middle, Barth pointed out that in such cases the truth is to be sought either on the right hand or the left, or perhaps a little more on the one hand than the other, and therefore *not* in the middle.]

[1][A response to Ernst's letter of 20 January 1966; see Appendix, 12.]

*   *   *

202
To Mrs. Elise Hilfiker-Diriwächter
Safenwil

Basel, 12 February 1966

Dear Mrs. Hilfiker,

Your letter did me good and I thank you for it. When I first saw it I asked myself, Who is E. Hilfiker-Diriwächter? But then I saw the number 95 and said, That is the year-group of my first confirmation class in Safenwil, and so it can be none other than Elisi Diriwächter, who listened to me in those days with such bright little eyes, and who, at the festival in Zofingen in 1961, made such a fine little speech in answer to the critical words of old Mr. Widmer.[1] Right? And now you are in the hospital and expecting an operation. Well, I have been very sick these past years, three times in the hospital, and have survived two operations with God's help. Do not be afraid. God will help you too, and doctors today are very clever.

You can see me on the enclosed prospectus and will note how the inexperienced young parson of those days looks today. He, too, has been through a lot since that time.

With sincere greetings and all good wishes to you and your husband,

Your former pastor,
KARL BARTH

[1]Cf. 13.

*　　　*　　　*

203
To N.N
Denmark[1]

Basel, 1 March 1966

Dear N.N.,

My sincere sympathies in the deep sorrow you are now feeling.

My reply to your question is as follows: We read in John 1:10 that he (Christ) was in the *world* and the *world* was made by him.

John 3:17: God sent his Son . . . that the *world* might be saved through him.

John 6:51: . . . my flesh which I (Christ) shall give for the life of the *world*.

2 Cor 5:19: God was in Christ and reconciled the *world* to himself.

Rev 11:15: Dominion over the *world* has been given to our Lord and his anointed (Christ).

John 1:29: Behold, this is the Lamb of God, which bears the sin of the *world*.

1 John 2:2: He is the expiation for our sins, yet not for ours only, but also for those of the *whole world*.

In the Bible the *world* is *all* humanity. If Jesus Christ is and does what we read here, then he also prays for *all* men: for those who *already* pray and those who do *not yet* pray.

With friendly greetings,

Yours,
KARL BARTH

[1]N.N., who had lost his wife, had read in Barth's *Vaterunser* (Zurich, 1965, p. 41) that Jesus prays for all humanity and he had asked Barth to mention some verses in the Bible which tell us this.

* * *

204
To Mrs. Margrit Brunner
Zurich

Basel, 7 March 1966

Dear Mrs. Brunner,

Your letter and the two appended lines by Emil[1] touched me very much. Tell him the time is long past when I shout No to him or anybody. We all can and should be glad to have a God who without any merits on our part says Yes to each of us in his own way.

Thanks to the care bestowed on me by Prof. Koller and other fine doctors, I am fairly well. The only thing is that I have to combat an inexplicable sadness which all the successes life brought me can do nothing at all to allay. Tell Emil that I live by nothing but the promise, Blessed are those who mourn, for they shall be comforted. He too should cling wholly to that. In a few weeks I shall be eighty years old and I wish that the celebration with all its speeches and articles, etc., were over. But with God's help I shall get through this, too.

If only I were a little better I would come over to exchange a few words with Emil. Greet him from me, and greetings to yourself, dear Mrs. Brunner. Thanking you for your letter, with all good wishes,

Yours,
KARL BARTH

[1]Prof. Emil Brunner had been ill in the Neumünster Hospital, Zurich, since 12 December 1965. He died there 6 April 1966.

* * *

205
To Two Ladies in Zurich

Basel, 16 March 1966

Dear Mrs. R. and Mrs. Sch.,

You have both written me about N.N.'s lecture. Naturally what the man seems to have said is poor and silly teaching. But you should not get too worked up or upset by it. It is not just today but in every age that such poor witness has been given in the Christian church. The gospel has always proved to be stronger; if only there were still people who would believe its truth simply but firmly and cheerfully and who would try to live according to its direction. This is what you, too, must now do. N.N. had a very orthodox father and now like a wild colt he must kick out for a time against the recollections of his youth. Perhaps he, too, will one day come to a different mind. Meanwhile we may rejoice and be thankful that even among the younger pastors in Switzerland there are today not a few who tread a better path and who indeed can represent and proclaim the true gospel better than was done fifty years ago. Cling to the fact that the good Lord is definitely not dead.

With friendly greetings and best wishes for the Good Friday and Easter season,

Yours,
KARL BARTH

* * *

206
To Mrs. Elise Hilfiker-Diriwächter
Safenwil

Basel, 1 April 1966

Dear Elisi Diriwächter,

I am simply going to use "Du" again like fifty-four years ago. Your letter gave me much pleasure and I was glad to hear the operation went well. Yesterday the T.V. people were here and told me they had talked with you and photographed you. If I am right all this and much else will be put on display to the world on 28 April (though this has yet to be decided). The two of us never thought, did we, that one day we should have become so famous? Don't speak too badly about good old Mr. Widmer. I simply laughed that day in Zofingen. But that you spoke up for me so bravely was very good of you. Greet all the members of your class, with sincere greetings and all good wishes for your health,

Your old pastor,
KARL BARTH

P.S. Why do you not attend church better? I know your present pastor and regard him as a good man.

*   *   *

207
To Pastor Peter Vogelsanger
Zurich

Basel, 4 April 1966

Dear Pastor,

Your letter of the second[1] touched me greatly—also because you wrote it.[2]

If I were more active after my two-year illness I would take the next train to press Emil Brunner's hand again.

If he is still alive and it is possible, tell him I commend him to *our* God. And tell him the time when I thought I should say No to him is long since past, and we all live only by the fact that a great and merciful God speaks his gracious Yes to all of us.[3]

With sincere thanks and greetings,

Yours,
KARL BARTH

P.S. Please give my greetings to Mrs. Brunner too.

---

[1] Vogelsanger, after a visit to Emil Brunner's sick-bed, sent a long letter to Barth on his serious condition, 2 April 1966.

[2] According to Vogelsanger, his hitherto good relation with Barth had been disrupted after the founding of the paper *Reformatio*, which Vogelsanger edited and whose policy Barth did not approve of.

[3]Vogelsanger received Barth's letter on the morning of 5 April, rushed to the hospital, where Brunner was weak but alive and conscious, and read the letter with Barth's greeting. A slight but beautiful smile came over Brunner's features and he quietly pressed Vogelsanger's hand. A few minutes later Brunner went into a coma from which he did not awake, dying peacefully near midday on 6 April. Barth's seems to have been his last earthly greeting.

*   *   *

208
To Prof. Eberhard Jüngel
Berlin

Basel, 13 April 1966

Dear Colleague,

On 9 May my eightieth birthday will be celebrated here in Basel.

I should be very pleased to see you among the invited guests because I have learned to know you as one among today's younger theologians who has studied me thoroughly and has the willingness and ability to do independently and fruitfully the further work which is needed today.

Please do all you can to make your appearance on the above occasion a reality.

With sincere greetings,

Yours,
KARL BARTH

*   *   *

209
To Mrs. Margrit Brunner
Zurich

Basel, 16 April 1966

Dear Mrs. Brunner,

You have perhaps wondered why I did not write at once on receiving news of the death of your husband.[1] But you know from my previous correspondence with yourself and Pastor Vogelsanger[2] that my thoughts were genuinely with him in his passing. And I for my part have been recollecting at least some of the things, both good and not so good, that happened to him.

Naturally I have been considering, too, the question how it really was, and how it came to be, between him and me. How glad I would be to have you tell me personally and orally how our relation appeared from his and your standpoint. From my standpoint the fact was that God not only led him and me on very different paths, but in his unfathomable goodness and wisdom willed us already to be very different people—so different that properly there could be no question at all of strife or suffering between us. And yet we did strive and suffer on both sides. And if I am right he suffered more at my hands than I did at his, once I had let off steam in 1934. Naturally I have read and pondered all that he wrote and published afterwards, but it never bothered me, at least not in such a way that I felt any need to attack him or to defend myself against him. From my standpoint the situation was simply this: I was so busy with the task set for me that I had no time for continual quarreling with him. Perhaps that was what caused him suffering as far as I was concerned? Perhaps you can say something that might shed light on the matter? And if it should be that I did more, and offended him with positive words or acts that I no longer remember, please do not hesitate, dear Mrs. Brunner, to draw my attention to them. I write all this because I am almost eighty years old and would like to have as clear as possible a picture of my responsibility in relation to this part of my past. But do not let yourself be upset by this question which the death of your husband has raised for me. If you are ready to reply at all, give yourself plenty of time.

With sincere sympathies in your great sorrow,

Yours,
KARL BARTH

[1] Emil Brunner died on 6 April 1966.
[2] See 204 and 207.

*　　　　*　　　　*

210
To Prof. Helmut Gollwitzer
Berlin

Basel, 23 April 1966

Dear Helmut,

Yesterday evening the parcel arrived with complimentary copies of "our" book on Job.[1] I thank you sincerely for your dedication and for the great amount of work you have done a second time on my behalf. I also admire your skill in seizing on what is important as this comes to light in your introduction and the transitions. Your account of the very different book on Job by Bloch[2] naturally interested me too. But— yes, but! I know, Helmut, that one should not look a gift-horse in the mouth. But what if one finds that the gift-horse has only three legs instead of four? You wanted to give people my exposition of Job as such. But where are pp. 522-531 [ET 453-461]; where are my illuminating elucidations of the theology of the three friends?![3] An able scholar like you could hardly fail to see that the whole point is to be found on these pages. And now you leave them out, although in your version on p. 68 you expressly refer to a fourth time that I turn to the book of Job. And no hint as to the reason for this omission! I really cannot think what reason there could be. Helmut, how could you? Nelly can bear witness that all through our mid-day meal I was complaining about you and your wicked act. And if you were not you, I would publicly protest somewhere against this being regarded as my exposition of Job. I can still only weep quietly at the irreparable damage that has been done.

Well, in spite of it all, in friendship and therefore with warm greetings,

Yours,

Karl Barth

[1] K. Barth, *Hiob*, ed. H. Gollwitzer, Bibl. Studien 49 (Neukirchen, 1966); a reprint of the exegetical excursuses of *C.D.* IV, 3 § 70, 1, with introduction and connecting summaries of the dogmatic material by the editor.
[2] E. Bloch, "Studien zum Buche Hiob," *Auf gespaltenem Pfad. Festschr. z. 90. Geburtstag von Margarete Susman*, ed. M. Schlösser (Darmstadt, 1964), pp. 85-102.
[3] Gollwitzer had inadvertently overlooked the fourth excursus on Job. It was printed separately in *Nachtrag zur Biblischen Studie Nr. 49*.

*   *   *

211
To Prof. Ernst Wolf
Göttingen

Basel, 21 May 1966

Dear Ernst,

In the last four weeks such an unbelievable amount has been going on around me that I hardly recall to whom among the interviewers and

T.V. people I said and eventually promised what. So Dr. Brenneke can do what he wants with the interview.[1] Is it the one in which I said something about the eastern frontier?[2] With reference to this I received a slanderous anonymous letter in which I was addressed as a worthless old fellow; it would be a good thing if I were to die soon and not see the glorious restoration of the German empire. The author also promised me that I shall be greeted by a bomb. Three (or two and one-half) important men from East Germany spent three and one-half hours with me: Götting, Seigewasser, and the Union Press man Wirth.[3] They came in a frightful car of Russian make (visible to the residents of the Bruderholz for three and one-half hours in front of my house) and laden with gifts like the three wise men from the east (Meissen china, etc.). I was not able to get permission for Bishop Scharf to come.[4] The chaplaincy agreement[5] played a more decisive role in this respect than I had expected.

With sincere greetings to you and Asta,

Yours,
KARL BARTH

P.S. I have just received word of the death of P. Althaus.[6]

---

[1]Wolf had passed on to Barth the request of Dr. Gerhard Brennecke of East Berlin for permission to print an eightieth birthday interview between M. Linz and Barth. Brennecke published it under the title "Kirche und Theologie heute. Ein Gespräch mit Professor Karl Barth," in *Die Zeichen der Zeit*, 20 (1966), 285-289.

[2]Ibid., p. 288.

[3]Götting was General Secretary of the Christian Democratic Union of East Germany. H. Seigewasser was Secretary for Church Affairs in the East German government. For Barth's eightieth birthday the Union Verlag of East Berlin published the collection *Karl Barth, Klärung und Wirkung. Zur Vorgeschichte der K.D. und zum Kirchenkampf,* ed. W. Feurich (Berlin, 1966).

[4]Kurt Scharf of Brandenburg had been forbidden re-entry to East Germany after a visit to West Berlin and later (on 1 January 1973) his bishopric was limited to that part of his diocese in West Berlin.

[5]This agreement had been worked out between West Germany and the Evangelical Church in Germany on 22 February 1957, and regulations for Evangelical military chaplaincies in West Germany were issued by the church on 8 March 1957.

[6]P. Althaus died 18 May 1966. Althaus had written a letter of sympathy to Barth on his illness on 3 March 1965 but Barth's reply on 5 March 1965, his last letter to Althaus, has not been found.

*　　　*　　　*

212
To Prof. Hans Küng
Tübingen

Basel, 21 May 1966

Dear Colleague,

Many thanks for your note, invitations, and *excellent* enclosures. All honor to Miss O.'s[1] photography. It is just a pity she herself is not seen on any of the snaps or at least did not focus more on the other lady[2] than on my weathered head. I have been reading these days the *Theologia Protestantium* that the Gregorian Witte[3] presented to his listeners. What poor stuff! I will write a letter soon to Cardinal Bea[4] to ask him modestly whether my visit planned for the end of September will be welcome (not to speak but to listen to the clever people in the Vatican and its environs). Perhaps you can also give me a tip some time about whom I should hear, if God wills and we live. But since I shall be accompanied by my Roman Catholic doctor and a Roman Catholic nursing sister my earthly frame at least should be secure. With warm greetings (also to be passed on to Miss O.),

Yours,

KARL BARTH

P.S. I swim in an ocean of about 1000 letters and 150 telegrams, and am provided with enough cigars (for guests) and tobacco (for myself) for the rest of my life.[5]

[1]Odette Zurmühle, Küng's secretary at the time.
[2]Another guest during Barth's visit to Küng in Sursee on 26 April 1966.
[3]J. Witte, S.J., *De Theologia Protestantium* (Rome, 1964-5).
[4]See 213.
[5]Greetings and gifts for his eightieth birthday.

*   *   *

213
To Augustine Cardinal Bea

Basel, 2 June 1966

Dear Cardinal,

You may recall that you were once kind enough to ask me, through Prof. Küng of Tübingen, whether I might possibly accept a personal invitation to take part in the Council as an observer.[1] To my deep regret I could not give an affirmative answer at the time because I was in the middle of a serious sickness. This did not prevent me from sympathetically following the labors of the Council from a distance and pondering its results so far as they were accessible to me. Since then, even though I am still under medical supervision and need all kinds of attention, my health has substantially improved and with it my mobility.

And now I have a lively desire to come to Rome, at least *post festum*, in order to learn what are the thoughts of the Vatican and its immediate environs, the central precincts of the Roman Catholic church and its theology, as it looks back on the finished Council and looks ahead from it. On this the following observations:

1. I should very much like to get in touch with you personally, honored Cardinal, and with the other most important personalities representing all the current tendencies within the authoritative ecclesiastical and theological circles in Rome.

2. I should come to Rome solely on my own personal responsibility, with no commission from any academic or ecclesiastical court, and personally not as a Protestant but simply as an Evangelical Christian and theologian who, like yourself, honored Cardinal, is concerned about the unity of faith and church which we seek but which is also to a large extent already present.

3. My aim would not be to speak in Rome but as much as possible to listen, to receive, to understand, to learn, and only perhaps to reply appropriately to any questions that might be put to me.

4. I have no journalistic purpose in planning this trip and obviously I will treat with the highest discretion anything I might come to hear.

5. Since my health, as noted, is not fully restored, I shall not be able to do without medical and nursing assistance on the journey. My physician, Dr. Alfred Briellmann, and nursing sister N.N., both Roman Catholics of Swiss nationality, will thus accompany me. Since both of them share the interest that brings me to Rome, I should be pleased if they could be present at any interviews that might occur; indeed this is desirable in view of any assistance they might have to give me. This applies particularly if I might perhaps be granted an audience with His Holiness Pope Paul VI—which I ask for as a superadded gift. I can vouch for the discretion of the two as for my own.

6. As the time for our stay in Rome we have in mind the days between 22 and 29 September of the present year. In Rome we would lodge in a hotel near the Vatican.

It obviously cannot be taken for granted that you, honored Cardinal, take the same interest in my whole plan or that its execution at what is still some distance ahead is welcome. If it is, may I ask for your advice and recommendations, based on your exact knowledge of people and circumstance, in selecting from among the different possibilities available. In any case, please tell me in good time whether you regard my whole project as meaningful and acceptable.

In Christian fellowship, and with great respect for your person, plans, and activities in the service of our common Lord,

Greetings,
Yours truly,
KARL BARTH

[1]Cf. 113 and 144.

*   *   *

214
To Prof. Hans Küng
Tübingen

Basel, 16 June 1966

Dear Colleague,

Thanks for your many news items. Tomorrow, Friday the seventeenth, I expect a visit from J. Feiner[1] direct from the session of the Bea commission,[2] and today midday I expect one from a man from the Freiburg Salesianum.[3] As is apparent in the fine photographs of you and me that you sent, it cannot really be said I have no ecumenical concern. But what are we to think of the pigeon-holing of the five conciliar decrees?[4]

Your visit with the twelve on the twenty-fourth is noted.[5] You will be very welcome.

With sincere greetings to you and compliments to Miss O.,

Yours,
KARL BARTH

[1]Cf. 215.
[2]Theological advisers to Cardinal Bea, head of the Vatican Secretariat for Christian Unity.

KARL BARTH

³Theological hostel at Freiburg, Switzerland.
⁴Perhaps an allusion to the establishment of five new curial commissions to replace the council commissions of the same names, 3 January 1966.
⁵Visit by Küng and colleagues in the Institute for Ecumenical Research at Tübingen University, 24 June 1966.

*   *   *

215
To Prof. Johannes Feiner
Chur[1]

Basel, 18 June 1966

Dear Colleague,

I hope that yesterday you got back to Zurich in time on your TEE train. I have good memories of your visit. Thanks for giving me so much time.

How far are we really separated brethren? Your infallible teaching office, your Mary (without mariology), your strange genuflections before the transformed host as I have seen them when visiting St. Klausen's close by,[2] your use of holy water and the like—these we can quietly allow you, especially as you have yet to achieve unity among yourselves on these and other matters. Meanwhile you can quietly allow us the relative austerity of our worship and the danger of pushing ahead without a teaching office, notwithstanding the tricks of some of our theologians at the moment and other criticisms you might bring against us. As far as I myself am concerned, I shall come to Rome, according to the direction of the Council, with two Catholic lay persons, the one on my right and the other on my left.[3]

Regarding Isa 43:18f. I can give you comfort. Your "only" or "merely" runs dead against the wording and meaning of the passage. Yesterday evening I learned from my son, a professional Old Testament scholar,[4] that the former and past things do not refer to the election and deliverance of Israel but to the judgment which came on Israel in the form of the destruction of the temple; over against this stands the new thing in the form of the coming return from exile. In your context, then, the former and past things would be the anathemas of Trent, the St. Bartholomew massacre, the misdeeds of Henry VIII of England, the Villmergen wars[5] and the battle of Gislikon,[6] the shocking articles against the Jesuits and monasteries in the Swiss Constitution.[7]

For our accommodation in the Kolumbus it should be added that my room ought to have a private toilet as well as a bath so that the sister may be able to care for me as necessary at any time.

Yesterday I telephoned my doctor and wrote a note to the sister, who now works in Sursee, to tell them that God willing everything will be shipshape in Rome; I cannot be grateful enough to you and your people in the Secretariat for all your help.

Perhaps we shall meet again before then. For the time being, with very sincere greetings,

Yours,

KARL BARTH

[1]Barth came to know Feiner through the Rome trip; cf. 212f.
[2]The Roman Catholic Church on the Bruderholz, Basel.
[3]The doctor and nursing sister.
[4]Christoph Barth.
[5]Wars between Zurich and Bern on the one side and Schwyz and its allies on the other. Schwyz won the battle of Villmergen on 23 January 1556 and Zurich and Bern the battle of Villmergen on 25 July 1712.
[6]The battle of Gislikon on 23 November 1847 ended the brief attempt of the Roman Catholic cantons to defend cantonal sovereignty. They were defeated by federal troops under General G. H. Dufour.
[7]The Constitution of 1874, Arts. 51 and 52 (cf. K. Barth, "Jesuiten und Klöster. Die umstrittenen Verbote in der Schweizerischen Bundesverfassung," *National-Zeitung* [Basel], 7-8 October 1967, pp. 1f. The articles were repealed by referendum in 1973.

*　　　*　　　*

216
Circular Letter to Those Who Congratulated Barth on His Eightieth Birthday[1]

Basel, June 1966

Dear and Esteemed Sisters and Brothers, Friends, Ladies and Gentlemen,

The tenth of May and my transition from the eighth to the ninth decade of my allotted span is already a month behind me and therefore behind you, too. Many of you will have wondered—I hope with not too much concern—why I have not given some sign in the intervening period of having received all the good things that you conveyed to me by word of mouth and letter and telephone before, on, and after that day, and also all the fine presents that were sent in such overwhelming abundance.

The reason for the long delay was simply the abundance of all the beautiful and moving and in their different ways refreshing things that have descended on me like a pleasant and fruitful former and latter rain. Just consider: Apart from printed matter there were about 1000 longer and shorter letters, no less than 150 telegrams, and several dozen larger or smaller packets and even boxes; then the articles dedicated to me and whole anniversary numbers in papers and journals; and finally solemn but friendly addresses by whole bodies and organizations. All this— and how much printed material may have escaped me, since I neglected to hire an agency or the like for the occasion—had to be read, or partly read, and tasted and appreciated. And time was needed—is still needed— for this, as well as the span of attention and assimilation that is no longer at my disposal in old age. I say this to explain and excuse the delay. But the moment has come to end the delay and to reply to the many greetings at least in this form of countergreeting.

What shall I say? First and above all that I am thankful to God and men that around that day so many had friendly thoughts of me and wanted to bear such unmistakable witness to their sympathy with my life and work. As a whole and individually this great outpouring has truly touched me, as we often say today. And now I ask each of you who has taken part in this great expression and acclamation to take the thanks which I here convey in general and relate it very personally to yourself as an individual and to your part in the joyful refreshment prepared for me. I hope that no matter what may come to me in the future by way of joy or suffering, I shall never forget the kindness you have so richly lavished on me. I hope further that in the quieter sphere of my present life, so far as I can, I will prove to be worthy in some measure of the confidence displayed on every side by further confidence in God and further trust in the people around me. Do not be angry if I should sometimes fail again in the form of all kinds of ungrateful acts or omissions. I shall have to pray afresh each day for God's forgiveness and sanctification in respect of my great disregard of the grace that he has shown me all along, and therefore before, on, and after 10 May. May you, too, continue to hold me dear even though later on, as in the past, you do not always see me on the heights on which you saw or thought you saw me that day according to your very sincere statements.

I have just used the word *grace*. Along with all else the word may include, grace, for those who experience it, is always something unexpected, unmerited, non-self-evident. Thus the remarkable radiance with which I saw myself invested on my eightieth birthday, and for whose manifold rays, as I said, I thank both God and men, was really something astonishing for me.

One truly astonishing thing is that I have lived to see this day and thus become so old when so many of my former contemporaries in age and colleagues in debate, both near and far, have been no longer among us for longer or shorter periods. And this after a two-year time of sickness in the course of which it might have happened more than once that I would have to join the company of those who have passed on. This did not take place. To be sure, I still need constant oversight and care, but in body and mind I am more cheerful and even more mobile than I had been long before those two years. That is unexpected, unmerited, and non-self-evident grace.

Also astonishing to me was the depth and intensity of the wave of love, gratitude, and regard that overflowed me. While modesty has never been one of my outstanding qualities, I have never at any stage in my life thought much about the range of my life and work, and never at all in the last years. What have I done and accomplished—first as pastor and then as theological teacher and writer—but simply, like many others, the thing which (among diversions of many kinds) seemed to be precisely what was demanded, given, and possible in different periods, surroundings, and situations. And now, hardly escaped from the hospital, it has been surprisingly brought to my attention on my eightieth birthday that through the decades my little bits of thinking, speaking, and doing have had for many in the church, and even to some extent in the world, a significance which I myself, having the closest knowledge of what I can and cannot do, would never really have ascribed to them. Their known radius was greater than I had imagined. This is for me a very astonishing thing. Something must have happened that did not depend on my own qualities and achievements, so that I myself, as I was and as I am, was present only as an assistant or a nursing sister is present with his or her qualities and capabilities at an operation, and has to be so, while someone other and higher does the real work. Here again the unexpected, unmerited, and by no means self-evident grace of God must have been at work. And all the praise you have so kindly and generously lavished on me should really be the praise of this grace. Insofar as I received it in this sense, I could take real pleasure in it. That is what I did, and still do in recollection. It was a beautiful celebration and in understanding it in the way I have just explained, and in living through it with you all, I thank God first for all the dear people who helped to make it so beautiful for me, too.

To all to whom this is addressed, my sincere greetings and my wish that in the best sense all will go well with you in the service in which you stand, each in his own appointment and limits,

KARL BARTH

[1]First published in *JK*, 27 (1966), 409f.

* * *

217
To Prof. Hans Küng
Tübingen

Basel, 27 June 1966

[In this letter Barth recalled his meeting with Küng on 24 June. He asked whether they had been separated brethren or not when eating together. He commented on the work on Calvin, *Calvin und Vatikanum II* (Wiesbaden, 1965), by Küng's assistant, A. Ganoczy, noting that a Roman Catholic Calvin scholar (and friend) was new to him, and suggesting that Calvin might have approved of chaps. 1-7 of the constitution on Peter's office, but not of chap. 8, which Ganoczy wisely ignored. Having heard Bach's *Magnificat* the previous day he mentioned that the Magnificat was the one great statement of Mary in the New Testament, but this Mary would surely have laughed at later mariology and such friends as Ratzinger and Hasenhüttl, an assistant of Küng's who had indulged in mariological speculation during the discussion. Barth enclosed a copy of Fra Filippo Lippi's *Madonna* to show how he thought Mary would view such matters. He advised Küng not to use the word *revolution* in relation to the Council.]

* * *

218
To Prof. Johannes Feiner
Chur

Arbaz s.Sion, 10 July 1966

[Barth thanked Feiner for making arrangements for his Rome visit, and asked him also to thank P. Magnus Löhrer, professor at the Pontificium

Athenaeum Anselmianum in Rome. He asked that some time might be allotted for a meeting with the Waldensians, suggesting this might be arranged through his former student Valdo Vinay, professor of church history on the Facolta Valdese di Teologia in Rome. He expressed surprise at Ratzinger's understanding of Mary as mediatrix in his introduction to the *Dogmatische Konstitution über die Kirche* (Münster, 1965) and asked about its authenticity, on which Küng seemed to hesitate. He expressed pleasure at the way the Council's decisions were being implemented in worship in the area, and also at the curé's sermon, which he found both biblical and practical.]

*   *   *

219
To Prof. Hans Küng
Tübingen

Arbaz s.Sion, 16 July 1966

[Barth first told Küng he was enjoying his vacation and feeling much better. He expressed interest in the *Konzilsreden*, which Küng had edited with Y. Congar and D. O'Hanlon (Einsiedeln/Zurich/Cologne, 1964), and said he was recommending it all round, for example, to an obstinate Protestant like Walter Lüthi. He then continued:]

I liked much less Karl Rahner's book on Mary [*Maria, Mutter des Herrn*, Freiburg i.Br., 1965], though it dates back to 1953 and is thus a specimen of preconciliar theology. Nevertheless, I should have expected better of this author even then. [. . .] How do you explain the fact that he regards mariology (p. 79) as one of the central truths that the church has to proclaim? And how do you explain the other fact that in the *Konzilsreden*, so far as I can see, it is commemorated only once (p. 123)?

As concerns the *Reden*, I find the structure you have given to the widely differing material especially good. The only question is whether Paul VI arranged the program in this way. In his speeches I do not really find this to be so, at least not with the same logic and perspicuity.

You will be glad of the vacation, which now that I am retired I can enjoy without restriction.

With thanks and friendly greetings (also to Miss Odette),

Yours,
KARL BARTH

220
To Augustine Cardinal Bea
Rome

Arbaz s.Sion, 17 July 1966

Esteemed Cardinal,

You wrote me a friendly letter on 15 June. I have since been in personal and written contact with Msgr. Johannes Feiner in Chur, who has acquainted me with the careful arrangements that have partly been made and are partly being made to make my September visit materially fruitful.[1]

It is now for me, in my own name and that of those who will come with me, to express directly to you, Eminence, sincere thanks for the encouraging words with which you bade me welcome in your letter. I have been workng hard at additional detailed study of the Council texts, so far as they are available to me, and also of the most important decisions made at the Council. It is a pity that the convenient Aschendorff Latin-German edition of the definitively proclaimed constitutions[2] seems to be making such slow progress.

I greatly regret, Eminence, that I shall be able to see and speak with you only on the last days of the week. But it may be an advantage that I shall be able to talk with you only after meeting the other fathers and brethren. In view of the kindly attitude of yourself and your coworkers in the Unity Secretariat I have no doubt that this venture, which I have undertaken with an expressly friendly purpose, will, D.V., be rewarding for myself at least, and for the cause which is our common concern.

Meanwhile with respectful greetings,

Your devoted servant,
KARL BARTH

[1]Cf. 215 and 218.
[2]The official promulgations of Vatican II, 1964-1967.

*　　　　　*　　　　　*

221
To Eberhard Busch
Binningen (Basel-Land Canton)

Villa [La Sage], 21 July 1966

Dear Mr. Busch,

Many thanks for your letter and its rich contents. Your services to me (note how the Catholic literature I am steeping myself in is coloring my speech) are immeasurable. Is it clear you are invited to spend not one but many evenings in my house [. . .]?[1] I am doing very well at 1700 m. With the necessary caution I can even go higher. Escalation! And music is heard here too, on the stereo my son[2] has put in his chalet.

With sincere greetings, also to Miss B.,

Yours,
KARL BARTH

[1]Barth had given permission to his assistant E. Busch, with his fiancée Beate Blum, to use his study while he himself was on vacation.
[2]Markus Barth, in whose chalet in Valais Canton Barth spent part of his vacation.

*   *   *

222
To Miss Ingeborg Heitmann[1]
Bicken (Dillkreis)

Basel, 6 August 1966

Dear Miss Heitmann,

Since God does in fact address man in his Word, he obviously regards and treats him as addressable in spite of the fact that man as a sinner closes his ears and heart to him. And as God awakens man to faith by his Holy Spirit, he himself posits the necessary point of contact. But he is greater than our heart,[2] making the deaf to hear and the blind to see.[3] That's the way it is.

With friendly greetings,

Yours,
KARL BARTH

[1]In a letter dated 1 August 1966 Miss Heitmann had asked Barth for his view of the point of contact and man's ability to be addressed by the Word.
[2]1 John 3:20.
[3]Cf. Mark 7:37; Matt 11:5.

*   *   *

223
To Pastor Martin Vömel
Frankfurt am Main

Basel, 10 August 1966

Dear Pastor,

For the first fifty to one hundred pages Moltmann's *Theology of Hope* seemed to be such an olive leaf,[1] but not after that, because his hope is finally only a principle and thus a vessel with no contents. But the true dove, perhaps many doves with the true olive leaves, will come one day. Noah waits patiently and meantime is closely occupied with what is happening in Roman Catholicism (Vatican II). Do not let yourself be either disturbed or afraid.

With warm greetings and all good wishes,

Yours,

KARL BARTH

[1]An expression used by Vömel and relating to the interview, "Karl Barth sagt: 'Ich fühle mich wie Vater Noah,' " *Frankfurter Allgemeine Zeitung*, 16 May 1964.

*   *   *

224
To Prof. Gerhard Gloege
Bonn

August 1966

Dear Colleague,

May I reply in this summary fashion[1] to your letter of 1 May, which greatly touched and pleased me. I welcome the suggestion regarding Gogarten and have accordingly made a note for 1 January 1967.[2]

Thanks, sincere greetings, and all good wishes,

THE ABOVE

P.S. Do you have to retire?[3] I went on to seventy-five.

[1]A hand-written P.S. to a copy of the circular letter (216).
[2]Gloege had suggested Barth send greetings to his former friend Gogarten on the latter's eightieth birthday, and hinted that Gogarten would welcome them. In the end, Barth did not write because he could not strike the right note.
[3]Gloege, then sixty-five, had said he would be retiring soon.

*   *   *

225
To Pater Prof. Magnus Löhrer
Rome

Basel, 18 August 1966

[Barth thanked Löhrer for arranging the details of his Rome visit, told him that since his nurse could not come, his wife Nelly Barth would be replacing her, and asked for a corresponding change in the hotel reservations. He noted that H. U. von Balthasar had sent him a copy of *Mysterium Salutis* (ed. J. Feiner and M. Löhrer; Einsiedeln/Zurich/ Cologne, 1966) and that he hoped to study this along with the pile of conciliar materials still waiting his attention.]

*   *   *

226
To Dr. R. Meyendorf
Waldshut

Basel, 2 September 1966

Dear Fellow-Student Meyendorf,[1]

Your letter of 30 August delighted me in the best sense.

God is dead? Many things have been very earnestly advocated and have now vanished. "He who sits in heaven laughs at them,"[2] and we on earth should do the same.

Westfalenhalle?[3] An even greater abomination to me. The walls of Jericho will certainly not fall down through the blowing of the thousand trumpets there. Tillich? He was a charming man and you certainly need not burn his books. But I would advise you not to direct your devotion to his ground of being.

With friendly greetings,

Yours,
KARL BARTH

[1]In a letter dated 30 August 1966 Meyendorf, alluding to Barth's statement in *Evangelical Theology* that one is either a student of theology to one's death or has never been one at all, had addressed Barth as "Dear Theological Student."
[2]Ps 2:4.
[3]Mass demonstration of the movement "No Other Gospel" on 6 March 1966 in Dortmund. Cf. "Ein Brief Karl Barths zur 'Bekenntnisbewegung' " (16 March 1966), *JK*, 27 (1966), 327f., to be reprinted in the volume of Open Letters.

*　　　　*　　　　*

227
To Prof. Hans Küng
Tübingen

Basel, 16 September 1966

Dear Dr. Küng,

I have found a decisive proof of the correctness of your thesis re the reversal of the ecclesiastical pyramid.[1]

In the decree on the lay apostolate—why do Catholic authors always make this neuter, not masculine?—at the end of Art. 4 Mary is called the perfect example of spiritual and apostolic life and also the queen of the apostles,[2] i.e., the queen even of Peter and his college and therefore of the whole hierarchy. Does it not follow unavoidably that the lay apostolate is superior to the hierarchy? May mariology live—in this case!

I find the declaration on religious freedom[3] absolutely terrible. Could you do nothing to stop this monstrosity? I have formulated some pertinent or impertinent questions on it which I will try to put to someone in Rome,[4] though naturally not to His Holiness himself.

Before you leave try to keep a day for a meeting either here or in Sursee.

With sincere greetings (also to Miss Odette),

Yours,
KARL BARTH

[1]Cf. H. Küng's *Die Kirche* (Freiburg/Basel/Vienna, 1967; already in print), esp. pp. 215-230, 429-562 (ET 1968).
[2]*Decretum de Apostolatu Laicorum* (1965), *LThK*. 2nd ed., Suppl. Vol. II (1967), p. 620.
[3]*Declaratio de Libertate Religiosa* (1965), *LThK*, Suppl. Vol. II (1967), pp. 712-747.
[4]Cf. K. Barth, *Ad Limina Apostolorum* (Zurich, 1967), 2nd ed., pp. 41-43.

*　　　　*　　　　*

228

To Prof. Ernst Wolf
Göttingen[1]

In Urbe, 27 September 1966

Dear Ernst,

I am now spending a week in Rome with my wife and my fine doctor. I have already had four three-hour discussions on the council texts with a chosen group, a private audience of one hour with S. Santità,[2] many trips in a papal Mercedes put at our disposal, and also several good meals. Today: Ottaviani[3] and company. Everything is very rewarding, ecumenical, serious, and pleasant. I will appear in passing at a current theological congress.[4] In short, everything is going very well and even my lower organs are cooperating obediently.

All the best to yourself and Asta,

Yours,

K. BARTH

[1]Cf. this and the following letter with the account of his journey given in *Ad Limina Apostolorum*, esp. pp. 9-19.
[2]Pope Paul VI.
[3]Alfredo Ottaviani, Vatican Secretary of State.
[4]International Congress on the Theology of Vatican II with twelve hundred participants, 26 Sept. to 1 Oct. 1966; cf. "Theologie nach dem Konzil," *Herder-Korrespondenz*, 20 (1966), 489-492 for an account; also "Ansprache Pauls VI an den Internationalen Theologenkongress," ibid., 513-516.

*　　　*　　　*

229

To Prof. Ernst Wolf
Göttingen

Basel, 3 October 1966

[In the first part of this letter Barth filled in some of the details of the activities described in 228. He mentioned that the Pope had given him a handsome autographed copy of the Codex Vaticanus in facsimile, that only Ottaviani and Parente had given him rather dark looks, and that at the congress he had been seated near the cardinals and the president had read him a Latin address. He then asked:]

What next? A public account is out of the question, since I promised discretion in my statement in April.[1] Perhaps my questions with a short introduction?[2] But I must first reach agreement on this with the Unity secretary (Bishop Willebrands—a very good man).[3] The net result: church and theology have been set moving to an extent I could not have imagined. Do you know the book by Paul Hacker, *Das Ich im Glauben bei Martin Luther* (Styria Verlag, 1966)?[4] I am reading it almost breathlessly and can hardly wait to see what and how our own Luther studies will reply to it.

We should see one another again soon. Meanwhile greetings to Asta and Uvo,

Most sincerely yours,
KARL B.

[1]Cf. 213.
[2]These, along with an essay and a letter to Roman Catholic theologians, constitute the book *Ad Limina Apostolorum*.
[3]Cf. 230. Bishop Jan G. M. Willebrands was then secretary of the Secretariat for Christian Unity. As Cardinal Willebrands he succeeded Bea as its chairman in 1969.
[4]Graz/Vienna/Cologne.

*   *   *

230
To Bishop Jan G. M. Willebrands
Rome

Basel, 11 October 1966

Dear Bishop,

As I hear, you have long since returned from France to Rome and it is high time that I gave some sign of life regarding my (or our) week in Rome.

Primarily I wish to thank you formally for all you did at the time to make my visit to Rome the success it will continue to be in my recollection of it. Exactly what I had in mind when I planned that rather risky undertaking came to pass. I was able to get to know post-conciliar Catholicism at the source in the form of some of its most important figures and I am incomparably much more in the picture than I was previously regarding what is now going on in your church. With hardly an exception the numerous personal meetings and discussions I had there were as instructive, as fraternal, as free and cheerful, as I could expect as a separated brother. In what a friendly way my not entirely innocuous questions were accepted and answered everywhere with learning and good conscience! That all this worked out so well is certainly to be attributed not least of all to the careful planning which you, Excellence, devoted to the matter—and to the skillful way in which, not without considerable sacrifice of time and energy, you constantly accompanied me. For this I want to thank you expressly and sincerely.

And now I only hope that I for my part have not left behind any unfavorable impression or stirred up opposition either with you or among the various groups to which you introduced me. I recall with some critical feelings only the evening with His Eminence Bea, in which I was truly surprised not to hear him present his good cause with an even better theology, so that I reacted rather nervously, as my companions later told me. Fortunately nothing of this kind happened at the audience which the Holy Father paid me the honor of granting. I was greatly impressed by his sincere and human piety and admired the loving skill with which a couple of times, when problematical points threatened to arise, he assured me of his prayers that certain deeper insights might still be given me in my old age, in the direction he desired. Does he have the same good recollections of me?

May I put a practical question to you, Eminence? You can imagine that news of my visit to Rome (and especially, of course, the official announcement of my audience at the top) has caused quite a stir here. Various newspapers and even the radio here want to know a good deal more from me. In close circles I have certainly told something, but strictly avoided any public utterance on the ground that I promised His Eminence Bea to be discreet in relation to what I might hear in Rome.[1] My question is whether there is any objection to publishing my own questions in an Evangelical theological journal or the like with a general technical elucidation, but without naming any particular places or people in Rome or broadcasting the answers I received?

In the NZZ I read a report of the seven points in which Rector Dhanis of the Gregoriana summarized the findings of the theological congress over which he presided. If the report is accurate, the course of this event has been astonishingly hopeful in its results.[2]

I must not omit to convey to you the thanks of my wife and my friend Dr. Alfred Briellmann for the kindness experienced through your help (not forgetting the magnificent Vatican car) and also to pass their respectful greetings. You will be hearing directly from Dr. Briellmann: he told me that the photograph on which I had the pleasure of appearing beside him under one of the gates of the Colosseum turned out very well.

Accompanying this letter I am sending you a package with my *Evangelical Theology* and my last two volumes of sermons.[3] It is no mere politeness if I tell you that among the many enjoyable things the days in Rome brought me one of the most worthwhile was the opportunity to get to know you, Excellence, and to be with you in so fruitful a way. If your path should ever bring you to Switzerland and especially Basel, you will always be welcome in my modest home, which does not bear comparison, of course, with the various palaces into which you conducted me there.

With sincere regards, best wishes for your future work, and greetings,

Yours,
KARL BARTH

[1]Cf. 213.
[2]"Der Theologenkongress in Rom. Schlussrede des Papstes," *NZZ*, 3 October 1966.
[3]K. Barth, *Einführung in die evangelische Theologie* (Zurich, 1962); *Den Gefangenen Befreiung* (Zurich, 1959); *Rufe mich an* (Zurich, 1965).

*   *   *

231
To Prof. Helmut Gollwitzer
Berlin

Basel, 20 October 1966

Dear Golli,

Your sending me your new address gives me occasion to write three things.

1. In future don't tell people I'm telegenic. Because of this the folk from Hamburg fell on me with all their equipment and troublesome political questions and claimed me for hours.[1] Only the accidental arrival of my friend and physician Dr. Briellmann (who went with Nelly and me to Rome) saved me from worse things.

2. Do you know the book by Paul Hacker, *Das Ich des Glaubens bei Martin Luther* (Verlag Styria, 1966)?[2] I can hardly wait to see how Lutheran theology and Luther research will deal with it. It gave me occasion to thank the Creator yet again that he did not have me born

a Lutheran and thus pledge me to human loyalty to this father. I always suspected him. And the book touches on the very point why this was so, why, for example, the Weimar edition in my study is hidden behind an Indonesian rug.

3. Is what I have been told by our common friend E. Thurneysen true—he is not always a wholly accurate informant—that at certain high points in pastoral counselling you set up a crucifix, light candles, and deck yourself in a robe[3]—a cultic act whose decor far exceeds in pomp what goes on in the Roman confessional? Is this true? If so, it causes me another of those deep sighs which sometimes escape me when I observe the actions of even my truest and dearest theological friends. Tell me that it isn't true but that Eduard must have become the victim of a nightmare.

Nelly sends greetings. She, too, has been under the doctor's care and must modify her tempo of life a good deal. So between her and Lollo I am (physically) the relatively healthiest creature.

> Unchangeably yours,
> KARL BARTH

[1]Interview on North German Radio, 13 Oct. 1966.
[2]Cf. 229, n. 4.
[3]Gollwitzer, whose reply has not survived, told the editors there was truth in the story. He had used forms of penance and absolution after the manner depicted by Barth, but gave them up in 1966.

*   *   *

232
To Prof. Edmund Schlink
Ziegelhausen near Heidelberg

Basel, 21 October 1966

Dear Friend,

Sincere thanks for sending me your book on the Council,[1] which I have read with great interest. Your account deserves high praise and will, I hope, be diligently consulted on our side.

I do not quite agree with you on the danger of the traditional complex of dogmas which is still in force among the Romans.[2] Naturally they cannot retract what was proclaimed by earlier popes and councils. Nevertheless, from what I know of them, and have just seen confirmed in various bodies in Rome, they have the wonderful ability either (1) to explain away these honorable relics, or (2) to push them on the margin of what they now really want to think and say, or (3) to commemorate them with deep bows, or (4) to keep solemn silence about them. So long as one does not disturb them at this game, but encourages them to seek help along these lines, it has been my experience that one can engage in good and fruitful discussion with them. As a separated brother one may then look a little more hopefully than you do to the future of what is now going on there, in a way that seems to me to be irresistible.

Paul VI, with whom I had an hour-long conversation, impressed me as a man worthy of respect and even love but also as one to be pitied in some sense. After a little praise from me he began with the almost touching statement how hard it is to carry and handle the keys of Peter committed to him by our Lord. He is obviously under pressure from the older men around him and also (and even more so) from the younger men who want to push backwards and forwards. Did you note the relation between the rather troubled warning message he gave to the international congress of theologians and the seven theses in which Rector Dhanis of the Gregoriana summed up the results of the congress?[3] When I visited this speech-making event a confessional mixed chorus of young Swiss who happened to be there greeted me with the song: "All Morgen ist ganz frisch und neu. . . ."[4] I was then seated alongside a row of cardinals (whom I envied only for their red hats) and was complimented and solemnly welcomed by the above Dhanis. All this simply as an indication of the way I experienced the ecumenical movement for six days there and contributed a little to it.

With best greetings (also to your wife) and thanks again,

Yours,

KARL BARTH

---

[1]E. Schlink, *Nach dem Konzil* (Munich/Hamburg, 1966).
[2]Ibid., pp. 165-178.
[3]Cf. 228, n. 4 and 230, n. 2.
[4]By Johannes Zwick (c. 1541): "All the morn is fresh and new. . . ."

*   *   *

233

To Mrs. Elise Hilfiker-Diriwächter
Safenwil

Basel, 22 October 1966

Dear Lisi,

You shall have the pleasure of a few lines from me. Your whole letter of the sixteenth gave me much joy. You need not worry about my cold showers. I have taken them with pleasure for decades—in the old manse at Safenwil I had to use a big sponge for lack of the necessary installation—and it is perhaps because of them I have lived so long. I am glad to hear that you are in tolerably good health and wish you further recovery. I also enjoyed your description of the old people's outing to Emmental with the recollections of Jeremias Gotthelf, who was also so dear to me.

Lisi, I will admit that for fifty years I have been sorry that your life could not have taken a different course. You had the gifts with which to reach—I will not say a higher, but at least another calling. But God makes no mistakes and he has certainly led and been with you well and faithfully.

Perhaps you might be interested in the enclosed journal with the essay on me.[1] Its author is my grandniece, granddaughter of my brother who died in 1940,[2] the pastor of Madiswil in Bern Canton.

Perhaps we can see each other on 6 November, the date on which, if all goes well, I shall be saying a few words in the church at the anniversary.[3]

With sincere greetings,

Your old pastor,
KARL BARTH

---

[1] Christine Barth, "Karl Barth," *Mitteilungen aus der neuen Mädchenschule* [Bern], 105 (1966), 79-87.
[2] Peter Barth.
[3] Centennial of Safenwil church.

*　　　　*　　　　*

234
To Prof. Eberhard Jüngel
Zurich

Basel, 25 October 1966

[Barth congratulated Jüngel on his professorship and told him he would be glad to see him to meditate, sigh, and laugh a little about modern theology. He mentioned his little colloquium on the constitution on divine revelation, held at the not very good time of three to five P.M. on Saturdays.]

*   *   *

235
To Pater Prof. Magnus Löhrer
Einsiedeln

[Barth enclosed a newspaper clipping which stated that in a phone conversation with Bishop Willebrands the Lateran University had refused to let the "head of heresy" come within the walls where the heads of the two apostles Peter and Paul were kept.]

Basel, 21 November 1966

Dear Pater Magnus,

What must I now read? Did this telephone conversation really take place? If the news is true, then the fathers and brethren in the Lateran are literally more papist than the Pope.

One thing is sure. My "head" is authentically my own, whereas I have some doubts as to the heads of Peter and Paul supposedly to be found in the Lateran.

A pity that we cannot deal with this matter at once over a glass of Frascati!

With sincere greetings,

Yours,
KARL BARTH

*   *   *

236

To Dean Sung Bum Yun
Seoul (Korea)

Basel, 2 December 1966

[Barth thanked the recipient for news of his plans for a Korean gift. He expressed interest in Dean Sung's project of a work on Barth's life and theology but did not feel he could write a preface to it as requested. He thought it better that the work should speak for itself. He also reminded the Korean scholar that if his life and theology were properly understood the focus of the work would not be on himself but on the matter or cause he always tried to represent. He closed with the hope this might be advanced in Korea. The book came out as a memorial to Karl Barth in Korean, published by the Christian Literature Society in Seoul in 1970.]

*   *   *

237

To a Pastor in Germany

Basel, 4 December 1966

Dear Pastor,

Your urgent letter of 2 November still lies unanswered in front of me and so (for the last week) does your fiery poem "Germany's Path," which points in the same direction. I thank you for them. Excuse me if I am brief. I am no longer able to draw up longer statements.

This brings me at once to your wish, which you have even presented to me in the form of a citation to appear before the judgment seat of the Lord of the church. Amidst all the speaking and shouting in Germany, loud enough as it is, you want me to issue a kind of roar of the lion of Judah in the style of certain utterances at the beginning of the thirties.[1] Dear pastor, you are not going to hear this roar. "For everything there is a season and a time."[2] That I am not at one with Bultmann and his followers I have shown publicly and clearly not only in my booklet *Ein Versuch, ihn zu verstehen*[3] but also in the whole *C.D.*, especially the last volumes.[4] And *C.D.* is in fact being read quietly much more, and more attentively, than you seem to realize. And since the good Lord, in spite of reports to the contrary, is not dead, I am not concerned, let alone do I feel constrained, to act as the defender of his cause in a confessional movement (that you yourself associate this B.B. ["Bekenntnis-Bewegung"] with Brigitte Bardot is no accident). For one thing I have other and more useful things to do.

This brings me to the second thing concerning yourself. As you tell me, you have just come from three months of persistent depression in the hospital, and you have already had other periods like it. After this "down" you are now in an "up." Good, thank God for it, but see that worse does not befall you. It is not thanking God, nor is it good therapy, to use this "up" to proclaim the *status confessionis hodie*, to imitate Luther at Worms or Luther against Erasmus, to compose thoughtlessly generalizing articles and paltry battle-songs, to write me (and assuredly not only me) such fiery letters, to pour suspicion on all who do not rant with you, indeed, to punish them in advance with your scorn, etc. Instead you should be watching and praying and working at the place where you have been called and set, you should be reading holy scripture and the hymn-book, you should be studying carefully with a pencil in your hand the theological growth springing up around you to see whether there might not be some good grain among the tares. Lighting your pipe and not letting it go out, but refilling and rekindling it, you should not constantly orient yourself only to the enemy—e.g., to senilely simplistic statements such as those recently made by the great man of Marburg in the *Spiegel*[5]—but to the matter in relation to which there seem to be friends and enemies. Then in the modesty in which is true power (*hic Rhodus, hic salta!*) you should preach good sermons in X, give good confirmation lessons, do good pastoral work—as good as God wills in giving you the Holy Spirit and as well as you yourself can achieve with heart and mind and mouth. Do you not see that this little stone is the one thing you are charged with, but it is a solid stone in the wall against which the waves or bubbles of the modern mode will break just as surely as in other forms in the history of theology and the church they have always broken sooner or later? Dear pastor, if you will not accept and practice this, then you yourself will become the preacher of another Gospel for which I can take no responsibility. You will accomplish nothing with it except to make martyrs of your anger those people who do not deserve to be taken seriously in this bloodthirsty fashion and whom you cannot help with your "Here I stand, I can do no other." With the modesty indicated, be there *for* these people instead of *against* them in this most unprofitable style and effort. In this way, and in this way alone, will you thank God for your healing. In this way, and in this way alone, can you help to prevent new depression overtaking you tomorrow or the day after.

This is what I want to say to you as your old teacher, who also has real knowledge of the ups and downs in the outer and inner life of man even to this very day, but who now knows how to greet in friendly fashion the remedy which there is for them.

With sincere greetings, which I ask you to convey also to your wife and sister-in-law,

Yours,
KARL BARTH

[1]The recipient had asked Barth to intervene with a polemical writing in contemporary debates and also to be more sympathetic to the confessional movement "No Other Gospel."
[2]Eccl 3:1.
[3]K. Barth, *Rudolf Bultmann. Ein Versuch, ihn zu verstehen*, ThSt, 34 (Zollikon-Zurich, 1952).
[4]Cf. esp. *C.D.* IV, 1 (Foreword).
[5]"Ist Jesus auferstanden wie Goethe? Spiegel-Gespräch mit dem Marburger Theologieprofessor Dr. Rudolf Bultmann," *Der Spiegel*, 20, No. 31 (1966), pp. 42-45.

*   *   *

238
To Prof. Josef Lenzenweger
Bochum

Basel, 5 December 1966

Dear Colleague,

Sincere thanks for your friendly letter of 11 November.[1] What you write rests formally on a slight error. I did in fact speak about a repetition of the mistakes made in Neo-Protestantism as a danger which threatens Catholic progressives—yet I did not do so in a contribution to the problem of monasticism,[2] but on the occasion of my visit to Rome last September,[3] from which the statement must have reached Linz in peculiar ways.

Materially I stand by what I said or hinted at there. And for a few days I wanted to accept your invitation to expound what I said rather more explicitly in your old and famous journal. On closer reflection, however, I have to tell you this would not be a good thing. What I have in my heart against Neo-Protestantism, and therefore implicitly against certain tendencies in modern Catholic theology, I stated long ago in some sections of my *C.D.* But I do not want to come on the modern scene as an "accuser of my brethren,"[4] whether my Neo-Protestant or my progressive Catholic brethren, as would almost necessarily have to happen in the essay you desire. It has been taken care of on our side that the Neo-Protestant trees should not reach to heaven. And it will be taken care of on their side too—without my running the risk of conveying water to the other mills which I heard working in Rome and whose anxious clatter I have no wish to help to strengthen. I ask you kindly to understand this old soldier if he cannot accept the undoubtedly interesting proposal you made.

With regards,

Yours truly,
KARL BARTH

[1] Lenzenweger had asked Barth to put his warning against the repetition of Neo-Protestant mistakes by progressive Catholics in essay form in the *Theol. Prakt. Quartalschrift* [Linz].

[2] G. M. Braso, ed., *Visioni attuali sulla vita monastica* (Montserrat, 1966). The book contains fifty-six answers to the question of monastic life by representatives of different confessions, including Barth (pp. 43f.).

[3] Cf. K. Barth, *Ad Limina Apostolorum*, p. 17.

[4] Cf. Rev 12:10.

*   *   *

239
To Pastor Dr. Tjarko Stadtland
Wirdum/Emden

Basel, 18 January 1967

Dear Dr. Stadtland,

Many thanks for your letter of 29 November 1966. You remind me in it that I have been owing you an answer for a longer period. Since you have taken such pains in studying certain trains of my thought during my theological youth I must not remain in your debt any longer. When you kindly sent me your book[1] some months ago, I read it entirely at once, but as you know an older man has to follow a slower tempo and I had many other things to do, so that I did not get around to expressing my thanks to you for sending the work and telling you what I thought of the presentation in it. That I will do now.

What am I to say about your work? First, that I undoubtedly followed with interest and some curiosity what you assembled, presented, analyzed, criticized, and evaluated with such industry, care, and scholarship in your dissertation. The interest—and curiosity—focused especially on the way you apprehended and treated the theme which you had chosen and I had long before laid claim to, the problem of eschatology. The interest—and curiosity—also focused on how I would fare in your analysis as the object of your scholarly skill. Having finished the reading I should like to say that in both respects I perused your exposition with total sympathy and much profit; that in the former respect I learned with assent things that were not self-evident but which you boldly stated; and that in the latter I learned with pleasure things that I myself did not remember saying in my youthful zeal, not to say arrogance. I like it that in the one respect you try to follow paths that differ from the trail of Rudolf Bultmann, which is strangely followed by so many people today, and that also differ from the favorite route of the Pannenberg school. Furthermore, in the other respect you have been able to present a more nuanced and faithful picture than my Basel friend Hans Urs von Balthasar[2] of the change between the first edition of my *Romans*, which is still strikingly dependent on my theological forebears, and the better known second edition.[3]

You can imagine that I did not read all your statements with agreement and that I did not read them only with pleasure. Though it does not affect my praise of your book, I must develop a little more explicitly my critical attitude to it. Concerning first your presentation of the theology of my early period: are you always right in your account of me, do you always place the accent correctly, have you distributed the weight sufficiently? Do you really hit the mark when you characterize me with such labels as "negative natural theology," "identity mysticism," "Barth is doing anthropology," and the like? Is your thesis tenable that in *C.D.* I return via the detour of the second edition of *Romans* back to the first? It seems to me that many questions may be raised concerning your expositions, statements, and judgments. At any rate, since I do not feel that I can recognize and understand myself at places in your book, I do not accept everything you say. But you don't expect me to act like a Barth scholar or a Barth expert (a hobby I leave to others) or even to strike up an apologetic song in my own cause (which could hardly be successful, since I think I see clearly the sins of my youth). In this connection I would simply like to give you the following friendly but serious advice. In the future avoid (as far as you can) something you obviously have a tendency toward, namely, making do with slogans and handy formulae. For me it would be a canon of all research in theological history, and perhaps in all history, that one should try to present what has engaged another person, whether in a good way or in a way less good, as something *living*, as something that *moved* him in some way and that can and indeed does move *oneself* too; to *unfold* it in such a way that even if one finally takes some other route the path of this other has an enticing, or, if you like, a tempting attraction for oneself. Disregard of this canon, I think, can only avenge itself by rendering the attempted historical research unprofitable and tedious. In reading your treatise I had the strong impression that you had taken special care not to allow your chosen subject—granted its shadow side—to shine forth in any way, not to develop it as an attractive, or if you like, a seductive thing. Rather, after colorfully heaping up quotations, you rushed on too quickly to slogans, formulae, and labels such as "apriorism," "Anselmianism," "Osiandrism," "christological compression," and the like. If you will pardon me, these and the many other concepts found in your work sound to me like coffin-lids and gravestones; and you cannot seriously think that, so long as it is not shown what is meant by them, a work decked out with such titles can seriously move or entertain even me, or keep me in suspense.

But now I must turn for a moment to the real theme of your work, your discussion of the problem of eschatology. You obviously have something seriously against me in this regard. And *a priori* I cannot deny you the right to take me to task in this area. I sincerely hope I am not shortsighted or dull of hearing regarding the objection that, as in everything else, so perhaps especially in relation to the theme of eschatology, I have said no final words but only penultimate and prepenultimate words. I think I have at least said these, and I am really surprised by the vehemence with which you so radically question whether I have "ever had a futurist eschatology" and whether I am now in a position to write about it in view of my "starting-point." In reading these observations of yours I am reminded of the story how as a little boy of four I am supposed to have asked my mother, "Mother, where is eternity?" It seems as if I never lost sight of this question on my theological pilgrimage, and it further seems as if even now—if I had the necessary powers—I could give to the question an answer which is a little better based, which rests on more solid ground, than what is being presented all over the place today as the "theology of hope." The objections you bring against my earlier theology, and which you think can be brought against *C.D.*, too, are not at all original: there is in me "no true" conflict, only a "palpable" monism of grace; the future brings "nothing new," "only" something noetic; and so it must be asked whether one can speak of "any" eschatology at all in me. It wearies me a little to tell you the reasons why this old story—partly because I have heard it so often—still makes no deep impression on me. I look around and try to understand the objections and see beside you a row of theologians telling this tale—and you are about to join them. They do indeed espouse an eschatology that will meet your postulates. In it there is indeed a "genuine" conflict. A "monism of grace" is obviously avoided. The future will plainly bring "something new." But in fact this eschatology can hardly be recognized or taken seriously as *Christian* eschatology. Instead of starting out joyfully with the confession of Jesus Christ it seems to have painfully pasted his name on its own futurism. It certainly promises all kinds of fine things in terms of *his* individual and social perfection but at root, in the light of what is now being proclaimed in full chorus by futurologists, champions of the principle of hope, and conjurors up of the future of every type of belief and unbelief—yes, I must throw back your objection in all seriousness—it announces *nothing new*. No, it seems best to me not to follow this track but approximately the track I proposed before—although not by a long way pertinently, radically, or consistently enough—if we are to find an answer to the problem of eschatology. We must concentrate strictly on the one thing by which Christian eschatology distinguishes itself from all other possible eschatologies, namely, on the *one* person, the *new* person, in whom God "was and is and is to come" (Rev 4:8). We would not be speaking of him as he is and as he reveals himself to be, we would not be speaking of the God who is eternally rich[4] and kind,[5] the coming God, if we were to speak of him *only* as the one who comes and not also and at the same time as the one who was and is. Eschatology is *not* the framework in which to speak of this living God but he is the framework in which to speak of eschatology. Thus your rejection of my criticism of the pan-eschatological dream is obscure to me. Either you are concerned about the excellent formal truth that in treating one aspect of dogmatics one must touch on all others—in which case you are, as you know, running through an open door as far as I am concerned—or else your enterprise leads to the setting up of an idol which ought to be cut down promptly, which will sooner or later fall, and which will do so primarily, you can count on this, through the power of him beside whom is no other God, not even one decked out with the title of "Eschatos" or "Point Omega." And if I do indeed insist that the Eschatos is no other than the Protos, that he who "is to come" is identical with him who "was and is," and that the meaning, novum, and proprium of his coming is—fortunately—very definitely determined and already characterized by the fact that he has come and is, I fail to see to what extent this rules out a futurist eschatology and does not even now invite us to hope zealously and expectantly for this coming of his. And if I also especially emphasize that his coming makes manifest with him the extent to which God has been and continues to be, not for nothing or in vain, the God of loving-kindness who has bound himself to man, so that no creature has escaped or evaded his love—if I emphasize this, I cannot really understand how people can say that this event is not something new but only something noetic. They say that as though *this* future did not include everything that one may and can only expect, as though anything more in this respect would not really be something less!

I break off, for I suspect that not having grasped my understanding of eschatology as it may be read in my books you also will not grasp it now. It remains only for me to wish you the very best for your work as a pastor and especially for any further studies you may undertake on the question of Christian eschatology. Since so far, apart from a few hints, you have in the main shown only how a Christian eschatology ought not to be thought of and formulated, I wonder greatly if you will not one day take back much of the criticism you have brought against me when you move on to a *positive* exposition of the doctrine of eschatology. May it then be granted to you to say something more illuminating, clear, and full of promise concerning this frightening but above all comforting theme of Christian hope than was ever given to me on my theological pilgrimage. If so, then I suspect it will be better grounded than that which your attitude toward my eschatology now hints at.

With friendly greetings,

Your old teacher,
KARL BARTH[6]

[1]T. Stadtland, *Eschatologie und Geschichte in der Theologie des jungen Karl Barth* (Neukirchen, 1966).

[2]H. U. von Balthasar, *Karl Barth. Darstellung und Deutung seiner Theologie* (Cologne, 1951; 2nd ed. 1962).

[3]K. Barth, *Der Römerbrief* (Bern, 1919, rpt. Zurich, 1963; 2nd ed. Munich, 1922, rpt. Zurich, 1967).

[4]From M. Rinckart's "Now Thank We All Our God" (1636), v. 2 ("bounteous").
[5]Titus 3:4.
[6]For extracts from Stadtland's reply on 25 January 1967, see Appendix, 13.

*   *   *

240
To Pastor Ulrich Jost
Linthal (Glarus Canton)

Basel, 20 January 1967

[Barth thanked Jost for his letter of the fifteenth and answered his concern that he (Jost) had not been one of the strong in spirit in 1946-50 by suggesting that many who had been had since proved to be theologically blind, which Jost was certainly not.]

*   *   *

241
To Pastor Dr. Otfried Hofius
Eiserfeld

Basel, 24 January 1967

[Barth congratulated Hofius on the opening of his new church, which rather well realized Barth's own idea of a model reformed church (cf. K. Barth, "Das Problem des protestantischen Kirchenbaus," *Werk* [Zurich], 46 [1959], 271) except that it was perhaps *too* open on all sides, so that the congregation might be blinded by too direct light or distracted by what they might see in this light.]

*   *   *

242
To Dr. Setsuro Osaki
Göttingen

Basel, 26 January 1967

Dear Dr. Osaki,

Some days ago you sent me your extensive dissertation,[1] and having immersed myself at once in reading it I want to thank you today for sending the work and for your kind accompanying letter. I hope you will receive this letter of mine before you conclude, as indicated, your lengthy stay in Europe and return to distant Asia. Having come to know you well from your literary product (I studied with interest the *vita* accompanying the thesis with its various dates, as, for example, your baptism which obviously occurred during your school years), I am really sorry not to have come to know you personally, too. At any rate you may be assured that as I now know you a little I shall accompany you with good thoughts and wishes on the way which leads you back home and which you will then follow further in the land of the rising sun.

Well, you want to know what I think of your work on what is, as you realize, a very decisive aspect of my theology. So I will tell you so far as I can in my present situation. What I have to say to you first and especially is that I have read all your book, from the first page to the last, and have read it with genuine pleasure. You have shown the ability to assemble, survey, and expound the material relevant to the theme with industrious and competent scholarship. Further, as I watched with growing interest, you have reproduced and followed my thoughts and discussions, especially in *C.D.* II, 2,[2] which I wrote with a joy of discovery I experienced perhaps in no other volume, in a way that is understanding, vital, and, so far as I can see, correct. You have also—and I especially liked this—enriched, deepened, and illuminated your discussion at all points by intelligently engaging the by no means little flood of secondary writings that either wash favorably or rage violently around my works and also—which is even more profitable—by skillfully surveying reformation and older orthodox materials on the theme you have treated. And finally you have been able in your work to show in a clear and clarifying fashion, and to make understandable, the predominant importance of this theme, the theme of predestination, for the thrust and meaning of any theology, and the joyfulness of the theme which I found so liberating at the time. All this is very good and worthy and merits the highest praise. This is the more so since you as a Japanese undoubtedly faced great difficulties of language and comprehension in your work on the theme and have obviously—one might truly call this too an ecumenical achievement—successfully overcome them. If theology is going to be pursued in Japan in the way you have actually pursued it in this work, one may look forward without worry to the future of the Japanese church, and granted the situation there is certainly not easy but difficult, one may equally and even more certainly view it as full of hope. In short, I have for the most part been able to follow you in your presentation with agreement, just as you could for the most part follow me and my understanding of predestination as God's free election of grace in Jesus Christ.

There is also, of course, something of a minor disagreement between you and me and I would be glad if we could clear it up. In what I now have to say to you I am not really criticizing your work but simply formulating a question, though ultimately a question with many implications, namely, whether you have really *understood* what you *seem* to have understood very well in your book. On the last page of your dissertation you state against me the objection that in my work in general, and my doctrine of predestination in particular, there is a dangerous tendency to ground theological statements ontologically at the cost of reality, history, and human decision, instead of accepting their truth only in the "situation of proclamation" as you propose in contrast. Frankly I was not prepared for this objection after all the agreement you had shown in the other parts of your book. Frankly I do not by a long way see the point or scope of your criticism which arises so abruptly in the concluding portion. It almost seemed to me that you were not presenting your own opinion here but quickly making a polite bow in passing to your mentor, my late friend,[3] who, as I know, had much against me more or less along the lines you indicate. If this is so, then I understand why your criticism of the ontological grounding of predestination statements has so little cogency; clearly your work itself accompanies your criticism with the emphatic and contrasting recognition that this ontological grounding is very closely connected with the christological concentration which I represent and you approve.

Or did you perhaps have something more serious and significant in view in your objection? Sometimes I had the impression that for you the special issue in it was a rejection of what you perceived to be in me a tendency toward a poor "orthodoxy" in which it is simply maintained that this and that is thus and thus, and that for good or evil, and more evil than good, man has simply to swallow it, and therefore he is not really taken seriously in his own true reality. If you fear this in me, then in this respect—I think with a good conscience—I can calm your fears and reassure you that today no less than when I dealt with predestination I regard such a theological procedure to be as foolish as it is tedious and unspiritual. When you allege specifically against me that my reflection on the two natures of Christ implies a static and to that extent ontological thinking on the relation between God and man, I may simply appeal to your reading of *C.D.* and ask whether I really regard speaking about the two *natures* of Christ as legitimate and permissible except in the context of his *history*. (If in your work you had consulted just a little more intently Vol. IV, 3 of *C.D.*[4] with its consideration of the prophetic office of Christ, your suspicion regarding the role of the two natures of Jesus Christ in my books would have cleared up of itself.) And when you also urge against me that in my thinking on the problem of election I have not given strong enough consideration to the "situation of proclamation," perhaps I need only remind you that in what I said in Vol. II, 2, including what you call there the ontological grounding, I had what is at least the fairly recognizable intention of directing my thoughts only according to the rule (to quote Luther), "My heart must rest on God and trust his goodness which his precious Word proclaims to me. . . ."[5] That all the predestination statements depend on this proclamation of the Word, and are true and actual in it, to whom do you say that, dear Dr.? Now in the course of the years I have learned to note more clearly than I did earlier that this divine proclamation— to our salvation—is not identical with what usually takes place in the pulpit between ten and eleven on Sundays. I can hardly think that maintaining this identity would be a helpful, comforting, or even necessary thought for you in understanding the wonderful truth and reality of the divine election. And it seems to me that if you insist on it, then there will finally—and really—emerge an orthodoxy which is undoubtedly a good deal worse than that you now think you detect in me.

Or is there something different and even more important in your objection to my doctrine of predestination? Am I right in assuming that perhaps the real point of it is that you find yourself forced to regard as offensive and dangerous as such the ontic concepts which here and there I use so uninhibitedly and joyously. Naturally, all concepts are relative. If you have better ones, then use them boldly and not mine. The matter denoted by them, of course, is for me so important that I cannot well drop them. As you yourself have noted, for me the fact that I may and must use concepts like "ontological" does not rest on the need to deduce lower being from a higher or highest being that can be referred to a fixed point (in spite of reports to the contrary I am no Platonist). It rests simply on the mode and manner in which the revelation that has taken place in Jesus Christ is to be understood. "Ask ye who is this same: Christ Jesus is His Name . . . He and no other one (God)," as Luther again said, and I would truly repeat "no other" than this. But when we say this "no other" God, when we say that we are not to find and seek a different and superior God behind the God who reveals himself in

Jesus Christ, we already enter the sphere where it is meaningful and where we are commanded to speak not only of the action but also of the being of God. Where it can never be sufficient simply to say that God reveals himself, but at the same time it must also be confessed that God is the one as whom he reveals himself, that he does not contradict himself in his speech, that he does not proceed arbitrarily in his action, that he does not act "as if" in declaring himself, that once and for all, even though and even while he constantly meets us in new and different ways, he is "no other," but the same yesterday, today, and forever,[6] the faithful God in all his speech and action and self-declaration. But if God is known as such, we cannot close our eyes to the fact that herewith—in sharp contrast to the ungodly and unprofitable attempt to "ascribe" ontological content to his action—we are already on the point of knowing him as the one who not merely through our service (or reality or decision), but antecedently, from the very first, is he of whom it is rightly to be said: "What God has done is well done."[7] In the beginning, dear Dr., there was for me, too, no abstract being but *the Word*, yet this *was* in the *beginning* with God.[8] And I fail to see how, in the attempt to acknowledge and denote this, man is made "secure" and his reality is not taken seriously enough, or how the former is avoided and the latter achieved if the ontological implications of God's action and the antecedently valid reality of his Grace are left open, or put in the background, or declared to be uncertain, or even ignored or contested. Indeed, I rather think that if a serious place is given to this idea in theology (as today a host of theological contemporaries desire), we shall set ourselves on a steep slope that can lead only to the dangerous abysses of the nineteenth century. On this steep slope the first step is obviously that of beginning to pay homage to a distinctive dualism between a God *in himself* who no longer concerns us and an all the more relevant God *for us*, between an ontologically grounded God and a God who is actual only in the "situation of proclamation." The second step which usually follows is that in the interests of a better understanding of this God a move is made to take with terrible "seriousness" the reality of man, his history, his sin, his decisions. And then the third step is not long in coming, for in consequence of taking man and his reality with increasingly reverent seriousness, God becomes an increasingly indefinite, obscure, and uncertain factor and finally (you know what I mean) he is even declared to be dead. *Obsta principiis*, dear Dr.! I believe at any rate that there are good reasons not to join in sliding down this steep slope. Now as always I believe that the task of theology is to bear witness to the "bounteous God"[9] (no less, but genuinely bounteous through the poverty he assumed in his Son), and to his unchangeably certain grace (unchangeably certain also and precisely in the hiddenness and vulnerability it endured in his Son). And I believe that in face of *this* God, man with his whole reality does not come off too badly but will be and is taken with what is for the first time genuine *seriousness* by God in his mercy. And it seems to me finally that the reality, history, and decision of man, when all this is understood as the sphere in which man may live in the circle of revelation and make *answer* to it, are in practice taken more seriously than in the turgid and superficial and dreary attempts of man to take himself seriously.

These, then, are my observations on the question which you put to me and which, as I said, I did not fully understand. I hope that they will help you a little to a further clarification of your theological position and I greet you with good wishes for your further service as a Christian theologian.

Yours,
KARL BARTH

[1] S. Osaki, "Die Prädestinationslehre Karl Barths," Diss. Göttingen 1966.
[2] K. Barth, *C.D.* II, 2, chap. VII.
[3] Prof. O. Weber, Göttingen (d. 19 October 1966).
[4] *C.D.* IV, 3, § 69.
[5] From Luther's hymn "Aus tiefer Not. . . ."
[6] Cf. Heb 13:8.
[7] Beginning of a hymn by Samuel Rodigast, 1674.
[8] Cf. John 1:1.
[9] Cf. 239, n. 4.

*   *   *

243
To Pastor Richard Karwehl
Osnabrück

Basel, 1 February 1967

[Barth thanked Karwehl for earlier greetings and told him he was waiting for the "bounteous God" to show him what was wanted from the rest of his life. He said he had given up the idea of an autobiography since it would unavoidably have too much reference to himself, and went on to describe his visit to Rome and his work on *Ad Limina*

Apostolorum. He commented on affairs in West Germany, on the fact that divisions in world communism were deeper than those in Christianity, and on Pharaoh Johnson, who in spite of all the plagues, and the new disaster in the space program, could only harden his heart the more in relation to Vietnam. Regarding his audience with the Pope he recounted the Pope's desire that he might get profounder insights regarding the Virgin in his old age, and also said that he had advised his wife not in any circumstances to go down on her knees to the Pope but simply to make a deep bow. He closed with personal news and greetings.]

*   *   *

244
To Wilhelm Zech
Bad Oeynhausen

Basel, 24 February 1967

Dear Mr. Zech,

Be cheerful and of good courage. The statement that God is dead comes from Nietzsche and has recently been discovered and trumpeted abroad by some German and American theologians and now by certain schoolboys.[1] But the good Lord has not died of this; he who dwells in the heaven laughs at them.[2] This is all I have to say on the matter.

With friendly greetings,

Yours,

KARL BARTH

[1] A school magazine in Bremen had contained an obituary, published in *Der Spiegel*, 20, No. 30 (1966), p. 90.
[2] Ps 2:4.

*   *   *

245
To the Seminar for Reformed Theology via Prof. Paul Jacobs
Münster

Basel, 28 February 1967

Dear Fellow-Teachers and Fellow Students,

I have heard with interest, emotion, and pleasure what has obviously been going on these last weeks and months in the Theological

Seminar at Münster.[1] I myself, though moving on to my eighty-first birthday, and in spite of all the less enjoyable signs of my age, have been and am very busy the present winter semester. With a number of students in my own Theological Seminar I have been finding edification in the constitution on divine revelation of Vatican II,[2] which is excellent on the whole though not always so in detail. Meanwhile you have been engaged in express and incisive discussion of no less a figure than—Karl Barth. Has it all been as delightful and enjoyable and even merry there as it has been, on the whole, here? Has anybody acquired the desire and insight to do everything much better than I was able to do? Above and alongside the theme of your seminar has something of the great and glorious theme by which every Christian theologian (and not he alone but he especially) stands or falls, has something of this theme become clear, or perhaps not yet become truly clear? At any rate I hope seriously that your study and reflection on what the old man of Basel might have meant here and there has not been tedious and painful to you, that in particular the pipes of those who have the hang of it have not gone out, and finally that when the seminar is over you can all proceed merrily and patiently and courageously on your ordained paths.

I greet you all: you, honored colleague, and you whose signatures have given me pleasure, with friendly greetings,

Yours,
KARL BARTH

[1]Seminar on Karl Barth, winter semester 1966/67. The participants had sent greetings to "the former professor and honorary doctor of their faculty."
[2]*Dogmatic Constitution on Divine Revelation* of the Second Vatican Council. Text in *LThK*, 2nd ed., Suppl. Vol. II (1967), pp. 504-583.

*   *   *

246
To Pastor A. A. Spijkboer
Amsterdam

Basel, 4 March 1967

[The recipient had raised the question in the Amsterdam Classis of adding the Barmen Declaration to the confessional statements of the

Dutch Reformed Church with an addition concerning weapons of mass destruction. He had asked Barth whether later emendations might properly be made, and Barth replied that they could so long as they were specified as such. Thus a mere addition in the present instance would be anachronistic in view of the non-existence of such weapons in 1934 when the Barmen Declaration was composed and published. Barth gave the recipient permission to print the letter, which he did (in Dutch) in his article "Een Antwoord over 'Barmen,' " *In de Waagschaal* (Amsterdam), 22 (1966/67), 251ff. (cf. p. 252).]

*   *   *

247
To Prof. Hans Küng
Tübingen

Basel, 10 March 1967

Dear Colleague,

Many thanks for your card from Paris and thanks even more for your *Kirche*[1] which arrived this morning and which I began reading at once.

I began with the Epilogue, where I found every page worthy of praise. I then moved on to what you say about baptism, since I am just now writing a foreword to my book on baptism, which is being printed as a Fragment from IV, 4. You will see there that I view Spirit baptism and water baptism as more neatly related and distinguished than you do. Curious as I am, I then turned to M in the Index to learn what you might have made of chap. 8 of *De Ecclesia* in your ecclesiology.[2] But oh, oh, p. 369![3] I remain obstinate in my view that St. Joseph—if only he were—is to be preferred to Our Lady with her crown of glory ("The Serving Church").[4]

Rather wild things seem to be happening in the Catholic church or Catholic theology of the USA. Along with your volume the post brought me a letter from my eldest son in Pittsburgh who has been busily moving in and out of all kinds of Catholic seminaries and colleges: "They are reading almost nothing but Protestant literature . . . and are in clear revolt against their bishops and everything conservative. They are lacking in wise older authorities. So they fall sometimes into the silliest stuff, worry about demythologizing and Bishop Robinson, and neglect too readily a serious study of Thomas Aquinas."

The March issue of *Herder-Korrespondenz* was also full of the noise of cracking timbers everywhere.

Well! Greet Miss Odette.

> In all things,
> Your separated brother,
> KARL BARTH

P.S. Will you be able to visit us again before the distant summer? My wife will do all that can be done for you regarding dessert and everything else. Miss Odette is naturally included.

---

[1]H. Küng, *Die Kirche* (Freiburg/Basel/Vienna, 1967; ET, 1968).

[2]The mariological chapter in the Dogmatic Constitution on the Church of Vatican II (Münster, 1965), esp. chap. viii, "Our Lady," pp. 142-161; cf. 123, n. 5.

[3]"Mariendogmen" in the Index to p. 369, where Küng says that papal primacy and infallibility (and in this connection the new Marian dogmas) form the main obstacle to unity. In his copy Barth underlined the words in parentheses.

[4]Cf. 62, nn. 4-6.

*   *   *

248
To Prof. Kurt Aland,
Münster

Basel, 17 April 1967

Dear Colleague,

Many thanks for sending your latest work on infant baptism.[1] Its contents trouble me greatly. For one thing, the proof that it can first be found in the sources only after 200 A.D. Again, at the end, the claim that it results—necessarily—from the theological presuppositions of baptism and the baptismal teaching of the New Testament. And again, the absence of any attempt to show that this really is so or how far it is so. Are we to take this procedure (I have in mind the article on baptism[2] in *RGG²*) as a canonical one in modern historico-critical research? And apart from material things, what especially troubles me about your essay is that it bears on the jacket a title I once invented, that of *Theological Existence Today*. New Series, of course (very new!).

Excuse this sigh; I could not suppress it.

With friendly greetings,

> Yours,
> KARL BARTH[3]

[1]K. Aland, "Die Stellung der Kinder in den frühen christlichen Gemeinden—und ihre Taufe," *ThExh*, N.F. 138 (1967).
[2]"Taufe," *RGG*, 3rd ed., VI, 626-660; cf. esp. sec. II, "Im Urchristentum," by E. Dinkler, 627-637.
[3][For Aland's response, see Appendix, 14.]

*   *   *

249
To Prof. Kurt Aland
Münster

Basel, 25 April 1967

Dear Colleague,

Many thanks for your letter of 21 April.[1] You can imagine it will not please me if the outcome of our correspondence on your latest book on baptism[2] is simply that not merely one of us but both are disillusioned and troubled. You know as well as I do that the question dealt with in your book is usually discussed and debated with cross faces and hardened minds. But I should be pleased if with some at least, including you, I could go my way in peace in the matter. Do not be angry with me, then, for what I said about your treatise.[3]

Naturally, I did not begin reading it only on the next to the last page. And obviously I confess my respect for the industrious scholarship with which you have dealt with the problem of infant baptism in this and your earlier work.[4] I have gratefully learned many interesting details from them.

My objection to both booklets, which you obviously find so disturbing, does not apply so much to those last pages but to the strange contradiction between those pages and what precedes. How is one to explain it if—in face of the attitude of the church to infant baptism, as you know it well enough in Westphalia—there is laid on the table a purely historical investigation, as you call it, which exposes the notorious non-existence of infant baptism in the early church, but which, according to your letter, is especially, and very incongruously, presented for the instruction of opponents of this baptism? How is one to explain it if the conclusion and point of the investigation is precisely that what is established purely historically is not so important, normative, or shattering that another baptismal practice which so obviously contradicts your own objections cannot obtain, and does not have to obtain? How else can one explain this than by assuming that the churches and their leaders are invited to treat the protest against modern baptismal practice, which comes down to us from early Christianity, as a purely historical one which is to be feared only when the Bible is used mechanically, so that they can go on sleeping in the matter. You see, dear colleague, that your work puts me in a difficulty. I should have liked it better if you had been more of a pure historian in your treatise.[5]

With friendly greetings all the same,

Yours,
KARL BARTH

[1]See Appendix, 14.
[2]Cf. 248, n. 1.
[3]See 248.
[4]K. Aland, "Die Säuglingstaufe im NT und in der alten Kirche. Eine Antwort an Joachim Jeremias," ThExh, N.F. 86 (1961).
[5]Aland later took issue with Barth's teaching again in his Taufe und Kindertaufe . . . (Gütersloh, 1971).

*   *   *

250
To Carl Zuckmayer
Saas Fee (Valais Canton)

Basel, 16 May 1967

[In this letter Barth told the writer Zuckmayer, with whom he struck up a friendship, that he had just been reading with pleasure his Als war's ein Stück von mir. Horen der Freundschaft (Frankfurt, 1966). He then introduced himself with a brief synopsis of his life and tastes, noted his prior acquaintance only with Zuckmayer's Des Teufels General and his own authorship of theological books, and described his retirement. He sent Zuckmayer two samples of his work, his most recent Ad Limina Apostolorum (Zurich, 1967) and his earlier Wolfgang Amadeus Mozart 1756/1956 (Zollikon, 1956).]

*   *   *

251

To Pastor Johann Christoph Hampe
Hohenschäftlarn near Munich

Basel, 16 May 1967

Dear Pastor,

The Kösel-Verlag has very kindly sent me the first volume of the work you edited called *Die Autoritat der Freiheit*.[1] If I am not mistaken they did so at your request. And so I send you my sincere thanks, which I ask you to pass on to the publishers, too, as occasion offers.

I have already read with pleasure and used with profit your first little collection (*Ende der Gegenreformation?*).[2] The same applies even more to your second and more comprehensively structured enterprise. Until now, I have been able to study intensively only some parts particularly important to me, but I shall be busy perusing and working over the rich materials presented to us in it. The title of the whole symposium is to be called almost a stroke of genius: This is exactly how the problem must be denoted, understood, and tackled on both sides. To judge from your choice of non-Catholic contributors you have in mind a special Lutheran-Roman peace, but I cannot demur, because for one thing (if not the only thing) I for my part have been an ecumenist on my own responsibility from my own particular position.

So I can only congratulate you on this whole work and wish you the best for its continuation. Shall I live to see the second and third volumes? The span of life before me is nearing its natural term and my receptive and creative intellectual forces have much narrower limits than earlier.

With friendly greetings and emphatic thanks,

Yours,

KARL BARTH

P.S. A detail on p. 8: You say 120 churches met for the New Delhi Assembly. Were there not 210?[3]

My latest book *Ad Limina Apostolorum* will have been long since in your busy collector's hands. Otherwise I would have gladly sent a copy.

---

[1]*Die Autorität der Freiheit . . .*, ed. J. C. Hampe, 3 vols. (Munich, 1967). At the request of the publishers, Barth wrote a piece on the work which came out in their *Nachrichten . . .*, 26 (Munich, 1967), pp. 23f.

[2]J. C. Hampe, *Ende der Gegenreformation? Das Konzil—Dokumente und Deutung* (Stuttgart/Berlin/Mainz, 1964).
[3]The figure was corrected in the rest of the edition.

*　　　*　　　*

252
To Rector Eberhard Bethge
Rengsdorf near Neuwied[1]

Basel, 22 May 1967

Dear Pastor,

You were kind enough to send me a copy of your masterpiece on Bonhoeffer.[2] Having studied it attentively from the first page to the last, I must not delay expressing to you my sincere thanks for the gift. It is a good and instructive book, and when people ask me whether they should buy and read it I say indeed they must.

I have learned many things about Bonhoeffer for the first time, or they have first made an impact on me, in your book.

It was new to me that it was specifically on an early visit to Rome that Bonhoeffer came to a living view of what the church (and penance within it) should be, and was in this way challenged to break with the school of Seeberg, Harnack, and Holl.[3]

Especially new to me was the fact that in 1933 and the years following, Bonhoeffer was the first and almost the only one to face and tackle the Jewish question so centrally and energetically.[4] I have long since regarded it as a fault on my part that I did not make this question a decisive issue, at least publicly in the church conflict (e.g., in the two Barmen Declarations I drafted in 1934).[4a] A text in which I might have done so would not, of course, have been acceptable to the mindset of even the "confessors" of that time, whether in the reformed or the general synod. But this does not excuse the fact that since my interests were elsewhere I did not at least formally put up a fight on the matter.[4b] Only from your book have I become aware that Bonhoeffer did so from the very first. Perhaps this is why he was not at Barmen nor later at Dahlem.

It was also new to me that he was as seriously intent on a trip to India as you tell us.[5] Even now, however, I do not quite get the point of his intention.

Again, it was new to me that with Bishop Bell[6] I myself was always so important a figure to him—until at the end he charged me with a "positivism of revelation,"[7] an objection I could never clearly understand. Until now I have always thought of myself as one of the pawns, not the knights or castles, on his chessboard.

More important than this and similar discoveries was the stimulation that reading your book gave me to reflect afresh on the whole of the unfinished path of your brother-in-law and friend. I think I must distinguish in it three lines which were certainly related for him but which are not wholly clear (even in your depiction and perhaps also to himself).

1. First is what Andreas Lindt in his new essay in *Reformatio* has called Bonhoeffer's way from Christian faith to *political* action.[8] This was my theme, too, when I left theological Liberalism, in the case of religious socialism in its specifically Swiss form. Did Bonhoeffer ever closely study Blumhardt, Kutter, and Ragaz, who were then my mentors? This theme slipped into the background for me when I got involved in the *Romans* and especially when I went to Germany in 1921. I made less of an impression on my German readers and hearers in this regard than in what was now my primary effort to reinterpret the reformation and make it relevant. In Germany, however, burdened with the problems of its Lutheran tradition, there was a genuine need in the direction which I now silently took for granted or emphasized only in passing: ethics, fellow-humanity, a serving church, discipleship, socialism, the peace movement, and in and with all these things, politics. This gap, and the need to fill it, Bonhoeffer obviously saw keenly from the very first, and he felt it with increasing intensity and expressed it on a broad front. This supplementation which had been missing so long and which he represented so vigorously, was and still remains to a great extent at least (and we hope decisively) the secret of the impression that he has rightly made especially when he became a martyr, too, for this specific cause.

2. The second thing seems to me to be the renewal of personal and public worship which Bonhoeffer clearly intended. I sense what was in his mind here and might perhaps sum it up in the term *discipline*. If this is right, then I can only endorse his intention as such but I must admit that not even from your book do I get wholly clear instruction in the matter. Obviously he had in view—was this the "arcane discipline" of which he finally spoke?—something different from the Berneuchener or that of Taisé. But what? His yearning for India was very obscure to me, as you know. One would have had to be at Finkenwalde,[9]

as you were, to get a better idea of it. For the rest, has Bonhoeffer awakened as much interest, found followers, and formed a school in this area as in the matter we touched on a moment ago?

3. Wholly obscure to me, even after reading your book, is the matter on which discussion has raged from several angles since it was provoked by *Letters and Papers from Prison*:[10] the renewal of theology in both the narrower and the broader sense as he envisioned it. What is the "world come of age"? What is meant by "non-religious interpretation"? What is the "positivism of revelation" ascribed to me? I know all the things, or most of the things, that the experts have made of this right up to Heinrich Ott.[11] But to this day I do not know what Bonhoeffer himself meant and planned with it all, and very softly I venture to doubt whether theological systematics (I include his *Ethics*)[12] was his real strength. Might he not later have simply dropped all those catchy phrases? Even when he uttered them, did he himself really know what he meant by them? Even though I might be wrong, I would maintain that in the prison letters we have only one (if the last) of the stations on what was from the first an agitated intellectual pilgrimage, that it was definitely not the goal of this pilgrimage, and that he was capable of the most astonishing evolutions in a wholly different direction. We do him serious wrong if—ranging him with Tillich and Bultmann—we now interpret him only in the light of those passages (or regard him as his own prophet in his orientation to them), whether finding in him a brave new middle-class Liberalism, construing him as a representative of East German ideology as H. Müller[13] does, or viewing him as a new Lutheran father as R. Prenter does.[14] Putting myself in his place, I hate to think of what people might have made of me if I had suffered a natural or violent death after the first or second *Romans* or after the first volume of my *Christian Dogmatics* in 1927.[15] What I would not have wanted in such a case I would rather not see inflicted on Bonhoeffer, least of all in the way it has been done most recently by H. Ott.

Please understand all these expectorations as signs of the gratitude and interest with which I have read your book.

With friendly greetings,

Yours,
KARL BARTH

---

[1]This letter was first published in a slightly abbreviated form in *EvTh*, 28 (1968), 555f.

[2]E. Bethge, *Dietrich Bonhoeffer* . . . (Munich, 1967; ET 1975).

[3]Bethge, pp. 89, 93.

[4]Bethge, esp. pp. 321-326, 357-365.

[4a][numbering of Swiss ed.] Cf. K. D. Schmidt, *Das Jahr 1934*, Vol. II of *Die Bekenntnisse und grundsätzlichen Äusserungen zur Kirchenfrage* (Göttingen, 1935), pp. 22-25, 93-95, for the Declarations of 3-4 January and 24-31 May 1934.

[4b][numbering of Swiss ed.] Cf. 260.

[5]Bethge, pp. 138, 183f., 209, 280f., 307, 379, 468-472.

[6]George Kennedy Allen Bell (1833-1958), Bishop of Chichester from 1929.

[7]*Letters and Papers from Prison.*

[8]A. Lindt, "Dietrich Bonhoeffer und der Weg vom christlichen Glaube zum politischen Handeln," *Reformatio*, 16 (1967), 251-257.

[9]Seminar on preaching held by the Confessing Church under the direction of Bonhoeffer, 1935-1937; cf. Bethge, pp. 488-662.

[10]D. Bonhoeffer, *Letters and Papers from Prison*, ed. E. Bethge (Munich, 1951; 13th ed., 1966); cf. the series *Die mündige Welt*, Vols. I-IV (Munich, 1955-1969) and also E. Feil, *Die Theologie Dietrich Bonhoeffers* . . . (Munich/Mainz, 1971), bibliography, pp. 402-422.

[11]H. Ott, *Wirklichkeit und Glaube*, Vol. I (Göttingen, 1966).

[12]D. Bonhoeffer, *Ethik*, ed. E. Bethge (Munich, 1949; 7th ed., 1966; ET 1965).

[13]H. Müller, *Von der Kirche zur Welt* . . . (Leipzig and Hamburg-Bergstedt, 1961).

[14]R. Prenter, "Dietrich Bonhoeffer und Karl Barths Offenbarungspositivismus," *Die mündige Welt*, III, pp. 11-41; "Bonhoeffer und der junge Luther," ibid., IV, pp. 33-51; "Jesus Christus als Gemeinde existierend . . . ," *Luth.Monatshefte*, 4 (1965), 262-267.

[15]K. Barth, *Die christliche Dogmatik im Entwurf*, Vol. I (Munich, 1927).

*   *   *

253

Circular Letter to Those Who Congratulated Barth on His Eighty-First Birthday

Basel, end of May 1967

Dear Relatives and Friends Both Near and Distant,

My eighty-first birthday is behind me and again many of you have sent me friendly greetings in different ways. Not such an overwhelming number as last year,[1] but I did not expect that. The number eighty-one is relatively insignificant, although research in the symbolism of numbers might find in it a fourth power of three, and therefore a four-dimensional vestige of the Trinity which *C.D.* did not reckon with, or a reference to the four Evangelists or the four beasts of Revelation. Nevertheless, the birthday mail was so vast that I could not think of answering you all individually and must beg you, for all the loyalty you have shown me so warmly and sometimes in such rich terms, to let me reply and express my thanks collectively. I really have cause to rejoice that people are thinking of me with such affection and understanding in so many places, although in every respect my feet can now move only in a small compass. Gone are the trips and runs and walks and rides of the past, gone the addresses to large groups, gone the participation in conferences and the like. Everything has its time,[2] and for me all that kind of thing, it seems, has had its time.

Yet I am not unoccupied and hence I am not really unhappy. I managed a well-protected train journey to Rome and some conversations there.[3] And speedy cars often take me short journeys—e.g., every Sunday afternoon to my dear and formerly so capable assistant Charlotte von Kirschbaum at the Sonnenhalde in Riehen, or to the sessions of my well-attended dogmatic colloquia in the theological seminar. And if the mountain can no longer come to the prophet, there are still some major and minor prophets who sometimes come on visits to the mountain. I can also read to an extent I previously did not enjoy. So I do not lack edifying or less edifying news from past, present, and most recent times, nor the chance to interact more or less profoundly with this or that. And I can still on occasion produce a little, especially in the form of rewarding letters to persons I regard as especially adapted for or in need of them, though routine correspondence is increasingly difficult for me and many people help by relieving me of it. What is not to be expected is a continuation of the autobiography I began in the winter of 1965/1966[4] or of Vol. IV, 4 of *C.D.*, whose appearance some over-optimistic friends seem to be looking forward to. What will in fact come out this year is a relatively important fragment of what was to be discussed in the volume: Baptism.[5] No one is obliged to do the impossible, though I am pleased and honored that people are still eagerly asking about further productions from my pen. If I should be impelled, not by an assignment but spontaneously, to speak out on this or that, and still have the necessary strength to do so, I shall certainly not refrain from coming forth again in writing.

My physical weakness has not been totally overcome—I usually call the place it makes itself felt Zurich-Niederdorf—and it is painful for me and a burden to those around me, though not for the moment dangerous. The activity of my little head is obviously not hampered by it. When I think of all the loyal help and care and attention I experience on all sides—and also of my beautiful place here at my desk and in our little house and garden on the Bruderholz—and also of the many people of the same age, and many younger ones, too, who have to put up with much worse than I do—then I have every reason to be grateful to God and sometimes, even if with a rather brittle voice, to sing a psalm.

Dear brothers and sisters and fellowmen, let these lines be enough this time, and be sure that I think of you all and wish the best for you in time and eternity, and pray for you,

KARL BARTH

[1]Cf. 216.
[2]Eccl 3.
[3]Cf. the letters on the Rome visit, most of those from 212 to 235.
[4]Cf. 198.
[5]K. Barth, *Kirchliche Dogmatik*, IV, 4 (*Fragment*): *Das christliche Leben. Die Taufe als Begründung des christlichen Lebens* (Zurich, 1967; ET *C.D.* IV, 4 [*Fragment*], Edinburgh, 1969).

*   *   *

254
To Pastor Max Schoch
Fehraltorf (Zurich Canton)

Basel, 9 June 1967

Dear Pastor Schoch,

Many thanks for your letter. I myself am not a Barthian according to your definition or in any other sense.[1] Luther's *Romans* was one of the books I read and had ready to hand at Safenwil in 1916-1918.[2] But even then I had some mistrust of the man which became stronger during my fifteen years at German universities—the German soul is by nature Lutheran—and here at Basel when I held a seminar on Luther and the fanatics.[3] Calvin is not my man at every point, but he was and is the superior teacher.

With friendly greetings,

Yours,
KARL BARTH

[1]In his letter to Barth on 7 June 1967 Schoch had said: "I am not a Barthian. I understand by this one who draws certain principles from your works and fights with these principles."
[2]Schoch had said that in Barth's first *Romans* (1919) he found no trace of any use of Luther's 1515-16 *Romans* and asked whether Barth knew this work at the time.
[3]Winter semester, 1954/5.

*   *   *

255
To Pater Prof. Magnus Löhrer
Rome

Basel, 9 June 1967

Dear Pater Magnus,

The important Vol. II of *Mysterium Salutis*[1] arrived this morning from Einsiedeln. What hard workers you are in the vineyard! Probably because you are not kept back from concentrated effort by the eye-flirting and other more serious impulses which trouble us poor non-celibates! Have you any idea—or could you find out (though not by way of Willebrands this time[2])—why I have received no acknowledgment from the highest place in Rome of the receipt of my *Ad limina* . . .?[3] But I realize they have other concerns there. Switzerland is unequivocally for Israel.[4] On the fourteenth I am to give a lecture on *Dei Verbum* in the Maria-Stein-Kreis.[5] If you are sometime (I hope soon) back in your homeland do not hesitate to come to Basel and visit with the doctor and me . . . you know already. . . !

With warmest greetings,

Yours,

KARL BARTH

P.S. Do you read *Orientierung*? In it H. Küng has a noteworthy article on Charles Davis.[6]

---

[1]J. Feiner and M. Löhrer, eds., *Die Heilsgeschichte vor Christus*, Vol. II of *Mysterium Salutis* . . . (Einsiedeln/Zurich/Cologne, 1967).

[2]Allusion to an incident in Barth's visit to Rome in 1966.

[3]Barth received an acknowledgment a day or two later on 12 June 1967.

[4]The reference is to the Six Day War (5-11 June 1967).

[5]Barth is referring to a discussion he held with a Roman Catholic group on the *Dogmatic Constitution on Divine Revelation*, *Dei Verbum*, of Vatican II.

[6]H. Küng, "Eine Herausforderung an die Kirche, Zu Charles Davis' Kirchenaustritt," *Orientierung; Katholische Blätter für weltanschauliche Information* (Zürich), 31 (1967), 123-126.

* * *

256
To Prof. Hans Küng
Tübingen

Basel, 14 June 1967

Dear Dr. Küng,

You will by now have received my affirmative and encouraging exclamation as a reply to your article on Davis.[1] While I still rejoice in this and its effect, I should like to take the occasion to whisper in your ear the following, which I regard as opportune in relation to the progress of the forward movement in Catholicism.

For some time you have been very eloquent on the credibility which has been so lacking in your church.[2] But is it not time to think of a slight shift of theme from stressing *veracitas* to what is ultimately no less and indeed even more important: *veritas*, in whose name you could still say all that you are now saying so stirringly, but say it with a different and much stronger accent?

Why should I wish that you would soon exhaust this fine and impressive theme of credibility, conscience, etc.? Because with only these words, which truly must not be abandoned, unless you add solid counterpoints in the sense of thinking from above to below, you can easily be led into proximity to our (Protestant) eighteenth-century Enlightenment, or fall into the corresponding twilight, thus exposing yourself to the attacks and censures of their eminencies and excellencies Felici, Ruffini, Ottaviani, Parente,[3] etc., not to speak of the more serious warnings of an H. U. von Balthasar.

This matter is related to a concern of mine which you already know and which I cannot suppress for all my sympathy with the work of the progressives in Catholic theology. These friends of mine on the other side have not been sufficiently careful to avoid certain errors which have been made in the past and in the present on this side (among us Protestants). Did I not read the day before yesterday an address on the council by the distinguished Cardinal Léger[4] who with his well-intended but flat identification of revelation and holy scripture reminded me uncannily of our seventeenth-century orthodox as well as our modern Fundamentalists? And on the other side, you know what I think of the Bultmannianism of Dr. Hasenhüttl,[5] who is so close to you and who in other respects is so good and worthy. And now I see you roaming over land and sea with your "credibility" and I think uneasily of our past Neologists, who in their way were also strong and forthright people, and of whom I catch only too clearly a distant echo in the statements of my honored teacher Wilhelm Hermann.

Please do not take amiss this little admonition, but do not ignore it either. I suspect your clever Miss Odette Zurmühle—greet her for me—will understand what I am saying.

With warm greetings,

Yours,

KARL BARTH

P.S. Have you noted what Herbert Mühlen has written on mariology in the remarkable symposium *Autorität der Freiheit* (I), pp. 486ff.?[6] And on it E. Wolf in the March/April number of *Materialdienst des Konfessionskundlichen Instituts* (Darmstadt)?[7]

This evening I am to have the pleasure of discussing *Dei Verbum* with the Mariastein-Kreis here.[8]

I should love to be there at your lectures on the sacraments at Tübingen.[9] Have you already done baptism and are you now dealing with the eucharist? And what about your five other sacraments?

---

[1]After receiving Küng's article (cf. 255, n. 6) Barth had sent off a postcard with the words: "Well roared, lion! Karl Barth."

[2]Cf. Küng's later *Wahrhaftigkeit. Zur Zukunft der Kirche* (Freiburg/Basel/Vienna, 1968). Cf. also 306.

[3]Conservative Roman Catholic cardinals.

[4]Paul Emile Léger gave an address on Vatican II at Montreal on 1 October 1964, published under the title "Vorrang der Offenbarung vor Lehramt und Tradition," *Die Autorität der Freiheit*, I, pp. 114-116.

[5]Cf. G. Hasenhüttl, *Der Glaubensvollzug. Eine Begegnung mit Rudolf Bultmann aus katholischen Glaubensverständnis* (Essen, 1963); cf. also his essays, *Füreinander dasein* . . . (Freiburg/Basel/Vienna, 1971).

[6]H. Mühlen, "Neue Perspektiven der Mariologie."

[7]E. Wolf, "Ekklesiologie und Mariologie nach dem II.Vatikanum," *Materialdienst*, 18 (1967), 21-28.

[8]Cf. 255, n. 5.

[9]Delivered in the summer semester of 1967.

*　　　　*　　　　*

256a
[second edition]
To Mrs. Helene Heim
Zurich

Basel, 12 July 1967

Dear Mrs. Heim,

I have no fewer than eleven honorary doctorates but consider this: None has given me more pleasure than your little letter in which you told me last week that my books affect you and your even older friend so much and are so understandable and useful in your lives.[1] I myself constantly need comfort and encouragement and I am truly grateful to you for the kind words you addressed to me. God keep you and your friend and grant to both of you much of his incomparable light.

With very sincere greetings,

Yours,
(recently eighty-one,
too, on 10 May)
KARL BARTH

[1]Mrs. Heim had written to Barth on 5 July 1967 to tell him that two old ladies in the city home in Zurich thought of him with much gratitude. "I, who am eighty-one years old, read to my ninety-eight-year-old friend . . . your sermons *Deliverance to the Captives* and some pieces from the Barth Brevier. She is almost blind and very hard of hearing and it is for both of us a great boon that I can read to her through a special hearing tube. Sermons which had especially much to say to us and those that we found hard to understand the first time we read two or three times and always with close attention. This gives my friend food for thought in her many lonely hours when she cannot do anything. It then happens that she can explain to me something that we did not properly grasp the day before. You see that we who are 'captives' in so many ways have every reason to rejoice in our freedom in spite of everything. Thank God for your work, your ministry. With sincere remembrances, Helene Heim."

*　　　　*　　　　*

257
To Carl Zuckmayer
Saas Fee

Basel, 15 August 1967

[Barth recalled a visit to Zuckmayer's house, calling it the high point of his vacation in the Valais mountains. He thanked him for the gift of his *Meistererzählungen* (Frankfurt, 1969), which had impressed Barth because of their sympathetic depiction of human darkness and their sense of God's all-embracing goodness. In the light of a discussion of predestination in Saas Fee Barth sent on a copy of II, 2 of *C.D.* along with his sermons *Deliverance to the Captives*. He told how his vacation had been cut short by a recurrence of his ailment which had meant his return to Basel by ambulance and a spell in the hospital. He closed with greetings to Zuckmayer as a friend or younger brother whom he had only recently discovered, but discovered with gratitude.]

*　　　*　　　*

258
To Prof. Ernst Wolf
Göttingen

Basel, 18 August 1967

Dear Ernst,

Thanks for your Declaration.[1] If it did not say explicitly "We Germans" at one point[2] I would ask if I might sign it with you. From what we now know it might just as well read "and we Swiss."[3] See that it is published abroad in all languages. The Szagorsk pronunciamento is a scandal.[4]

With warm greetings,

Yours,
KARL BARTH

[1]At Szagorsk on 4 July 1967 the working commission of the Christian Peace Conference had issued a Declaration on the Mideast situation condemning Israel's policy (cf. *JK*, 28 [1967], 453f.), but several German members, led by K. Immer and M. Rohkrämer, issued a counterdeclaration to which Barth is referring here (cf. *JK*, 28 [1967], 504f.).

[2]Point 6 of the Counterdeclaration begins with the words "We Germans."

[3]The Germans had confessed their guilt toward Israel and Barth is pointing to the culpability of Switzerland vis-à-vis Jewish refugees from 1933 on; cf. A. A. Häsler, *Das Boot ist voll . . . Die Schweiz und die Flüchtlinge 1933-1945* (Zurich, 1967).

[4]Cf. n. 1.

*　　　*　　　*

259
To Corps Commandant Dr. Alfred Ernst
Muri

Basel, 3 September 1967

[Barth thanked Ernst for a letter and his friendship and expressed the need for less complaint and more praise on his own part in view of the many blessings in his personal life and his life in the church and even the world. Having just heard a radio sermon he was confident God has not abandoned his community in this age. He remarked that he also listened to the Roman Catholic sermon each Sunday, and the preaching was getting "more biblical," although, perhaps due to the celibacy of the preachers, it failed to move on from the gospel to life, apart from general moralizing. He had then heard Mozart's flute concerto in G major to his great comfort and refreshment. New medication was for the time being holding his sickness at bay.]

*   *   *

260
To Dr. Friedrich-Wilhelm Marquardt
Berlin

Basel, 5 September 1967

Dear Dr. Marquardt,

I have just finished reading your book.[1] For two and one-half days it kept me holding my breath or breathless. I thank you sincerely for this gift and for all the things you point out and develop in it.

I still remember clearly how one day—I forget the year—you made a remarkable journey up the Rhine and turned up here as one of two "Bultmann corpses," as I then called those who had been hurt in some way by the virulent spread of Bultmannitis, but who had been sent here by their fathers, or had come on their own volition, as to a hoped for sanatarium. In the case of the other one, whose name I do not recall, the cure did not work; he became a jurist, which is also a good thing. But you went on to build with great originality and independence a theological house which now even stands formally on Baslerstrasse Berlin[2] and is a light that holds promise of lighting all who go in and out.[3] But to get to the point.

You have discovered and expounded my doctrine of Israel with great skill and finesse, and historically and materially I can raise no objection. This doctrine of mine as you depicted it was so impressive and convincing to me (before I came to §5) that I was almost tempted to tip the hat to myself—only seldom do I rummage about in my books, but you have shown point by point that this is the way it is. I myself could never have brought it to light in this way. And so the praise that this doctrine of Israel merits is really yours. Please let me thank you for taking the trouble to bring out the truth in this matter by following the banister of my ways and works. I am looking forward with joy (though also not without a certain anxiety) to what more you may say on this and other matters now that you no longer need the banister.

You had good cause to develop the criticism made in §5. At this point there is indeed a gap in my work. I can only say two things, not by way of excuse, but by way of explanation.

1. Biblical Israel as such gave me so much to think about and to cope with that I simply did not have the time or intellectual strength to look more closely at Baeck, Buber, Rosenzweig, etc. as you have now done in such worthy fashion.

2. I am decidedly not a philosemite, in that in personal encounters with living Jews (even Jewish Christians) I have always, so long as I can remember, had to suppress a totally irrational aversion, naturally suppressing it at once on the basis of all my presuppositions, and concealing it totally in my statements, yet still having to suppress and conceal it. Pfui! is all I can say to this in some sense allergic reaction of mine. But this is how it was and is. A good thing that this reprehensible instinct is totally alien to my sons and other better people than myself (including you). But it could have had a retrogressive effect on my doctrine of Israel.

A partially consoling factor here is that in your work you have also noted the beginnings of improvement in me, or at least a serious attempt at it. Please let me give you some other indications. Here is the text, worked out in my 1954 seminar, of a supplement to the declaration on the theme of "Christ—the Hope of the World" which was then occupying the World Council of Churches.[4] In view of the protest of the Lebanese ambassador in Washington it was not adopted by the full assembly. Again, a summons from as early as 1938, drawn up by W. Vischer, subscribed by me, and also strenuously defended by me against Emil Brunner.[5] Also to my credit, my reservations concerning the Romans in my work *Ad Limina Apostolorum*, p. 33, question 5 and pp. 39f., questions 6-7. Also to be considered, my contribution to a panel discussion held in Chicago in 1962.[6] I also sent you eight days ago (N.B.: before I took to heart your §5) my introduction to a book coming out in the Union Press Berlin (though they certainly will not print it).[7] I realize that all this is not enough to fill the gap to which you have drawn attention in the doctrine of Israel as it is presented in my other writings and as you have so finely sketched it.

The only thing is—and I feel rather unsure at this point—what about your own doctrine of Israel as you fill this gap and draw out the lines in my treatment in the desired direction? I need not point out to so clever a person as yourself what dangers might arise and affect this enterprise. *Incidit in Scyllam, qui vult vitare Charybdin!*[8] May this not happen to you in the projected improvement of my first attempt! May you do it with no less wisdom than courage!

And now again thanks for everything, best wishes for your further activity in research and teaching, which you have begun with such promise, and sincere greetings,

Yours,

KARL BARTH

[1]F.-W. Marquardt, *Die Entdeckung des Judentums für die christliche Theologie. Israel im Denken Karl Barths* (Munich, 1967).

[2]Marquardt's address.

[3]Cf. Matt 5:15.

[4]Unpublished.

[5]"Das Heil kommt von den Juden (Memorandum)" (Oct. 1938), in *Juden—Christen—Judenchristen. Ein Ruf an die Christenheit*, publ. by the Swiss Evangelical Auxiliary for the Confessing Church in Germany (Zollikon, 1939), pp. 39-47. The debate with Brunner took place 8-9 December 1940 on whether salvation is or was of the Jews (John 4:22).

[6]"Introduction to Theology; Questions to and Discussion with Dr. Karl Barth, Wednesday, 25 April 1962 and Thursday, 26 April 1962, 8 P.M., Rockefeller Memorial Chapel, University of Chicago," in *Criterion; A Publication of the Divinity School of the University of Chicago*, 2, No. 1 (Winter, 1963), pp. 3-11, 18-24.

[7]*Stärker als die Angst*, ed. H. Fink (Berlin, 1968). As Barth foresaw, his introduction was not published, but Marquardt included it in his essay "Christentum und Zionismus," *EvTh*, 28 (1968), 629-660, on 654. It included severe criticism of the Szagorsk Declaration and commendation of the Counterdeclaration; cf. 258, n. 1.

[8]Philippe Gualtier de Chatillon, *Alexandreis* (1277), v. 301: "Incidis in Scyllam, cupiens vitare Charybdon."

*   *   *

261
To Pastor Emeritus Dr. Otto Lauterburg
Wabern (Bern Canton)

Basel, 8 September 1967

Dear Liberal Brother Otto,

Thanks for your sympathy as to my health. The relapse I suffered can be remedied by using new medication. So I have recovered fairly well and sit at my desk and smoke my pipe, something you have impressively sung about for sixty years but never done, so far as I know.

What I think about conversion you may learn from the enclosed[1] (cf. also *Ad limina*, p. 18). But this does not stop me thanking you for sending the writing of J. Böni.[2] That he is a freemason will certainly not prevent me reading him attentively. But we shall have to see whether he will be interesting and congenial to me in other respects.

With sincere greetings and best wishes (also for your wife's health),

Yours,

KARL BARTH

[1]A reprint of letter 104 in *Kerk en Theologie*, 18 (1967), 266f.
[2]Josef Böni, originally a Roman Catholic priest, had been the Reformed pastor in Trogen (Appenzell Canton) for twenty years.

*   *   *

262
To Prof. Eberhard Jüngel
Zurich

Basel, 9 September 1967

[Prompted by Max Geiger, Barth asked Jüngel to take part in a conference to be held at the Bruderholz Restaurant on 22-23 Oct. 1967 by contributors to *PARRHESIA,* the *Festschrift* for Barth's eightieth birthday. (Jüngel came, but did not, as suggested, read a paper on christology along the lines of his contribution "Jesu Wort und Jesus als Wort Gottes," *PARRHESIA*, pp. 82-100.) Barth also recalled a recent visit paid him by Jüngel and Prof. R. Smend of Münster. He suggested that they had spoken too much about himself, though he thought there might be something in the saying that having made history once he had now become history.]

*　　　*　　　*

263
To Carl Zuckmayer
Saas Fee

Basel, 12 September 1967

[The previous Sunday Barth had heard Zuckmayer's play *Katharina Knie* on the radio and had been moved by it to reply to Zuckmayer's letter of 20 August. He said he had found the latter's *Meisterdramen* no less vital than his *Meistererzählungen*. He found the poems more difficult and was a little worried by the idea of worshipping God in the form of the bark of an Alpine tree. While one might worship God the Creator this way, if the author was to perform the *priestly* service Barth discerned in his work, the God at issue must be God the Reconciler of the creation that has fallen from him and contends with him, the same God, but now acting and speaking in Jesus Christ alone, so that it is to him we must direct our worship, and only indirectly to God in the tree-bark. Even according to Vatican II (the *Dogmatic Constitution on the Church*), the priestly ministry of the laity is an analogous participation in the priestly office of Jesus Christ. This makes worship of God in the tree-bark highly problematic, even when rendered by the layman or indeed the poet. Barth also wondered whether Zuckmayer had known and what he thought of the actor E. Ginsberg, who had died recently. He gave a not very encouraging report on his health in spite of the efforts of his wife and doctor, and closed with a personal request and greetings.]

*　　　*　　　*

264
To Bishop László Ravasz
Leanyfalu (Hungary)

Basel, 19 September 1967

Dear Bishop Ravasz,

As I hear, in the next few days you will have to pass and will be able to celebrate your eighty-fifth birthday. This reminds me of our common relationship: the relationship of memories of earlier and serious but also cheerful meetings with you; the relationship, for good or ill, in the fact that we have both become old and even very old people; above all the relationship in the same service to the same good Lord in whom the two of us—you there and I here—have been allowed to stand and may still stand a bit longer. In this relationship I greet you sincerely and wish you on the occasion of your jubilee every good thing—or rather the one good thing in which everything that is good "in life and in death"[1] is enclosed.

With very friendly greetings,

Yours,
KARL BARTH

[1]Cf. Heidelberg Catechism, question 1.

*   *   *

265
To Pastor Emeritus Dr. Otto Lauterburg
Wabern (Bern Canton)

Basel, 29 September 1967

Dear Otto,

Many thanks for sending me the two books by J. Böni.[1] I have read both of them completely and attentively. But mark you: I found neither the personality of the author congenial nor the intellectual level of his work impressive. Do you not also find that already on the title page he seems to be really more interesting in the mists of his earlier Catholic life than later as a supposedly liberated Reformed child of God? But I have long since accustomed myself to the thought that God has very different people who like one another to different degrees. The books of J. Böni annoyed me in any case because these days I had to write an article for the *National-zeitung* in *opposition* to the Jesuit and monastery clauses in the constitution.[2]

With warm greetings and good wishes to you and your wife,

Yours,
KARL BARTH

[1]J. Böni, *Bekenntnisse eines Konvertiten*: Vol. I, *Erinnerungen aus meinem Leben*; Vol. II, *Gedanken zu Fragen unserer Zeit* (Bern, 1966).
[2]Cf. 215, n. 7; K. Barth, "Jesuiten und Klöster...," *National-Zeitung* [Basel],

7/8 October 1967, pp. 1f. Böni wanted the clauses retained (Böni, Vol. II, pp. 170-202), and wrote a reply to Barth in Part 1 of his article: "Unfreundlichkeiten und Torheiten," *Alpina*, 93 (1967), 315f.

*   *   *

266
To Dr. Louis Glatt
Geneva

Basel, 29 September 1967

Dear Dr. Glatt,

Thanks for your letter of 19 September. The special concern which led you to write me[1] sincerely interested me. So I will not delay any longer discussing the question you put to me regarding the guilt of men for the crucifixion of Jesus.

I can already understand it in some way when you try to answer the question your letter posed. Only too often it has been answered in a totally unevangelical way. Only too often it has been answered in such a way as to give rise to various types of folly and mischief, especially in the relationship between Christians and Jews. Yet I do not think that because of a wrong understanding of the guilt of men for the crucifixion of Jesus one can simply draw the conclusion that they were wholly without guilt. I fear that if guilt is totally removed the crucifixion (and perhaps the whole incarnation) will become a purely fatalistic event. In your letter there is a dubious trace of this. But in this case real man would not be received there by God in his grace, for he, the sinner, would not be really received there by God in his grace.

What is at issue at the cross? That God's eternal election, his good will toward men, even and precisely toward sinful and wicked men, is fulfilled. Indeed, as this good will of God is fulfilled, it is for the first time truly *manifest* that both Jews and Greeks, all are under sin (Romans 3:9). And this is how the story of the crucifixion actually goes. As Jesus did his work for men, the guilt of the Jews and also of the Gentiles (in the form of Pilate and his people), to whom the Jews delivered Jesus, is brought to light. Neither of them, with their acts that are there shown to be sin, could contribute anything at all to the work of God, to the fulfillment of his love. God in his love does not will sin, and therefore they could render no service to him by sinning, but only contradict his work. On the other hand neither Jews nor Gentiles in the persons of their representatives could stop God's work with their sin. In their own ways they could only confirm their wickedness, but with it they could not extinguish or evade the fact that God is kind and gracious to them, sinners though they be. If one understands the matter thus, I do not see how one can avoid speaking of the guilt of Jews and Gentiles for the crucifixion of Jesus—of a guilt, be it noted, that one can recall only in the context of the hymn: "Thou hast borne all sin, otherwise we should despair; have mercy on us, O Jesu."[2]

This by way of a hint and spur to your own further thinking. My health has not been so good these days and weeks. I hope, however, that you are tolerably well.

With friendly greetings,

Yours,
KARL BARTH

[1]Glatt had asked Barth whether or not the Jews or the Romans or both had incurred guilt by condemning and executing Christ.
[2]From the hymn "O Lamb of God" by N. Decius.

*   *   *

267
To Pope Paul VI
Rome

Basel, 3 October 1967

Holy Father,

You celebrated your seventieth birthday on 26 September. Forgive me that having been hampered by health problems last week I am only now sending you my good wishes for this day. I shall always remember with gratitude and joy 26 September 1966 when Your Holiness had the kindness to receive myself, my wife, and my friend Dr. Alfred Briellmann for a rewarding, pleasant, and to me instructive discussion.[1]

May the new year on which you have now entered be for you, in the lofty service in which you stand, a divinely blessed time of wise resolves and courageous actions.

I have learned with sincere sympathy that Your Holiness has lately been ill in body, and perhaps still is. It cannot be my affair to comfort you. But it may interest Your Holiness to hear that I have twice had the surgery that your doctors are obviously considering and at least in a limited way I am still capable of work despite my eighty-one years. May it be granted to you, too, to be able to confess with the apostle: "When I am weak, I am strong."[2]

So far as it is possible from the newspapers, I am following very attentively news of the work of the synod of bishops now meeting in Rome.[3] Its program is a very rich one and highly significant at every point for the future of the church committed to the bishops' guidance and also for us separated brethren. The prayer *Veni, Creator Spiritus*, which Your Holiness is undoubtedly in these weeks addressing without ceasing to the One who alone can fulfill it, is also the prayer of us all— as a prayer for your church and for the whole people of God.

With respectful greetings, Holy Father (*una cum Patribus Synodi*),

Yours truly,
KARL BARTH[4]

[1]Cf. 228-230, 232.
[2]2 Cor 12:10.
[3]The synod ended 29 October 1967.
[4]For the answer of Pope Paul VI see Appendix, 16.

*　　　　*　　　　*

268
To Pastor Max Schoch
Fehraltorf (Zurich Canton)

Basel, 17 October 1967

Dear Pastor,

I have read your book[1] from beginning to end and will express my thanks while my impressions are still fresh.

Frankly after our discussion a year ago I had some doubts about your plan because the insights and intentions you then uttered seemed somewhat diffuse. I am now pleasantly surprised both as a whole and materially. The book is intelligently written and interested me—how else could I have read it through with such rapt attention? You have rightly perceived and finely presented the positions and the various new positions of the younger, middle, and older K.B. and the continuity of the whole. I find particularly worthy of praise the way you have also brought into the picture the figures of my contemporaries and partners in debate, although naturally according to your own selection, knowledge, and judgment. I was especially pleased, for example, that you gave such a full account of Kutter. On the other hand, Eduard Thurneysen, who introduced me to Blumhardt and Kutter and with whom I had such penetrating and fruitful exchanges in my period of development, is treated rather too briefly. My philosopher brother Heinrich ought also to have come in somewhere in his originally peaceful and later not so peaceful relation to me. Question marks need to be put here and there, for example, with regard to the relations, events, and people in Germany. Regarding my discussion with Brunner, it is to be noted that he unfortunately had no understanding of the church conflict, that his Nature and Grace attacked me from the rear at the worst possible moment,[2] and that (apart from the basic issue) this helps a little to explain much of the sharpness of my No.[3]

Your book really annoys me only at points where I annoyed and obviously still annoy you, namely, in all matters concerning West Germany, and in connection with it the whole problem of East and West. It is plainly not without penalty that for half a lifetime you have been a reader and co-worker of the NZZ,[4] which has clearly become and still is a kind of official paper of the Bonn government. Hungary 1956! I could go on at length about that but cannot and must not do so here. I will ask you at least, in face of all that has happened since on the part of the lions of East and West (and among ourselves), who was really right then? Those who shouted out then or myself, who opposed their shouting only with provocative silence? One day we must get all this straight between us orally. Unfortunately in the next weeks I have no time for this, since I face another semester with a seminar (on De Ecclesia in Vatican II).[5] But some day the opportunity will come. The main thing is that for all your disapproval in this whole context you still vouch for the fact that in this respect too I am faithful (all too faithful as you see it) to my theological line. In your sermon on 1 Cor 9 (p. 10)[6] you grant the apostle Paul the freedom to be at one and the same time a Christian of both East and West? Why do you not grant it to me too? Well, I will spread a cloak of love over this chapter of your book and rejoice that on the whole it is such a good and understanding and in its way impressive work. So I thank you.

With friendly greetings,

Yours,
KARL BARTH

[1]M. Schoch, *Karl Barth. Theologie in Aktion* (Frauenfeld/Stuttgart, 1967).
[2]E. Brunner, *Natur und Gnade* . . . (Zurich, 1934).
[3]K. Barth, *Nein! Antwort an Emil Brunner*, ThExh, 14 (Munich, 1934).
[4]*Neue Zürcher Zeitung*.
[5]Announced in the Basel lecture schedule for the Winter semester, 1967/68 as "Dogmatic Colloquium: Second Vatican Council: The Dogmatic Constitution on the Church."
[6]M. Schoch, "Predigten über 1 Kor. 9," *Von des Christen Freude und Freiheit* (Zurich), 24, nos. 277-279 (Nov. and Dec. 1966, Jan. 1967).

*   *   *

268a
Eberhard Busch to Pastor Dr. Gerhard Bergmann
Halver (Westphalia)

Basel, 17 October 1967

[Bergmann had sent Barth a copy of his *Kirche am Scheideweg. Glaube oder Irrglaube* (Gladbeck, 1967). Through Busch, Barth recognized that in the face of Liberalism they had a common concern but stated that he did not wish to be used as a figurehead by the confessing movement in its "battle for the Bible" and that he did not like the style of theology ("theology with a flail") which he found in the book. He missed two things: first, a sense of shock, partly "that there are now Christian brethren who are so little recognizable to you as such," but above all that we are all people of unclean lips, so that "one cannot make a single statement about God and his revelation without always having to pray afresh for the Holy Spirit"; and second, a failure to witness in such a way that the gospel is heard as "a liberating, comforting, edifying, pleasing, and indeed a glad word." Barth closed by suggesting that since God has set up the cross in this world as a visible sign of his eternal grace and faithfulness, it cannot be shaken, and does not need to be defended or protected against attempts to shake it. "So a Christian can go his way freely and peacefully . . . and confidently speak his little word of testimony to God's grace in the cross of Jesus Christ—a little word which will not be as such a liberal word of little faith, and even less an apologetic word of little faith, but a much more modest and therefore a much more cheerful little word."]

*   *   *

269
To Superintendent Pastor Walter Herrenbrück
Hanover

Basel, 31 October 1967

[In this gossipy letter Barth mentioned that he had sent off a copy of his *Ad limina*, asked whether a certain Adenauer who admired him was related to Konrad Adenauer, and mentioned his article on the Jesuit articles in the Swiss constitution. Barth recalled a saying from forty years before when he had compared our participation in salvation to that of a condemned man in his execution. He added that he was now reading for the first time Dorothee Sölle's *Stellvertretung. Ein Kapitel Theologie nach dem "Tode Gottes"* (Stuttgart/Berlin, 1965), and that he saw in the author an example—or "model" as she would say—of how one can be at one and the same time both utterly brilliant and utterly without understanding.]

*　　　*　　　*

270
To Dr. Martin Rumscheidt
Toronto

Basel, 1 November 1967

Dear Dr. Rumscheidt,

Sincere thanks for your recent letter with all its news. I am glad to hear that there in Canada you not only think of me personally but spend a good deal of your time studying and interpreting the early Barth. The days when I tussled with my venerable teacher Harnack, he not liking me nor I him,[1] are long, long since behind me. Then, as you have well observed, I spoke no final words. And so I may hope that in heaven we may still perhaps reach an agreement. As things were on his side in those mad and stirring twenties, this was not practically possible, and I for my part could only resist him and for good or ill be unintelligible to him. It has been your task to traverse again the hotly contested front of that time. And I can only hope that you have been able to do it with the necessary caution but also resolution, so that in your Canadian setting, in which not all have studied cautiously or resolutely enough what then took place, a trumpet blast may be sounded which is rousing but, I hope, joyful too and not just shattering.[2]

In brief answer to your various questions:

1. There is no objection on my part to your publishing the little collection of essays you have translated and assembled.[3]

2. I am naturally interested that you think a new translation of *Romans* is necessary and might be undertaken, especially as I, too, have heard criticisms of the first one. But I can take no initiative in this; it is your affair. If you or someone else is prepared to do it, I wish you good success.[4]

3. Regarding your translation of the essay comparing Kierkegaard and me,[5] perhaps you had best approach Eberhard Busch, as proposed. But I can at least tell you that I am as little an opponent of Kierkegaard now as I was earlier. On the other hand, not even in *Romans* was I a real friend of Kierkegaard, let alone a Kierkegaard enthusiast. I have seriously let his words be *spoken* to me—and let him who wants to be a theologian see to it that he does not miss him. But I have also let his words *be* spoken to me and then gone merrily on my theological way— for I still think that he who meets him and stays with him must take care that the gospel does not become for him an irksome and legalistic thing.

My best wishes, especially for the new work you have obviously begun, and friendly greetings,

Yours,

KARL BARTH

[1]Cf. A. von Harnack's open exchange with Barth in *CW*, 37 (1923), 6-8, 89-91, 142-144, 244-252, 305f.; also K. Barth, *Theologische Fragen und Antworten. Ges. Vorträge*, Vol. III (Zollikon, 1957), pp. 7-31; also J. Moltmann, ed., *Anfänge der dialektischen Theologie*, Part I (Theol. Bücherei, 17; Munich, 1966), pp. 323-347.

[2]Rumscheidt later published his dissertation under the title: *Revelation and Theology. An Analysis of the Barth-Harnack Correspondence of 1923* (Cambridge, 1972).

[3]K. Barth, *Fragments Grave and Gay*, trans. W. Mosbacher, ed. with a Foreword and Epilogue by M. Rumscheidt (London/Glasgow, 1971).

[4]The new translation was never done.

[5]A. McKinnon, "Barth's Relation to Kierkegaard: Some Further Light," *Canadian Journal of Theology*, 13 (1967), 31ff.

*   *   *

271
To Carl Zuckmayer
Saas Fee

Basel, 1 November 1967

[Barth thanked Zuckmayer for a recent letter and gift of wine, hoped he was recovering from his sickness, and congratulated him on an award. He spoke of the opening of his seminar on *De ecclesia* of Vatican II with some sixty students, commented on the national election returns, referred to the Pope's illness, and mentioned that Christoph Barth and his family had now settled in Mainz. He told Zuckmayer that he had received an invitation to give three lectures at Harvard (which he declined on 5 Dec.) and closed with a story about Pablo Casals: "The man is ninety years old—so much older than both of us—and he still practices four to five hours every day. When asked why, he answered: 'Because I have the impression I am making progress.' "]

*   *   *

272
To Prof. Helmut Gollwitzer
Berlin

Basel, 7 November 1967

Dear Helmut,

I have just read D. Sölle's book,[1] for previously the reviews had given me no desire to get to know it first-hand. Now I am glad I read it. What a woman! What an equation of great brilliance and even greater lack of understanding! [. . .] But [. . .] a considerable part of the community (who are the friends she mentions at Göttingen?)[2] seems to take pleasure in her excited folly.

Well, she has merited one service from you (you have granted her others in your chivalrous fashion), namely, that of being stirred to write a reply,[3] which I had also set aside up to now. Helmut, I find this to be one of the most impressive, instructive, and in the best sense edifying things to come to my attention from your pen, for, quite apart from your convincing exposure of what is wrong in Dorothee, you have dealt with the matter as a dogmatician of considerable independent weight, and known how to speak for yourself in such a way that it is a joy to follow you. How much more so than in your controversial work against the primitive Herbert Braun[4] and especially your rather confusing exchanges with your philosophical friend in Berlin.[5] This time you must have had a good angel at your side to write as you do. For this time the horse does not limp on three feet but gallops as it needs to on all four.[6] This time everything is in place, or rather everything flows out from the center and back to it again. I thank you and I thank God that you have succeeded so admirably.

I was just a little dissatisfied with what I read on pp. 111ff., because in you (as in Moltmann and others) it is not clear what is to be understood by redemption and similarly by hope. If I am right, you seem to avoid my view of the eschaton as "apocalypsis" of the "tetelestai."[7] But what then? The title of the book also seems to me to be too cumbersome and not very illuminating. Why did you not simply have *Stellvertretung* with a reference to the book by D.S. in a sub-title? But materially and as a whole what you offer is indeed sufficiently enlightening, strong, and comforting.

Yesterday we received a letter from Gertrud Staewen in which, anxiously seeing her own reflection in the fifty old and very old women around her, she tells us gratefully that you visit her regularly. Similarly I rush off each Sunday at midday to see our dear Lollo.[8] What indeed is man?—but stop, the continuation runs: "That *thou* art mindful of him?"[9] And that he is so, stands triumphantly over all the trouble that we ourselves and so many others near and far who are dear to us have to endure. For three weeks I have been surprisingly well in a relative sense. Nelly is also getting through from day to day. And in some way Lollo is graciously preserved from experiencing subjectively the severity of her condition.

Each Saturday from ten to twelve I am studying *Lumen gentium* with some sixty students.[10] I am already in the third semester of my modest academic convalescence and I have grown so cocky that for the summer semester of 1968 I have announced another colloquium—on Schleiermacher's Speeches (Note: 1768 - 1968.[11] How do you plan to keep this anniversary in Berlin?)

[The letter closed with a paragraph of greetings and reminiscences in part evoked by the death of Gogarten on 16 October 1967.]

---

[1]D. Sölle, *Stellvertretung. Ein Kapitel Theologie nach dem "Tode Gottes"* (Stuttgart/Berlin, 1965).

[2]D. Sölle dedicated her book to friends in Göttingen in the hope of church reform.

[3]H. Gollwitzer, *Von der Stellvertretung Gottes. Christlicher Glaube in der Erfahrung der Verborgenheit Gottes. Zum Gespräch mit Dorothee Sölle* (Munich, 1967).

[4]H. Gollwitzer, *Die Existenz Gottes im Bekenntnis des Glaubens* (Munich, 1963; ET 1965).

[5]H. Gollwitzer and W. Weischedel, *Denken und Glauben. Ein Streitgespräch* (Stuttgart, 1965).

[6]Cf. 210.

[7]On Barth's understanding of the eschatological consummation as the manifestation of what has been done by Jesus Christ ("tetelestai": John 19:30), cf. *C.D.* III, 2, p. 462.

[8]Charlotte von Kirschbaum, in a nursing home in Riehen, near Basel, since the beginning of 1966; cf. 200.

[9]Ps 8:4.

[10]Cf. 268, n. 5.

[11]1768 was the year of Schleiermacher's birth. For the anniversary H. Bolli published a *Schleiermacher-Auswahl* (Munich/Hamburg, 1968) for which Barth wrote an epilogue, pp. 290-312.

*   *   *

273
[written in English]
To Sarvapalli Radhakrishnan
Madras

Basel, 7 November 1967

Dear Mister Radhakrishnan,

I thank you very much for your letter from 26 Oct. and for the honour, that you want a contribution from me to the planned volume commemorating the birth centenary of Gandhiji.[1]

Please, understand me kindly when I must answer to your question that it is impossible for me to write an article for this volume. I regret that I am forced to give you this negative answer. The main reason for this is the fact of my old age, by which I am hindered to do such a work which you wish from me.

Indeed, I regret this because I estimate Gandhiji as a good representative of humanity and I think of him with great respect. Therefore I approve of your plan in memory of his engagement for the humanization of the world and I wish you cordially a good success.

Yours sincerely,
KARL BARTH

[1]Gandhi was born 2 October 1869 and the volume came out under the title *Mahatma Gandhi—100 Years*, ed. S. Radhakrishnan (Bombay, 1968).

*   *   *

274
To Prof. Helmut Thielicke
Hamburg

Basel, 7 November 1967

Dear Dr. Thielicke,

I want to thank you expressly for the gift of your latest work[1] and also to say a few words in reply to your kind letter.[2]

I read your book at once at a single sitting and in its totality, and I can only endorse its essential thesis and its tenor. For a long time I have been rather disconcerted by your great ability to say anything and everything to our fellowmen in a precise, definite, and instructive way that I could never match. But this is related to your gift of comprehensive understanding and also to your astonishing temperament. And in the matter on which you write I feel a certain competence and therefore I am pleased to be able to express to you my material agreement.

Have you come across my youthful utterances on the same theme which *ZThK* 1909 immortalized under the wonderful title "Moderne Theologie und Reichsgottesarbeit"[3] and which I then had to defend against two professors of practical theology?[4] How remarkably different are the times. My difficulties face to face with my approaching office were ultimately the same as those of young people today, but I was not really gripped by any anxiety at moving on from the lectures and seminars of Harnack and Herrmann to the pulpit, etc. In those essays I simply wanted to state that these were the presuppositions on which *tant bien que mal* I would have to preach and teach. And I did just that for years—sure (only too sure) of my cause—until quite naturally (again with no special trauma that I can remember) there came about the discovery of other presuppositions. This did not happen, of course, without some later shame at all the historicism and individualism I expected of the people of Geneva and Safenwil in those first beginnings of mine.[5] But in fact I did pretty well with the meager pound I brought with me to the work. If we were then misled by our Kant and Schleiermacher, were we not more substantially provided for and stimulated to more lively speech and action than the moderns are with their Heidegger and Sartre? Or did we live only in the great naivety of the years before the earthquake of the First World War? It is hard to say, but for my part at least I did not receive from anyone the direction you give to young people in your book.

Tomorrow morning Thurneysen will be back here and will undoubtedly have much to tell me about what could be his last journey on the high seas.[6] I do not begrudge it to him that at least in old age his feet have been set in the broad place[7] where I had such an eventful time when younger. If you should pay a visit here I should be pleased to see you again—but please, none of the honored and venerable professor. I never was this and shall not be or become so in my remaining days.

With friendly greetings,

Yours,
KARL BARTH

[1]H. Thielicke, *Über die Angst des heutigen Theologiestudenten vor dem geistlichen Amt* (Sammlung gemeinverständlicher Vorträge und Schriften aus dem Gebiet der Theologie und Religionsgeschichte, 247), Tübingen, 1967.

[2]See Appendix, 15.

[3]*ZThK*, 19 (1909), 317-321.

[4]Barth's article evoked reactions from E. C. Achelis, "Noch einmal: Moderne Theologie und Reichsgottesarbeit," ibid., 406-410 and P. Drews, "Zum dritten Mal: Moderne Theologie und Reichsgottesarbeit," ibid., 475-479. Barth closed the debate with his "Antwort," ibid., 479-486.

[5]Barth served as assistant in Geneva, 1909-1911, and pastor in Safenwil, 1911-1921.

[6]A guest semester in Hamburg.

[7]Ps 31:8.

*　　　*　　　*

275
To Prof. Karl Rahner
Münster, Westphalia

Basel, 14 November 1967

Dear Colleague,

It is really time I told you how pleased I was to read your letter of 23 October[1] and your "Notes on the Reformation."[2]

For a long time I have wanted to have closer contact with you like that I have with Hans Küng. Not by a long way have I read all you have written but all I have read I have absorbed with great interest, though not without the need for some counterquestions. Do not hesitate to use your next visit to Basel (to H. U. von Balthasar, the author of *Cordula*?!)[3] for a meeting with me.

I can gladly agree with your "Notes" not only on the whole but also in almost all the details. They are a true reformation sermon—another proof to me of what you say on p. 234 about "common faith," "not from the church but toward it" (p. 230). Let us henceforward stand and move together in this sense even as separated brethren. I shall never forget how P. Maydieu, OP, of Paris, who unfortunately died some years ago, and who once, long before the council, regularly visited me supposedly for the "strengthening of his faith"—I was much more polemically inclined then than I am now—how he said to me: Let us not talk about the pope, let us talk about Jesus Christ. That sometimes we have to talk a little about the pope, too, and Mary, etc., has not escaped me in reading your fine essay. But it is wonderful that today we can discuss such problematical things without biting and devouring one another. In relation to you particularly we also have to reckon with the appearance of some special doctrines such as that of anonymous Christianity[4] which one can applaud only with a *Placet juxta modum.*

Your desire that we on our side should produce authoritative spokesmen[5] in the form of institutionally empowered church leaders will, I fear (no, I must say, I hope), be fulfilled only in the eschaton when every impossibility will be realized. When someone becomes a president or bishop among us, then one can count on it with the greatest probability that if ever he was a good theologian he will cease to be so, or at least to speak and act as such. Is the opposite really the rule on your side? Did not all or most of the good things that were said at the council and expressed in the texts come from the Periti who were prompting certain accessible bishops behind the scenes? And as concerns the unity of doctrine at least in necessary things, on our side it is only too true today, as it has been for the last two or three centuries, that the situation is dreadful. Do you know the book *Stellvertretung* by D. Sölle,[6] a lady of whom the only thing one can really say is that *that* woman should keep silence in the church?[7] But read too the fine book in which H. Gollwitzer has answered her.[8] Among us, everything depends on the Holy Spirit being there at the right time and seeing to it that the church remains at the heart of the village. He has done this faithfully through all our Pietism, Rationalism, Romanticism, Historicism, Existentialism, etc., so that in fact—without any official congregation of faith or the like—we have always survived and may definitely still hope to do so today. Indeed, what are we for our part to think of it that among you it can and does take place that with an episcopal imprimatur, Hasenhüttl[9] and the Dutch Robert Adolfs[10] (whose book I came to know through the November issue of *Herder-Korrespondenz*) can extol as theological leaders, even if they cannot beatify, not only Bultmann but even the English Robinson? Are not those who speak authoritatively by virtue of their office equally poor on both sides and equally well taken care of by the prayer *Veni, Creator Spiritus*, or the constant hearing of that prayer?

I was very pleased at what you wrote on p. 233 and p. 235 about our future fellowship in the Lord's Supper, which is so very different from what we Reformed still hear today from the Lutherans, at least in principle. Think of it: A year ago I was in Rome, where on Sunday I was at a Catholic service, and was seriously tempted to go with my Catholic doctor to the communion rail, refraining only so as not to embarrass the officiating priest who had previously greeted me, and not to cause offense later among the Roman Waldensians. Conversely I do not think there are many Evangelical pastors (apart from some obstinate Lutherans) who would forbid a known Catholic to partake of our Lord's Supper.

What do you think of Schillebeeckx's book on transubstantiation (or, as he says, transignification or transfinalization)?[11] If you have the time and desire, read what Heinrich Bullinger, Zwingli's successor in Zurich, wrote in this connection in Articles XIX and XXI of the Second Helvetic Confession of 1562.[12] Did Sch. know this text? Would he not be a little scared to find in whose close company he is with his doctrine, which is undoubtedly such a noteworthy one for us? Should you not be studying our classical theology with as much diligence as I at least have rooted around for years in Denzinger, Möhler, and especially Scheeben?[13] In my old days I spent more time reading all kinds of Catholica than I did the more or less tasty fruits growing in our own garden. Now I am giving a seminar on *Lumen Gentium*[14] which is attended at the moment by a handful of students from Freiburg i.B. whose teacher (Kolping) happens to be dealing with the same theme this winter. So I am poring over the (wickedly expensive) volumes of Barauna,[15] the first volume of your *LThK* on the council,[16] the volumes of Hampe (where I found an essay by you),[17] and many other relevant materials.

A last question: for a long time I have been regularly listening on the Sunday radio to a Roman Catholic sermon side by side with the Evangelical one, and I may sometimes be found in the Bruder Klaus Kirche on our Bruderholz hill. What am I to make of it that so far I have not heard in any of these sermons even a mention of anything mariological? And what am I to make of it that in spite of *Lumen Gentium* chap. 8[18] brother Küng has managed to avoid any such mention in his very important book *Die Kirche*?[19] This is fine with me. But how does it relate to your statement (made at least in a past book) that mariology

is one of the "central truths" of Catholic Christianity?[20] (I raised this
w th you, if I recall, in our short meeting in Rome, but what now?)

Enough for the moment. I fear you must regard me as a talkative
old man. The letter has become so full because I wanted to indicate to
you that we shall certainly not be short of things to discuss if you ever
visit me in my little house. I would then introduce you to my dear
doctor whom I am constantly exhorting to practice his lay apostolate.

With friendly greetings, then, and all good wishes,

Yours,

KARL BARTH

[1]In this letter Rahner had thanked Barth for his article "Jesuiten und Klöster" (cf.
265, n. 3).

[2]K. Rahner, "Anmerkungen zur Reformation," *Stimmen der Zeit*, 180 (1967),
228-235.

[3]H. U. von Balthasar, *Cordula oder der Ernstfall* (Einsiedeln, 1966). In this book
Balthasar has many counts against Rahner (pp. 84ff.).

[4]Cf. K. Rahner, "Die anonymen Christen," *Schriften der Theologie*, Vol. VI (Ein-
siedeln/Zurich/Cologne, 1965), 454-554. Balthasar is critical of this theory.

[5]Cf. the essay referred to in n. 2, p. 232.

[6]Cf. 272, n. 1.

[7]Cf. 1 Cor 14:34.

[8]Cf. 272, n. 3.

[9]Cf. 256, n. 5.

[10]R. Adolfs, *Wird die Kirche zum Grabe Gottes?* (Graz, 1967); cf. on this
Herder-Korrespondenz, 21 (1967), 497-501. Adolfs refers chiefly to J. A. T. Robinson,
The New Reformation? (London, 1965).

[11]E. Schillebeeckx, *Die eucharistische Gegenwart* ... (Düsseldorf, 1967); Dutch,
Christus' tegenwoordigheid in de Eucharistie.

[12]*Confessio et expositio simplex orthodoxae fidei.*

[13]Barth had three editions of H. Denzinger's *Enchiridion Symbolorum* ... (Freiburg i.Br., 1922[14-15], 1937[21-23], 1965[33]). He used J. A. Möhler's *Symbolik oder Darstellung der dogmatischen Gegensätze der Katholiken und Protestanten* ... (Mainz/Vienna,
1834[3]) and M. J. Scheeben's *Handbuch der Katholischen Dogmatik*, 4 vols., 1874-1903
(Freiburg i.Br., 1925) and *Mysterien des Christentums* ... , 1865 (Mainz, 1925).

[14]Cf. 268, n. 5.

[15]*De Ecclesia. Beiträge zur Konstitution "Über die Kirche" des Zweiten Vatikanischen Konzil*, 2 vols., ed. G. Barauna (Germ. ed., Freiburg/Basel/Vienna/Frankfurt a.M.,
1966).

[16]*LThK*, 2nd ed., Suppl. Vol. I, *Das Zweite Konzil. Dokumente und Kommentare*
(Freiburg/Basel/Vienna, 1966). Rahner was a coeditor of *LThK* and a contributor to this
volume.

[17]K. Rahner, "Kirchenlehre des Konzils und künftige Wirchlichkeit des Christen,"
in *Die Autorität der Freiheit*, ed. J. C. Hampe, I, 344-359; cf. K. Rahner, *Schriften zur
Theologie*, VI, 479-498.

[18]"De Beata Virgine Deipara in mysterio Christi et Ecclesiae," *LThK*, 2nd ed., Suppl.
Vol. I, pp. 326-347.

[19]H. Küng, *Die Kirche* (Freiburg/Basel/Vienna, 1967).

[20]K. Rahner, *Maria, Mutter des Herrn, Theologische Betrachtungen* (Freiburg i.Br.,
1965[5]). In answer to Barth's question Rahner told the editor that certain Marian dogmas,

even though they belonged to christology, were binding for him; that insofar as they are part of the apostolic faith they are central truths; but that since Vatican II speaks of a hierarchy of dogmas they need not be defended as such.

*　　　　*　　　　*

276
To the State Secretary for Church Affairs Hans Seigewasser
Berlin (East)

Basel, 14 November 1967

[Barth recalled Seigewasser's visit for his eightieth birthday and explained that he had not been able to answer two later letters because of his academic activities, his Rome journey, and his health problems. He hoped that Seigewasser might be able to visit Basel again so that they could have a personal discussion of such matters as peace, atheism, etc. He remarked that his son Markus Barth, in an article on "Church and Communism in East Germany" (*The Christian Century*, 83 [1966], 1440-1443, 1469-1472), had described Seigewasser as an *anima candida* and said that if a new church conflict should arise "the fault will not be his."]

*　　　　*　　　　*

277
To Prof. Bruno Corsani
Rome

Basel, 21 November 1967

[Barth thanked Corsani for reminding him of his pleasant days in Rome by sending some photographs of himself with the Waldensian Faculty, though he expressed horror at how old he looked in them. He mentioned the further study of Roman Catholicism he was engaged in, assured Corsani he was no Roman Catholic and did not expect to become one, but expressed concern at the thinness of Protestant theology in Germany and the USA and hoped the Waldensians would take care to avoid this by continuing to do good theology. He asked for more prints to pass on to his physician.]

*　　　　*　　　　*

278
To a Theological Student in Basel

Basel, 28 December 1967

Dear N.N.,

Many thanks for your kind letter. But what an obstinate fellow you are! You write that you were very impressed by what I told you last week in the Theological School.[1] And now you manage to put down on paper again all that nonsense about the kingdom of God that we must build. Dear N.N., in so doing you do not contradict merely one "insight" but the whole message of the whole Bible. If you persist in this idea I can only advise you to take up any other career than that of a pastor. But why should you not come to a new mind on this decisive issue in the new year which is about to dawn?

For both the New Year and also the rising of a new, the only true and bright light, I wish you all the best.

With sincere greetings,

Yours,

KARL BARTH

[1]On 21 Dec. 1967 Barth had answered student questions at the Church Theological School in Basel.

*   *   *

279
To Pastor E. Warmers
Office for Mission and Social Work
Brunswick Church, Wolfenbüttel

Basel, 2 January 1968

Dear Pastor,

Many thanks for your kind letter of 18 December.[1] It interests me to hear that you are holding a conference for non-theologians on no less a subject than K.B. I sincerely wish the very best to all those who participate and who thus gather solemnly around myself and my little thoughts. How will it go with them at this "no light undertaking," as you call it? I hope in such a way that the participants will not find it dull and tedious but will find some joy in it and even laugh a little.

There is only one thing in your letter, dear pastor, that does not really please me, namely, that you call your enterprise a conference for non-theologians. I think that if you, pastor, could impress it on your fellows, and the participants could grasp the fact that in the church of Jesus Christ there can and should be no non-theologians, but that each man or woman, however simple, is called upon to be an even *better* theologian than K.B., you would have *understood* me and my theology.

With friendly greetings,

Yours,
KARL BARTH

[1]Warmers had asked Barth to send a greeting to those taking part in a conference on Barth's theology for non-theologians.

*   *   *

280
To Theological Student Kurt-Peter Gertz
Wuppertal-Elberfeld

Basel, 29 February 1968

Dear Mr. Gertz,

It was a real pleasure to me that you and your fellow-students wanted to take part in my seminar and did take part so intensively.[1] Also pleasing was the visit of Kolping's seminar to my modest home. The dog which wanted to get in was, like Faust's dog, Mephistopheles trying to bring confusion into our irenical-critical harmony.[2] I have affectionate memories of you all.

Yesterday we had a remarkable gathering in a well-situated Evangelical home in the hill-country of Basel-Land Canton:[3] five Roman Catholic bishops, a Christian Catholic, the corresponding Evangelical hierarchy, representatives of two semi-official commissions for "dialogue," and a few associates. In the morning I myself—only released from the hospital last Saturday—gave a rapidly sketched address and in the afternoon H. U. von Balthasar spoke with his usual perspicacity and profundity.[4] As I heard it the tone was wise and gentle, not, I hope, in the sense of dampened. Everybody was satisfied. And God's sun shone with amazement but peacefully on the whole scene. Is the millennium really just "round the corner"?[5] The fact that Mozart was also played and listened to twice might be a hint in this direction. I recommended to the lord bishops that a movement might be set going in Rome, not for his canonization, but for his beatification.

I will remind my colleague Max Geiger about you.[6] He is a very busy man.

Greet your fellow-students,

Yours,

KARL BARTH

[1]Gertz belonged to a group of Roman Catholic students at Freiburg who regularly visited Barth's colloquium in the winter semester 1967/8.

[2]In the afternoon of 11 December 1967 Barth had invited the conservative Freiburg theologian Dr. Adolf Kolping and seventeen of his students to a discussion of the church, churches, etc. at his house. The discussion was interrupted when Kolping's housekeeper entered the room with her dog.

[3]Leuenberg Home, Hölstein near Liestal.

[4]Barth's lecture on "Kirche in Erneuerung" and Balthasar's on "Die Vielheit der biblischen Theologien und der Geist der Einheit im Neuen Testament" were both published first in *Schweizer Rundschau* [Solothurn], 67 (1968), 152-158 and 159-169; then in *Freiburger Zeitschrift f. Philosophie und Theologie* [Freiburg, Switzerland], 15 (1968), 161-170 and 171-189; then as the second ecumenical paper of the *Zeitschrift* under the title "Einheit und Erneuerung der Kirche" (1968), pp. 9-18 and 19-37. Balthasar's essay was expanded in the two later versions and given the new title of "Einigung in Christus."

[5]Barth was probably recalling the saying at Amsterdam when he was working with the Anglican A. M. Ramsey, "The millennium must be round the corner."

[6]The reference is to a planned publication by Gertz, though the project fell through.

*   *   *

281

To Pope Paul VI
Rome

Basel, 16 March 1968

Holy Father,

You had the kindness to honor and please me on 14 November with an unusually full and friendly handwritten letter[1] passed on to me through the nuncio's office at Bern. And then in January of this year I was greatly pleased to receive as a personal gift from Your Holiness the fine edition of the Vulgate rendering of the two New Testament epistles ascribed to Peter,[2] published in preparation for the approaching anniversary in 1969 of the martyrdom of the apostles Peter and Paul.[3]

I ask you kindly to forgive me for being so long in replying. In the months of December and January my wife and I were both seriously ill and found ourselves in the hospital. So against my wishes even the most important things have had to be set aside for a long time. You may be assured, Holy Father, of my sincere thanks for all the attention you have paid me.

You will pardon me if I permit myself to say to you in all candor, Holy Father, that I have not read and pondered the book on Peter without serious theological, historical, and even aesthetic questions. I am surely not mistaken if I assume that in preparation for that anniversary a corresponding work is planned and is to be awaited on the apostle Paul, Your Holiness' own patron saint. While I have no authority to offer advice or even to express any wishes in this matter, I should not like to withhold from Your Holiness my opinion that if a biblical text is to be the main content of such a book, Paul's Epistle to the Romans might prove to be especially appropriate and significant for many reasons, including ecumenical ones.[4]

I followed with very great interest what Your Holiness wrote in the book on Peter concerning your attitude to the development of post-conciliar Roman Catholic theology.[5] I, too, as a separated brother, accompany this development with rapt attention, not least because I am in close personal contact with more than one engaged in it. And I may say that at least some of the concerns expressed by Your Holiness are no strangers to me too.

I must not delay on this occasion to express to you, Holy Father, my thanks, my joy, and my admiration at the bold, resolute, and patient words that are coming out of the Vatican today on the burning contemporary issues of international politics.

My respectful greetings, Holy Father, with best wishes for your personal welfare and the further blessed discharge of your high ministry,

Yours truly,
KARL BARTH[6]

---

[1]See Appendix, 16. The letter was written by a copyist and signed by the pope.
[2]*San Pietro, Epistole Cattoliche* (Vatican City, 1967).
[3]The anniversary of Peter and Paul was celebrated in 1967/68. Paul VI proclaimed it a year of faith, and when it ended on 20 June 1968 he sent a message to all the clergy affirming the dogmas of the real presence, Mary, the angels, original sin, the papal primacy, and the infallible teaching office.
[4]Cf. 303.
[5]Cf. n. 3, pp. 10-27.
[6]For Cardinal Cicognani's response, see Appendix, 17.

*   *   *

282

To Carl Zuckmayer
Saas Fee

Basel, 16 March 1968

[Barth mentioned that he had not written since 1 Nov. (cf. 271) but was giving Zuckmayer priority after the pope. He referred to his further hospitalization (along with that of his wife) and mentioned his participation in the "summit conference" (280). His present reading included Wilhelm Raabe and Jean-Paul Sartre and he asked for the recipient's opinion. He took issue with Zuckmayer's description of Frederick William IV as the most intelligent of the Prussian kings, especially in view of his handling of the 1848 revolution and his projected attack on Switzerland. He reported with amusement his election as a member of the Institute of France in place of a deceased brigadier general and spoke of the anniversary seminar on Schleiermacher which he had planned for the summer semester, closing with a plea that Zuckmayer would visit him "one way or another, as the greatest general of all times (Hitler) used to say or shout."]

*   *   *

283

To Prof. Karl Rahner
Münster, Westphalia

Basel, 16 March 1968

Dear Colleague,

Last Sunday I heard you on radio Beromünster, at first with pleasure, expressing by lively gestures to those listening with me my approval of individual statements. In the end and on the whole, however, I was completely stunned. You spoke much and very well about the "little flock," but I did not hear a single "Baa" which was in fact authentically and dominatingly the voice of one of the little sheep of this flock, let alone could I hear the voice of the shepherd of this flock. Instead, the basic note was that of religious sociology and the other favorite songs of what is supposed to be the world of modern culture. In the way you are speaking now, so some fifty years ago Troeltsch was speaking of the future of the church and theology. Get me right: I am not speaking a word against the seriousness of your personal faith and what I write is not even remotely meant to be an anathema. But take it from me, our Neo-Protestants were and are in their own way pious and even churchly people. To spend a few hundred years in eternity with their father Schleiermacher (whom I never think of as excluded from the communion of saints) would please me very much should I myself get to heaven—so long as I could have a few thousand years with Mozart first. But with such addresses as that you gave on Sunday, which lack spiritual salt—or "spirituality" as you like to say in Catholic terminology— you are not building up the church in time and on earth, as is our common task, nor building up "the church for the world."

With sincere and fraternal greetings,

Yours,
KARL BARTH

*   *   *

284

**To the Senior Class of Mary's School for Daughters of the Holy Cross
Essen-Werden**

Basel, 16 March 1968

Dear Graduating Seniors,

Your principal has surprisingly asked me to say a personal word to you on the occasion of the important end and new beginning you are now approaching. Since I do not have the pleasure of knowing your surroundings and course of instruction, and above all of knowing any of you personally, it is rather hard for me to respond appropriately to this invitation. But I will not evade it, for to me a great deal rests on every useful contact between the Catholic and Evangelical churches and their members on both sides.

1. You are now—compared to my almost eighty-two years—very young *Christians*, although in very different ways. Hold fast to one thing: No one can create for himself or give to himself faith in Jesus Christ, our Lord and Savior. But he himself, he in whom we may (not must) believe, is given to us all without exception from the supreme and decisive place. He simply waits for us to recognize him so that we may then live with and for him.

2. You are now young *scholars*. That means that before you stands

the task of achieving a solid starting point for thought and the little knowledge which is indispensable and attainable for a cultured person, or one becoming cultured. Enter then into the rich stimulations as well as the much fruitless chatter of our remarkable age—enter into everything which comes to you from outside or which may seem excellent and illuminating from within your own mind—but do so cautiously and in free humor so that you may learn better and better how to take firm, independent steps.

3. You are now becoming young *women*. This means that in some way the problem of love (of men) will become important in your lives, and may already have done so. If I may give you advice in this matter too, I would say two things. First, no playing around, but only responsible behavior in this area. I think you will understand at once what I mean. Then, no overhasty decisions. The right man may be waiting for you round the next corner of life but he may also be waiting round a very distant corner. Believe me as an experienced warrior in this field when I tell you: wisdom and patience, ladies.

This should be enough, since brevity is required. I wish you success in your examinations, and then along the three lines suggested the very best in the further stages of your development.

With friendly greetings,

Yours,
KARL BARTH

*　　　*　　　*

285
To Mrs. Elise Hilfiker-Diriwächter
Safenwil

Basel, 7 April 1968

Dear Lisi (for me Diriwächter),

How long since I last heard from you. I hope this is not because you have been ill again. I am enclosing a little address I gave on 28 February at Leuenberg BL[1] before an exalted gathering of Roman Catholic, Christian Catholic, and Evangelical bishops, presidents, etc.[2] It can and will undoubtedly interest you. I now have a great deal to do with Roman Catholics. Some weeks ago I held a kind of two-hour confirmation class for some thirty vicars of this confession, and fourteen days ago I wrote a fine letter to the Holy Father (the pope)[3] after getting one from him.

Our health has been poor this winter. My wife had a serious heart problem, and I myself in addition to my other troubles had a double lung inflammation, so that we both had to go to the hospital, my wife for two months and I for three weeks. We are both tolerably well again now. How one learns to be *thankful* for each day on which one can still do something. On the twenty-seventh I hope to do a little teaching at the university again,[4] and I am very busy with the necessary preparation.

Let us know if you can how things are with you and with Safenwil in general. Who will be your new pastor?

With warm greetings—you are and will always be one of the first of my women students—and with all good wishes,

Your (almost eighty-
two-year-old) pastor,
KARL BARTH

[1]Basel Land.
[2]Cf. 280, n. 4.
[3]Cf. 281.
[4]Cf. 272, near n. 11 in the text.

*   *   *

<h1 style="text-align:center">285a</h1>
[second edition]
To Pastor Albrecht Goes
Stuttgart

Basel, 27 April 1968

Dear Pastor,

What a *pity*, what a great pity that you were in Basel without visiting me. To be sure, I have to protect myself a little from many people, but I certainly would not have hidden from you behind my almost eighty-two years and the modest work I am still doing; I would have seen and heard you gladly. I have still not thanked you for your book of sermons,[1] in which everything that I read of its little fulness—especially the little homiletics at the end[2]—pleased me *very much*. Next Monday, when I am to meet for a second time with thirty Roman Catholic vicars, I will read it again to strengthen me in what I am to say to these young and very sincere but rather confused hotheads. And now you have sent me with your letter that really fine thing you have written on Bach and Mozart.[3] Oh how I envy you the breadth of your *hearing* as I envy the breadth of *seeing* of my other poet-friend Carl Zuckmayer. (Since last summer, when I visited him in Saas-Fee, I have been in lively correspondence with him, having read his autobiography and all his other important books.) Compared to you both I am really and truly small fry with my few theological intuitions.

This morning at the opening of my colloquium (on Schleiermacher's *Speeches*!!) I myself "spoke" for two whole hours without a stop—incorrigible schoolmaster that I am, yet also a fine specimen of the skill of modern doctors, for in the period 1964-1966 it could never have been guessed that I would be able to do such things in the fourth semester. Well, the Stop! sign will be given me any time now.

Sincere thanks for your gift and sincere greetings,

Yours,

KARL BARTH

[1] A. Goes, *Der Knecht macht keinen Lärm. Dreissig Predigten* (Hamburg, 1968).

[2] "Marginalien als Nachwort," ibid., pp. 159-173; also published in *Kanzelholz, Dreissig Predigten* (Siebenstern-Taschenbuch, 163; Hamburg, 1971), pp. 178ff.

[3] A. Goes, *Contessa Perdono, Variationen über ein unerschöpfliches Thema* (printed privately, 1968). The title is a quotation from the fourth act of Mozart's *Marriage of Figaro*.

*   *   *

285b
[second edition]
To Pastor Albrecht Goes
Stuttgart

Basel, 1 May 1968

Dear Pastor,

I have an uneasy feeling that in my little letter a few days ago I did not adequately thank or particularly praise either the *Servant Who Will Not Cry* or the *Contessa Perdono*.[1] Even today I cannot find the right words for the latter, probably because only the weightiest words would be enough. But I can tell you that the day before yesterday, at the end of a two-hour discussion with my Catholic vicars on the basics of theology as such and of preaching in particular, I read them *in extenso* your title-sermon on pp. 54ff.[2] and I observed that some of those present at once made a note of the book.[3] And today I gave the *Contessa* to my doctor[4] to read—he, too, is a Catholic and loves music and is open to all that is true and good and beautiful. As a needful return gift I am sending you an address that I gave at an ecumenical conference of Swiss leaders—Catholic bishops were to be seen there (no longer carrying a cross today) and excellent Reformed presidents and the like, all peacefully alongside one another.[5] It is rather sketchily put together for I had only left the hospital four days before. Therefore, *perdono!* Your brother at Uhlbach is already acquainted with it.[6] Please greet him for me as occasion offers.

With sincere greetings,

Yours,

KARL BARTH

[1]Cf. 285a, nn. 1 and 3.

[2]This sermon on Isa 42:1-8 is to be found in the collection with the same title on pp. 54-58 and also in the collection *Kanzelholz* (cf. 285a, n. 2), pp. 83-87.

[3]Cf. Barth's account of this conference on 29 April 1968 in "Am Runden Tisch. Evangelischer Professor und Katholische Vikare zur Sache der Verkündigung," *Orientierung: Katholische Blätter für weltanschauliche Information* [Zurich], 32 (1968), 134f.

[4]Dr. Alfred Briellmann.

[5]Cf. 280, n. 4.

[6]Pastor Helmut Goes.

*   *   *

285c
[second edition]
To Dr. Heinz Kloppenburg
Dortmund

Basel, 6 May 1968

Dear Mr. Kloppenburg,

I have just heard that your birthday, like mine, is on 10 May. I have also heard that you are concerned about my really blazing anger last summer at the Szagorsk Declaration.[1] That event and my reaction to it also slightly estranged G. Casalis and my loyal Martin Schwarz. I am not really concerned about the Israelis, whose recent parade in Jerusalem[2] did not please me, but the problem is that I did not come across any friend, or indeed anyone at all, who took upon himself the responsibility of praising their parade, whereas the Szagorsk Declaration was unequivocally in praise of Soviet policy toward Israel. This, then, concerns me—as long before I was concerned about the Pan-Christian Peace Conference, whose cadence and products did not in any way enlighten me. But I have never spoken out *publicly* against it—just as it is only my surprising silence that has made me suspect and more than suspect among the rabid mob of Anti-Communists. But you must allow me freedom for such silence and also freedom to give my reasons for it sometimes *in private*. Or have I upset you specifically by a private utterance of this kind? This is not impossible, for our local discussions of things and persons have often been lively. I cannot remember, however, that I ever made you specifically a target.

However that may be, I want us to enter this new year of our lives at peace with one another. That you mean well and want the very best is obvious to me even though we differ about Prague in general and Szagorsk in particular. Regarding Prague, a Pastor Kutschera,[3] previously unknown to me, has just paid me a visit from there, and I at once came to a basic understanding with him. Why should this be not only possible but also a reality between you and me, too, at some future date?

Be ready to want all that is good in the other matter as well, and in agreement within the disagreement, greetings,

Yours,
KARL BARTH

[1] Cf. 258.
[2] A military parade on 2 May 1968 on the twentieth anniversary of the founding of the state of Israel. The march of 4,500 Israeli soldiers with 99 tanks, etc. led through the parts of Arab Jerusalem occupied in the June War of 1967. The United Nations Security Council and General Secretary U Thant appealed in vain to Israel not to hold the parade.
[3] Pastor Zdeněk Kučera of Prague visited Barth on 2 May 1968.

*　　　　*　　　　*

286
To Carl Zuckmayer
Saas Fee

Basel, 7 May 1968

[Barth apologized for not writing earlier and pleaded health problems and the time taken by his university course. He announced with joy that they now had a very capable housekeeper (Frau Stöckli), regretted that his wife would be in Adelboden when Zuckmayer planned to visit him on the seventeenth, thanked him for his poem "Den Vätern im Stammbuch" (published in the anthology *Die Väter* . . . , ed. P. Härtling [Frankfurt a.M., 1968], p. 40), and sent on a copy of his own seven rules for older people in dealing with the young (printed in *Evangelischer Digest*, 10, No. 5 [May 1968], p. 23). He then went on to speak of Bonhoeffer, the new Roman liturgy, and Schleiermacher:]

I knew Dietrich Bonhoeffer well. What he would have thought and planned and achieved had he lived, no one can say. The fragments of his theology (especially from his final years) have unfortunately become the fashion. To know him properly the standard book is the great biography by Eberhard Bethge (Christian Kaiser Verlag, Munich). I would not say with Max Born that natural science is responsible for the modern intellectual and spiritual debacle. On the contrary I would gladly concede that *nature* does objectively offer a proof of God, though man overlooks or misunderstands it. Yet I would not venture to say the same of natural *science*, whether ancient or modern.

I can understand your aesthetic problems with the postconciliar Catholic liturgy. The example you give ("guided by divine instruction" before the Lord's Prayer) is indeed poor. But is it not true that the shaping of the liturgy is first and last a problem of church and theology? Could it and should it be expected in the long run that Christians in Ghana or Korea or even Basel and Valais should be edified in Latin? And how glad I am I do not have to pray the rosary, for I should find it hard to say "among women" in view of the present-day associations of this expression. [. . .]

Schleiermacher: When you come I will show you two of my books in which I tried to expound him to the best of my ability. If you like them I will have them sent on to you with pleasure. I am dealing with him in a seminar with many boy and girl students and for the moment I am enjoying it (with the old love/hate and the even older hate/love).

[Barth then told of his second conference with Roman Catholic vicars, of the visit of a crazy woman who thought she was the woman of Rev 12 and a reincarnation of Mary, and of an immature Canadian who asked him what reason meant for his theology, to which Barth simply replied, "I use it." He closed by mentioning Yadin's book *Masada* and commenting on the strange things that take place on earth.]

* * *

287
Circular Letter to Those Who Congratulated Barth on His Eighty-Second Birthday

End of May 1968

Thanks and Greetings

To all the many people, that is, who before and on and after the tenth of May wanted to give me pleasure, and did give me pleasure, by sending me for my eighty-second birthday letters, cards, telegrams, flowers, and edible, potable, smokable, readable, and audible gifts of all kinds. If it is by no means to be taken for granted—when most of my companions and friends of past days are no longer here—that I at eighty-two should still see the sun and moon shining, and that I should still take real pleasure in being alive, it is especially not to be expected that so many both near and far should think of me with such love and acceptance and constantly let me know this with such generosity. But since all this is true, I take it as a free gift from God's hand, and also from the hands of men, as what is freely given should be taken.

The eighty-second year that is now behind me was a troubled one both outwardly and inwardly. But even with all the vexation, anxiety, weariness, humiliation, and melancholy, all in all I look back on it gladly and at peace.

I will indicate only briefly the shadows that lay over it. The worst was that my dear wife Nelly, with whom, like Philemon and Baucis in the book, I celebrate a most harmonious evening of life, suddenly found herself in December 1967 very near the end of the strength she had used so faithfully and zealously all her life. (After a long stay in Bethesda Hospital, which I know so well, and subsequent care at home,[1] she is at the moment spending some time in the mountains and her reports cheerfully indicate marked improvement. She will be seventy-five years old on 26 August.) But in my case, too, brother body has made himself notably unpleasant. The dramatic high (or low) point was last July when I unexpectedly had to make a night journey by ambulance from a considerable height up in Valais direct to Basel Hospital, where I also had to spend a few weeks in January because of other troubles. There were (and are) also many burdens to carry in the narrower and wider family circle. The similar accompaniment of events in world politics and in the spectacularly changing intellectual and living conditions of our common human life, and not least what has happened and is still happening in the field of theology (with some hopeful exceptions), was and remains an unsettling business.

Yet the positive things I think of as I look back and also as I look at my present situation are incomparably greater.

I will begin with a few small but not unimportant things. I can shower in cold water every morning both summer and winter (only in the hospital was this impossible). Again, whereas many others have long since become, either willingly or unwillingly, dejected non-smokers, I have still had my pipe (even in the hospital). And late in the evening I can take a small glass of white or red wine, or occasionally a little beer.

Furthermore, I have my dear study with my practical modern desk. And we also have our small but pretty and quiet garden (our Gertli, as my wife says in her incorrigible St. Gall dialect), which is waiting for the real arrival of spring and summer.

Again, in February we found in the person of Frau Marie Stöckli an intelligent, willing, and able helper for housekeeping, cooking, and the personal care we both of us now need. I am also grateful to her for many a new insight into the depths of the life of the Swiss people both yesterday and today. May she long sustain us!

Again, to my refreshment my Roman Catholic physician and friend Alfred Briellmann, who is forty years younger than I, comes at close intervals for ever new discussions of things medical, personal, and also Christian and ecclesiastical. My even younger friends also come regularly—again to my refreshment: my trusty assistant Eberhard Busch, who shares everything at a basic inward level, and can find his way about far better than I can in the wilderness of books and papers old and new that surround me, along with his no less clever than charming wife, Beate (née Blum).

And how shall I not also and especially think with gratitude of our children (and children's children) both here and abroad? We really have a close and beautiful life with them, along with a few disagreements. And this year, for all that they are busy with their own affairs and problems, they have stood by us old people with special love and patience and practical help.

And then, of friends from older days, Eduard Thurneysen at least is still here, sincerely devoted to me and available by phone and personally with comfort and encouragement.

Among truly positive things in the personal sphere I count the hour I spend each Sunday with dear Lollo von Kirschbaum at the Donnenhalde in Riehen. Without her dedication and activity the whole of the middle period of my life and work would have been unthinkable. Now because of her brain illness she is only as it were in a heavily veiled fashion what she once was. But the good sisters there tell me she is a patient they like. And what did she herself tell me a couple of weeks ago: "Everything is so hard and so beautiful and so much more interesting." And when I left: "We are well off, are we not?" On 25 June— always a year ahead of the century—she will be sixty-nine. Even in her frailty she always edifies me.

Now some broader matters in my life. From the autumn of 1966 I have been able to take up again a little of the academic work I discontinued in 1962. A little, namely, in the form of a two-hour colloquium (or seminar) each week, in which I try to practice again with fifty or sixty students my old teaching method: Learn to read by means of the texts of Vatican II, Calvin, and—hear this to your surprise!—Schleiermacher.[2] If at times my health hinders me, Eberhard Busch steps into the breach for me with verve and authority.

Furthermore, since I went ad limina apostolorum[3] in 1966, it has come about almost of itself that I have been engaged in a small ecumenical movement of my own. It has been so in my dealings with the Roman Catholic congregation here assigned to Brother Klaus, whose pastor recently hailed me publicly as the church father of the Bruderholz, and on whose council my doctor-friend discharges his lay apostolate obligation as vice-president. It has been so in discussion with a lively group of Catholic vicars from Basel and environs. It has been so in April[4] of this year with a little address at a summit conference of Catholic, Christian Catholic, and Reformed churchmen. And each dear Sunday morning we both listen to not just one but two sermons (on the radio), one Catholic and one Evangelical. There is no need for concern that I might become a Catholic! For I see only too clearly the plight they are in, too. My own concern is rather that some Catholics might become much too Protestant.

Again, my book on baptism,[5] by human reckoning my last, has now come out. My first impression of its effect: it will be read and pondered by clever people (theologians and non-theologians of both churches); it will be viewed favorably by those who regard themselves as especially historico-critical; it will be pigeon-holed by church leaders who are full of respect for the fine old man and even more full of caution regarding its possible consequences. Even so, what is true in what I have said will still prevail.

Finally, in high old age a remarkable new friendship has been my lot, namely, with the poet Carl Zuckmayer, whom I visited last summer in Saas Fee just before I fell ill and with whom I have entered into a lively correspondence.[6] He has just paid a fruitful visit to me (on the occasion of the Basel premiere of Des Teufels General), and he looked fairly good between my rigid walls of books. What a man he is! He can be very serious and also very merry.

Clearly in and with all this, music, that is, Mozart, has unceasingly accompanied and still accompanies me, as Schleiermacher said of his religion.

But enough! Dear readers of this letter, as a sign of my thanks for your remembrances on 10 May I wanted to tell you as briefly and concretely as possible how things are with me. In retrospect I have no serious complaint about anyone or anything apart from my own failure today, yesterday, the day before, and the day before that—I mean my failure to be truly grateful. Perhaps I still have some difficult days ahead, and sooner or later I certainly have the day of my death. What remains for me is that in relation to yesterday and all the days that preceded it, and all those that may follow it, and finally the last day that will surely come, I should constantly hold up before me and impress upon myself: "Forget not all his benefits."[7]

I commend you too to him, dear readers of this letter,

Yours,
KARL BARTH

[1] February; Barth was in the hospital 2-24 February 1968, and his wife from the middle of December 1967 until January 1968.

[2] Winter semester 1966/67, cf. 234, n. 2; winter semester 1967/68, cf. 268, n. 5; summer semester 1968, cf. 272, n. 11.

[3] Cf. Barth's book of this title (Zurich, 1967) on his Rome trip (22-29 Sept. 1966).

[4] The conference was in fact on 28 February 1968; cf. 280, nn. 3, 4.

[5] K. Barth, C.D. IV, 4 (Fragment): The Christian Life. Baptism as the Foundation of the Christian Life (Zurich, 1967; ET 1969).

[6] Cf. 250, 257, 271, 282, 286, 302.

[7] Ps 103:2.

*　　　*　　　*

288

To Dr. Ernst Johann
General Secretary of the German Academy of Speech and Poetry
Darmstadt

Basel, 1 June 1968

Dear Dr.,

You passed on to me on 27 May the completely astonishing news that the presidium of your academy has resolved to confer on me the Sigmund Freud Prize for 1968.

Have I really earned an award for academic prose? It is from your academy that I have first heard this stated so solemnly and respectfully. So far, when the public has paid attention to me, it has as a rule spoken more about what I said than the way I said it. If my prose is really meritorious and even worthy of a prize according to the judgment of your academy, then in all the decades of my writing there must have been resolutely at work (apart from my conscious concern to write respectably) what Sigmund Freud would have called my unconscious or subconscious. But be that as it may, I naturally accept this interesting honor with pleasure and thanks.

Since I am already over eighty-two years old and no longer in very good health, I do not know for sure whether I will be able to come to you in person. If not, I will have my son Christoph, Old Testament professor at the University of Mainz, act as my representative.[1] But I hope and plan that if it can be managed I myself will be in Darmstadt on 26 October, accompanied by my wife and for safety's sake by my doctor, Mr. Alfred Briellmann, who is very close to me both personally and intellectually. You will then be kind enough to let me know all the details in good time, and also whether a speech will be expected of me. Giving addresses is no longer the thing for me. At best I could handle only a brief salutation.

With high regards,

Yours,
KARL BARTH

[1]Barth was not in fact well enough to go and was thus represented by his son Christoph Barth.

*   *   *

289
To Prof. Heinrich Stirnimann, O.P.
Freiburg (Switzerland)

Basel, 3 June 1968

Dear Colleague,

I have received your letter of 30 May and issue 15, No. 1 of your *Freiburger Zeitschrift*, and I thank you sincerely for both.

I read and considered your review of my baptism fragment[1]—you have teasingly chosen to put the title in this ambivalent form—immediately upon receiving it and on the following day. It really represents more than a small contribution, as you call it in your letter. It does honor to me—and also to yourself—that you have obviously sifted the book so thoroughly and have so well expressed and criticized its positive and negative content.

In my view it would be better for us to discuss personally the few reservations I have about your text. They are not so important or interesting for third parties as to merit a printed reply. It is enough for me that you merely do not agree fully with all my conclusions. I think I hear the cracking in the timbers that I have credited to H. U. von Balthasar and Hans Küng more clearly in you than in them.

One argument against my contesting of baptism as a sacrament that gives me trouble, since it is taken directly from *C.D.* itself, you seem to have missed completely. A subtle (Reformed) Dutchman discovered and stated it.[2] But I will tease you now and tell you about it at the earliest in our next personal meeting.

With friendly greetings,

Yours,
KARL BARTH

P.S. It may interest you to hear that there are Evangelical bishops in Germany who proceed with fire and sword against pastors who keep the law and baptize the infants of others but not their own. Not merely an almost but a totally persuaded Catholic pastor among my readers could never get into this difficulty—unless he had the most indulgent bishop!

---

[1]H. Stirnimann, "Barths Tauf-Fragment. *KD* IV, 4," *Freiburger Zeitschrift für Philosophie und Theologie*, 15 (1968), 3-28.

[2]J. M. Hasselaar, "Vragenderwijs bij kennisname von Barths doopleer," *In de Waag-*

schaal [Amsterdam], 23 (1967/68), 327-329, 339-342. Hasselaar thinks Barth's doctrine of baptism calls in question his ecclesiology in *C.D.* IV, 2, § 67 and his "classical" doctrine of the threefold form of the Word of God in I, 1, § 4.

*　　　　*　　　　*

290
To Mrs. Helga Noth
Bonn

Basel, 20 June 1968

Dear Mrs. Noth,

The news of the death of your husband[1] took me completely by surprise since I did not know of his illness and thought he was fully occupied in his beloved work. And now he has already been buried for a while in the city of David. I have read all that came from his hand, have estimated it highly, and have distinct personal memories of him from my time in Bonn after the war.[2] Nothing of the love you both showed us at that time has been forgotten. I deeply sympathize with you in the loss of your life-partner which you are now suffering, and remember you with sincere affection.

Yours,
KARL BARTH

[1]Martin Noth, emeritus professor of Old Testament at Bonn, died on 30 May 1968 near Beersheba.
[2]Barth was a guest professor in Bonn for the summer semesters 1946 and 1947.

*　　　　*　　　　*

291
To Prof. Karl Schefold
Basel

Basel, 21 June 1968

Dear Colleague,

Warm thanks for your letter of 12 June. I was delighted to hear that in carrying out your planned cycle of academic lectures on the theme of the "future"[1] you thought of bringing me in as one of the speakers. I believe that on this theme, which is such a zealous concern in every area of scholarship today, I have something to say from my own theological standpoint, particularly since it has interested and accompanied me in the last years especially. Thus, although I really have a strong desire to experience something of what may and will come, even more I perceive the importance of the task of drawing attention to the distinctiveness of Christian hope in relation to everything "futurological" that engages other minds.

All the same, respected colleague, I am forced to make a negative response to your invitation. As circumstances are, I can still express myself in short articles, hold discussions in more or less small groups, or even do a little teaching, though for the most part I prefer simply to listen and learn. But what I very definitely cannot do is give the kind of academic lecture that you so kindly ask for. I beg you to understand my situation and therefore the refusal that I unfortunately have to make in this letter,

Yours,
KARL BARTH

¹The exact title of the series was "The Future of Man in Modern Science."

*　　　　*　　　　*

292
To an Engineer in East Germany

Basel, 21 June 1968

Dear Mr. N.N.,

Warmest thanks for the trouble you took in your detailed letter of the twelfth, which I read with great pleasure. I was glad to hear what you are doing in your particular position, both in your job and especially in your free time.¹ And I can only hope that you will continue to do well and bravely what you obviously have to do. As one who recently (as an Evangelical) has observed and followed attentively and hopefully what has been going on in the Roman Catholic Church, I am particularly interested that you have had the opportunity and desire to build a kind of ecumenical house-church in your close family circle—something which impresses me, although only if those concerned are *good* Evangelical and *good* Roman Catholic Christians. The article in the *Kirche*² that you mention is not as yet known to me, nor do I recall how it originated. What did I then tell the world—I hope it was not too bad? If it is not too much trouble for you, I should be grateful if you could send me a copy of the article as occasion allows. So that you do not misunderstand me in relation to what is (rather superficially) called "student unrest," I certainly do not agree with all that is trumpeted forth or even set in motion by the agitated minds of young people, and I strongly believe they should give themselves to their studies with zeal and seriousness and humor, but in one respect, I think, they are wholly in the right against the angry critics who castigate them, namely, that keeping quiet is not the primary civic virtue, especially in West Germany, which has still to learn the ABC's of democracy.

But now to the question which has bothered you for a long time.[3] Well, it is something of a surprise to me that you in East Germany should be bothered by the fact that I belonged for a while to the Social Democratic Party. I believe there is no real reason for this to concern you any longer. It sounds very fine and good that as a Christian one should not belong to any political party, but this is true only when it is a matter of belonging in principle. Being a Christian, however, is not just an inward and private matter. (In this regard we may calmly be taught a little and warned a little by Karl Marx.) Faith in God's revelation has nothing whatever to do with an ideology which glorifies the status quo. (Here again we should be bold to read Marx attentively.) Serious service of God should always include a political service of God. Christians cannot get by in some other and cheaper way. As Christians they must also make political decisions. This means that in specific cases, in relation to specific points and tasks, they can and should join up with a party which stands for the right thing.

In specific cases! When as a young parson in Safenwil in the Aargau I saw the unjust situation of the workers, who were deprived of their rights, then I believed that as a theologian I could meet both them and the other members of the community only by taking their side and therefore becoming in practice a Social Democrat. In so doing I was less interested in the ideological aspect of the party than in its organizing of unions. And "my" workers understood me on this matter. For them I was their "comrade parson" who was even ready on one occasion to march with them behind a red flag to Zofingen, just as they for their part were prepared (sometimes) to become zealous hearers of my sermons. With that concern, I used the fathers and doctors of socialism to enlighten them as to their rights and possibilities both politically and especially in relation to unions, I successfully taught them to make use of their rights and options, and at times I even represented them at various congresses. Once I was almost elected to the Aargau council of government by the Socialists.[4] Who knows, if I had not in the meantime found other and perhaps more important things to do, I might finally have ended my days as a famous Swiss politician!

The other time I had to consider supporting Social Democracy was shortly before the Nazis seized power. At that time my joining the party[5] was above all a protest against the increasingly dangerous spread of the darkness of Hitlerism. In view of the way the Socialists were being restricted and contested at the time, and in view of the way they contradicted and resisted the rising Thousand Year Empire, I regarded it very simply as the right thing, quite apart from all other political motives, that I should accept solidarity with them as I did.

Today I am no longer a member of their party, and indeed I see with vexation and distress that in both Switzerland and Germany this party has now become such a crippled one. But that is another story which I won't bother you with just now. Without belonging to the party, however, I have constantly put in my little word, and still do so, that the walls and barriers to the east which have been put up so zealously and passionately in the west should be torn down. You will have heard this, and I hope it does not trouble you. It is also my serious hope that after these explanations you will no longer have any worries in this whole matter when you think of me.

With friendly greetings, also to your Roman Catholic wife and especially to your [. . .] son,

Yours,
KARL BARTH

---

[1]The recipient was an office-bearer in the church. His family was Roman Catholic.

[2]"Polnische Christen besuchten Karl Barth," *Die Kirche. Evangelische Wochenzeitung* (Berlin, East Germany), 23 (1968), 1f. The account, taken from the Polish monthly *Jednota* (Nov. 1967), relates a visit to Barth on 13 September 1967, when Barth is reported as saying that "ten students who read the Bible play a much more important role than a group of demonstrating students . . . The worst sermon is a more important contribution to world renewal than anything else. At the time I was a student it was thought we should devote a lot of time to psychology. Today the same is said of sociology. But Christians ought to know how to say something new and distinctive. What we need today is a kind of new pietism."

[3]The recipient was bothered by Barth having been a Social Democrat, argued that the Christian should not belong to any political party, and could not understand membership in "what is finally a Marxist party, which as such condemns the Christian faith."

[4]The election was to the Greater Council (Parliament) of Aargau Canton, not to the

Council of Government; cf. Barth's letter to Thurneysen on 8 March 1921, *Briefwechsel*, Vol. I: 1913-1921 (Zurich, 1973), p. 474.
[5]On 1 May 1931 in Bonn.

*　　　*　　　*

292a
[second edition]
To Dr. Carl Zuckmayer
Saas-Fee

Basel, 29 June 1968

[In this letter Barth began by saying that he wanted to answer Zuckmayer's letter of the fifth of June before the month ended. He observed what a pleasure it was to have Zuckmayer stay with him and meet some of his close friends. Barth also expressed pleasure that the Zurich doctors had merely given Zuckmayer some warnings and joined with him in thinking that what we really fancy does us good in the complicated paths linking soul and body, although in enjoying God's good gifts Zuckmayer should remember that "we would like to see you with us for a long time in 'the land of the living,' as the Old Testament puts it."[1]

He was put at ease by Zuckmayer's own opinion that his play *Des Teufels General* did not do too well in Basel because "in your view, too, the situation of 1933-45 is no longer our situation, and its problems, no matter how they excited us then, can no longer be our problems today." In contrast Zuckmayer's *Seelenbräu*,[2] for all its local setting, "expresses and addresses something timeless," and Barth thought that for this reason it would have a more lasting effect.

This led him to wonder whether the new work which Zuckmayer had in hand[3] really had the right material, for no matter how well the 1944 conspiracy against Hitler were to be handled, who could really work up enthusiasm for the inner problems of the Kreisau Circle[4] when attention was now focused on Vietnam, Paris, Biafra, or Bonn? Even when he first heard of the conspiracy from Dietrich Bonhoeffer Barth himself had felt that it was hopeless, and when the only survivor of the 1944 coup, the President of the Bundestag,[5] became its prophet he could see no promise for the future in it.[6] Perhaps Zuckmayer's work would shed new light. Barth thought Zuckmayer might be interested in a book that he himself was reading at the time, *Linke Leute von rechts*, by

O.-E.Schüddekopf (Kohlhammer, 1960), which gave the wider historical context of the episode.

Passing on his own news, Barth referred to his ecumenical activities—he had sent a sample in *Orientierung*[7]—and also to his spring and summer seminars on Schleiermacher. He would send on a selection from the latter's works with a longer autobiographical epilogue[8] on his own relations with him. He then told about the award of the Sigmund Freud Prize for his "academic prose" and of his projected trip to Darmstadt to receive it[9] and also to see the cathedral where a terrible thing took place according to one of Zuckmayer's works.[10]

He asked Zuckmayer whether he could give any plausible explanation for the fact that his "thanks and greetings"[11] gave pleasure to his wife and to those outside the family but not to other closer members of it.

A reference to working with a television team evoked from him the familiar Latin tag: *O tempora, o mores.*[12]

He closed with sincerest greetings and remembrances to Zuckmayer's wife.]

---

[1]Ps 27:13; 116:9; Isa 38:11; 53:8, etc.

[2]C. Zuckmayer, *Der Seelenbräu* (1945) in *Meistererzählungen* (Frankfurt a.M., 1967), pp. 119-189.

[3]On his visit to Barth on 15 May 1968 Zuckmayer had told him that he planned to write a play on the resistance to Hitler and the attempt on his life on 20 July 1944. Cf. C. Zuckmayer/K. Barth, *Späte Freundschaft— in Briefen* (Zurich, 1977; 3rd ed., 1978), esp. p. 79.

[4]The Kreisau Circle, led by James Graf von Moltke, took part in the conspiracy which led to the attempt on Hitler's life in 1944.

[5]Eugen Gerstenmaier.

[6]Cf. K. Barth, "Neueste Nachschriften zur neueren deutschen Kirchengeschichte?" in *Kirchenblatt für die reformierte Schweiz*, 101 (1945), 216-218; reprinted in "Karl Barth zum Kirchenkampf. Beteilung—Mahnung—Zuspruch," *ThExh*, N.F. 49 (1956), 84-89.

[7]Cf. 285b, n. 3.

[8]K. Barth, "Nachwort" in *Schleiermacher-Auswahl*, ed. H. Bolli (Munich/Hamburg, 1968), pp. 290-312.

[9]Cf. 288 and 313.

[10]C. Zuckmayer, *Die Fastnachtsbeichte* (1959) in *Meistererzählungen*, pp. 355-476.

[11]287.

[12]Cicero, *In Catilinam*, I, 1, 2.

*   *   *

293

To Pastor Karl Honemeyer
Düsseldorf

Basel, 13 July 1968

Dear Pastor,

I was pleased to read your essay on the placing of the organ.[1] I gladly endorse your proposal, believing it is at least the second best solution. The best, in my view, is that the organ, which is out of place in divine worship, belonging to the concert hall and not the church, should be replaced by four wind instruments as the basis of congregational singing. But I am as little likely to live to see this as I am to see a weekly Lord's Supper (in the presence of the whole congregation) or the replacement of infant baptism by an act of penitence, prayer, and confession performed in common responsibility by both the congregation and the candidate.

With friendly greetings,

Yours,
KARL BARTH

[1]K. Honemeyer, "Grundsätzliches zum Standort der Orgel," *Musik und Kirche*, 38 (1968), 97-106.

*   *   *

294

To Corps Commandant Dr. Alfred Ernst
Muri

Basel, 17 July 1968

[Barth referred to Ernst's impending retirement, mentioned an article written by Ernst, and in the light of his own military interest wondered whether Ernst might not devote some time to theology in his retirement!]

*   *   *

295
To Dr. Rudolf Giovanoli
Bern

Basel, 23 July 1968

Dear Dr. Giovanoli,

I do not understand why you are so worked up over the Biafra matter.[1]

On the political issue between Nigeria and Biafra one may hold different views. Shrewd observers tell us that there is a little more right on the side of Biafra. But however that may be, millions in Biafra are hungry and have to be helped. What option have we but to do the little we can?

With friendly greetings,

Yours,
KARL BARTH

[1]Giovanoli had criticized a Pro-Biafra Committee on the ground that it involved propaganda against Britain and the Soviets.

*   *   *

296
To Eberhard Busch
Langrickenbach (Thurgau Canton)

Basel, 29 July 1968

[Barth asked how Busch was doing, told him of his intention to read Marcuse's *One-Dimensional Man*,[1] reported on his fair but weakening physical condition, and exhorted Busch to follow Phil 3:14 in his work on Bengel, the theme of his dissertation.]

[1]On the title page of his copy of this work Barth wrote: "And now, Lord, for what do I wait? My hope is in thee" (Ps 39:7).

*   *   *

297

To Mrs. Hannelore Hansch
Rittnerthof near Karlsruhe

Basel, 29 July 1968

[Barth thanked Mrs. Hansch for sending a copy of a manifesto on the use of force. He referred to his other reading (Marcuse) and the paper *Dinge der Zeit*. He hoped that the recipient and Ernst Wolf would come to see him even though a previous visit had had to be cancelled, but could not promise any further specimens of his prizewinning academic prose. In a postscript he expressed amazement at the flood of writings now engulfing the good old church conflict.]

*　　　　*　　　　*

298

To Prof. Ernst Wolf
Göttingen

Basel, 10 August 1968

[Barth mentioned his recent reading of the *Marburger Hermeneutik* (1968) of Ernst Fuchs, Marcuse's *One-Dimensional Man*, and the July number of *EvTh* (28, 1968) devoted to Cybernetics,[1] in which he read on p. 364 that "the horse bit the girl." He wondered what he might have done as a theologian and a writer if he had studied cybernetics and bought a teaching machine! He also wondered whether programmed man might be able to produce a better theology than the Holy Spirit! In conclusion he asked Wolf whether G. C. Berkouwer's book on the Vatican Council[2] was as "breathtakingly important" as Oberman claimed[3] and whether it was therefore worth buying.]

[1]With contributions by H.-D. Bastian, K. Steinbuch, G. Frey, and M. Frank.
[2]G. C. Berkouwer, *Das Konzil und die neue Katholische Theologie* (Munich, 1968; Dutch ed. Kampen, 1965; ET 1965).
[3]H. A. Oberman, *EvTh*, 28 (1968), 388.

*　　　　*　　　　*

299
To Chief Postal Inspector N.N.

Basel, 17 September 1968

Dear N.N.,

You have put to me two questions inexhaustible in scope. Permit me to answer you briefly as follows:

1. What do you regard as the most important and essential thing in the life of a man?

That he should use his understanding in such a way as to learn to live responsibly.

2. What do you regard as the most important and essential thing in the life of a theologian?

That he should exercise his responsibility in such a way as to learn to reflect (think after).[1]

With friendly greetings,

Yours,
KARL BARTH

[1]Cf. K. Barth, "Denken heisst: Nachdenken" (A reply to M. Bense's "Warum man heute Atheist sein muss," printed with this under the title "Atheismus—pro und contra"), *Zürcher Woche*, 14 June 1963, pp. 5-7; also *Kirche in der Zeit*, 21 (1966), 203ff.

*　　　　*　　　　*

300
[written in English]
To Mrs. Virginia Menzies
Kamloops (Canada)

20 September 1968

Dear Mrs. Menzies,

Many thanks for the nice book with the pretty pictures of the Civil War.[1] I am happy that you are so kindly interested in my interest on this strange event of the last century. Perhaps you are astonished that I (as a theologian and as a peaceful man, who prefers pacifism to militarism) like the history of wars and especially of this war. I am astonished too. Probably only psychology is able to solve this paradoxy.

However, I thank you very much for this gift.
With good wishes,

Sincerely,
KARL BARTH

[1]*A Civil War Album of Paintings by the Prince de Joinville*, Preface by the Comte de Paris, text by André Maurois and General James M. Gavin (New York, 1964).

*   *   *

301
To Dr. Albert von Erlach
Bern

Basel, 24 September 1968

[Barth regretted he had had not been able to have such lively contact with von Erlach as in the past, sent his sympathies on the latter's severe illness, and assured him they were in the best of hands, to which they for their part should cling. He remembered happy days with von Erlach and his deceased wife at their place on the Gerzensee and told him he was in his thoughts and prayers.]

*   *   *

302
To Carl Zuckmayer
Saas Fee

Basel, 26 September 1968

[Barth told Zuckmayer of severe physical ailments which had necessitated a hurried operation (on the night the Russians marched into Czechoslovakia). In his sleep after it, according to the nurse, he gave incessant expression to some lofty but to her unintelligible ecumenical and other theology. He had to be fed intravenously and had learned to know what real thirst was, but survived, and wondered whether God was telling him to leave further talk to the younger generation or giving him a period of grace to do a few more little things at his desk. He then asked Zuckmayer what he thought of current events: the Near East, Biafra, the encyclical on the pill (*Humanae vitae*, 1968), Suez, and whether one ought not to postulate the near return of Christ, which Bengel expected in 1836, the very year of Strauss' *Life of Jesus*. Two practical questions which bothered him were whether he could offer his winter colloquium on predestination and whether he could make his projected trip to Darmstadt and Mainz, but he was confident God would provide (Gen 22:8).]

*   *   *

302a
[second edition]
To Dr. Carl Zuckmayer, Saas Fee
(First draft of the first paragraph of 302)

[In this first draft Barth expressed concern that apart from a card he had not heard from Zuckmayer since writing to him on 29 June. He hoped that this was not connected with a decline in health, but even more so that it was not because of displeasure at Barth's doubts about Zuckmayer's next project.[1] Barth realized that he had no real right to interfere in a field that was not his own and so, quoting the Latin tag *si tacuissem, philosophus mansissem*,[2] he says that he will not mention the matter again and assures Zuckmayer that everything he has written or will write moves and concerns him almost "as if it were a part of me."[3]]

[1]See 292a.
[2]This quotation is from Boethius, *Philosophiae consolationes*, libri V (II, 7).
[3]". . . als wär's ein Stück von mir"—an allusion to the title of Zuckmayer's autobiography, *Als wär's ein Stück von mir. Horen der Freundschaft* (Frankfurt, 1966).

*   *   *

303
To Pope Paul VI
Rome

Basel, 28 September 1968

Holy Father,

On 30 July through your state secretary and the nuncio in Bern you again delighted and honored me with two valuable and equally significant gifts: the Pauline volume with the text of and a commentary on

Romans,[1] and the facsimile of the Bodmer papyrus.[2] You will permit me to express profound thanks for these two highly interesting presents.

Your Holiness may perhaps recall that in my letter of 16 March[3] I took the liberty of suggesting that for the anniversary year 1967 the Vatican might publish a Pauline book as well as a Petrine, or, more precisely, that to complement the reproduction of the two Epistles of Peter it might consider a work which has been so important in the history of the whole church, Paul's Epistle to the Romans. Your Holiness can imagine my joyful surprise when I learned that this had in fact been done. It was all the more joyful because in view of the short period between my letter and the publication of the book I could only assume that my modest suggestion could not really have had anything to do with it but had to conclude that in this special instance too, whether by accident or not, the thinking in Rome and in Basel—if I might for a moment mention the two places together—had been moving in the same direction. I am glad about this and I know that I am at one with you, Holy Father, in the hope that as previously, so in the future, the same might happen in even more important matters between Rome and—Geneva.

(I might mention incidentally that the artistic reproductions in the second volume have given me incomparably greater pleasure than those in the first. The great Michelangelo!)

In the meantime many unusual things have happened in both the world and the church to lay upon the whole of Christianity ever new cares and questions and tasks. Kyrie eleison! Believe me, Holy Father, that as I have reflected on these things from my own restricted corner, the power of the keys, whose transmission to the church and to Peter our Lord spoke of,[4] has not been the last thing on my mind. In our meeting almost two years ago one thing that made a lasting impression on me was the seriously troubled way in which Your Holiness mentioned the burden which this in particular laid upon you. You may rest assured of the sympathy with which, as I follow Roman Catholic matters with ever-increasing attentiveness, I continually think of the ways of your special Peter-ministry, confident that it will be given to you, and given to you again and again, to fulfil this ministry with joy, no matter how great the burden may be.

As concerns your encyclical *Humanae vitae*[5] in particular, I have studied its significance and reception with the special help of many Roman Catholic statements, but I will not take up any position here in relation to its material content. My Roman Catholic physician and friend, Dr. Briellmann, who was with me two years ago, would be better equipped to do that. The problem of church authority, which has become such a burning issue by reason of the encyclical, is also, for us others, a matter which must be discussed and settled in the Catholic Church (in the narrower sense). The point which engages me in this discussion is the basic theological problem of the momentous appeal of the encyclical to natural law, or rather, its estimate of natural law as a kind of second source of revelation,[6] and on the side of critics of your text, ascribing a similar function to the conscience of the individual and of the individual Christian. During the long course of my engagement with theology it has become impossible for me to agree with Thomas Aquinas on this issue, whose path is followed not only by Your Holiness but also by both friends and critics of the encyclical and also by many non-Roman Catholics. In this regard I for my part cannot reconcile the encyclical with the fine constitution *Dei verbum* of the recent council,[7] in which I do not find anything said about either natural law or conscience as sources of revelation. In spite of this serious difference, however, you may be assured of my great respect for what might be called the heroic isolation in which, Holy Father, you now find yourself along with your closest advisers.

My only remaining task is to apologize for the long time I took to react to your important gifts. It is due to the fact that I have been ill again and even had to have another fairly serious operation. Its success (along with the light burdens that followed it) I have taken as a sign that I should refrain from the big words I have tried to speak in no small measure during my long life and be content to contribute only a few little words from time to time. As one such little word, Holy Father, I beg you to understand this letter too. How glad I would have been during the past weeks to come to Rome a second time with my doctor and wife—who is fairly well and sends her respects—and to exchange a few confidential and contemplative thoughts with you, Holy Father.

With sincere loyalty and devotion,

Yours,
KARL BARTH[8]

[1]*San Paolo, Lettera ai Romani* (Vatican City, 1968); text in Latin and Italian, with reproductions of the frescoes of Michelangelo from the Capella Paolina in the Vatican.

[2]*Petri Epistolae ex papyro Bodmeriana*, with a companion volume, published by order of Pope Paul VI, May 1968. The Bodmer Papyrus is an incomplete MS of the NT dating from the third (?) century.

[3]Cf. 281.

[4]Matt 16:18f.; 18:18; John 20:22f.
[5]Cf. 302.
[6]Cf. esp. *Humane vitae*, §4.
[7]Cf. *LThK*, 2nd ed., Suppl. Vol. II (1967), pp. 497-583.
[8]For the reply of Cardinal Secretary Cicognani see Appendix, 17.

*　　　　*　　　　*

304
To Mrs. N.N.
Württemberg[1]

Basel, 30 September 1968

Dear Mrs. N.N.,

Your note of 18 Sept. so cheered me—in the best sense—that I am going to do something not very common and send you a brief personal reply.

1. Mozart's church music is an area of his work about which even his good and indeed his best friends usually speak with some disconcerted reserve. And now a Swabian lady previously unknown to me (young? old? I myself am in my eighty-third year) confesses to me that she is greatly attracted precisely by Mozart's church music. How right you are!

2. You write hinting clearly enough at your faith, or lack of faith, your knowledge of faith and its limits, your difficulties with many dogmatic theses including my own, and then describe how you find your "unbelief" and problems constantly diminished and even removed precisely by Mozart's church music. My own little knowledge of faith has arisen and operated for decades and decades in the same setting (Mark 9:24). You can find my dogmatic theses recapitulated in all their strength and weakness in the texts of the Mozart masses. I might add that as a visual aid Grünewald's picture of the passion has hung before me for the last fifty years.[2]

3. At the end of your letter you conjectured that Mozart might have become an angel. This agrees remarkably with what was once whispered to me by Walter Lüthi, a man and a thinker whose contours were not at all Mozartean, but who has been our most important Swiss preacher, and who is just retiring from his ministry at Bern minster. According to my fairly explicit doctrine of angels[3] it might very well be possible. But naturally we cannot make it a dogmatic "thesis." Since I have the pleasure of being on good personal terms with the present pope (in spite

of the pill and some other differences),[4] I might suggest to him one day that the time has perhaps come for, not a canonization, but a beatification of Mozart.

With thanks and friendly greetings,

Yours,

KARL BARTH

[1]This letter was published in Dutch with the title "Correspondentie over Mozart," *In de Waagschaal* [Amsterdam], 24 (1968-69), 186.

[2]A reproduction of Matthias Grünewald's *Crucifixion* on the altar at Isenheim (c. 1512-1515).

[3]*C.D.* III, 3, §51.

[4]Cf. 303.

*   *   *

305
To Prof. Hendrik Berkhof
Leyden

Basel, 10 October 1968

[In this letter Barth discussed with Berkhof what their mutual friend J. Bouman had told him about the Lebanese, or, more precisely, the Arab Christians and their pietistic, semi-Islamic, anti-Jewish, and neo-Marcionite tendencies. He suggested the need for a new study of the relation between the Bible and the Koran.[1] He thanked Berkhof for his book on the theology of the Holy Spirit (*Die Theologie des Heiligen Geistes* [Neukirchen, 1968], mentioned his epilogue to the Schleiermacher selection edited by H. Bolli (Munich/Hamburg, 1968),[2] and referred to his own more comprehensive project for a theology of the Holy Spirit, which he could now view only from afar as Moses did the promised land. Incidentally the question had arisen whether Bouman should go back to Lebanon, and while Barth thought this theoretically the best thing, he could not take practical responsibility for it in view of the advice he had once given Bonhoeffer to return from London to Germany (in a letter dated 20 November 1933),[3] a return which had finally led to his execution.]

[1]Cf. J. Fangmeier, *Der Theologe Karl Barth* ... (Basel, 1969), p. 62.

[2]K. Barth, "Nachwort" in *Schleiermacher-Auswahl*, ed. H. Bolli (Munich/Hamburg, 1968), pp. 290-312.

[3]D. Bonhoeffer, *Gesammelte Schriften*, II (Munich, 1959), pp. 134-137.

*   *   *

306
To Prof. Hans Küng
Tübingen

Basel, 12 October 1968

Dear Hans Küng,

It was kind of you to have a copy of your *Wahrhaftigkeit*[1] sent to me. Sincere thanks. Putting everything else aside, I took it up at once and read it attentively from A to Z. I read this expression of your acute mind and resolute speech with the same sincere admiration with which I have assimilated all your earlier works and with which I expect to read any future ones as well. There was hardly a page on which I did not find something to kindle my glad agreement and applause, including what you have to say about us Evangelicals on pp. 103ff. (if I am not mistaken your Tübingen colleague Käsemann was the prototype you had in mind when you spoke of a fanaticism for authenticity!)—namely, our need for a reformation of the reformation (p. 150). You are taking a difficult path like that little monk at the Diet of Worms.[1a] But you are taking it so courageously and yet so circumspectly on all sides that I do not doubt you will tread it resolutely to the end. Nor do I doubt that with what you say and do you will plow a notable furrow in the history of the Catholic church and therefore of the whole Christian church, even if—which God forbid, though I have some fears in this regard—a new Pio Nono[2] should arise at the next papal election and Vatican II should be overturned with unpleasant consequences for your own position and activity.

But now I must take up this modern virtue (p. 96) of authenticity in relation to you too and must openly confess that for all the pleasure and agreement I found in reading your latest book I could not repress a certain deep-seated uneasiness (which I have sometimes indicated to you before in other contexts).[3] There are two related "bezwaren," as the Dutch say.[4]

Dear Hans Küng, I take you seriously not only as a masterly theological writer but also in the spirituality which has been more or less evident in all your work thus far. More or less, I say; for me it is to be found most clearly in your little book *God and Suffering*.[5] By the spirituality of a theological text I mean the strength and clarity with which what is thought and said and affirmed and delimited derives from Jesus Christ as the way, the truth, and the life.[6] But there are only distant signs of this strength and clarity in your latest book. Your theme, covered in great abstractness, is the virtue of authenticity in its special application to the modern church. But the true church as such is hardly mentioned or set forth, let alone the true ground of the existence and essence of the church, Jesus Christ himself. I did not miss the place on p. 21 where you referred to your earlier book.[7] But I ask you: When the church is at issue, can you proceed by presupposing that its truth, basis, meaning, and goal have already been dealt with in another book, and then cheerfully concentrate on what must be said by way of criticism and necessary change? I was disturbed already by the arrangement of Part I on p. 5. Should not the order of I, II, and III be reversed[8] if there is to be a sound theological grasp and execution—even though the twentieth-century passion for authenticity (a gratifying but rather dubious matter) can then be modestly introduced only as a hopeful example? With the partial ambivalence of the starting-point of what you say, can you convincingly and solidly arrive at the serious things you are after both on the conservative side and also on the progressive side? Will not less serious readers get the impression—I know, I know, contrary to your intention!—that your basic concern is to appeal to the modern church for God's sake not to delay reunion in face of a general modern trend? Why in the world did you not begin with the Holy Trinity or at least christology, then proceed to ecclesiology, and then descend from there—in a kind of nosedive—to your special theme?

Always for the sake of "authenticity," I may not conceal a second thing which bothered me in reading your book, good though it is in intention and in its own way so fine in execution. What do you really mean (on p. 12 and in other formulations passim) by the original gospel of Christ? If Paul correctly understood this gospel (as opposed to the inauthenticity of Peter, the first pope, in Galatians[9]), then authenticity has something, and something decisive, to do with the free and liberating grace of God. In John, too (8:36, cf. 32), the matter runs unmistakably in this direction: "If the Son shall make you free, you shall be free indeed *(ontōs)*." Then and only then! But we see hardly anything of this in your new book. According to the whole tenor of your presentation, what you express is a demand, a religio-moral appeal. In every context there appears what is to me as an old Kantian the very respectable little word "ought" or a synonym for it, whereas in Christian exhortation what we should hear is only a very clear and firm and even imperative "may."

I must now say something very dreadful to you, but you have a thick skin and can put up with it from an old friend (N.B. when you have really taken it to heart): Where in this book of yours is the author of the book on justification?[10] In its totality it has left on me a painful impression of *legalism*. With your diagnosis and therapy, with all your justifiable cry for *veracitas*, you are laying on people a yoke which is certainly not identical with the yoke of him who calls himself *mitis et humilis corde* (Matt 11:29), and which is also not at all easy and light, but only hard and burdensome. Nor can it lead to the finding of peace. If only you had struck up a Glory to God in the highest, and on earth peace (with the familiar and better translation "to men of [God's] good pleasure")[11] and thus joined with the heavenly hosts in their song of praise, and then, looking back from there, presented your doubts and postulates! In what a different light would these have appeared then! But of course you would then have had to start out very differently in the matter of my first complaint, and your cry for *veracitas* would have had to be from first to last an act of glad recognition and adoration of the *veritas*, comparable to the shouts of the disciples or the children on the entry of Jesus into Jerusalem.[12] Why do you not argue, criticize, protest, and postulate on the basis of the gospel (in its literal sense as good news)? Then your book might have been not only instructive but also helpful in the best sense. For all my respect for the work you have put into it, I could not call it that.

(Perhaps you might then have avoided also some overzealous repetitions which have crept in. But this may be connected with the origin of the book as described on p. 23. I will not stress it then. Paul could sometimes repeat himself deliberately according to Phil 3:1. With him, however, it was a matter of the "Rejoice" which underlies, illumines, and controls all the rest.)

But enough and more than enough. Now at least you know the line I would take with you if, as a member of the sacred office, decked out with a red hat, I had a seat and a voice in the action which will obviously be brought against you sooner or later,[13] or the matter which, if I were— a very abstruse idea—in the place of the pope, who is much to be pitied, things beings as they are, I would discuss with you face to face over a good glass of wine (unfortunately neither of you has mastered the art of smoking a peaceful pipe together).

I know for sure that neither by the Sempacher See, nor the Neckar, nor the Tiber, nor whatever other water you may be near at the moment, will waves of anger rise up after you read this letter. You know me well and are aware that materially and personally I am well disposed to you and desire no other than to see you do as mighty a work as possible in your own church and the whole church.

As always,

Yours,

KARL BARTH

[1]H. Küng, *Wahrhaftigkeit. Zur Zukunft der Kirche* (Freiburg/Basel/Vienna, 1968; ET 1968).

[1a]Allusion to the supposed remark of Captain Georg von Frundsberg concerning Luther in 1521.

[2]Pius IX (1792-1878), pope from 1846 to 1878, who issued the polemical encyclicals *Quanta Cura* and the *Syllabus of Errors* (1864) and also proclaimed the dogmas of the Immaculate Conception (1854) and Papal Infallibility (1870).

[3]Cf. 256.

[4]Objections.

[5]H. Küng, *Gott und das Leid* (Theol. Meditationen 18; Einsiedeln, 1967).

[6]John 14:6.

[7]H. Küng, *Die Kirche* (Freiburg/Basel/Vienna, 1967; ET 1967).

[8]I. The Passion for Authenticity in the Twentieth Century; II. Historical Background of the Neglect of Authenticity; III. Authenticity as a Requirement of the Message of Jesus.

[9]Gal 2:11-14.

[10]H. Küng, *Rechtfertigung. Die Lehre Karl Barths und eine katholische Besinnung* (Einsiedeln, 1957; ET 1964).

[11]"Men of God's good pleasure" instead of "men of good will," Luke 2:14.

[12]Matt 21:15f.

[13]The Holy Congregation had already begun an investigation into Küng's *Die Kirche* in 1967 and similar proceedings were begun against his *Unfehlbar?* (ET *Infallible*, 1971) when it was published in 1970.

*   *   *

307
To Mrs. Lieselotte Schwenzel
Darmstadt

Basel, 16 October 1968

[Barth regretted having to inform Mrs. Schwenzel that because of his health and the risk to his wife Nelly he could not visit Darmstadt and Mainz as planned. He had had to give up his colloquium and he quoted

Gerhardt's refrain that "everything has its time" ("Alles Ding hat seine Zeit"; cf. Eccl 3:1ff.).]

*　　　*　　　*

308
To Mrs. Käthe Smith
Glasgow

Basel, 16 October 1968

Dear Mrs. Smith,

I was deeply and sincerely moved to hear of the sudden death of your husband.[1]

I shall never forget meeting him and then you—the impress of his lively personality, balanced between great cheerfulness and profound resignation—the way in which he and I understood (and did not understand) one another—your marriage in the church on the other bank of the Rhine[2] when you were both astonished to hear me trying to declare to you the saying: "I am the resurrection and the life"[3]—these and many other things as well, including the story of a blackbird which played a role in the life of your husband.[4]

It was clear to me from the outset, and merely confirmed later, that I could not win him over to my own theological path. But I never aimed to form a theological school and therefore I was never cross with anyone (least of all your husband) who thought he should see and say things in a more original and a sounder way than I myself could.

And now I think of you with great sympathy, dear Mrs. Smith, as you have to go on your way alone. Believe me, in my very different way I, too, know what parting means. I wish I could impart to you something of the hope which is for me the bright lining of so much separation and solitude.

Sincerely yours,
KARL BARTH

[1]Prof. Ronald Gregor Smith died 26 September 1968.
[2]See 92, n. 3.
[3]John 11:25.
[4]Cf. 92, n. 2.

*　　　*　　　*

KARL BARTH

309
To Pastor Richard Karwehl
Osnabrück

Basel, 30 October 1968

[Barth invited Karwehl to come to see him in Basel now that he was less than 100 kilometers away, told him of his further operation, and mentioned that he could not go to Darmstadt to pick up his Sigmund Freud Prize, and that he had had to give up his seminar on election. He planned, however, to take part in a Mozart program on the radio on 17 Nov. and also to appear on the radio twice again in January in programs on "What it Means to be Liberal" and on "Roman Catholic and Evangelical Radio Preaching" (for the text of these broadcasts see K. Barth, *Letzte Zeugnisse* (Zurich, 1969; ET *Final Testimonies*; Grand Rapids, 1977). He was also interested in recent books, including one edited by Dantine and K. Lüthi on the profound question whether he was outdated (*Theologie zwischen gestern und morgen* ... (Munich 1968), Marcuse's *One-Dimensional Man*, and Moltmann's *Perspektiven der Theologie* (Munich, 1968). Regarding Roman Catholicism he referred to his reading of *Herder-Korrespondenz*, his exchanges with Paul VI, the rampages of Roman Catholic Bultmannians, Küng's stand on the church, and the desire of the German Roman Catholic laity for a joint conference with Evangelicals, which the cardinals and bishops were trying to prevent for not very obvious reasons. He closed with some personal tributes to those who had meant a great deal to him in his sickness, his wife and doctor, Eberhard Busch and his wife Beate, the poet Zuckmayer, and Thurneysen; with a reference to the many who had passed on, Merz, Gogarten, Brunner, and his former student Erica Küppers; and with a quotation from Schiller's *Xenien* that speaks of the old man quietly making it to port on his rescued boat.]

*　　　　*　　　　*

310
To Markus Unholz
Basel[1]

Basel, 30 October 1968

DEAR MARKUS,

YOUR LETTER GREATLY PLEASED ME. THANKS FOR YOUR

GOOD WISHES. PERHAPS YOU WILL LATER BECOME A PROFES-
SOR, TOO, AND EVEN GET TO BE EIGHTY-TWO YEARS OLD AS
I AM NOW. GREETINGS TO YOUR PAPA AND YOURSELF.
WITH LOVING GREETINGS AND SOME SUGAR CANDIES,

PROFESSOR BARTH

[1]Markus Unholz was six and one-half years old and had written Barth the following
letter:

LIBR HAR BROFESER BART. DER PAPI HAT LETSCHTES SEMESCHTER SCHDU-
DIRT BI INEN. ICH HAT GEÖRT ES GET INEN NICHT SO GUT. ICH WÜNSCHE
INEN GUTE BESERUNG. FILE LIBE GRUSE,

MARKUS UNHOLZ

Dear Professor Barth. Papa studied with you last semester. I have heard you are not
so well. I wish you a good recovery. Loving greetings,

Markus Unholz

*   *   *

311
To Mrs. Anna de Quervain
Bern

Basel, 1 November 1968

Dear Mrs. de Quervain,

I was sincerely moved to read of the passing of your husband.[1] He
was one of the outstanding figures of our vanishing generation whose
particular history and mission in our troubled century with all its changes
he not only shared but also in his own specific place and way helped to
shape and determine. He always did this with great loyalty to the cause
but also with great independence and originality. And through the decades he had to live under the constant trial of physical frailty while
the rest of us were only thinking and teaching and writing about it.
How bravely he lived through every stage of his life's work! What he
did as a sufferer, but never as a complainer, will never be forgotten by
the many he was able to serve in Germany[2] and Switzerland.[3]

Regarding my personal relation to him, I am conscious that I did
not give him all the attention and devotion I should have. I was totally
absorbed in my own tasks and problems and was also greatly restricted
in the last years by physical limitations. But believe me, dear Mrs. de
Quervain, I always thought of your husband with deep attachment and

I always respected his achievements. It is with great sympathy, then, that I think of the sorrow which has come upon you especially, though his death had something of the nature of a release.

With sincere greetings,

Yours,

KARL BARTH

P.S. My wife joins me in this letter of sympathy.

[1]Prof. Alfred de Quervain died 30 October 1968.
[2]A. de Quervain was a pastor in Frankfort on Main and then, during the church conflict, he served the Dutch Reformed congregation in Wuppertal-Elberfeld.
[3]In 1944, after teaching in Basel, de Quervain became professor of theological ethics at Bern. His main work was *Ethik*, I and II (1,2,3) (Zollikon-Zurich, 1945-1956).

* * *

312
To Mrs. Gertrud Staewen
Berlin

Basel, 5 November 1968

[Barth sent Mrs. Staewen a copy of his letter to R. Karwehl (309), referred to the approaching election of her brother-in-law Gustav Heinemann as President of West Germany (1969-1974) (he wished he had a better understanding of his politics), passed on greetings to Gollwitzer and Pastor Kanitz, and in a postscript asked how Wolf Dieter Zimmermann came to write such a stupid book of anecdotes about Dibelius (*Anekdoten um Bischof Dibelius* . . . [Munich, 1967]).

* * *

313
To Dr. Gerhard Storz
President of the German Academy of Speech and Poetry
Darmstadt

Basel, 13 November 1968

Dear Dr. Storz,

Now that the ceremony of conferring the 1968 Sigmund Freud Prize by your Academy is a few days past,[1] and the money associated with the award has arrived and even been apportioned in what seems to me to be a meaningful and appropriate way, I may express to you my very real thanks for the honor you have paid me.

I have to admit that this honor gave me special pleasure, perhaps because it was for me the most surprising and unexpected that I have ever received. And those who know me closely are as astonished as I am that a prize which bears such a respected name and is awarded for this particular achievement should be granted to me. In my life's work my express concern was to remind theology that it should listen to its theme, be measured only by this, and orient itself to this alone. It should not let itself be tied, then, by the fetters of any discipline, including psychology, but be bound only by its distinctive subject. It should always have regard to the content of its statements and not their form. When you still judged that my theological work, written according to this rule, should be honored with this particular prize, none of all this prevented me from modestly but gladly accepting the award, and accepting it gratefully as something that just simply falls in one's lap, in keeping with the biblical saying, "Seek first his kingdom . . . and all these things shall be yours as well."[2]

Personally I was very sorry that the condition of my health extinguished my hope of being present myself at the ceremony in Darmstadt. May I ask you once again to excuse my absence? Here at a distance I could at least hear extracts from the ceremony and especially the address of Golo Mann,[3] which in its own way certainly deserved a prize.

With good wishes and regards,

Yours,

KARL BARTH

[1]26 October 1968; cf. 288 and 307.
[2]Matt 6:33.
[3]Golo Mann received the Georg Büchner Prize on the same occasion and gave an address on "Georg Büchner und die Revolution," printed in the *Annual* of the Academy, 1968, pp. 88-103.

*   *   *

314
To Mrs. Roswitha Schmalenbach
Basel

Basel, 18 November 1968

[Mrs. Schmalenbach had interviewed Barth on the radio program "Music for a Guest," and in this note Barth told her that from the mail he had received they had made something of a hit. He suggested that, along with Mozart, her skill in keeping him on track was responsible. He sent on one of the letters he had received, wondering whether she could deal with it.]

*   *   *

315
To Bishop Dr. Jan G. M. Willebrands
Rome

Basel, 20 November 1968

Dear Bishop,

I was greatly moved to hear of the death of Augustine Cardinal Bea.[1] In him the whole church has lost a pious and judicious servant, a man of prudent and kindly thinking, one who in the high office entrusted to him[2] spoke and acted consistently in terms of its true basis according to the measure given to him. I would ask you to make known to all who work with you in the secretariat for Christian unity my sincere sympathy in this painful loss.

Cardinal Bea will live on in my memory as the soul of candor. The hours I spent with him at his home on the Via Aurelia, dear Bishop, I recollect with pleasure,[3] although, paradoxically, it was precisely in discussion with him that I waxed a little polemical when we touched on the difficult complex of nature, natural law, and natural rights. I am glad that the high dignitary, who was five years my superior in age, obviously did not take it amiss. The lofty calm with which you yourself watched the proceedings, understanding both aspects, is also something I cannot forget: it certainly contributed to the fact that no shadow of any kind could remain between the cardinal and me.

How I would have liked to have seen and talked to him again! Perhaps it has come to your ears that for a year now I have been in loose correspondence with the Vatican itself. The Holy Father has sent me some valuable literary gifts and singled me out by writing in person,[4] so that everything suggests that even as a separated brother I am not *persona non grata* in that highest place of all. In my last answer there[5] I touched on the delicate problem of the most recent encyclical and let it be known that my greatest difficulty in relation to it was not that of the means of prevention nor that of ecclesiastical and especially papal authority over against instituted authority, but the very point that had

—326—

been at issue in my talk with Cardinal Bea, namely, the complex of nature, etc. in the encyclical, and in connection therewith the concept of conscience stressed by opponents of the encyclical. Three days ago I received a letter from Cardinal Cicognani, composed at the express request of and representing the pope, in which he kindly attempted to instruct me in the arguments for these things, though these are, of course, familiar enough to me and in no way adequate. (Since I have not yet replied[6] I would ask you to treat this as confidential for the time being.) If you are ever in Basel again I will be pleased to set the whole convoluted matter before you so you can see what it is all about.

I still have a lively interest in everything that is going on in the Catholic sphere—which is by no means little. I am particularly anxious, of course, to see what the answer will be to the question of Cardinal Bea's successor in the unity office.[7]

Assuring you of my great respect, and of my hopes for you in your future work,

With regards and friendly greetings,

Yours,
KARL BARTH

[1]Bea died 16 November 1968.
[2]President of the Roman Secretariat for Christian Unity.
[3]Cf. 230.
[4]Cf. 229; 281, n. 3; 303, nn. 1 and 2; Appendix, 16.
[5]Cf. 303.
[6]Cf. 321 for Barth's answer on 28 November 1968.
[7]Willebrands himself was Bea's successor.

*　　　*　　　*

315a
Eberhard Busch to a Theologian in East Germany

Basel, 21 November 1968

[This theologian had raised with Barth the question whether, precisely for the sake of the seriousness of faith, little children should be spared prayers and Bible stories and the like. Barth agreed that faith should not be forced, but wondered whether the recipient had not misunderstood what Christian education is. While the question was a good one, would it not be arrogant to withhold Christian instruction on a regular basis?— as though only adults could really believe and not confuse prayer and

Bible stories with other things. Are not adults foolish, too, and should we not take the truth of Matt 11:25 literally, seeing that even children can understand that God was in Christ (2 Cor 5:19)? Indeed, is not the God that was in Christ as well or better grasped by children than adults,[1] and cannot the mystery of it be brought home directly through the Bible stories without our clever interpretations? The Christian education of young children may be quietly continued, for if misunderstanding arises with them it does so with adults too, and the fact that it does is no reason to stop the instruction but rather to do it better. "As we ourselves constantly need the correction by God of our obstinate misunderstanding, we may be comforted and hope that more than misunderstandings will be left among the children, and that these will not always remain, so that when the children become adults they will of themselves put away childish things (1 Cor 13:11). So, pray on with your children. Tell them Bible stories. Well or badly—but do it!"]

[1]In support, Busch refers to Dostoevski (E. Thurneysen, *Dostojewski* [Munich, 1921; Zurich/Stuttgart, 1963], pp. 36f., 99f.).

*   *   *

316
To N.N. in Switzerland

Basel, 26 November 1968

Dear Mr. N.N.,

You very kindly sent me your writing along with an accompanying letter. I thank you for this but I also have to admit quite openly that I took no pleasure in reading it.

As opposed to what you learned from the other side, I have to say that precisely "in essentials" I am not at one with you and that I do not expect this publication of yours to have any salutary effect.

Why not? Because I do not detect in your work the slightest trace of what is called in holy scripture the peace of God that passes all understanding.[1]

You say many correct things. But what is correct is not always true. Only what is said kindly is true. You do not speak kindly in a single line.

You utter a powerful No on all possible sides. It is indeed necessary to say No too. But the right No can only be one which derives from and is upheld by an even more powerful Yes. I hear you say only No.

You accuse. That, too, has to be done. But again, if this is Christian accusation, it has to be enclosed in the promise, in the glad tidings of God's grace. In you it is naked accusation.

You demand that others repent. Sometimes one must dare to do this. But only he may do so who himself repents and lives in repentance. You preach down from your high horse, righteous amid the unrighteous, pure among the impure.

Dear Mr. N.N., I am in my eighty-third year; I am ahead of you by many years along with their experience of life, and I can only say: It cannot be done as you are trying to do it in your book. A Christian should not speak as you do either to his fellow-Christians or to his fellow-men, nor should the church speak thus to the world.

I hope you will not feel dressed down by what I say as you were by that Zurich pastor. I concede that you mean well. But in my serious opinion you must mean well in a better way.

In conclusion, to judge from the quality of paper and printing (you yourself are the N.N. press), you must be fairly well off. Please, no more works of this kind! Give the equivalent to the Evangelical Swiss Church Auxiliary, account 80-11 15, for church development. This is appropriate today and will be well done.

With friendly greetings,

Yours,
KARL BARTH

¹Phil 4:7.

*   *   *

317
To Mrs. N.N.
Württemberg

Basel, 26 November 1968

Dear Mrs. N.N.,

Since you have still not decided to visit me in Basel, I may express my opinion that it would be good, if not necessary, if you were to come and tell me openly and expressly about your great concern and the problem of unbelief. I could then listen attentively and productively and say what I can say in reply. Certainly not as "a representative of a world of faith"—a dreadful word for something that does not even exist, and especially not as a "world of conventional faith."

I promise you:

1. that I will make no presupposition in relation to you except that you, too, dwell in the Father's house, which, as we know, embraces many dwellings,[1] and

2. that I will keep even this presupposition to myself, or at least not harass you in any way with it.

I have thus tossed back the decision to you.

With friendly greetings,

Yours,
KARL BARTH

[1]Cf. John 14:2.

*　　　　*　　　　*

318
To Dr. Joachim Kahl
c./o. Rowohlt Taschenbuch Verlag
Reinbek near Hamburg

Basel, 26 November 1968

Dear Dr. Kahl,

Someone has sent me a copy of your recently published rororo book *Das Elend des Christentums . . .*[1] and I did not just skim through it but read it all immediately.

Some of your observations really amused me, e.g., what you say on p. 105 about hermeneutical brainwashing, or on p. 130 about cathedrals and freeways, or on p. 33 about the peace of Nanking.

I am astonished by the temple-storming zeal with which you point to the many bad fruits on the fig-tree of our poor Christianity. The only new thing, of course, was what you said about nightshirts on p. 53— the rest has been familiar to me and to many others for a long time.

The philosophical and historical method (so far as one can speak of such a thing in relation to your book) with which you have carried through your fierce *Carthaginem esse delendam*[2] is not at all clear to me. I am surprised at the breadth of the plunge of the damned into hell as you describe it; compared to it Michelangelo's depiction in the Sistine

Chapel has the appearance of a very narrow brook. From the biblical authors by way of the fathers and the reformers to Herbert Braun and Dorothee Sölle, who studied with you under Gogarten—all on the wrong path! "Ferryman, tell me truly. . . ."[3] With what breadth and depth have you as a twenty-seven-year-old studied all those you handle so roughly to enable you to do so with validity and authority?

Finally, what alternative have you to set over against the sorry plight of Christianity as you have unmasked it? Only your Yes could make your devastating No both interesting and credible. What I miss is something instructive, charming, inviting, and helpful about "humanity without God." But you are lucky; you are still fifty-five years younger than I and have plenty of time to fill in what is in my view the most serious gap in your book, with the help of philosophy, sociology, and political science, to which you have turned after starting out with theology. Good luck, brave man! May you also show yourself to be a wise one!

With friendly greetings,

Yours,
KARL BARTH

[1]J. Kahl, *Das Elend des Christentums, oder Plädoyer für eine Humanität ohne Gott*, rororo aktuell 1093 A (Reinbek near Hamburg, 1968).
[2]Cato's plea for the destruction of Carthage on the occasion of the Third Punic War.
[3]"Schiffsmann (Barth has Fährmann), sag's mir ehrlich, ist's denn so gefährlich"; the third verse of a Bavarian folk-song.

*   *   *

319
To Dr. Gotthold Müller
Schopfheim

Basel, 27 November 1968

Dear Colleague,

It was kind of you to send me your book on Strauss.[1] As I am now able to do as an "honorary invalid" (p. 197), when something interests me I read it more or less at a sitting and very thoroughly (apart from skimming pp. 279ff.). Many thanks both for the gift as such and for the instruction I received from the book.

So far as I can see and judge without your special qualifications, you have dealt with your theme, the presuppositions of poor David Friedrich Strauss, who became so famous in 1836, not only with a display of astounding diligence in research, but also with clear and convincing results. May your warning with respect to the present age (p. 264) be heeded![2]

I have no objections to bring. But in relation to all the interesting material on the specific background of Strauss in Württemberg, I wondered whether by pp. 234ff. at the latest you should not have investigated Brenz[3] and the particular Württemberg position in the kenosis debate.[4] The question of "identity and immanence" has something to do with the Lutheran *genus maiestaticum*[5] which the Tübingen group represented more faithfully than their Giessen opponents and the Decisio Saxonica.[6] You could certainly have produced something of intellectual value concerning this earlier connection. And perhaps digging even deeper into the past—with the help of available local geological writing—you might have given us (in fine print) a fascinating reminder of the chthonic character of Swabia and the way in which this could have shaped its theology and philosophy.

As far as I myself am concerned, how is it that my statements on the question of apokatastasis are put in a special showcase on pp. 337f.?[7]

Your projected ethics within the concept of discipleship has my full attention, as you could gather from my *C.D.* fragment on baptism.[8] If IV, 4 had not remained a fragment, I should have tried to expound in the main part that which Christians should or may do in keeping with what Jesus prayed for and with the disciples. May you do it as I would have done, or differently and better! A pity I shall hardly live to see your work if you go about it as thoroughly as I expect.[9]

With best wishes for your research and teaching,

Yours,

KARL BARTH

P.S. What are we to make of it that the Basel Faculty had nothing to say on the occasion of the Schleiermacher anniversary on 21 November?[10]

---

[1]G. Müller, *Identität und Immanenz. Zur Genese der Theologie von David Friedrich Strauss. Eine theologie- und philosophiegeschichtliche Studie* (Zurich, 1968).

[2]Müller saw it as the main value of his study that it warns us against allowing contemporary philosophy to determine the theme and results of theology.

[3]Johannes Brenz (1499-1570), Swabian reformer.

[4]Debate between the faculties of Tübingen and Giessen on the divine attributes of Christ in his humanity.

[5]Participation of the man Jesus in the divine majesty of the Son of God.

[6]Declaration by Electoral Saxony in favor of Giessen (1624).

[7]Müller has as an appendix a bibliography on the question of apokatastasis (pp. 321-338) which includes references from and to Barth (pp. 337f.).
[8]Cf. *C.D.* IV, 4, esp. pp. 147, 154.
[9]G. Müller, *Verantwortliches Leben. Grundfragen christlicher Ethik* (Stuttgart, 1973).
[10]F.E.D. Schleiermacher was born on 21 Nov. 1768.

*   *   *

320
To Prof. Erik Wolf
Oberrotweil, near Freiburg i.Br.

Basel, 27 November 1968

[Barth regretted that he had had an appointment with the dentist and had missed seeing Mrs. Wolf on a visit the previous week. He thanked Wolf for the copy of his edition of the letters of G. Radbruch (Göttingen, 1968) which Wolf's wife had left. He had been impressed both by the way Radbruch had survived the Hitler period and maintained a serious resistance of "inner emigration," and by the combination in him of the eminent jurist and the active literary and art critic. Barth approved of Radbruch's liking for Fontane and also of his insistence that reconstruction after 1945 should not begin with parties and constitutions and parliaments but with communities. After some reminiscences of his post-war course in Bonn (in which he met Walter Ulbricht) and a lecture in Heidelberg around 1932 (in which he greatly annoyed Marianne, wife of Max Weber), Barth closed by asking Wolf to come to see him again in Basel, since he himself could not travel now, although he was more concerned about his wife's health than his own.]

*   *   *

321
To Amleto Giovanni Cardinal Cicognani
Rome

Basel, 28 November 1968

Reverend Cardinal,

It was an honor and pleasure for me to learn from your letter of 11 November[1] that the Holy Father was interested in the contents of my last letter to him[2] and had instructed you to reply on the critical issue of what I said about the encyclical *Humanae vitae*. And I thank you, Eminence, for the friendly and excellent way in which you have discharged this commission.

It cannot be my business to claim your time and energy with an express statement of my observations on the content of your letter. At issue is the basic formal and material question of all Christian, ecclesiastical, and theological thought and speech, which has been considered and discussed in all churches of all confessions, countries, and centuries, and which will certainly continue to occupy them to the end of all times. So I will be content with a very brief formulation, in relation to your letter, of where I myself stand in answering this basic question.

1. We (the Holy Father and yourself as his representative on the one side, and my humble self on the other) agree that the revelation of God to which the Christian church has to attest is to be found in the true sense only in holy scripture, though naturally with due respect to tradition.

2. We also agree that this attestation is the task of the whole people of God and within this community especially of the teaching office and theology.

3. We also agree that this attestation, being committed to specific men, takes place in the realm of nature and conscience which has been determined and delimited by God the Creator.

4. We agree finally that nature and conscience co-determine the form of this attestation in every time and place.

5. Should we not agree also that while there is no necessary antithesis there is a fundamental distinction between the revelation of God on the one side and on the other side the nature and conscience which co-determine its attestation in the sphere of God's creation?

6. Could we not also agree on the nature of this distinction? God's revelation is God's own personal Word; it has been spoken by Him loudly and definitely in the epiphany of His Son and as such it needs no elevation. Nature and conscience, however, join in with neither speech nor language nor audible voice (Ps 19:3), so that they have absolute need of elevation by God's free grace if they are to be the means of attestation of his Word. "In Jesus Christ . . . it was not Yes and No . . . but Yes and also Amen through him" (2 Cor 1:19f.). This can be said of neither nature nor conscience. In them as such is both Yes *and* No and no Amen. Can we not agree on this?

7. While I can see real consensus regarding Questions 1-4, and possible consensus regarding 5-6, we now come to the critical question in which I see no consensus: How far is it right or possible to do as is done in the encyclical, in its opponents, and also in your letter, and set nature and conscience alongside revelation as equally divine: the temporal

means on the one hand and the eternal theme of Christian knowledge and therefore of Christian witness on the other? Where does this equation occur in holy scripture? Where is it prescribed or even permitted for the church in holy scripture?

May I ask you, Eminence, to discuss these seven points with me further and also to present them, as occasion allows, to him who commissioned you?

Only hesitantly do I permit myself to add to what has been said the following suggestion regarding the much debated encyclical. In my view it would have been possible to shape the text of this document in such a way that

a. the excellent intention of the Holy Father regarding the true relation between marriage and parenthood could have been not only safeguarded but even strengthened in terms of clarity and Christian authority;

b. the irremovable distinction between the unequivocal Word of God on the one side and the ambivalent voices of nature and conscience on the other could have been strictly upheld, the one being treated as the solid side of the papal statement and the other as its variable side,

c. the whole would not have the character of the proclamation of a law but rather of an apostolic admonition and entreaty in Christ's name (2 Cor 5:20), the character of a proclamation of the gospel.

I am firmly convinced that along these lines the Word of the Holy Father would have been received with joyful applause by the whole episcopate and all serious Christians of all churches and that the document—unsought, *per se*, as a demonstration of the Spirit and of power (1 Cor 2:4)—would have resulted in a powerfully higher estimate of papal authority.

I sincerely ask you, Eminence, and the Holy Father through you, not to regard this last part of my letter as presumptuous but rather to gather from it with what lively concern and inward sympathy I take part in what is going on today in the Petrine Catholic Church and the special burdens of its supreme leadership.

I may say that I consider it a highly unusual distinction to be able to speak directly about these things to the Vatican, the center of the Petrine Catholic Church. Assure the Holy Father of my gratitude and of my readiness to perform any service in the cause of church agreement that lies within my powers.

With respectful greetings,

Yours,
KARL BARTH

[1]See Appendix, 17.
[2]See 303.

*　　　　*　　　　*

322
To Pastor Karl Feer
Menzingen (Zug Canton)

Basel, 30 November 1968

Dear Pastor,

Sincere thanks for your friendly lines. Do you not also think that Mozart should be at least beatified?

Could you keep me a copy of your *Crisis theologiae* ... if it is still in print?[1] I have very good relations with modern Catholic theology and would like to read your 1931 work.

With warm greetings and thanks also for the Ravenna doves!

Yours,

KARL BARTH

[1]Feer had written in response to the radio program on Mozart and told Barth about his 1931 Latin dissertation, extracts of which had been published in German: K. Feer, "Weltanschauliche Annäherung?" *Schweizerische Kirchen-Zeitung*, 102 (1934), 276-278, 284f., 300-302.

*　　　　*　　　　*

323
To Prof. Hendrik van Oyen
Basel[1]

Basel, 4 December 1968

Dear Friend and Colleague,

You are perhaps surprised and—not unjustly—disturbed that I have been so completely passive and silent during the whole period of your birthday and retirement celebrations.[2] Though this is no excuse, all kinds of other things urgently claimed my attention. In any case, I ask you, if I now write you a few words as a mere straggler, to accept them kindly if with some shaking of the head, rather along the lines of the opening words of Schiller's *Wallenstein*, Part II: "You come late, but you still come. The long road, Count Isolan, excuses your delay."[3]

I have been thinking of you as I read about the celebrations and heard that you have now passed over the classical boundary from the seventh to the eighth decade and will have become an honorary instead of a regular professor, if the new university rule goes through as proposed. Whether we should feel promoted or degraded by this, or whether, in spite of the external changes it brings, we should simply carry on as before, content in the best sense of the word, that is the issue for us, is it not?

In the symposium edited by the same Mr. Puchinger who, as you see from the enclosed, enlivened my Schleiermacher colloquium last summer with his statements,[4] you say with a slight tinge of regret that during the long period we were both teachers you never got very close to me or to the others at Basel.[5] There is undoubtedly something in this. And I recognize at once that it could and should have been different.

But look, in all the years it was only occasionally, if at all, that I cultivated any close relation with most of the other members of the faculty, not to speak of my own brother Henry, with whom I was on pretty cool terms here for thirty years.[6] Each of us turned to his own way,[7] partly for practical and technical reasons, and partly for deeper ones. This was far from being an ideal situation. It is again connected with the fact that some at least, if not all of us, yourself included, were very intensively claimed by our own works, and it may also be said in (limited) vindication that each of us had something considerable afoot, which was not yet true, or true only to a limited extent, of our younger colleagues, who obviously have some need to catch up in regard to collegial (or, shall we say, human) relations.

As far as the special relation between you and me, I think that at least we never lived or worked either in opposition to or indeed apart from one another, but we clearly found it difficult to give concrete expression to our being together. The same thing that bound us manifested itself to us—the good Lord obviously has very different clients—in such different lights and connections and meanings that there could never be any cooperation in the true sense or any of the corresponding give and take. We each read what the other wrote but were not in a position to determine, stimulate, or activate one another in any depth. From my standpoint, it was the same as with E. Staehelin,[8] or, in a wholly different way, the recently deceased de Quervain,[9] whose work I knew and respected without any notable meshing of the gears. In the wide world of scholarship, too, there may and perhaps must be sincere greetings from afar,[10] even though better than this is surely conceivable.

My only remaining task is to wish for you in your retirement the same busy indolence and indolent business which I have truly enjoyed in spite of some physical weakness and limitation. We differ, of course, at the present stage in the sense that, unlike you,[11] I can no longer envisage finishing my unfinished work. I simply read more industriously than before all kinds of literature both great and small, and on occasion, in speech or letters or limited publications, say just what I have a mind to say. For the past two years I have held my Saturday morning[12] colloquium, which was good fun but also very hard work; I have now had to give it up. I am anxiously awaiting the account which, as intimated, your assistant Mr. Dekker will give of the second Schleiermacher session of the past summer semester and of my largely extemporaneous statements at it.[13]

Aware of my shortcomings in relation to you but with friendly greetings from the Bruderholzallee to the Thiersteinerrain,

Yours,
KARL BARTH

P.S. I am aware that I still have the book on Schleiermacher by the young Richard Niebuhr,[14] which you kindly lent me and which I called dilettante—he undoubtedly has other merits unknown to me. I will see you get it back.

---

[1]Published in a Dutch translation under the title "Laatste brief van Karl Barth" in the newspaper *Trouw* [Amsterdam] on 8 February 1969.

[2]Van Oyen reached the age of seventy and retired on 20 October 1968.

[3]F. Schiller, *Wallenstein, Ein dramatisches Gedicht*; "Die Piccolomini," Act I, Scene 1.

[4]G. Puchinger, "Colleges over Schleiermacher (I)," in *De oude Barth zoals wij hem hoorden in colleges en gesprekken*, ed. A. Dekker and G. Puchinger (Kampen, 1969), pp. 95-113.

[5]G. Puchinger, *Christen en Secularisatie* (Delft, 1968), pp. 187f.

[6]Cf. K. Barth, "Philosophie und Theologie," *Philosophie und christliche Existenz. Festschrift für Heinrich Barth* . . . (Basel/Stuttgart, 1960), pp. 93-106.

[7]Cf. Isa 53:6.

[8]Ernst Staehelin, professor of church history at Basel, emeritus from 1961.

[9]Cf. 311.

[10]The opening words of a patriotic Swiss folk-song by J. G. Krauer, "Erinnerung an das Rütli" (1820).

[11]Van Oyen published several essays after 1968: *Verantwortung und Freiheit* (Gütersloh, 1972).

[12]Barth used here the Dutch term *Zaterdagmorgen* employed by Puchinger.

[13]A. Dekker, "Colleges over Schleiermacher (II)," *De oude Barth* (see n. 4).

[14]Richard Reinhold Niebuhr, *Schleiermacher on Christ and Religion: A New Introduction* (New York, 1964).

*   *   *

324
To the Chr. Kaiser Verlag
Munich

Basel, 4 December 1968

Dear Kaiser-Verlag,

Please send me at once (and charge to my account) 8 (eight) copies of the *Predigten* by Eberhard Jüngel.[1] They are excellent, better than much (or all) the Kaiserverlag has published!—and I will see to their distribution at Christmas.

Tell the author—I will also tell him direct—that in a second edition he should leave out the whole of his homiletical epilogue. I have nothing against its content. Being so schoolmasterish, however, it is stylistically disruptive. And the volume could be a little cheaper without it.

With Advent and Christmas greetings,

Yours,
KARL BARTH

[1] E. Jüngel, *Predigten. Mit einem Anhang: Was hat die Predigt mit dem Text zu tun?* (Munich, 1968).

*   *   *

325
To Prof. Erik Wolf
Oberrotweil, near Freiburg i.Br.

Basel, 6 December 1968

Dear Friend,

You will be welcome on Tuesday 10 Dec. at any time after one o'clock.[1] Perhaps you can phone me from your brother's to let me know the exact time of your arrival and whether you want black coffee or tea. No. 352779.

With sincere greetings to you both,

Yours,
KARL BARTH

[1] When Wolf and his wife came at the time arranged on 10 Dec. 1968 they found that Karl Barth had died the previous night.

APPENDIX

1
To Letter 2
Prof. K. H. Miskotte to K. Barth

Voorst, 16 May 1961

[In this letter which evoked Barth's reply in Letter 2, Miskotte told Barth that he had been flabbergasted by his speech at the seventy-fifth birthday celebration on 10 May 1961. He could not understand how Barth could speak of a "strong man" who might destroy his work or his readiness to abandon this work even though he said at the same time that he saw no reason to retract. Miskotte thought that perhaps Barth had said these things out of a desire to end the isolation of his obvious superiority. He sustained himself with the fact that no matter what Barth might say God does not end things and Barth would simply have to put up with his superiority.]

*   *   *

2
To Letter 2
Prof. K. H. Miskotte to K. Barth

Voorst, 29 May 1961

[In this reply to Letter 2 Miskotte thanked Barth for his prompt answer and admitted that in the light of it his fears had been largely unfounded. He did not agree, however, with Barth's analysis of his own earlier reaction. As a former opponent of Barth he explained that what he had come to defend in Barth's work was its ecumenical character. It was for this reason that he was horrified at the idea of a "strong man," not improving his work as Barth had suggested in the letter, but smashing it, and thus breaking the continuity he valued so highly. He told Barth he had been too bashful to raise the matter personally just after the tenth but now that Barth had pointed his finger at him he recognized that this bashfulness could be a fault. In a postscript he pointed out that in Dutch "phenomenon" means a surprising fact, so that no hierarchy arises when, as in his article in *In de Waagschaal*, three phenomena are associated, namely, Barth himself, his theological discoveries, and the laziness of those who do not follow up these discoveries in inner freedom.]

*   *   *

3
To Letter 3
Questions to Karl Barth

From Dr. Clark:

1. Was it reasonable for Paul to endure suffering in his ministry (or is it reasonable for us) if all are in Christ and will perhaps be saved anyhow, and if, as you once said, Feuerbach and secular science are already in the Church?

2. In your Anselm (ET, p. 70) we are told that we can never see clearly whether any statement of any theologian is on one side or the other of the border between divine simplicity and incredible deception. Does not this make theology—your own included—a waste of time?

From Dr. Klooster:

3. On *Geschichte* and *Historie*: (a) Has this distinction a biblical basis? (b) How does one distinguish *Geschichte* which may be the object of *Historie* from that which may not? (c) Are there two kinds of *Geschichte*, and if so how do they differ? (d) Could the cross and the resurrection be *Geschichte* even if proved most improbable to *Historie*? (e) Are the cross and the resurrection datable in the sense intended by the creeds and confessions? or only (f) as those who perceive them are datable?

4. On humiliation and exaltation: (a) If these are not successive, can the cross and the resurrection be datable? (b) If they are not successive, is the resurrection a "new" event only in a non-chronological sense? (c) Is the resurrection a true past event, or is it only a timeless event manifested and preached in time?

From Dr. van Til:

5. If resurrection is an object of expectation as well as recollection (*K.D.* I, 2, p. 128), (a) does this refer to Christ's resurrection? If so, (b)

in what sense is it a datable, objective, past event?

6. If the cross and resurrection as *Geschichte* are the basis of salvation for all, (a) is this consistent with the orthodox view of their nature as past events? Or (b) is there a connexion between the orthodox view and orthodox lack of appreciation for a "biblical" universalism, so that the historicity of the cross and resurrection must be amended in the interests of this universalism?

*   *   *

4
To Letter 68
Prof. J. L. Hromádka to K. Barth

Prague, 13 May 1963

Dear Karl,

Only today am I getting round to answering your letter. I hoped for some time we might have a longer personal conversation during your Prague visit so that I could listen to you attentively and tell you frankly what is on my heart. And this letter is written precisely at the time when we had hoped to have you in Prague. I ask you to receive it kindly along with our good wishes for your seventy-seventh birthday.

I understand why you declined, for I can put myself in your position. I, too, note the pressure of age and am always unsettled at the prospect of a longer journey abroad. Nevertheless, I am disturbed, not least because reports have come about your attitude toward me, and your declining the invitation has been interpreted as a kind of criticism of me. Your letter to me on 18 December 1962 has become relatively well known, though not its full contents, and it is circulating in some circles in West Germany, as I learned a few days ago from a well-informed German brother. My personal interest in seeing and hearing you in Prague was not that I expected from your visit a strengthening of my own position; on the contrary, your presence in Prague would have strengthened those circles in our church whose attitude to me is critical. You should never forget that here at home I have to deal with the same suspicions you have sometimes expressed concerning me these past years. What you have said and written is in the air and corresponds to the mood in fairly extensive church circles which cannot accept the present situation but have little resolution to wrestle manfully with our problems on the spot. These circles would have been encouraged in this mood by you and your suspicions and statements. But I still longed to have you here with our faculty and our congregations and their pastors in order that the air might be cleared and I might be compelled to fight on more responsibly and intensively and perhaps also to correct myself.

I have never claimed that I am in the right and that the manner of my activity is the only possible one. What you object against me is motivated by my understanding of the gospel. Yet I am aware that the place and atmosphere of my activity have shaped me and still do so. You cannot deny the same in relation to yourself. We all have to wrestle unceasingly with ourselves and search our final and deepest motives. But it is also true that each of us must stand in a certain solidarity with the problems, difficulties, sins, and exaggerations of our people in personal and public life. You take Swiss neutrality seriously and orient yourself to it. Even your criticism of the past and present of your people has certain limits. Whether you realize it or not, your best utterances on political and public questions bear the mark of your homeland for all their theological profundity. This is what gives relevance and urgency to what you say. Your reservations in relation to me are not purely theological. They are shaped by what is a well-founded or not so well-founded and perhaps even irrational anxiety face to face with our East European world. I remember how in a personal conversation you once admitted that you have an uneasy feeling—even goose flesh—regarding the Eastern sphere in which I live. I do not take this amiss. I try to understand you aright and to learn from your criticism. What I expect from you is not full agreement but a little imagination so that you can understand those statements of mine which put you off. When I see how modern Christianity, including many Christians in the Czech republic, still cannot understand or take seriously our historical situation, I have no choice but to present our problems in historical perspective. I am in fact puzzled that you, too, repeat the familiar arguments about my so-called philosophy of history and that you even suspect me of wanting to glorify the 1917 revolution theologically. In reality I have a much deeper vision of the problems and tasks of our activity in our Socialist countries. First, I have never maintained that the Western world and its civilization are moving toward their decline and fall. And I always try to hammer it home to our Czech Christians that the future does not lie exclusively in the hands of the Communists but depends also on whether we Christians—including those of the West—can understand the situation of present-day humanity and bear living and practical witness in the freedom of the gospel, the sovereignty of faith, and love for men, not in opposition to Communism, or the Soviet Union, or China, but in a positive way. You must read my statements in the framework of my theological books and essays and not in the light of current simplistic interpretations. I have several times considered at different levels what you wrote in your letter. I would not presume to think I am always right. But in my basic position I think I stand where I have been put by my faith in the incarnation of the living Word of God in Jesus of Nazareth. I am not ashamed to write about this, for I have spoken and written about it innumerable times. I have always believed that you look at modern problems and facts with wonderful freedom and openness. I am still sure today that you are not of the company of men like Emil Brunner and Reinhold Niebuhr, who for a long time grasped the world situation bravely but then stopped at a particular point and with unbelievable stubbornness and appeal to principle ceased to wrestle freely with the new and unexpected situation. I need not assure you that you are still our great teacher and that we shall always listen to you attentively.

In conclusion a brief word about Picasso's dove and the anti-American hawk. I understand your reservations but this statement is a distasteful one on your lips. Since 1951 I have attended several conferences of the peace movement in both a passive and an active capacity. One may criticize or endorse the individual resolutions or conclusions. But from my own experience I can say that there has been a real attempt, and still is, to get into touch with the Westerners and to have authentic dialogue with them. On the other side everything has been done to ignore, defame, and silence the movement. Our Christian Peace Conference works on another level, but its concern is to clarify and discuss the differences, contradictions, and antitheses, as well as our own exaggerations, to find a tolerable solution, and therefore to contribute to real peace, penitence, and reconciliation. Naturally one has to be on the spot to understand our weaknesses and temptations and trials, but also our hopes and concerns.

Once again I greet you most sincerely in the name of the Comenius faculty, and with the best of wishes I remain,

Ever yours,
JOSEF
(L. HROMÁDKA)[1]

[1][For Barth's response, see 93.]

*   *   *

5
To Letter 131
Eucharistic Confession
Karl Handrich

Summer 1963

Dearly Beloved,

We are now celebrating the Lord's Supper which our Lord and Savior Jesus Christ instituted and commanded us to keep.

He himself is our host who now invites us all to come to his table that we might receive from his hand bread for life and wine for rejoicing and at his command eat and drink with him (to eternal life).

With bread and wine, in his body broken for us and his blood shed for us, he gives himself as the paschal lamb of God which bears the sin of the world, so that he is in us by his Word and we abide in him by his Holy Spirit.

As often as we eat this bread and drink this cup we remember in faith, full of praise and thanksgiving, that Jesus by his sacrificial death on the cross of Golgotha reconciled the world to God and brought to all of us the forgiveness of sins.

At his table we all eat of the one bread and we all drink of the one cup, and so as members of his body we are all united in love with our Lord and Head, who is with us to the end of this world.

In the fellowship of the body and blood of Christ we are also reconciled with one another and united as brothers and sisters who love and help one another.

At the supper of the Lord we attest and proclaim with great joy our hope that he will soon come again in power and glory, and redeemed on his day we shall celebrate the great wedding-feast with him in the kingdom of God.

*   *   *

6
To Letter 131
Eucharistic Confession (Draft)
Karl Handrich with Corrections by Karl Barth

20 September 1963

Dearly Beloved,

1. We are now celebrating the Lord's Supper which our Lord and Savior instituted and commanded us to keep.

2. He himself is our host who now invites us all to come to his table.

3. As we now receive and take bread and wine according to his direction, he is among us in his body broken for us and his blood shed for us; he himself is the promise of our eternal life and our eternal joy.

4. As often as we do this we remember in faith, full of praise and thanksgiving, that by his sacrificial death on the cross he reconciled the world to God and has brought to all of us the forgiveness of sins.

5. As we all at his table eat of one bread and drink of one cup, we recognize and confess that we are all members of his body with whom he himself will abide to the end of this world.

6. In this fellowship with him we also recognize and confess that we are brothers and sisters, mutually reconciled and united, and loving and helping one another.

7. And in this fellowship we attest and proclaim with great joy our hope that he will soon come again to make all things new.

*   *   *

7
To Letter 131
Eucharistic Confession
Karl Handrich/Karl Barth

Dearly Beloved,

We are now celebrating the Lord's Supper which our Lord and Savior Jesus Christ instituted and commanded us to keep. He himself is our host who now invites us all to come to his table. As we here receive and take bread and wine together according to his direction, we find comfort and joy in the presence and power of his body that was broken for us and his blood that was shed for us and therefore in the promise of our life in his coming kingdom.

We bear witness in so doing to our gratitude for the reconciliation of the world with God that has taken place in him.

We also confess herewith that we are brothers and sisters who are united to one another, who love one another, and who should help one another.

And we confirm herewith our hope of his final manifestation when he will come and make all things new.

*   *   *

8

To Letter 172
Prof. J. Moltmann to K. Barth

Bonn, 4 April 1965

Dear Dr. Barth,

The long, personal, and kindly letter which you wrote from the hospital regarding my *Theology of Hope* came a long time ago and keeps looking at me questioningly as I go on with my work. I would have thanked you for it, and answered it, long ago if I had been able to find the quiet to do so. Only now have I reached the point of telling you how much your letter moved me and still does. That you should have read my fragmentary theological effort so thoroughly causes me shame, as does all that you wrote, since it was only with great trepidation that I ventured to submit it to you. I cannot deny a certain inspired pre-occupation with this one eschatological or messianic idea. You are perfectly right in thinking that we have here only prolegomena to eschatology. I gratefully accept your reference to a lack of concrete eschatology. I will devote the immediate future intensively to meditations on the apocalyptic texts in the New Testament. In the chapter on the ethical consequences of Christian hope I have deliberately stopped at a certain point so as to avoid the suspicion that all that is said systematically up to that point simply serves to exercise a certain criticism of church and society. In the lectures on social ethics I gave at Bonn I tried to move ahead here to a theological concept of work, etc. Perhaps this will issue one day in a volume on the practice of hope.

The nub of your criticism caused me the most cogitation, namely, that in place of eschatology—to escape its dominating onesidedness—the doctrine of the immanent Trinity should function as an expository canon for the proclamation of the lordship of Jesus Christ. I must admit that in studying *C.D.* at these points I always lost my breath. I suspect you are right but I cannot as yet or so quickly enter into this right. Exegetical friends, namely, Ernst Käsemann, have forced me first of all to think through eschatologically the origin, course, and future of the lordship of Christ. In so doing I thought I could so expound the economic Trinity that in the foreground, and then again in the background, it would be open to an immanent Trinity. That is, for me the Holy Spirit is first the Spirit of the raising of the dead and then as such the third person of the Trinity. In recent times the doctrine of the Holy Spirit has come to have a wholly enthusiastic and chiliastic stamp. Joachim is more alive today than Augustine. Thus some depict direct knowledge as a transcending of faith and others depict faith as a transcending of the Christ event. Through an eschatology christologically grounded in the cross and resurrection of Jesus both, I think, might be taken up again into the history at whose eschaton God will be all in all, and they might be changed thereby.

Since I studied in Göttingen with O. Weber and E. Wolf, *C.D.* has been my constant companion. It is far from my intention to try to replace it with anything else. From this castle I simply wanted to make a sortie into the lowlands of lesser conflicts. If in so doing I broke rank a little and at many points followed up the author's criticisms of his earlier statements with criticisms of his later statements, this was not intended to be a parting of the ways. Polemics always makes one a little onesided. But according to my impression the present theological and intellectual situation is such that I must champion the truth polemically and onesidedly in the hope that it will itself emerge in the process.

When I sit at my desk, *C.D.* always faces me with a question. Often I, too, look at it with questions. How could it be otherwise? It bears witness to me not only of peace but also of promise, and for that I am truly thankful.

With friendly greetings and all good wishes,

Yours,
JÜRGEN MOLTMANN

*   *   *

9
To Letter 173
From Corps Commandant Dr. A. Ernst to K. Barth

Muri, 11 November 1964

[In this letter Ernst expressed pleasure that Barth was recovering from his illness and also that he showed interest in his own military career. He said how hard it had been to take the post of corps commandant when he had planned to retire at the end of 1965, for he did not want to be a mere symbolical figure nor just to have more gold on his hat. He had thought at first that he could do something significant only if he had been chosen as chief of the general staff, but he now believed that he could still do it, since his position was fairly strong, opposition could not last, he owed something to his supporters, and even if he failed he would at least have tried. He quoted the third verse from P. Fleming's hymn "In allen meinen Taten," which speaks of taking what comes from God, asked for Barth's prayers, and said he could now see more clearly what a dreadful catastrophe a war would be, so that he could not approve of even Swiss militarism. He closed with good wishes for Barth's health and a request that he might perhaps visit him again some time later.]

*   *   *

10
To Letter 174
Prof. W. Pannenberg to K. Barth

Mainz-Gonsenheim, 9 May 1965

Dear Professor Barth,

Please permit me to send you sincere greetings for your birthday tomorrow with the hope that in the meantime you have completely overcome your illness, which Mr. Ritschl told me about in the winter. May I also thank you for the letter which you wrote me in December about my book on christology. It moved me greatly, especially when I heard from Mr. Ritschl how far from well you were at the time, that you should have read my book so thoroughly and taken the time and energy to write so full a letter to me. Of course, I cannot say that I feel you have understood me. After your friendly reaction to my first effort I was bold enough to hope that you would perceive in my work a continuation of the basic thought of your theology of revelation in a changed intellectual climate. Have I really found in christology the symbol of a general anthropology that has its basis elsewhere? Have I not rather tried to understand the event of Jesus of Nazareth as a mutation of its own—as of all earlier and later—general historical presuppositions? It has been my concern not to begin with the generality of a soteriological-anthropological interest or a christological concept of God-Man-unity but rather with the highly particular and unique fact of the historical event of Jesus of Nazareth. It has thus seemed unavoidable that I should start with the historical question of Jesus of Nazareth, since otherwise his historical particularity would be concealed at once by general theological or other concepts. My different approach to the significance of historico-critical biblical investigation for theology (in spite of the many ways in which philosophical considerations constrict the modern historical method) is the prominent sign of the change of intellectual climate in comparison with your own work. Even from my student days in Heidelberg it has seemed to me, of course, that a change at this point was being unavoidably forced even on those who will not give up the basic features of their theological opposition to Neo-Protestant anthropocentrism. If you cannot see the problem which inevitably arises at this point for those who have studied with you, as I gather from your remarks on the historical study of scripture, then I can understand, of course, that you regard my effort as a superfluous and, as you put it, "reactionary" enterprise. But might there not also be here a limitation in your awareness of the problem with which you once started, in what was for the most part a justifiable antithesis to the theological historicism of a Troeltsch or a Harnack? I venture to put the question here only because I would like to express my conviction that even though a critical turn is made in this question it will still be possible to continue your concentration of theology on the truth of the revelation of God in Jesus Christ, which transcends all our human questioning and speaking. I shall never cease to be grateful that I learned from you to focus all theological work on this center.

With the request that you will give my kind regards to your honored wife and to Miss v. Kirschbaum,

Yours respectfully,
WOLFHART
PANNENBERG

*　　　　*　　　　*

11
[written in English]
To Letter 196 (n. 2)
Inscription on Barth's former desk in the foyer of the library
of Pittsburgh Theological Seminary

THE DESK OF KARL BARTH

In 1884 my mother, Anna Sartorius Barth, gave this desk as a wedding present to my father, Fritz Barth. He worked on it first while he was a minister in Reitnau in the canton of Aargau (Switzerland); later, since 1886, in Basel, as a teacher at the Evangelical Seminary for Preachers (*Evangelische Predigerschule*); finally as an instructor and then as professor at the University of Berne until he died in 1912. At this desk he wrote, among other things, his books *Die Hauptprobleme des Lebens Jesu* (1900) and *Einleitung in das Neue Testament* (1908).

In 1922 I inherited the desk. Sitting at this desk in Goettingen, in Muenster in Westfalia, in Bonn, and since 1935 in Basel, I wrote all of my books published from 1922 on, including *Die Christliche Dogmatik im Entwurf* (1927), *Theologische Existenz heute* (1933), and all the volumes of *Kirchliche Dogmatik* published since 1932.

The chair has served me since the year 1936.

> KARL BARTH
> Basel, Switzerland
> September 1964

*　　　　*　　　　*

12
To Letter 201
Corps Commandant Dr. A. Ernst to K. Barth

Muri, 20 January 1966

[Ernst suggested to Barth that in view of a recent issue of *Vaterland* the truth might be somewhere between the two extremes in relation to the Swiss situation in 1940. Regarding Markus Feldmann, who opposed Barth over East Europe in 1950, Ernst believed that Feldmann was afraid Barth's theological view would weaken resistance to communism, while in matters of toleration Feldmann failed to distinguish clearly enough between a dogmatic and a practical political approach. Though he respected Feldmann, Ernst declared himself on Barth's side. Some "Barthians," however, got on his nerves, though he admitted that some of his own supporters were also more extreme than he himself was. The debate had at least brought about a rethinking of the relation of church and state.]

*　　　　*　　　　*

13
To Letter 239
Dr. T. Stadtland to K. Barth

Wirdum, 25 January 1967

Dear Professor,

Thanks for your letter of 18 January 1967. In spite of its sternness (or precisely because of it), it was a genuinely pastoral letter.

I was pained by your charge that I treated my (historical??) subject, your early theology, without love. For I wrote the work not only as one who still felt himself your student but also with a final passion for the theme itself, and I do not think I am an obscurantist but have at least tried to find some joy in the theology of that time. But you are in the happy position of never having taken an advanced degree. When one is compelled to assemble, analyze, and criticize everything with thorough German scholarship, often the last bit of spirit is swept out of such work. [. . .]

Our ultimate problem is that it is not clear to us what we have to do alongside you if we are too arrogant merely to go behind you. Your *C.D.* blocks our vision like a gigantic mountain. And although the few younger ones among us who tread the whole mountain step by step are richly rewarded, we are just as timid as those who at the sight of the mountain give up and simply grumble without knowledge. [. . .]

To ask whether you could ever develop an eschatology from your starting point is not, as you say, a serious criticism, but simply stupid. I sorrowfully retract it as a sin of my youth.

Do you detect that my whole letter is one long perplexed question? We just have no unequivocal front against which to fight. Was not your own age and that of your friends an age that was "blessed" by the church conflict, etc.? [. . .] If I may venture an undoubtedly lopsided illustration to show what I mean by this dissatisfaction (and the cheeky arrogance to which it often gives rise), your theology is in many ways like a vast and wonderfully beautiful garden with many different flowers and al-most no weeds, but staying forever in this garden finally proves tedious, so that we are tempted to take flight, or at least to look over the wall at the neighbor's garden, even though we realize there is not much there and everything is so much poorer. And then we are misguided enough to justify this effort, and even to trumpet it forth with self-assurance in order to conceal its poverty. We cultivate a quest for real trial (many call it the theology of the cross) because we are too young to give up fighting. To be sure, there are dangers enough in Germany against which to fight, whether in politics or the church societies, whose doings are much more dangerous to our congregations than a thousand Braunians could ever be. But either the fronts are cemented fast or the enemy is not worth any theological effort because he will not understand. [. . .]

A final question: When you hear our sermons, and those of your other friends in Germany (over eighty percent of them preach à la Barth), you will find them all sound, but in spite of everything will you not often be overcome by a queasy feeling in face of the monotony? This is how it is with me, though I do not know how to improve things. One is glad, then, when a sturdy heresy arises . . . as a sign that someone is experimenting (he can fail quietly). [. . .]

*   *   *

14
To Letter 24
Prof. K. Aland to K. Barth

Münster/Westphalia, 21 April 1967

Dear Professor,

Many sincere thanks for your letter which I received today. May I say that I, too, am disturbed. For your criticism relates exclusively to the last two pages of my work,[1] which form an addition. The work itself, as the title and all the contents show, is meant to be a purely historical investigation. It aims to establish what can be said about children (and their baptism) in the first two centuries.

You do not deal at all with my main concern and the significance of the work, if it has any, and so I feel, if you will pardon me, that I have not merely been misunderstood but really unjustly treated. In my view the material assembled and discussed in this and also in my previous work on infant baptism[2] is indispensable to the modern discussion, and especially to those who nowadays reject the baptism of infants or children.

I, too, must justify myself. Perhaps all that I miss is presupposed in your letter, but as it now reads I cannot help being disillusioned and disturbed.

With respectful greetings,

Yours sincerely,
K. ALAND

¹See 248, n. 1.
²See 249, n. 4.

*   *   *

15
To Letter 274
Prof. H. Thielicke to K. Barth

Hamburg, 1 November 1967

Dear Professor Barth,

A happy friendship with Eduard Thurneysen, a reading of the book he brought with him, your *Ad Limina Petri*, and an obscure sense of standing behind you on our modern fronts—often with the same irony!—have all encouraged me to send you the enclosed little book. [. . .¹]

Naturally I do not expect any expression of thanks for this slender volume. I am pleased to hear that you are now much more lively in the main and it would be a sin to be the cause of interrupting your work with routine matters.

Eduard Thurneysen and his wife stayed in my country cottage where I wrote the first volume of my dogmatics, which is now in print. How blessed is the hilaritas of two old men who desire and are able to drink up the last drops.

When I read the introductory report of your Rome book it became clear to me how you differ from all the others whose books one must read professionally. To be sure, it is the *doctrina* that makes this difference. But the charming thing is probably more a by-product of this *doctrina*: the cheerfulness of the climate, the beauty, the great joy in telling, the laughter of world-overcoming. Thus one closes the book warmed and uplifted as after drinking an old and fiery and gentle Mosel. Where is there a theologian who can achieve such effects with his theme—and not just because after all the jollity he stands his ground? This, for me, is the difference. [. . .] In you is none of the terminological and hermeneutical make-up with which the ravaged face of theology is adorned but theology that always has a freshly washed and laughing face; one might not even miss the freckles that spot the likes of us.

But what frivolous talk to such an eminent person. You will certainly not take it amiss. I shall always see you now through Eduard's spectacles and on this view all will be well. With respect and gratitude,

Yours,
HELMUT THIELICKE

[1]Cf. 274, n. 1.

*   *   *

16
To Letter 267
Pope Paul VI to K. Barth

To Professor Karl Barth, Basel   *The Vatican, 14 November 1967*

Dear Professor,

With joy and satisfaction we have received your valued letter in which you send us your good wishes on the completion of our seventieth year.[1] We would thank you for the friendly thoughts and the sympathetic words addressed to our person and our office.

We recall with pleasure your visit in September last year and the talk we were able to have with you, esteemed professor, in an atmosphere of mutual understanding. In you we met a scholar who boldly seeks the truth and for whom the concept of brotherly fellowship in Christ is a real concern. We confidently express the hope that our efforts to find the path of unity will always be directed and blessed by the Lord.

We commend yourself, esteemed professor, and also your wife to the special protection and help of God, and we sincerely hope that many years of health and peace may yet be granted to you.

We pray the Lord that, with his grace, our understanding may grasp the truth with ever increasing depth and our hearts may increasingly be penetrated by it, so that in the light of a full knowledge of it we may find our way to one another.

Paulus PP.VI[2]

[1]See 267.
[2][For Barth's response, see 281.]

*　　　　*　　　　*

17
To Letter 303
A. G. Cardinal Cicognani to K. Barth

The Vatican, 11 November 1968

N.121503

Dear Professor,

His Holiness has received the delicate letter you recently sent him[1] and I am pleased to be the interpreter of his feelings to you.

The Holy Father, noting your expression of thanks, is glad to know that his recent parcel with the epistles of St. Paul and St. Peter has met your wishes and become for you another sign of hope on the way to the reunion of the churches.

The Sovereign Pontiff is also pleased by the affectionate attention with which you take to heart his cares as pastor at the head of the church that the Lord has committed to him in a conjuncture which gives him the duty of testifying boldly to the truth. And since your interest stirs up dialogue, you have expressed in terms that have evoked his lively attention your views on certain points in the encyclical *Humanae vitae*.

Regarding this subject, it is obvious that natural law and conscience are not, in the strict sense, sources of revelation. And you are right to emphasize, with the constitution *Dei verbum* (10),[2] that holy scripture and tradition constitute the unique sacred deposit of the Word of God entrusted to the church: revelation in the true sense, supernatural, public, and external.

But the Redemptor God is also the God who created man according to his own image and likeness, and in spite of sin man continues to discover "in the depths of his conscience the presence of a law which he did not give himself but which he is obliged to obey" (conciliar constitution *Gaudium et spes*, 16).[3] This way of finding God's will, even though it is often obscured and distorted, is not radically deceptive; it is by it that those who have not been able to know God's purpose in any other way will be judged (Rom 1:20, 32; 2:7). As for Christians, revelation does not suppress natural law, which is equally divine; it simply elucidates it, completes it, makes its observance possible through the Holy Spirit, and above all orders it to the supernatural calling of the children of God which remains their sole salvation. This fact, that natural law finds itself thus ordered to salvation, explains why its prescriptions can be the subject of the church's magisterium. Aiming only to lead men to salvation, the magisterium must pronounce not only on the contents of revelation but also sometimes on natural truths that are necessarily linked to salvation.

The Holy Father is glad to have had this chance to reply thus, through myself as intermediary, to the observations you made to him. He also sends cordial wishes for your health and invokes on Mrs. Barth and yourself the blessing of the Lord.

I myself am honored to have interpreted to you the thoughts and sentiments of the Sovereign Pontiff and I beg you to accept, Professor, the assurance of my religiously affectionate feelings,

A. G. Card. Cicognani[4]

[1]Letter 303.

[2]*Constitutio dogmatica de divina Revelatione Dei verbum* of Vatican Council II, Art. 10, *LThK*, 2nd ed./Suppl. Vol. II (1967), pp. 526-529.

[3]*Constitutio pastoralis de Ecclesia in mundo huius temporis, Gaudium et spes* of Vatican Council II, Art. 16, *LThK*, 2nd ed./Suppl. Vol. III (1968).

[4][For Barth's response, see 321.]

INDEXES

CHRONOLOGICAL LIST OF LETTERS

Abbreviations:

L = Letter
PC = Postcard
LC = Lettercard
H = Handwritten
T = Typed

A: Original not available
*   This sign denotes that a (partial) précis is given instead of the full text.

26. To Pastor D. Hoch
    L T   3/3/1962   35

27. To Mrs. G. Staewen
    L H   3/15/1962   36

28. To Prof. W. H. Schultze
    PC H   3/26/1962   36

29. To Councillor W.-D. Zimmermann
    L T   3/28/1962   37

30. To Prof. C. C. West
    L T   4/1/1962   38

32. To Prof. D. F. Fleming
    L T   4/2/1962   39

32. To Bishop A. Hege
    L T   4/3/1962   40

33. To Pastor F. Middendorff
    L T   4/5/1962   41

34. To M. Zellweger
    L H   4/18/1962   43

35. To M. Zellweger
    L H   5/19/1962   45

36. To Pastor M. Schwarz
    L H   5/19/1962   47

37. To an Assistant at Radio Basel
    L H   5/22/1962   47

38. To Pastor U. Hedinger
    L T   6/6/1962   48

39. To Pastor E. Hubacher
    L T   6/6/1962   49

40. To Dr. J. I. McCord
    L T   6/11/1962   50

41. To Prof. D. Ritschl
    PC H   7/11/1962   51

42. To Prof. H. Rheinfelder
    L T   7/14/1962   52

43. To Dr. R. Leuenberger
    L T   7/15/1962   53

44. To N.N.
    L T   7/16/1962   55

45. To Prof. K. H. Miskotte
    L T   7/16/1962   56

*46. To Prof. E. Fascher
    L T   7/16!1962   58

47. To Prof. A. Krebs
    L T   7/16/1962   58

*48. To Pastor H. Goes
    L T   7/17/1962   59

49. To Prof. H. Gollwitzer
    L T   7/31/1962   60

50. To Prof. W. Kreck
    L T   7/31/1962   63

*51. To W. Finck
    L T   7/31/1962   65

*52. To Prof. L. Schrade
    L T   8/4/1962   65

53. To Theological Student C. Besmer
    LC H   8/17/1962   65

54. To Prof. G. Dehn
    L H A   9/13/1962   66

55. To Prof. M. Fischer
    PC H   10/26/1962   68

*56. To Bishop H. Dietzfelbinger
    L T   10/27/1962   69

*57. To Prof. P. Althaus
    PC H   10/28/1962   69

58. To F. Sanders
    PC H   10/29/1962   70

59. To Dr. E. Jüngel
    PC H   11/3/1962   71

60. To a Former Student in America
    L T   11/7/1962   72

61. To Prof. E. Wolf
    PC H   11/8/1962   73

62. To Prof. O. Cullmann
    PC T   11/25/1962   74

*63. To Miss A. Hirzel
    L T   11/28/1962   76

*64. To Mrs. H. Bürri-Fahrni
    L H   11/30/1962   76

65. To Superintendent U. Smidt
    PC T   12/11/1962   76

65a. To Dr. A. Buchholz
    PC T   12/12/1962   77

66. To Dr. J.-F. Konrad
    L T   12/17/1962   78

67. To Prof. F. Buri
    L T   12/18/1962   79

68. To Prof. J. L. Hromádka
    L T   12/18/1962   82

69. To Prof. H. Küng
    PC H   12/19/1962   84

70. To Prof. E. Wolf
    LC H   Jan. 1963   85

LETTERS IN APPENDIX

SCRIPTURE REFERENCES

Genesis	
1 and 2	78
22:8	11, 60

Numbers	
16	109, 163

2 Kings	
22:14	115

Psalms	
2:4	219, 243
8:4	275
19:3	334
23	28
23:5	110, 153
27:13	305f.
31:8	278
39:7	308
90:10	31, 163, 193
98:1	42
103:2	298
116:9	305f.

Proverbs	
1:7	20
15:33	20

Ecclesiastes	
1:2	43, 49
3:1ff.	6, 229,254, 320

Isaiah	
6:5	271
21:11	110
38:11	305f.
40:9	115
40:31	165
43:18f.	210
53:6	337
53:8	305f.
60:1–9	148

Jeremiah	
20:9	19

Lamentations	
3:22	164

Zechariah	
14:13	124

Matthew	
5:4	200
5:15	261

5:45	163
6:23	60
6:33	325
6:34	116
7:16, 20	33
11:5	218
11:25	328
11:29	319f.
16:18f.	313, 315
18:18	313, 315
25:43	23

Mark	
7:37	218
9:24	315
9:36	39

Luke	
1:5ff.	179
1:42	294
2:1-20	28
2:14	319f.
2:35	15, 17
9:62	121
14:18ff.	68

John	
1	147
1:1	241
1:10	199
1:14	144
1:29	199
3:17	199
4:22	263
5:2ff.	132
5:4	172
6:51	199
8:36	318
11:25	102, 321
11:43	91
14:2	330
14:6	318
16:33	137, 148
19:30	128, 147, 275f.
20:22f.	313, 315

Romans	313
1:20	357
1:32	357
2:7	357
3:9	267
9–11	25
9:4f.	26
11	100

1 Corinthians	

2:4	335
4:20	98
9	270f.
13:11	328
14:34	279

2 Corinthians	
1:19f	334
3:17	85
5:1	164
5:19	67, 199, 328
5:20	335
12:10	269

Galatians	
2:11–14	318, 320

Philippians	
3:1	319
3:14	308
4:7	83, 328f.

Colossians	
1	147

1 Thessalonians	
5:24	165

Titus	
3:4	235

Hebrews	
1	147
13:8	242

James	
4:15	76, 207

1 Peter	285f., 313
3:19	155f.

2 Peter	285f., 313

1 John	
2:2	200
3:20	218
4:18	16

Revelation	
4:8	235
5:5	229
11:15	199
12	294
12:10	232

NAMES

Recipients of letters (or authors of those in the Appendix) are in **bold** type.
Persons referred to in the text are in roman type. Persons mentioned only in the notes
are in *italic* type.

Achelis, Ernst Christian 278
Adenauer, Konrad 77, 97, 272
Adenauer, Paul 272
Adolfs, Robert 279, 281
Aland, Kurt **246ff., 354f.**
Allmen, Jean-Jacques von **126**
Althaus, Paul **69f.**, 206
Andersen, Hans Christian 109
Andrews, James E. 51, **138f.**
Anselm of Canterbury 139, 342
Asmussen, Hans 16
Athanasuis 158
Athenagoras I 152f.
Augustine 349

Bach, Johann Sebastian 12, 214, 291
Baeck, Leo 262
Baldwin, James 130
Balthasar, Hans Urs von 71, 101, 103, 112,
  135, 219, 233, 236, 257, 278, 300
Bammate, N. 154
Barauna, Guilherme 280f.
Bardot, Brigitte 230
Barth, Anna (née Sartorius, Barth's mother)
  351
Barth, Catherine (Barth's granddaughter)
  115f.
Barth, Christine (Barth's grandniece) **184,**
  227
Barth, Christoph (Barth's son) xii, 12, 17,
  29, 32, 44, 45, 47, 57, 59f., 87, 115, 155,
  194, 210f., 274, 299
Barth, Daniel (Barth's grandson) 17, 29,
  115f.
Barth, Fritz (Barth's father) 351
Barth, Hans Jakob (Barth's son) 166
Barth, Heinrich (Barth's brother) 101, 149,
  270, 337
Barth, Marie-Claire (née Frommel, Barth's
  daughter-in-law) **17f.**, 29, **115ff.**, 119,
  194
Barth, Markus (Barth's son) xii, 21, 32,
  43, 45, 47, 57, 124, 153, 155, 169, 172,
  217, 245, 282
Barth, Nelly (née von Hoffmann, Barth's
  wife) 17, 196, 205, 219, 223, 224f., 243,
  246, 268, 275, 285, 290, 295, 299, 306,
  314, 320, 322, 351, 356, 358
Barth, Nicolas (Barth's grandson) 17, 29,
  115f.

Barth, Peter (Barth's brother) 227
Barth, Renate (née Ninck, Barth's daugh-
  ter-in-law) **166**
Barth, Ruth (Barth's granddaughter) **130**
Bartsch, Hans-Werner **20**
Bastian, Hans-Dieter 309
Bauer, Werner **160**
Baumgartner, Walter 54f.
Bea, Augustine Cardinal 127, 168f., **207ff.,**
  216, 222f., 326f.
Beauvoir, Simone de 67
Beethoven, Ludwig van 86, 152
Bell, George Kennedy Allen 250
Bengel, Johann Albrecht 308, 312
Bense, Max 310
Bereczky, Albert **10f.**
Berger, Joachim 38
Bergmann, Gerhard **271**
Berkhof, Hendrik **316**
Berkouwer, Gerrit Cornelis 7f., 110, 309
Bernstein, Michèle 169
Besmer, Clemens **65f.**
Bethge, Eberhard **250ff.**, 294
Beyreuther, Erich 62
Biedermann, Alois Emanuel 67f., 178f.
Bittlinger, Arnold **50**
Bizer, Ernst 96
Bizer, Herman **96**
Bloch, Ernst 175f., 205
Blocher, Gerhard 131
Blumhardt, Christoph 175
Blumhardt, Johann Christoph 251, 270
Bodelschwingh, Friedrich von 53
Böni, Josef 264, 266f.
Bolgiani, Franco **113f.**
Bolli, Heinz 276, 306, 316
Bonhoeffer, Dietrich 122, 165f., 250ff.,
  294, 305, 316
Bonjour, Edgar **22f.**, 40
Born, Max 294
Bouman, Johan 316
Bousset, Wilhelm 67
Bovet, Theodor 135f.
Brandt, Willy 98
Braso, Gabriel M. 232
Braun, Dietrich 155f.
Braun, Herbert 92, 109, 146, 150, 186f.,
  275f., 331
Breit, Thomas 16
Brennecke, Gerhard 206

Frugier, A. 169
Frundsberg, Georg von 320
Fuchs, Ernst 62, 71, 79, 110, 150, 192f., 309
Fulton, Leonard V. **88**
Fulton, Timothy 88

Gabriel, Martin **196f.**
Gallmann, Louise **191**
Gandhi, Mohandas Karamantshand (Mahatma) 276
Ganoczy, Alexandre 214
Gaulle, Charles de 173
Gavin, James M. 311
Geiger, Max 54, 74, 264
Gellert, Christian Fürchtegott 9f.
Gelzer, Charlotte **134**
Gelzer, Heinrich 134
George VI 197
Gerhardt, Paul 36, 42, 164, 320
Gerstenmaier, Eugen 306
Gertz, Kurt-Peter **284f.**
Ginsberg, Ernst 265
Giovanoli, Rudolf **308**
Gisevius, Hans Bernd 172
Glatt, Louis **267f.**
Gloege, Gerhard 103, **218f.**
Goes, Albrecht **290ff.**
Goes, Helmut **59**, 292
Goethe, Johann Wolfgang von 52, 68, 78, 87, 103, 142, 187, 189, 193, 195, 196
Götting, Gerald **146f.**, **188**, 206
Gogarten, Friedrich 179, 218f., 275, 322, 331
Goldschmidt, Dietrich 26
Gollwitzer, Brigitte 62
Gollwitzer, Helmut 10f., 15, 18, 26, 54, **60ff.**, 105, 131, 175f., 183, 194, **204f.**, **224f.**, **274f.**, 279, 324
Gotthelf, Jeremias 227
Gowalezyk, Ludmilla **189**
Graf, Urs 80f.
Graham, Billy 43f.
Grünewald, Matthias 315f.
Grundtwig, Nikolai Frederik Severin 99
Gualtier de Chatillon, Philippe 263

Hacker, Paul 222, 224
Haering, Hermann 195
Haering, Theodor 195
Häsler, Alfred A. 260
Hamann, Johann Georg 102f.
Hamel, Johannes **122f.**
Hammer, Karl 155f., 189
Hampe, Johann Christoph **249f.**, 280
Handel, George Frederick 12
Handrich, Karl **142f.**, **150**

Handrich, Wilma 150, **346ff.**
Hansch, Hannelore **309**
Harder, Günther 183
Harnack, Adolf von 250, 272f., 277, 351
Hasenhüttl, Gotthold 214, 257, 279, 281
Hasselaar, J. M. 300f.
Haupt, Ernst Friedrich 74
Haydn, Joseph 65
Hedinger, Ulrich **48**
Hege, Albrecht **40f.**
Hegel, Georg Wilhelm Friedrich 149
Heidegger, Martin 72f., 277
Heim, Helene **259**
Heinemann, Gustav 16, 324
Heiniger, Franz **95**
Heitmann, Ingeborg **217f.**
Henry VIII 210
Herrenbrück, Walter **109f.**, **272**
Hermann, Rudolf 181
Herrmann, Wilhelm 109, 187, 197, 258, 277
Hesse, Hermann Albert 55
Hilfiker-Diriwächter, Elise 21, **198f.**, **201f.**, **227**, **289f.**
Hindenburg, Paul von 173
Hirsch, Emanuel 69f.
Hirzel, Annie **76**, **118f.**
Hitler, Adolf 42, 62, 85, 172, 181, 197, 287, 304, 305, 307
Hoch, Dorothee **35**
Hochhuth, Rolf 135f.
Hofius, Otfried **237**
Holden, R. A. 32
Holl, Karl 250
Hollenweger, Walter J. 133
Honemeyer, Karl **307**
Hromádka, Josef L. 11, 23f., 39, **82ff.**, **94f.**, **103ff.**, 120, 122, 152f., **165f.**, **343ff.**
Hubacher, Ernst **49f.**

Ignatius of Antioch 109
Imboden, Max 144
Immer, Karl 55
Immer, Karl, Jr. 260
Israelsen, H. **107f.**
Iversen, Carl **92**, **99**
Iversen, Mrs. 99
Iwand, Hans Joachim 181

Jackson, Thomas J. (Stonewall) 22, 161
Jacobs, Paul **243f.**
Jaspers, Karl xi, 154
Jaspers, Bernd xiv
Joachim of Fiore 349
Johann, Ernst **299**
John XXIII 85, 94, 106, 118, 168
Johnson, Lyndon B. 243

SUBJECTS

WORKS OF BARTH CITED IN THE LETTERS

"Lebensregeln für ältere Menschen im Verhaltnis zu jüngeren." *Evangelischer Digest*, 10 (1968): 294

"Nachwort." In *Schleiermacher-Auswahl.* Munich/Hamburg, 1968, pp. 290ff.: 316

"Musik für einen Gast" (radio interview, 1968). In *Letzte Zeugnisse*. Zurich, 1969, 11ff.; ET *Final Testimonies*, Grand Rapids, 1977, pp. 17ff.: 322, 325f.

"Liberale Theologie. Ein Interview." Ibid., pp. 33ff. (ET, 31ff.): 322

"Katholische und evangelische Predigten am Radio." Ibid., pp. 49ff. (ET, 41ff.): 322

Note: The Swiss edition also includes the following references:

Leonardo von Montenuovo oder Freiheit und Liebe (unpublished play, 1901): letter no. 312

Gruppe 44 IV Kirchenwesen (unpublished, 1912): letter no. 111

"Landesausstellung" (sermon at Safenwil, 1914). *Neue Wege*, 8 (1914): letter no. 111

Evangelical Theology.... 7 records. Waco, Texas, 1963: letter no. 117

"Uns fehlt das Bewusstsein der eigenen Relativatät" (interview). *Die Woche*," (1963): letter no. 79

WORKS DISCUSSED IN LETTERS TO THEIR AUTHORS

Aland, Kurt. "Die Stellung der Kinder in den frühen christlichen Gemeinden—und ihre Taufe." *ThExh*, N.F. 138 (Munich, 1967): 246f.

Bergmann, Gerhard. *Kirche am Scheideweg*. Gladbeck, 1967: 271

Berkhof, Hendrik. *Theologie des Heiligen Geistes*. Neukirchen, 1968; ET *The Doctrine of the Holy Spirit*, 1976: 316

Bethge, Eberhard. *Dietrich Bonhoeffer, Theologe—Christ—Zeitgenosse*. Munich, 1967; ET, 1975: 250f.

Brunner, Emil. *Eros und Gewissen bei Gottfried Keller*. Zurich, 1965: 180

Buri, Fritz. *Dogmatik als Selbstverständnis des christlichen Glaubens*, II, *Der Mensch und die Gnade*. Tübingn, 1962: 79ff.

Casalis, Georges. "L'Eglise 'réduite à sa plus simple expression." In *Vers une Eglise pour les Autres*. Geneva, 1966, pp. 73–75: 132f.

Dehn, Günther. *Die alte Zeit....* Munich, 1962: 66ff.

Fleming, Denna Frank. *The Cold War and its Origins, 1917–1960*. 2 vols. London, 1961: 39f.

Gollwitzer, Helmut. *Von der Stellvertretung Gottes....* Munich, 1967: 274f.

Hampe, Johann Christoph, ed. *Die Autorität der Freiheit....* Munich, 1967: 249

Hedinger, Ulrich. *Der Freiheitsbegriff in der Kirchlichen Dogmatik Barths*. Zurich, 1962: 48

Honemeyer, Karl. "Grundsätzliches zum Standort der Orgel." *Musik und Kirche*, 38 (1968), 97–106: 307

Hromádka, Josef L. "Die Krise ist vorbei?" *Die protestantischen kirchen in der Tschechoslowakei*, 9, No. 9 (1962), 61ff.: 82

———. "Memorandum on the German Question." *Christian Peace Conference*, 4 (May 1963), 83ff.: 106

Jüngel, Eberhard. "Die Möglichkeit theologischer Anthropologie auf dem Grumd der Analogie." *EvTh*, 22 (1962), 535–557: 71

———. "Das Sakrament—was ist das?" *EvTh*, 26 (1966), 320–336: 192

Kahl, Joachim. *Das Elend des Christentums oder Plädoyer für eine Humanität ohne Gott*. Reinbeck bei Hamburg, 1968: 330f.

Kantzenbach, Freidrich Wilhelm, ed. *Zeugnis und Zeichen....* Munich, 1964: 156

Konrad, Johann-Friedrich. *Abbild und Ziel der Schöpfung....* Tübingen, 1962: 78f.

Kreck, Walter. *Die Zukunft des Gekommenen. Grundprobleme der Eschatologie*. Munich, 1961: 63

Kubly, Herbert. *The Whistling Zone*. New York, 1963: 111

Kung, Hans. *Kirche in Freiheit*. Einsiedeln, 1964: 190

———. ed. with Y. Congar and D. O'Hanlon. *Konzilsreden*. Einsiedeln/Zurich/Cologne, 1964: 215

_____ . Die Kirche. Freiburg/Basel/Vienna, 1967; ET, 1967: 245

_____ . "Eine Herausforderung an die Kirche. Zu Charles Davis' Kirchenaustritt." Orientierung, 31 (1967), 123–126: 257

_____ . Wahrhaftigkeit. Zur Zukunft der Kirche. Freiburg/Basel/Vienna, 1968; ET Truthfulness, 1968: 317f.

Leuenberger, Robert. "Pro et contra. Bemerkungen zu einer politischen Kontroverse in der Kirche." Reformatio, 11 (1962), 276–296: 53f.

_____ . "Ehrlich vor Gott! Bemerkungen zu dem Buch von John A. T. Robinson 'Gott ist anders' ('Honest to God')." Reformatio, 13 (1964), 456–477: 171f.

Marquardt, Friedrich-Wilhelm. Die Entdeckung des Judentums für die christliche Theologie. Israel im Denken Karl Barths. Munich, 1967: 261ff.

Marti, Karl, Kurt Lüthi, and Kurt von Fischer. Moderne Malerei, Literatur und Musik. Drei Entwürfe zu einer Begegnung zwischen Glaube und Kunst. Zurich/Stuttgart, 1963: 100f.

Miskotte, Kornelis Heiko. Über Karl Barths Kirchliche Dogmatik. Kleine Präludien und Phantasien, ThExh N.F. 89. Munich, 1961: 5f.

Moltmann, Jürgen. Theologie der Hoffnung. Munich, 1964; ET 1967: 174ff.

Morgenthaler, Walther. Der Mensch Karl Marx. Bern, 1962: 129

Müller, Gotthold. Identität und Immanenz. Zur Genese der Theologie von David Friedrich Strauss. Zurich, 1968: 331f.

Osaki, Setsuro. Die Prädestinationslehre Karl Barths. Diss. Göttingen, 1966: 237ff.

Pannenberg, Wolfhart. Grundzüge der Christologie. Gütersloh, 1964; ET Jesus, God and Man, 1968: 177ff.

Rahner, Karl. "Anmerkungen zur Reformation." Stimmen der Zeit, 180 (1967), 228–253: 278ff.

Riniker, Hans. "Die Existenz Gottes. Zu zwei theologischen Neuerscheinungen." Kirchenblatt für die reformierte Schweiz, 119 (1963), 294ff.: 131

Ritschl, Dietrich. Nur Menschen. Zur Negerfrage in den amerikanischen Südstaaten. Unterwegs No. 18, Berlin, 1962: 51f.

Schmid, Friedrich. Verkündigung und Dogmatik in der Theologie Karl Barths .... Munich, 1964: 170

Schoch, Max. Karl Barth. Theologie in Aktion. Frauenfeld/Stuttgart, 1967: 269f.

Schrade, Leo. "Joseph Haydn als Schöpfer der klassischen Musik." Universitas, 17 (1962), 767–778: 64

Smith, Ronald Gregor. "Hamann und Kierkegaard," in Zeit und Geschichte. Dankesgabe an Rudolf Bultmann zum 80. Geburtstag. Tübingen, 1964, pp. 671–683: 102

Stadtland, Tjarko. Eschatologie und Geschichte in der Theologie des jungen Karl Barth. Neukirchen, 1966: 232ff.

Steck, Karl Gerhard. "Die römisch-katholische Kirche." Materialdienst für die Männerarbeit der EKD, Botschaft und Dienst, 4 (1961): 29f.

Stirnimann, Heinrich. "Barths Tauf-Fragment. KD IV/4." Freiburger Zeitschrift für Philosophie und Theologie, 15 (1968), pp. 3–28: 300

Storch, Martin. Exegesen und Meditationen zu Karl Barths Kirchlicher Dogmatik, Munich, 1964: 158f.

Thielicke, Helmut. Über die Angst des heutigen Theologiestudenten vor dem geistlichen Amt. Tübingen, 1967: 277f.

Werner, Martin. "Karl Barths 'Einführung in die evangelische Theologie.'" Schweizerische Theologische Umschau, 33 (1963), 84–87: 114

Willems, B. A. Karl Barth. Een inleiding in zijn denken. Tielt Den Haag, 1963: 93f.

Wolf, Erik, ed. Gustav Radbruch: Briefe. Göttingen, 1968: 333

Wolf, Erik. "Karl Barths Entlassung. Die Tragödie einer Fakultat" (unpublished address): 192, 194

Zuckmayer, Carl. Als wär's ein Stück von mir. Horen der Freundschaft. Frankfurt, 1966: 248